UNBOUNDED PUBLICS

UNBOUNDED PUBLICS

Transgressive Public Spheres, Zapatismo, and Political Theory

Richard Gilman-Opalsky

LEXINGTON BOOKS

A division of ROWMAN & LITTLEFIELD PUBLISHERS, INC.
Lanham • Boulder • New York • Toronto • Plymouth, UK

LEXINGTON BOOKS

A division of Rowman & Littlefield Publishers, Inc.
A wholly owned subsidary of The Rowman & Littlefield Publishing Group, Inc.
4501 Forbes Boulevard, Suite 200
Lanham, MD 20706

Estover Road
Plymouth PL6 7PY
United Kingdom

British Library Cataloguing in Publication Information Available

Library of Congress Cataloging-in-Publication Data

The hardback edition of this book was previously cataloged by the Library of
Congress as follows:

Gilman-Opalsky, Richard, 1973–
   Unbounded publics : transgressive public spheres, Zapatismo, and political
theory / Richard Gilman-Opalsky.
      p. cm.
   Includes bibliographical references and index.
   1. Political sociology. 2. Communication—Philosophy. 3. Ejército Zapatista
de Liberación Nacional (Mexico) I. Title.
   JA76.G535 2008
   306.2—dc22   2007044343

ISBN-13: 978-0-7391-2478-9 (cloth : alk. paper)
ISBN-10: 0-7391-2478-1 (cloth : alk. paper)
ISBN-13: 978-0-7391-2479-6 (pbk. : alk. paper)
ISBN-10: 0-7391-2479-X (pbk. : alk. paper)

Printed in the United States of America

∞™ The paper used in this publication meets the minimum requirements of
American National Standard for Information Sciences—Permanence of Paper
for Printed Library Materials, ANSI/NISO Z39.48–1992.

This work is for all those who struggle to enliven new public spheres, for those committed to the common good in a world where a deep and abiding respect for others remains the lofty ideal it has always been.

I also dedicate this work to my partner in life, Robyn. Without her, this book would not have been possible. Her love, support, and friendship have been my beacons throughout.

Contents

Acknowledgments

This book would not have been possible without the support of a number of people, many of whom I acknowledge here. Courtney Jung has been an honest, committed, and careful reader of this work, and taking her advice has always served to make it better. David Plotke and Andrew Arato have also provided invaluable input and support, and I appreciate their assistance throughout. Andreas Kalyvas read the manuscript with remarkable closeness and clarity. Our few conversations have been immensely valuable to me and have improved the quality of this work. Finally, the most heartfelt thanks must be reserved for my lifemate, Robyn Gilman-Opalsky, for coming along for this journey and, in so many ways that I cannot express here, for leading the way.

General Introduction

Public spheres are the places where people come together to communicate, to exchange and consider ideas. But in defining the public sphere, political theorists go further—it is the place where political opinions and collective interests are formed, and ultimately, it is a means for registering opinions with power-holders, for speaking truth to power. Sometimes the public sphere gives rise to more than speaking, but to other forms of collective action and contentious politics. A public sphere must do more than host communication—it must work to form a collective political will and to bring this to bear on other actors.

Debates about the public sphere, its form and its function, can be and typically are mapped out along a continuum that starts with a national conception on one side and ends with a transnational conception on the other. This continuum, a line that traces the rethinking of the public sphere throughout the twentieth century, represents the development of the concept in the history of philosophy. Early theorizations of the public sphere assumed a national framework[1] until (and only very recently) the transnational public sphere was proposed as a compensatory antidote to the classical model—the latter now seen as outflanked by the preeminence of a transnational or even a "postnational" political topography.

I trace twentieth-century developments in theories of the public sphere, evaluating how the public and its political function have been defined and redefined. In Jürgen Habermas' classical, major study of the bourgeois public sphere, the ideal public fulfilled the intrastate function of democratic legitimation; it served as a conduit of influence between civil society and the state.[2] Today, Habermas and others regard the national public sphere as insufficient and even as an impediment to the development of a much-needed transnational public sphere. A transnational public is required for the task of legitimating or challenging numerous and increasingly powerful transnational actors, policies, and processes. In short, theorists now contend that public spheres must be theorized in a transnational framework. This newer argument has occasioned a reframing of the debate in the light of questions about globalization and transnational politics.

I argue that there has been and can be a different kind of public sphere, a *transgressive public sphere*, which inhabits the two frameworks complementarily. Some public spheres are simultaneously national and transnational; it is therefore often wrong for theorists and disadvantageous for actors to choose between a nationally or a transnationally oriented public sphere. Following this, I argue that the public sphere represents a potentiality for rethinking and expanding the parameters of political identity, civil society, and citizenship.

I make this argument bearing in mind that many theorists propose transnational cosmopolitan public spheres not as supplemental to national ones, but against them and in their stead. The presumption of a competitive tension between frameworks appears in numerous influential texts and often associates the national public sphere with ethnonationalist reactions (Habermas, 2001, 2002; Thompson, 1998; Nussbaum, 1996).

In this book, I challenge dichotomous thinking about national and transnational frameworks. Treating national and transnational frameworks as clear and distinct characterizes not only prevailing public sphere theories, but also many other discussions about politics that seek to locate power in either a national or a transnational context. I argue that public spheres and political theorists need not choose one or the other framework.

Power, politics, and people do not abide by these boundaries, and are not always clearly concentrated in one or the other domain. Rather, we must consider the "double-occupancy" of people and politics in both arenas at once.

It is typically held that wherever the public is made up of citizens of a particular country, and they speak as a collectivity to their own government, the public sphere is national. Here, the public sphere takes shape in cafés, community organizations, and other topical common spaces; its members can and often do meet and associate in person. In the best-case scenario, this public sphere plays a part in the democratization of its own polity.

Wherever a given public sphere is made up of citizens from various countries, and these citizens speak as an international collectivity to other people's governments, numerous governments at once, transnational nongovernmental institutions, or to each other, the public sphere is transnational. Here, the public sphere takes shape in the reading publics of both print and electronic media, and its members correspond in the metatopical common spaces of television, telecommunications, radio, and the Internet. This public sphere is made up of people who may or may not ever meet in person. In the best-case scenario, they bring their opinion and will to bear on the international system, checking and directing the will of foreign and/or multiple governments (the EU, for example), and/or institutions such as the World Bank or World Trade Organization.

Contrary to the analytical distinction sketched above, it is possible to discuss real public spheres that function at both of the levels outlined above. Actually existing public spheres are *not* always strictly national or strictly transnational. Throughout history, various publics have struggled to hold sway, to wield political influence, and often, these public spheres have been simultaneously national and transnational in important ways (we may think here of the movements of abolitionists, suffragists, environmentalists, working class people, immigrants, and indigenous people, just to name some). Such transgressive public spheres challenge the dichotomy of national and transnational frameworks, and this challenge has important consequences for political identity, the efficacy of movements, and normative political philosophy.

By rejecting a strictly national or transnational identity, publics can increase their political leverage at home and abroad. But the strongest case for transgression lies in the concept's normative commitments. The internal logic of the concept of transgression inextricably ties it to a radical democratic politics, to ideals of deepening inclusion, and to forming innovative complex political identities that can set the stage for social movements taking on the evolving problems of present-day capitalist societies. Ultimately, I propose my theory as a contribution to the post–Cold War development of socialist political theory. I understand my argument in this context because the most self-consciously transgressive public spheres have been formed by structurally disadvantaged people and/or people excluded for ideological reasons or reasons of misrecognition. In short, transgression has mainly been the innovation of what I would call "nonbourgeois public spheres," those publics that must struggle against exclusion, that are driven to create inroads of inclusion and recognition needed to achieve reciprocity in contemporary capitalist societies.[3] Furthermore, I contend that nonbourgeois publics formed the first effectively transnational public spheres because, from their position of socioeconomic disadvantage and marginalization, it was often politically necessary to reach out to publics and states beyond the boundaries of their own country. And finally, transgressive public spheres are not so much concerned with the democratization of capitalist states (although they do assist in that process) as they are with posing challenges to international trends in politics, culture, and economics that affect local and geographically disparate communities.

In Habermas' *Structural Transformation of the Public Sphere*, purportedly democratic states could only legitimate the claim that they were appealing to and representing the people at large if they had the express, voluntary affirmation of the national public—if they were influenced in policy and practice by the will and opinion of their own citizens. Today, Habermas argues that a transnational public sphere is desperately needed so that citizens around the globe can come together in collectivities and address their concerns to transnational actors, about policies and processes that lack legitimation from a public sphere. To take Habermas' favorite example, without a fully formed European public sphere to hold the European Union accountable, the EU faces a legitimation crisis.

My counterexample, and guiding illustration of the transgressive public sphere, is found in the case of the Mexican Zapatistas of the 1990s. The example of the Zapatistas is especially poignant for a number of reasons. First, their movement grew out of what was originally an ethnonationalist response to the Mexican government's assimilation and miscegenation policies toward its indigenous populations. The Zapatistas thus grew out of precisely the kind of movement that theorists of the transnational public sphere impute to the national paradigm and believe to be the most likely to resist cosmopolitan developments. According to the usual dichotomous thinking, such nationally framed movements, and particularly a movement like the Zapatistas that employs both ethnic and nationalist discourses, should be reactionary and actively resistant to cosmopolitanism. Yet, while the Zapatistas retained a particular nationalist rhetoric and orientation, they managed to recast indigenous politics as transnational and cosmopolitan at the same time. Their staunch double-occupancy in both the national and transnational frameworks cannot be downplayed or reduced. What's more, the Zapatistas' transgressive public sphere bears radical insights and implications for political identity, and topically, it cuts across all of the major cleavages in current debates about global justice and transnational politics.

Because every public sphere is made and activated by a group of people, public spheres always implicate some kind of collective identity. In the case of transgressive public spheres, this identity is neither national nor transnational. Transgressive public spheres require the regrouping of disparate collectivities and the recasting of political identities against exclusivist group identities. But transgressive public spheres are not simply cosmopolitan, for they refuse to abandon or undermine national identifications and national political projects, looking instead for new ways to affirm both.

As a normative political theory, transgression guarantees that a public sphere will be incompatible with exclusivist, antidemocratic, and fundamentalist politics. In order to be transgressive, a public sphere must oppose itself to national

chauvinisms and to biases that favor de facto dominant bourgeois opinion. To be transgressive they must make a broad invitation for membership at home and abroad, without
encouraging the erosion of group differentiation or assimilation.
So transgression is often a choice aimed to increase the emancipatory potential of a political movement, deepening its terms of
inclusion and consolidating leverage (again, the case of the Zapatistas shall illustrate this).

This book is divided into three parts (three chapters per
part): The first is devoted to the *national*, the second to the
transnational, and the third to the *transgressive* theorization of the
public sphere. I shall provide a basic sketch of the book's structure here.

In part I, I focus on the national framework. I begin with a
survey of the basic concepts and terms of early theories. I present a critical and historical review of the concept of the political
public sphere. This includes a consideration of Immanuel Kant's
international thinking on the public sphere that was more or less
lost to the nationally framed conception. I review Hannah
Arendt's definitions of public and private, and her theory of
communicative power. Consideration of Arendt's theory of communicative power inevitably segues to Habermas' arguments
about legitimation and the public sphere. I examine Habermas'
classical theory of the bourgeois public sphere, but I do so in
light of an account of nonbourgeois public spheres—an account
that was wholly and openly excluded from Habermas' early
study. Nonbourgeois public spheres were not granted any clear
political function in the classical theory. Ignored and marginalized, they had to struggle to define a political function beyond
the conventional channels of reciprocity between civil society
and the state. Certain nonbourgeois public spheres have been
historically misfit with the national framework.

In part II, I turn to discuss the transnational framework. I define globalization; I ask if it warrants a reframing of how to think
about civil society and the scale of political problems, and
mainly, whether or not it signals a new topography for the public sphere. I argue that while globalization is not a new process,
its recent economic and cultural phases do introduce new problems that demand special attention, and the public sphere must

be rethought in important ways. I thus consider existing theories of cosmopolitan and transnational public spheres and the ways in which most theorists have turned away from (and some against) the national framework. I explore numerous efforts to theorize transnational public spheres, and particularly, Habermas' influential recent thinking on cosmopolitan solidarity and transnational (and "postnational") public spheres. Ultimately, we see the dividing lines and shortcomings of the dichotomy between the national and transnational frameworks, and begin to move beyond this dichotomy toward a theory of transgressive public spheres. I initiate this transition by laying bare the deficits of transnational formulations and introducing public spheres that defy categorization as either national or transnational.

In part III, I consider and propose an alternative paradigm for the public sphere. I analyze an actually existing public sphere that employs such a paradigm in practice—that of the Mexican Zapatistas. It is following this example that I formulate my theory of transgression. I argue that it is not possible to understand the Zapatista public sphere if we neglect or discount its national or its transnational orientations and commitments. Simply put, the Zapatista public sphere always has orientations and commitments at both levels. I explore indigenous identity and the recasting of subject positions, showing that a transgressive politics entails transgressive identities. Finally, I make the case for the transgressive public sphere, arguing that it is strategically advantageous and normatively stronger than the other two paradigms. I thus conclude that transgressive public spheres are preferable wherever they are possible.

Taken together, I intend for this book to offer a wide-ranging and critical review of relevant and influential debates in the history of public sphere theory. Understanding the public sphere's various, major theorizations throughout history and its discrete and current reformulations is a necessary part of the present project. After all, introducing a new paradigm for thinking about the public sphere would be premature and perhaps unnecessary so long as earlier paradigms could be sufficiently defended against criticisms. Only after a thorough treatment of the national and transnational paradigms can we justify the necessity of an alternative.

In writing any book, I imagine most authors would like for their whole work to be read, for the critical insights of each chapter to be of interest and value to readers. Indeed, that is how I would envision the ideal "reading public" for this book. Those interested in exploring the principal questions of social movements, radical politics, globalization, cosmopolitanism, and political identity, should make the full journey. But acknowledging the reality of actual engagements with extensive scholarly works, I realize that many readers will come to this text for one reason or another, and not, as it were, for all of the same reasons for writing it. In light of this, I offer the following bit of guidance: Those interested in the history of public sphere theory in political philosophy should focus on parts I and II. Those who already have an in-depth understanding of public sphere theory, and who have come here to discover a new theory of the public sphere, should focus on part III. Those mainly attracted to the discussion of the Mexican Zapatistas will find chapters 6, 7, and 8 the most relevant to their interests.

In general, I hope the reader will discover the enduring appeal of the concept of the public sphere to generations of political philosophers, that s/he will derive from this book a richer understanding of the most influential thinking on the subject. Moreover, I hope to convincingly illustrate a necessary and vital new way to think about, talk about, and participate in public spheres today. Without transgressive public spheres, governments, corporations, and other institutions that function both within and beyond national boundaries grow increasingly unaccountable and elude the democratic control of peoples.

Notes

1. Immanuel Kant is an exception here, since he theorized the need for an international public sphere in the late eighteenth century; his thinking on the public and its political function is discussed at length in my book.

2. Habermas' classical account is 1962's *The Structural Transformation of the Public Sphere: An Inquiry into a Category of Bourgeois Society.*

3. This term is used in contradistinction to Habermas' idea of the "bourgeois public sphere" (1962).

I

PUBLIC SPHERES AND THE NATIONAL FRAMEWORK

Introduction to Part I

A central aim of this book is to show that certain social movements, particularly those that take the public sphere[1] to be their chief terrain (such as the Mexican Zapatistas, considered in chapters 6, 7, and 8), demonstrate the insufficiencies and risks of analyzing public spheres in either a national or a transnational framework (each of these analytical frameworks will be respectively treated in parts I and II). As we shall see, many publics transgress the boundaries between national and transnational and, politically, participate in a multifaceted politics in both national and transnational contexts. In this first part, we focus on the public sphere in a national framework, working to understand problems in the historical development of the concept and the deficits and dangers of tying the function of the public sphere to the political institutions of single states.

Oversimply, I shall argue that (1) some early conceptions of the political public sphere (i.e., Immanuel Kant's and that of the communists of the First International) provided a paradigm for transnational reading publics with an international political function, but that (2) the focus, role and understanding of public spheres were ultimately narrowed to a national framework during the twentieth century by influential theorists who were engaging the crises of their time. And, finally, I argue that (3) this led to neglecting a critical transnational dimension of important public spheres and to the misdiagnosis of the concept of the public sphere itself. But although I argue that an understanding of the deficits of the national framework was clear and present in early theories of the public sphere, only to be problematically obscured, I ultimately contend (in parts II and III) that a theory of the transnational public sphere is also insufficient. I analyze both the national and transnational frameworks in turn because it is precisely in their development, and in their juxtaposition, that we can best discover their shortcomings.

The historical development of the concept of the political public sphere prefigures its understanding as part of the democratic organs correlating to single nation-states, despite the fact that international reading publics had already formed an important political transnational public realm. Republics of letters, meaning discursively linked but geographically separated communities of people who take up the same texts, have existed and been understood as publics as early as the first circulated writings. Such reading publics worked to circulate and to evaluate arguments about the American and French Revolutions, for example, and were formed by revolutionary movements (such as the communists of the First International) for the express purpose of making those movements international. The political role of reading publics was both clear and clearly international as early as the eighteenth and nineteenth centuries.

But, although the circulation of texts has only grown throughout history, in tandem with printing and distribution technologies (now accelerated further by recent nontextual and electronic communication technologies), twentieth-century public sphere theory has almost always taken the individual national public as its unit of study. I will show that the reasons for this are historical, and have to do with the changing focus of political theory, particularly during and after World War II. The focus and function of public sphere theory was narrowed to a specific set of questions regarding the complexly manipulated condition of public opinion as it was situated in national contexts during the rise of Fascism, afterward during the Cold War, and otherwise throughout the twentieth century by each state's employment of evolving medias. Though it is understandable that these developments guided the discussion of public spheres for so long, they have culminated in the radical postponement of the very question of transnational public spheres and the obfuscation of their actual existence.[2]

In chapter 1, we survey the basic concepts and terms of the public sphere showing how in its early theorization, and particularly in Kant's work, the public sphere was not solely restricted to the state-bounded function of checking and influencing national governments. Rather, it worked across national boundaries circulating and processing propaganda and other texts making the attentive public itself a clearly transnational body. Later, in the works of C. Wright Mills and Hannah Arendt, in the midst of World War II and in light of the emergence of distinct media publics, the public sphere was increasingly seen as both a property of single states and as comprised of the participation of state-bounded civil societies.

In chapter 2, we see how Jürgen Habermas extended and deepened Mills' and Arendt's thinking using the concept of the legitimation crises of democratic states, states in want of the conferral of the public opinion of their own civil society. Ultimately in chapter 2, following Habermas, we see how the political public sphere was increasingly fixed and fitted to a strictly state-bounded political function. Here, we see how the historical development of the concept of the public sphere narrowed our understanding of its political function by so tightly linking it to a national framework that, outside of this framework, the public sphere would appear to have no political function at all.

In chapter 3, we focus on Habermas' longer and seminal study of the political public sphere, *The Structural Transformation of the Public Sphere: An Inquiry into a Category of Bourgeois Society* (Habermas' most extensive and influential study of the public sphere). Here, I argue that defining features of the classical theory must be rejected in light of a consideration of what I will call "nonbourgeois public spheres." A consideration of nonbourgeois public spheres, left out of the classical theory, provides the grounds for a critique of the bourgeois public sphere, for rethinking the scale and function of the public sphere in general, and the necessity of widening the definition of discourse to allow for more contentious, even revolutionary, forms of political action. Both the historical development *and* the state-boundedness of the public sphere must be rethought in light of a consideration of neglected, nonbourgeois publics.

In part I, we are not focused on more contemporary public sphere theories. We are not focused on Habermas' work in the 1980s or 1990s, for example (these more current works are discussed in parts II and III). Throughout part I, we shall discover how the concept has come to be better understood, but also, how it has come to be misunderstood in important ways. The concept of the political public sphere has been repeatedly refined in the answering of very specific questions about its changing role throughout the twentieth century (specifically in the contexts of totalitarianism, World War II, the subsequent Cold War, and the ongoing evolution of mass media). But in the course of this refinement, theories of the public sphere have neglected important insights that were clear and present in the prehistory of the concept. In concluding chapter 2, I will argue that some of these earlier insights not only remained relevant as they were being overlooked, but that they were actually growing more relevant. In particular, Arendt and Habermas, as well as others who later enlarged their discussions of the public sphere (some of these others are discussed in chapter 3, but more fully in chapter 5), have misidentified the public sphere as a strictly state-bounded political organ until around the early 1990s, just after the end of the Cold War and the English translation of Habermas' *Structural Transformation*.

In chapter 1, we assess Kant's idea of a transnational, cosmopolitan public realm, and in chapter 2, we learn how subsequent and influential theories of public realms and communicative power rethought political publics as distinctly state-bounded. In Habermas' classical account (chapter 3), the political public sphere is understood to serve the function of a conduit of public opinion and will from civil society (defined as a society of legal citizens) to its corollary beholden state. Yet we shall see by the end of part I that many public spheres have exceeded this strict functionality for strategic reasons or for reasons of material necessity.

Theorists today, in light of discussions about globalization and transnational politics, are trying to reconfigure the sense of the place, the scale, and the membership of public spheres. A number of theorists have tried to enlarge the concept beyond its previous, national confines so that the idea of the public sphere could provide a means for imagining the possibility of a cohesive, global civil society.[3] More specifically, so that the concept could provide a way to think about people in multiple civil societies coming together to self-identify and to communicate as a single collectivity that can challenge or feed back as such to multiple states and transnational institutions.

Perhaps what is most significant here is that the history of the concept of the public sphere has led analysts to think of it as inherently bounded by citizenship. So rethinking the public sphere transnationally has seemed to require rethinking citizenship transnationally, rethinking civil society in terms of global civil society. But the development and juxtaposition of these two paradigms, the national and the transnational, has obscured the possibility for (and the practice of) transgression, that is, the transnationalizing of the public sphere while *affirming* national identities and *retaining* national projects. I ultimately argue that recent efforts to transnationalize the public sphere do not properly address the shortcomings of the nationally conceived public sphere. To the contrary, theories of transnational public spheres have initiated too hard a turn away from the national framework. In these more recent formulations, enduring and critical potentialities of the national framework are ultimately overlooked, something of the concreteness of the classical public sphere is lost, and the importance of certain national identifications (such as those used to mobilize struggles against colonization) is dangerously neglected. It is for these reasons that a rather extensive historical understanding of public sphere theory is essential to my larger project.

When we examine what is unique about the Zapatista public sphere (chapters 6, 7, and 8), we find that all public spheres do not need to be either national or transnational, but that some public spheres could be, should be, or even must be, both national and transnational simultaneously. Not all nationalisms are bad and not all transnationalisms must preclude or supplant national orientations, national politics, and national identities. Indigenous rights politics (among others discussed throughout this work) clearly transgresses the boundary between national and transnational frameworks, in that "indigenous rights" has recently come (in some cases) to refer to highly localized crises and lifeways but always with links to others elsewhere and within the context of economic globalization and transnational politics.

What I will call "transgressive public spheres" are never merely political terrains for theorists to account for. A transgressive public sphere, like all other public spheres, is not simply an instrument without any normative content. As we shall see in the present chapters, the early and classical accounts of the public sphere discuss an arena that always worked toward increasing inclusion, and that has historically served the function of democratization and democratic legitimation. The concept of the public sphere, by itself, has variously upheld the ideals of inclusion, democracy, and human rights. Indeed, as the political public sphere is defined and redefined, we shall see that it always contains a normative commitment to these ideals that only gets deeper and more resolute over time. And the concept of the political public sphere upholds these ideals by its own internal logic (we shall see this in part I in Kant, Arendt, and Habermas). Yet the inclusivity, openness and communicative power of the public sphere, as we shall define and redefine it in parts I and II, is ultimately made even more expansive with the idea of the transgressive public sphere (part III).

Rethinking the political public sphere in varying contexts requires that we have some basic definition of what we mean by it. However, the concept of a political public has been defined multifariously throughout the history of political philosophy. Because different theorists have defined it differently, a survey of its definition does not leave us with a single, coherent term. Hence, a major task of chapters 1 and 2 is to synthesize the varying, most prominent, and most useful definitions of the notion of political publics into a clear and basic understanding that does not overlook major insights.

I begin with a selective prehistory of the concept of the political public sphere (1), and my guiding focus thereafter is on the works of Arendt (1) and Habermas (2 and 3). In this, I agree with the convention of taking Arendt and Habermas to be the founding figures of what is understood as contemporary public sphere theory. Arendt, indeed, offers the clearest exposition of the concepts of public and private that remain at the base of contemporary debates (in *The Human Condition*), and her concept of communicative power (as derived from chapter II in *On Violence*) clearly explicates how the public realm demarcates the most important space for the political action of people. Arendt's concept of communicative power goes far to establish the public realm as both a discursively formed arena and a means to the contestation and influencing of institutions of authority. These facts link us directly to Habermas' 1973 discussion of discourse and legitimation (in *Legitimation Crisis*) and his 1977 essay, "Hannah Arendt's Communications Concept of Power." Although these works were published after his *Structural Transformation*, they appeared in English over fourteen years before the latter and offered clear and concise statements of some of the basic contentions of the earlier work.

Nevertheless, a thorough study of theories of the public sphere will inevitably pay special attention to its "classical" formulation. Habermas' *Structural Transformation* (1962) remains, variously, the centerpiece and/or launching off point for contemporary debates on the subject. In it, nonbourgeois public spheres, those that form in the more "plebeian" sectors of civil society, are excluded from consideration. In light of this, theorists and historians have invoked revisionist histories in order to distinguish other public spheres from the bourgeois public sphere.[4]

Such theorists and historians have argued that an account of nonbourgeois public spheres proves that there has been a multiplicity of publics and reveals a diversity of initiatives within intrastate democratization processes. This is important, but in chapter 3 I make a further claim about the bearing of nonbourgeois public spheres on the classical theory and the national framework. I argue that there is an important lack of fitness between nonbourgeois public spheres and their structurally determined addressee, the state. Nonbourgeois public spheres often internationalize their political discourses and address themselves to other bodies than their own state. I argue not only that the status, strategies, and discursive content of the public sphere must be rethought in light of nonbourgeois public spheres, but also that the structurally determined political function of the public sphere, that is to say, at its best, its function as a conduit of influence between society and the state, must also be rethought. In short, a theory that evolves specifically to account for the bourgeois public sphere has a particular normative content (the democratic legitimation of a corollary, representative state), which cannot be simply appropriated and applied to the case of nonbourgeois public spheres. This is because nonbourgeois public spheres often function on a different scale and have fundamentally different methods, politics, and aims than their bourgeois counterparts (they may, for example, aim at rebellion, radical democracy, or revolution).

These points will be more fully illustrated by the case of the Zapatista public sphere. What I mean by this is that, as we shall see with the Zapatistas and others, nonbourgeois public spheres often have nationally focused initiatives, but are faced with institutions of governance that do not automatically or necessarily recognize them as political—hence, such nonbourgeois public spheres have to work hard and innovatively in order to hold political sway. The classical theory and the national framework, as explicated in chapter 3, do not guarantee any political function for nonbourgeois public spheres. Indeed, nonbourgeois public spheres must struggle to constitute their political function outside of established or expected conduits of reciprocity between civil society and the state.

In chapter 3, I present my culminating critique of the classical theory. I assess the analytical rubric according to which the criteria for a national public sphere in a Westphalian sense ground Habermas' theory. This analytical rubric enables us to see clearly how, why, and which public spheres are national. Here, in arguing that nonbourgeois public spheres have a special interest in constructing themselves and their discourses transnationally, the stage will be set for part II, which focuses on public spheres and the transnational framework.

In the context of the larger work, the following three chapters move us from analyzing the concept of the political public sphere in the history of philosophy to analyzing the possibility for alternative constructions of public spheres with alternatively constituted political functions (in contrast to the structure and the structural political function of the national, bourgeois public sphere). A richer, more contestatory account of the multiplicity of public spheres provides us with the necessary grounding for a discussion of transnational public spheres (part II), and eventually for the possibility of alternative constructions that could situate public spheres beyond the dichotomy of national and transnational frameworks (part III).

Notes

1. Until chapter 3, when I will discuss Jürgen Habermas' *Structural Transformation* directly, I speak generally of "public realms" or "publics," and not always of "public spheres." By all of these terms, I mean to refer to the same concept. My hesitation in using the term "public sphere" throughout chapters 1 and 2 derives from the fact that the phrase did not appear in the academic literature until the publication of *The Structural Transformation*.

2. The problems of this postponement and obfuscation will be discussed in greater detail in parts II and III, when I more expressly take up the question of transnational public spheres. There, I will show that this line of questioning ultimately produced another problem for theorizing public spheres, precisely the problem of seeking to understand them as either national *or* transnational. Though we are still far from assessing the problems of moving from a national to a transnational framework, the basic problematic is as follows: The insufficiencies and risks of conceiving of political publics as state-bounded eventually led theorists to turn from a national conception of public spheres to a transnational conception. Yet the transnational conception, on its own, (1) takes for granted the enduring problem-solving capabilities of the state, (2) takes for granted the positive potentialities of national identifications, and (3) therefore contributes to the further diminishment of the scope of state power and the further dissolution of the classical democratic relationship between civil society and the state.

3. I am alluding to theorists and theories that I will consider more closely in chapter 5.

4. See, among others, Oskar Negt and Alexander Kluge (1993), Geoff Eley (1992), Nancy Fraser (1997, 2002), Michael Warner (2002), and Jean Cohen and Andrew Arato (1999). I will make reference to the work of these and others throughout parts I and II.

1

Basic Concepts and Terms

Political Public Spheres and Communicative Power

Formative Lexicons of the Political Public Sphere: From Kant to Mills

In chapter 1, I intend to accomplish two distinct goals. First, I aim to provide the reader (and to begin this work) with a historical understanding of the theoretical lexicon for thinking and speaking about the political function of public opinion. In subsequent chapters, I shall accept the premise that political opinion forms in discursive arenas in civil societies and that organs of public opinion have, or at least can have, an indispensable role in influencing powerholders, ultimately, in shaping and reshaping political and social realities (from the domestic and foreign policies of states to the transformation of collective identities). Therefore, I must substantiate and explore the basic premise of the political function of public opinion in this opening chapter.

However, this contextual purpose, although it is the most rudimentary, is of lesser importance than the argumentative aim of chapter 1. In fact, the following review of the genesis of the concept of the political public sphere is crucial to the overarching arguments of this book, and observations made here will be revisited and invoked at the most important junctures in the development of my own theoretical paradigm.

The central claim of chapter 1 is that, if we begin with Immanuel Kant's minimal yet influential writing on public reasoning and its political significance, we shall find a clear theorization of transboundary public spheres, for example an understanding of actually existing international reading publics that foster cosmopolitanism. At the same time, however, Kant was reluctant to suggest a wholesale transition from national to transnational public spheres because he understood the enduring value of national frameworks for civic and political life. Indeed, we can find the seeds for a "transgressive public sphere theory" in Kant's work. Now, Kant did not develop such a theory himself, and we would have disagreed about acceptable forms of political action and the question of revolution. Still, my own thinking on the public sphere owes a great debt to Kant. In the end, I will distinguish the theory of transgressive public spheres from both early and contemporary formulations—to counterpose the transgressive public sphere to Kant's account, and to the classical national and the contemporary transnational models.

But Kant reminds us that the first paradigmatic transition in public sphere theory was not (as is typically represented) a transition from a national public sphere to a transnational one, but from an increasingly rational, international, and cosmopolitan public sphere (Kant) to that of a state-bounded, manipulated mass public (variously in Mills, Arendt, and Habermas, among others).[1] A proper understanding of this theoretical transition, why it happened, and how and why it has been overlooked, shall help to reveal the limitations of succeeding public sphere theories.

Hence, beyond setting the stage for a general discussion of the public sphere, chapter 1 also sets the stage for my own efforts to rethink the concept in light of contemporary theorizations. In the culminating argument of this work—that is, in making the case for transgressive public spheres—I return to and build upon many of Kant's insights.[2] Furthermore, we shall see that some of the chief concerns and observations of early theories of the public sphere help to refute arguments for a wholesale transition from the national to the transnational framework (which we encounter in part II).

I am not here interested in the etymology of the word "public," nor even with the development of the concept of a public realm as a particular social space, but only with the prehistory of the concept of an expressly political public realm with the distinction of being an organ of and within civil society. I begin with this already qualified political public realm because to start with any of its constitutive parts, for example, to trace the concepts of public and private as distinct zones, would bring us at least as far back as Diogenes, the fourth-century Greek philosopher who would challenge the public/private dichotomy by masturbating in public places whenever he felt a sexual need.[3] Such an accounting is both too vast and of insufficient relevance to the project at hand.

To better anchor my focus, let me begin with a working definition of my unit of study: By political public realm I mean *a subset of a larger and delimitable group of people, who become a defined subset by way of their engagement in a particular topic or topics of discussion, and who politicize themselves as a subset by attempting to influence outside bodies, whether institutional or other subsets of peoples, with norms, claims, and demands rooted in an opinion and will that they call their own, formed in collective discussion.* Very generally then, a political public is a collective of actively engaged discussants that need not consist of every member of civil society (though it may be open to every member), which intends to negotiate changes in the social and political reality outside of itself. Thus, sharing some kind of collective identity is not enough. A political public forms *within* a larger collectivity (civil society) by and in the active discussion of a group, and this group discursively assesses or develops a will and opinion, which it ultimately seeks to bring to bear on outside bodies.

In this working definition, civil society is also defined, loosely, as the larger and delimitable group of people within which political publics take shape as a subset. And civil society must remain loosely defined as such because it cannot (not yet at least) be simply or sharply distinguished from the political public realm. This is because members of civil society *enter* political publics by way of their communicative engagement with others over issues of common concern about which they become outwardly political. Political publics are essentially sectors of civil society engaged in a special type of activity (for now, we may think of social movements, politically organized ethnic groups, or other civil society organizations).[4] If we imagine a group of citizens bringing its collectively formed opinion and will to bear on outside bodies, we are thinking precisely of what is meant by the political public sphere.

That said, the public sphere is not synonymous with "special interest group," and the public sphere is not the domain of a lobbyist, both of whom are, by definition, foremost concerned with the interests of some particular party, and often openly, the private interests of a paying client, or the group's members themselves. Because of this, special interest groups represent a fundamental tension with the sense of "public" intended here—public means of, by, or for the general public, and public spheres must be able to make this claim of generality, to convincingly frame their concerns and issues as sufficiently public. Hence, if the wealthiest subset of the population calls for a regressive tax scheme that relieves them of a due proportionate to their income, the claims of this group do not form a public sphere—they certainly may be heard passing through one public sphere or another, but they cannot comprise such a space within civil society since they represent private interests and an initiative that is agreeable only to those few who share similar economic privilege.

But how is civil society defined? Conventionally, which shall suffice for the bulk of part I, civil society is defined as the society of legally conferred citizens of a particular city or state. That is, civil society is conventionally taken, and for the time being we may assume it, to map out over citizenship. However, as we shall see, the relationship between civil society and the state has been understood in importantly different ways.

With these general terms in mind, let us turn to explore some features of Immanuel Kant's discussions of political publics, particularly, his ideas of civil society, international right, and public justification. In this, we shall see that Kant had a good idea of the need for a transnational public sphere, that he argued for its realization, and that he already understood the political limits of a nationally bounded public sphere.[5]

Kant's definition of public reasoning in his essay "An Answer to the Question: What Is Enlightenment?" provides an early and important discussion of the concept of the public sphere. But it would be misleading to focus only on this short (under eight pages in any translation) essay of Kant's. It is also necessary to consider how Kant defines the requisite terrain of civil society on which public reasoning could take place, as well as the larger role public reasoning plays in determining principles of justice for a state and for international relations among states. To get a more comprehensive understanding of Kant's theory of political publics, I will also look briefly at selections from his *Metaphysics of Morals* and his essay, "Perpetual Peace: A Philosophical Sketch." Contemporary public sphere theory presupposes a legal framework that sufficiently secures people to participate in contentious public discourse; that is, it presupposes a kind of liberal democratic civil society. Kant, however, wrote during a time when the case still needed to be made for the protection and encouragement of public debate that might be critical of the government, of tradition, and of the interests of others in positions of power and authority. Hence, it was necessary for Kant to focus on the prerequisites for political publics.

In *The Metaphysics of Morals*, "The Theory of Right, Pt. II: Public Right," Kant insists that a basic social order, maintained by laws, is required for there to even be a terrain on which to engage others without fear of violent repercussions. External forces, embodied in political institutions, secure this terrain for civic engagement. Man "must accordingly enter into a state wherein that which is to be recognised as belonging to each person is allotted to him *by law* and guaranteed to him by an adequate power (which is not his own, but external to him). In other words, he should at all costs enter into a state of civil society."[6] Civil society is indeed the most essential prerequisite for the political public realm. A legally delimited civil society (again, citizenship meant membership in most cases), however, has not always meant the same thing.

The above definition of civil society is reminiscent enough of Jean-Jacques Rousseau's idea of the pact that puts us beyond the state of nature in his *Social Contract*. But although Rousseau stressed that the ruler or state was not the people's master but rather its agent of representation, he nevertheless severely restricted the contestatory inclinations of civil society to a concept of freedom rooted in subservience. The public might desire the good, Rousseau says, but it cannot always see the good, and, therefore, a "lawgiver" is necessary to, in a peculiar but very real sense, force the people to be free—to show the public what it desires and to calibrate the judgment that guides the general will.[7] The complexities of this argument cannot be taken up here, so it will have to suffice to say that for Rousseau the continual progress of a society is neither a responsibility nor a process that can be safely assigned to the voluntary negotiations of civil society, and this underlies his contention that democracy "is not suited to men."[8]

Far more extreme, and thus a far better counterpoint to Kant's view, is Thomas Hobbes' idea of the establishment of civil society as coincident with the establishment of political society—coincident with the establishment of the state. On the famous title page of Hobbes' *Leviathan*, one can see a clear illustration of the idea that the representative sovereign state takes its form in its subsuming of the people; its citizens comprise both its existence and its sovereignty to the extent that contestation with the state becomes a self-contradiction. This image could be overextended to make Hobbes' picture look a bit more absolutist than it is in fact, but it nevertheless represents a vision in which there is little to no distinction between civil society and the political state. But in Kant's "Enlightenment" essay, a distinction between the civil and the political by way of fostering a general refusal among citizens to defer their judgment to established authorities is much of the main point. In fact, Kant's theory of the power of public reasoning effectively redefines civil society as the realm in which a critical and somewhat autonomous citizenry grows up. Ultimately, the critical and rational autonomy of civil society becomes the measure of its maturity, or competence.

Despite this (which I will substantiate below), it has often been held that not until the political philosophy of G. W. F. Hegel was civil society reconceived as a corollary but autonomous field of political contestation. For Hegel, indeed, civil society constituted a political power that could function independently of the state, although to be political it must always ultimately engage in matters of the state, and in fact the highest ideal was for a people to self-identify (through *Sittlichkeit*) with their national state.

Still, Hegel defined the critical independence of (or differentiation between) society and state in his early pamphlet *The Magistrates Should be Elected by the People*, and later on in his *Philosophy of Right*. Hence, Charles Taylor invokes civil society in a "post-Hegelian sense" when referring to a civil society that could voluntarily, legally, and justifiably participate in clashes of various sorts with its own state.[9] This conception of civil society and the state in Hegel's work was appropriated and restated by Karl Marx, who viewed the relation of the one to the other as not only distinct but inevitably combative.

Kant, I contend, preceded Hegel's distinction of civil society as such in his "Enlightenment" essay where he argued for a civil society that was more than a mere attachment of or extension to the state, and more than a fully obedient populace. It is likely that this has been obscured to some degree by the fact that Kant remains cognizant at each step of the need for civil society to obey and preserve the authority of the state, and the fact that he incisively indicts revolution as an ineffective means to social change. However, what is more important to Kant is precisely the argument that civil society has been too intellectually subordinate to the complex of conferred authorities and specialists guiding and guarding society, and that this lack of differentiation in thinking is responsible for the widespread condition of self-incurred immaturity. Kant claims that a combination of (1) citizens finding it easier to defer to the authority and power of their guardians, and (2) untrusting leaders reluctant to encourage civil society to think for itself, to become critical and independent in its thinking, has stunted "Enlightenment," our overcoming of self-incurred immaturity. To become independent, critically thinking, speaking, reading and writing rational citizens, not just as individuals but also as a whole society, is the aim of Enlightenment. An enlightened society would not physically overthrow institutional authorities, but would reconfigure thinking on important issues, essentially overthrowing hackneyed and dangerous traditions that do not improve society as a whole. At bottom, Kant was calling for a politicization of civil society, not through revolution, but through the use of public reasoning. It is here that we find the first formulation of a discursive public power with a clearly political role.

Kant argues that our rational faculty can and should be divided between two uses, the public use and the private use. Public reason is that use of our reasoning that publicizes our rational reflections and critical insights. The publication of our rational reflections and critical insights has as its purpose the betterment of society. So, if you are a teacher, clergyperson, or taxpayer, and you have some expert grasp of the subject of your specialty, it is almost unthinkable that you will not discover problems within the existing systems of education, religion, and taxes. Not only is a critical analysis of such problems guaranteed, it is also likely that you will discover rational, implementable solutions. Given this, Kant argues that we must be completely free with regard to our public use of reason, that public reasoning is our duty as citizens, and that enlightened rulers are identifiable as such inasmuch as they encourage us to use our reason publicly.[10]

It is also here that Kant defines the idea of a public realm as a subset of civil society, even though discussing the public realm as a social space of any kind is not quite his intention. He argues that the reading or hearing public for publicized critiques ought to be specialized subsets of civil society to whom the critiques will make sense. So if you are a clergyperson, you address your criticisms to the Church; if you are a teacher, you address the school, other teachers, or the board of education; if you are a taxpayer, you address other taxpayers, or perhaps more importantly those who legislate tax laws. Others, outside the appropriate public may neither understand the critique of the specialist, nor need to. For example, if the teacher prevails, the students will benefit from the improvements made in the educational system. The public reasoning of the teacher persuaded the board of education and the school (faculty and/or administration), but the students and tax legislators were not addressed and did not need to be. Publics, in Kant's sense, are therefore somewhat exclusive, inasmuch as they come together around specialized subject matters.[11]

However, some issues may be more open and inclusive than others, such as a reading public for a popular book that proliferates some sort of criticism for the purpose of prevailing upon the thinking of a readership as large as is possible. In such a case, literacy and the accessibility of the text define its exclusiveness.

But we must also remember that Kant means by enlightenment a general enlightenment of the people at large, not just of leaders and guardians and other specialists, and so public reasoning must ultimately spread beyond the specialized subsets of its various addresses. Kant maintains that an unrestrained public use of reason works to proliferate critique and engender inquiry throughout the whole society, and that people in general will ultimately begin to emerge from their self-incurred immaturity. During this process, we are in what Kant calls an "Age of Enlightenment," and only when "men as a whole can be in a position (or can even be put into a position) of using their own understanding confidently and well in religious matters, without outside guidance" are they in an "Enlightened Age."[12] (It must here be noted that Kant distinguishes the example of religious matters to be of the gravest concern, since unthinking deference when it comes to matters of one's own spirituality is the direst predicament.) In the end, according to Kant, the unrestricted use of public reason should replace political revolution as a mechanism for change. Unrestricted public reasoning may bring change far more slowly than revolution, but the change yielded by the former would be a result of real reforms in thinking, not of coercion.[13]

But, says Kant, we must also employ the private use of reason. Citizens are repeatedly entrusted with important tasks whose ongoing completion constitutes the smooth functioning of society. In any occupation, we are assigned a set of tasks that must be completed. Indeed, our employment depends on our completion of these tasks. And the completion of these tasks requires the use of our rational faculty. From clergy entrusted to give sermons or lessons in spirituality to teachers working at schools, to mechanics repairing cars, all must employ their reasoning while at work, in answering questions, solving problems, and getting their jobs done with competence. Yet the reasoning employed here is private because it is employed for the purpose of completing entrusted tasks. This is a peculiar way to define "private," but what it essentially means is that we must, despite any and all rational-critical concern, remain purely passive in certain roles and during certain times, that we must work within the existing framework in order to keep it functioning, overall, for the good and security of the commonwealth. A taxpayer who disagrees with the taxes he is asked to pay must nevertheless pay them, and an officer who disagrees with a law must nevertheless uphold it. In these roles and during these times, our use of reason is not completely free, it is restricted, and it must be. For the legal framework that establishes and protects civil society to continue into the future, for the tax structure to remain functional even if flawed, for the Church and the schools to continue operating, it is necessary that our rational faculty is restricted in certain roles and during certain times and that obedience takes the place of critique. Therefore, our private use of reason is that use we make of it during moments of obedience. We may think critically while we obey, but we may not make such reasoning a public matter while obedience is appropriate.[14]

All of this, for Kant, is to say that there are proper times and places for critique and dissent, as well as for obedience. Also, that both critique and obedience are necessary, and that a competent member of society is understood as such when he or she not only knows when to use reason publicly and when to use it privately, but when he or she actually uses reason in both ways. What is interesting about this conclusion is that Kant does not assign to the state or to a lawgiver the enforcement of times and places for dissent and obedience, but rather, expects the mature citizen him or herself to learn how and when it is right to disobey. A competent citizen, according to Kant, works both toward a better society and to keep the existing one stable and functional. A person who goes to work all day and uses her reason privately in order to get her job done, and then, after work, gives public voice to her thoughts and criticisms on improprieties, deficiencies, and injustices in her field of work to the appropriate public is a competent citizen. Kant applies this paradigm of public criticism to the political state, saying ultimately that criticism of the government must be allowed, and even encouraged by the government itself, but that the government's mandates must simultaneously be obeyed for the preservation of both state and civil society.

Of course, Kant is not here particularly concerned with the problems of modern liberal democracy. What he is trying to establish is the right of public criticism in an age when rulers were

extremely paternalistic, in an age when they maintained a disposition toward civil society that presumed its incompetence. In
this analogy, civil society may be likened to a child who neither
contests nor evaluates parental wisdom and dictates. But Kant
challenges this paternalism and maintains that, although law
and order are to be obeyed and preserved, civil society must out-
grow its state of immaturity and critically interrogate the underlying principles and actual utility of all of the workings of
politics, economics, society, and tradition. Hence, alongside
stressing obedience and deriding revolt, we must find in Kant a
concept of civil society as a field for antagonistic questioning
that is markedly more defined as such than the conceptions of
civil society present in Rousseau's and Hobbes' work. And
Kant's ideas of civil society and public criticism lay the groundwork commonly imputed to Hegel's theory.

It might appear thus far that Kant is implying that the political role of public criticism inheres in its forming a kind of dia-
logical relationship between the public realm and the state,
delimiting the political public to a state-bounded function. But
such a contention is rigorously complicated by Kant's thoroughgoing cosmopolitanism. If public reasoning is the most useful
mechanism for effective and lasting social and political change,
and if politics must always look toward international ends, as it
must for Kant, then how do we rightly understand the state-
boundedness of political publics? To answer this question, we
must turn to Kant's essay on "Perpetual Peace, Pt. II: On the
Agreement between Politics and Morality according to the Transcendental Concept of Public Right," where he outlines a
broader role for the rational-critical public.

In "Perpetual Peace," Kant argues that for any principle to be
just it must be publicly knowable and conferred as just by the
public. This argument is an extension of Kant's categorical imperative. Kant maintains that all actions that impact the lives of
others are based on motivations and principles that should be, in
principle, acceptable to all those affected. In politics, when such
motivations and principles are kept out of the public arena,
when they are kept secret, it is precisely because they are unjust.
He writes: "All actions affecting the rights of other human beings are wrong if their maxim is not compatible with their being

made public."[15] In other words, it is necessary to publicize the maxims that would ground human rights to all those who would be affected by such rights in order to assess whether or not they are right. The assessment of political right, then, requires the scrutiny and approval of the public. For Kant, public right refers to the declarability of a maxim. If it is openly declarable, does not require secrecy, and if it is in principle acceptable to all, then it conforms to public right.

Here, Kant is linking justice to openness, binding politics to the public realm on a deeper level. The public realm is the testing ground for maxims, it is a discursive arena in civil society where the acceptability of principles is evaluated, and importantly, the wider the public is, the wider the validity of the principles. In "Perpetual Peace," Kant maintains that internal right (national) and international right are distinct zones, maintaining that we can speak of both a national and an international framework. International justice is achievable, Kant maintains, a declaration of international human rights is possible, but international right cannot be achieved until internal right is achieved (the fact that Kant does not simply choose one framework over the other, that, in other words, he insists on the necessity of both internal and international right will return as a major theme in the final chapter of this book, chapter 9). Yet Kant warns at length about the perpetually warring relation of states, observing that war seems to be "ingrained in human nature" and that it is "the desire of every state (or its ruler) to achieve lasting peace by thus dominating the world, if at all possible."[16] Because of this, a nationally conceived political philosophy is insufficient even if it is necessary as the first theory, for it does nothing to solve the problem of international warfare.

Hence, Kant argues "[t]here is only one rational way in which states coexisting with other states can emerge from the lawless condition of pure warfare. Just like individual men, they must renounce their savage and lawless freedom, adapt themselves to public coercive laws, and thus form an *international state (civitas gentium)*, which would necessarily continue to grow until it embraced all the peoples of the earth."[17] He refers to this lofty goal as "the positive idea of a *world republic*," and in it Kant presages the idea of a global civil society as a political power.[18]

This follows from the fact that international right, just like internal right, can only be determined in the publicity of the maxims that ground it to all those affected by the rights in question. Kant thus intends for global civil society to provide a security against the unjust domination of one state against others since what is politically right in one state may need to be modified after it is scrutinized in the light of international public criticism.

At this juncture, I shall conclude our discussion of Kant by making some important clarifications about his concepts of public reasoning and cosmopolitanism. Kant defined public reasoning explicitly as that use one makes of it in "addressing the entire *reading public* [Kant's emphasis]."[19] But what could Kant have meant by the entire reading public in 1784? It is not easy to say exactly, but we can be sure that he was himself, as reader and writer, a member of numerous reading publics. I briefly mentioned the war between the American colonies and Great Britain, which ran roughly from 1775–1783, and the French Revolution from 1789–1799. Kant was well aware of both revolutions; he was an enthusiast of the American Revolution and a critic of Great Britain during the war, and wrote his "Enlightenment" essay at its close. He wrote about the French Revolution at some length in his *Contest of Faculties* (1798), speaking of it as a "detached political observer."[20] Kant was not much for travel and his role as "detached political observer" was precisely that of a member of reading publics.

Kant, along with many other observers in the same reading public, spoke of the French Revolution as a peculiar kind of shared experience. Speaking of the enthusiasm of outsiders for the revolutionaries, Kant wrote "the external public of onlookers sympathized with their exaltation, without the slightest intention of actively participating in their affairs."[21] Hence, there existed an international reading public that was neither passively observing nor actively participating in the revolution, but was asserting solidarity with it from afar. Though the revolution was a major event in the history of the French nation-state, the reading publics of the world observed and discussed it, circulating signals that were also received by the governments of the world about a kind of moral cause that roused not just the French people but humanity. The public sphere that took up the texts and the questions of the French Revolution was international and comprehended the international resonance of the underlying moral principles of the revolution. Yet the revolution's primary import was mainly understood in terms of its bearing on the French reality. Certainly, though, there can be no question that Kant understood at least some "entire reading publics" to be transboundary.

For Kant, the public must justify political right not just in national but also in international affairs—publics across boundaries must affirm principles and policies that would apply across boundaries. But even in the national context, Kant insisted on thinking about political right in a cosmopolitan framework, with an ideal in mind that the end for states should be to arrive "at a lawful settlement of their differences by forming something analogous to a universal state."[22] Kant maintained that there was ultimately a need for something like a transnational public sphere that could provide public justification for a transnational state, a state that would be the logical outgrowth of the cosmopolitanism of numerous states. In such a state "the peoples of the earth have thus entered in varying degrees into a universal community, and it has developed to the point where a violation of rights in *one* part of the world is felt *everywhere*."[23]

In between Kant and Arendt, there have of course been many other important developments in theorizing political publics, but I must here exercise the promised selectivity of this account. One way (not the only way) to sum up Hegel's appropriation and revision of Kant's idea of civil society, and then Marx's appropriation and revision of Hegel's idea of civil society, would be to say that the role of civil society was increasingly redefined as more autonomous and potentially (or for Marx, inexorably) antagonistic, the distinction drawn by Kant between civil society and the state taken to an extreme. Kant's counterbalance of obedience in private reasoning and his general derision of revolution were increasingly supplanted by the growing popularity of revolutionary political thinking in the late eighteenth century (Kant's "Enlightenment" essay was written in the light of the American Revolution and in the dawn of the French Revolution) and throughout the whole of the nineteenth century.

Two key components of Kant's understanding of political publics persevered. First, from Kant through Marx, whether or not civil society became the terrain for political publics had much to do with the self-understanding of civil society and/or the disposition of the state. That is to say, how the people (or, for Marx, proletarians) understood themselves and their relationship to the state and to other powerholders would determine their proclivity for political or civic engagement. Indeed, for Marx, the self-understanding of the proletariat was a major factor in their mobilization as a class. Despite pointed remarks about the primacy of the *structure* in Marx's theory, the *superstructure* remained as a critical terrain, hence his own lifelong investment in propaganda and the widespread translation and publication of texts, correspondences, and debates. But the disposition of the state would also go far to determine popular inclinations toward political or civic engagement. For example, in a severe case, when it was discovered that the African slaves in America in the eighteenth and nineteenth centuries associated for political ends, their associations were often met with repercussions of extreme violence or death.[24] Though slaves were not legally integrated into civil society (via citizenship), the very prerequisite for political public realms, this example illustrates vividly a relationship to powerholders that preempted the emergence of subaltern or subversive political publics. Many other examples are available, such as the various pecuniary penalties that have served to deter the association of women for political ends throughout much of American history.[25] Kant lauded the enlightened leader as precisely that leader who would not preempt political publics by fear of reprisal, but rather would encourage them, and Kant encouraged civil society to understand itself as a rational-critical political agent capable of contestation with authorities.

The second component of Kant's understanding of political publics that persevered, at least for some time, was the international framework. The communists of the First International believed in beginning their project within the nation (as did Kant, not for revolution, of course, but for the establishment of political right), among its own proletariat and the objective reality facing that group, within their language and regarding their directly lived and shared experience of industrialization. However, the most important addressees of the First International were capitalism understood as a world system, never understood as a national system, and the world proletariat, never just that of a particular nation. Even if reformist and basically national in their orientation (such as the German Worker's Party was, according Marx), the communists were still addressing a world system managed by the "big bourgeoisie" and the world proletariat, and they made visceral attacks on all conceptions of politics that were fitted to a national framework.[26] Yet this trait, that of international political thinking, was ultimately obscured by the orientations of the public sphere theories of the twentieth century.

Indeed, the core of Kant's insights on political publics was essentially preserved in political philosophy until the development and proliferation of myriad forms of mass media and until these medias came to be seen as instruments of manipulation during the twentieth century. Beginning with the advent of radio and film, and culminating in the idea of mass publics propagandized through the use of these medias, scholars started to discuss complexly manipulated publics and the mobilization of biases. This would mark the next major revision in thinking about political public realms.

Social psychology, mixed with sociology and philosophy, and particularly, with Marxism, led to a new understanding of the situation of the public in the twentieth century. Indeed, the Frankfurt Institute for Social Research, where much of this interdisciplinary theorizing began as the development of critical theory, is both the school and the spirit in which Habermas wrote *Structural Transformation*. The concept of "masses," that is, the cumulative result of the mechanisms of mass production and mass communication, which produced, among other things, "mass consciousness" and "mass culture" radically altered the Kantian conception of the public realm.[27] Theodor Adorno and Max Horkheimer did much to explicate the dangers of mass consciousness, in light of Nazism, in their *Dialectic of Enlightenment*, the title of which is a sarcastic reference to the optimisms in Kant's concept of enlightenment and in Hegel's and Marx's concepts of dialectics. These concepts (Kant's, Hegel's, and Marx's) implied a necessary progression that, although tumultuous, was working toward a greater good. But for Adorno and Horkheimer, the Holocaust stood as a fearful refutation of such hopeful theses, fascism appeared to them to be taking elusive cultural forms in advanced capitalist societies, and there was no serious expectation to revitalize any theory of a potentially liberatory public sphere.[28]

This brings us to the final question of this prehistory: Were there any explicit reformulations of the public as a potential political power in light of the emergence of complexly manipulated publics that preceded Arendt's major works? Yes. In the postwar period, the next major figure to write directly and at great length about a public realm with clear political agency was, ironically, C. Wright Mills. I call this ironic because Mills is best known for the central argument in his *Power Elite* (1956), in which he claims that the political agency of citizens in America has been near totally eliminated by the consolidation of business and political power. Both Arendt and Habermas have acknowledged Mills' contributions to their subject, but have focused on Mills' conception of power in *The Power Elite*, where he does not offer an optimistic theory of political publics. What is lacking is a focus on his numerous essays investigating the still vital potency of public opinion in an era of mass consciousness and mass culture.[29] Mills' reformulation of a potentially liberatory public sphere in these works and during the 1950s matters for our larger thesis because it insists that public opinion cannot be wholly wielded by the pervasive special interests of a commercial media, and that even where mass consciousness is a dangerous cultural product the public realm remains a promising site for critical discourse with a political function.[30]

In 1950, Mills wrote an essay titled "Mass Media and Public Opinion" that offered an overview of the political history of public opinion. He generalized three phases. The first phase is the "classic democratic" phase in which people constitute a public by freely and voluntarily engaging in discussions of common concern, and form a public opinion that is used to measure and to enrich existing democracy. This idea should remind us of Kant's; Mills, however, is thinking here specifically about the situation of public opinion in the classical democratic conception.

The second phase is the "totalitarian" phase in which external forces infiltrate and control public opinion without revealing to the public that their own, self-identified opinions have been strategically manufactured. In the totalitarian phase, power-holders monopolize and employ mass media to canonize chosen topics for public discussion, framing them according to ideologies that suit their interests and support their goals. In this phase, public opinion is clearly important even if it is overtaken by special interests, since pains are taken to engineer it with particular penchants. Mills is thinking of totalitarian states here, but particularly of Nazism and of the Nazis' use of mass media to acclimate large subsets of the German population to an ideology that would lubricate the plans of the regime.

The third phase is the "synthesis" phase in which mass media continues to monopolize the means of communication and to delimit public discussion in civil society, but does not do so "totally." This phase of the public realm presents it as a still, even if narrowly, open space for competing interests that emerged in the late 1940s in the United States. According to Mills:

> The American public is neither a sandheap of individuals each making up his own mind, nor a regimented mass manipulated by monopolized media of communication. The American public is a complex, informal network of persons and small groups interchanging, on all occupational and class levels, opinions and information, and variously exposed to the different types of mass media and their varying contexts.[31]

In this phase, discussion circles could still challenge the official line of thinking and form a dissident public opinion, despite significant infiltration and control from the media. So publics are still possible, and they retain enduring political importance. This is because publics engender and host dissent and provide the classical democratic function of revealing the limits and improving the quality of representation.

It is crucial to point out that this view is more hopeful than Adorno and Horkheimer's influential analysis of American culture developed during their Californian exile in 1944. In fact, it is precisely in discussing this phase of public opinion that Mills reformulates an optimistic political role for the public in light of the emergence and his own acknowledgment of complexly manipulated publics. In Adorno and Horkheimer's 1944 analysis, America was almost wholly overtaken with mass deception manufactured by what they called the "culture industry," and although what they saw in America was very different than the totalitarianism they fled from in Germany, America's culture industry constituted a different kind of totalitarianism, they claimed, and one that did not promise to be any less ominous in the end.[32] Mills' "synthesis" phase admits the possibility of mass deception while denying it as a totality.

Much of this has to do with an important distinction Mills draws between publics and masses.[33] A public forms by the discussion of a primary public, that is, a public formed in and of the free and voluntary discussion of people. Often and more benignly, he maintains, the media serves to associate different primary publics around the country to particular topics of discussion publicized to widespread audiences. In this case, the mass media actually helps to animate and link otherwise disparate, unrelated publics (there is a revitalized version of this argument today in consideration of Internet technologies, which we will further explore in part III). However, a public is transformed into a mass wherever it is substantively restructured as a market. Publics may be restructured as markets without their populations noticing much of the difference. This transformation is brought about, in part, through repeated addresses of the commercial media to the public in which the latter is treated as a field of consumers whose interests and wishes can be influenced to suit the needs of industry. For Mills, publics do face the danger of becoming masses, but mass media itself is intrinsically neutral, as it can be yielded to enliven and enrich publics as well as to restructure them into masses. Interestingly, the transformation of a public into a mass market is much of what Habermas means when he later discusses the depoliticization of the public sphere, or its structural transformation.

Given this tension between publics and masses, Mills argues that the distribution of cultural products is perhaps the single most important issue complicating the "synthesis" phase of public opinion. According to Mills, *cultural products* are things, such as movies, books, music, radio, television shows, and other artworks. *Cultural publics* are publics whose membership consists of their consumption of cultural products. Hence, publics also always serve as markets, at least to some extent, so it is difficult to determine at what juncture a public should be reclassified as a mass, or even if this transformation is ever complete. Consumers of, or audiences for, any given cultural product belong to the same cultural public.[34] The *cultural workmen*, those who create cultural products for various cultural publics, do not control the means of the distribution of their products. Because a new cultural product is created does not mean that it will be made widely available, and there are underlying economic and political reasons why certain products are distributed and others are not. It can be said then, that the struggle of the "synthesis" phase of public opinion is not a struggle over the "means of production," the centerpiece of Marx's conception of class struggle, but rather, over the "means of distribution" and the "means of communication." Controlling the latter is tantamount to being able to establish a cultural mainstream, which Mills calls the establishment.[35]

Yet something further must be observed here. In Mills' analysis publics appear for the first time to be somewhat rigidly state-bounded. In part this stems from the ways in which Mills defines and analyzes publics—from the fact that publics are not theorized in general as much as they are analyzed in specific cultural contexts (Mills studied, for example, public opinion in small localities, such as Decatur, Illinois, to measure opinion on the news items of the day). His focus on the American public as the paradigmatic "synthetic" case of public opinion after World War II, coupled with his idea of the establishment, suggests that highly particularized phases of cultural development shaped by the distribution and communications networks of local and national cultural mainstreams should be the focus of any assessment of any public. In Mills, we speak of particular publics and not of the public in general.

And this was not simply a methodological point. For beyond the empirical orientation of Mills' work was also the international thinking of the Cold War period, based on an understanding of national blocks consisting of states with communist or capitalist identifications. In America, Mills claims, cultural workmen are dependent on bourgeois businessmen who own and/or run the colleges, the museums, the libraries, and the other commercial avenues for the distribution of cultural products. So in the United States, the "cultural establishment" is commercial, and this is the only way that we understand the cultural mainstream (as commercial). However, Mills pointed out that in the Soviet Union, the cultural establishment was not commercial, but rather political. That is, the selection, distribution and canonization of cultural products were not determined by bourgeois businessmen, but rather by the state and its politics. The colleges, museums, libraries, and the other avenues for the distribution of cultural products were all supervised by the Soviet state.

Hence, in the wake of World War II and in the dawn of the Cold War, Mills reconceived the public optimistically, as a critical political power; at the same time, he held that publics could be properly assessed only as they concretely existed in varying national contexts. One of the key issues we see here, at the end of this brief and selective prehistory of the concept of the political public sphere, is a procession from a far-reaching, potentially transnational political function for the public (in Kant) to a more concretely anchored, intrastate function for the public (in Mills). This narrative has much to do with the evolving imaginary of what civil society is and/or could be, though we will consider different ways to imagine civil society throughout this work.

The turn away from Kant's transnational thinking, a turn here represented by Mills, is made more resolute by the classic public sphere theories of the twentieth century. Through a consideration of Arendt and Habermas, we shall better understand the historical development of the concept of the political public sphere and why this development problematically discounts important forms of political action.

Arendt on the Public, the Private, and Communicative Power

For Arendt too, the political public realm is ultimately statebounded. Her concept of communicative power effectively hardens the theoretical turn toward situating public realms as organs of civil society whose political role is understood in national contexts. This contextual definition provides the grounding for the larger difficulty of envisioning public spheres transnationally, a topic that will be further treated in chapter 2. For now, we seek to understand Arendt's influential general theory of political publics and their state-boundedness.

With Kant, we have only defined and compared public and private reasoning, which has not directly provided us with general conceptions of public and private realms as broader arenas for human activity (though we have inferred such social spaces). In *The Human Condition*, Arendt defines "public" as that which is broadly communicable to a large group of individuals. The experience of physical pain, she explains, is not necessarily public because it may be difficult or even impossible to communicate to others. The term "public," Arendt says, "means, first, that everything that appears in public can be seen and heard by everybody and has the widest possible publicity."[36] So she is speaking here primarily, not about spaces but about experiences and events, ideas and arguments. Public refers to the communicability of experiences, events, ideas, and arguments—that is, their possible publicity.

But Arendt also defines public as a realm. The public realm refers to spaces in civil society that are open to all citizens, as opposed to exclusive spaces that are privately owned and managed as "off limits" to unauthorized citizens such as one's home or office, or a "members only" club or association. For Arendt, the public realm is not merely open to citizens but is also *actually* populated by them, and deliberation and communication about common interests are not just possible, but *actually* take place in the public realm. Thus, the public realm does not simply exist because it can, but rather, its existence must be activated by participation. Public means open, available, and communicable to a potentially large constituency of willing members of civil society who voluntarily participate and, through that involvement, constitute the public realm.

Seyla Benhabib captures this part of Arendt's theory well:

> [A] town hall or a city square where people do not act in concert is not a public space in this Arendtian sense. But a private

dining room in which people gather to hear a *samizdat* or in which dissidents meet with foreigners become public spaces; just as a field or a forest can also become public space if it is the object and location of an action in concert, of a demonstration to stop the construction of a highway or a military air base, for example.[37]

This passage clearly highlights the fact that Arendt's concept of the public realm entails action in concert. But we also discover something else of great importance in this "associational view of public space."[38] Arendt does not believe in formally possible public realms, but only in those that are substantively made by the extant associations of people in some kind of collective action. Because of this, Arendt always imagined political public realms as physically assembling bodies. You cannot point to an empty park and call it public, even if it is legally open to the public. Surely, this is part of the reason why the theorization of transnational public realms—realms that would have to be comprised by the collective action of geographically disparate people who could not easily associate in person—was not a part of Arendt's conception. As we shall see, Habermas agreed with the indispensable importance of in person association, stressing the vital role that salons and cafés played in providing the spaces for and for sustaining the actions of the public sphere. This requirement reveals why for both thinkers the political function and the scale of the public sphere would have to be state-bounded—because the idea of substantive association always points us toward the lived experience of people actually interacting in their own communities.

Arendt defines "private" as that which lacks or forcibly delimits the broad communicability and the participatory openness characteristic of the public. Private refers to that which is not seen and heard by all citizens, and the private realm refers to spaces that are not open to all of civil society. It is possible for something that is private to be potentially public without being actually public (for example, a kept secret), which underlines the fact that the public realm requires actualization. Feminists who have defined political action, in large part, as publicizing the inequities, abuses, and dissatisfactions that have been historically relegated, sealed, and preserved in domestic privacy have mined this point to great effect. So private and public are not immutable binaries. People are more or less private by way of the degrees to which they are seen and heard by others. The more public person puts herself in common spaces with others, speaks and acts publicly, and spends more time in open rather than in closed, private spaces. But the act of putting herself in front of others, the actual spending of time in open spaces, does not only form her public personality. It is a part of the process of forming the public realm itself. Our park, for example, may be public in some cases, yet private in other cases. If it is legally public and remains completely unpopulated, there is no substantive sense (for it is only public by name) in which we could understand it as an actual public realm. Its legal status is formal; it is always insufficient.

For Arendt, the private realm includes everything from unpublicized reasoning, kept secrets, the place and responsibilities of one's employment, to legally exclusive parks and pools, and even to ineffable pains and experiences. Her conception of the public realm is of a space in which we find all of the open and populated parks and pools, and all of the experiences, events, ideas, and arguments that are broadly communicable and actually shared. Arendt's distinctions between public and private realms are consistent with those generally assumed in present-day discussions of political public spheres, and thus serve as grounding for those discussions.

But the public realm only becomes expressly political in Arendt's discussion of "communicative power" in her *On Violence*.[39] Communicative power is the power of the opinion of the public and can therefore only be generated in the public realm. Communicative power is formed in the realization of common interest and the development of common judgment among a large enough group of people that their collective opinion effectively confers or contests political institutions, plans and policies, or purportedly representative bodies. Power

> remains in existence only so long as the group keeps together.
> When we say of somebody that he is "in power" we actually
> refer to his being empowered by a certain number of people to

act in their name. The moment the group, from which the power originated to begin with (*potestas in populo*, without a people or group there is no power), disappears, "his power" also vanishes."[40]

According to Arendt, communicative power, essentially communicatively produced agreement, is so powerful that political institutions collapse in want of its conferral. In this, Arendt joins Kant in locating the locus of power in public criticism. Governments that rule without resorting to tyranny require widespread popular support. Tyranny is the violent or coercive maintenance of sovereign rule, and is thus only necessary from the standpoint of the ruler when public opinion opposes his rule. If a government were in general agreement with the will and opinion of the people, it would have no need for violence or coercion to maintain its rule, and would have no need for tyranny.

In this way, communicative power is the opposite of violence. Violence in any political situation is used wherever people are not in voluntary agreement with its wielders, and this lack of the people's affirmation indicates a lack of real power. So wherever real power exists violence is unnecessary. This is not a small point. Max Weber, for example, understood power as the ability to force one's will on another, which is indeed a common way of thinking about power—as force.[41] But one does not need to force compliance to a maxim that is already voluntarily agreed to, so having agreement is having power.

But we cannot think of power and violence as simple oppositions, for there are degrees of each one that admit for degrees of the other. Power and violence are only simple opposites in the analytical rubric of opposing poles marked by extreme power on the one hand and extreme violence on the other.

> All political institutions are manifestations and materializations of power; they petrify and decay as soon as the living power of the people ceases to uphold them. This is what Madison meant when he said "all governments rest on opinion," a word no less true for the various forms of monarchy than for democracies. . . . The extreme form of power is All against One, the extreme form of violence is One against All. And this latter is never possible without instruments.[42]

The analytical rubric that pits power clearly and cleanly against violence deals in extremes that are possible and have precedent, but are not as likely in the world as the existence of governments that are more or less upheld by communicative power, that are more or less violent in measure with the degree to which the people are for or against them. In the extreme where everyone agrees, or nearly agrees (All against One), the one is overpowered, and in the other extreme where the general population is forcibly imposed upon by a small faction or by one person (One against All), the one must be coercive and will require instruments of violence to maintain his position. But the more likely combinations of Most against Some and vice versa, or of Minorities against Majorities and vice versa, complicate the question of agreement versus violence. This is because it is unclear at what point instruments of coercion or violence would be deemed necessary at any juncture toward the center of the two extremes.

For example, imagine that an important government policy contradicts the opinion of a large public, but agrees with the opinion of a still sizable minority public (public opinion polling produces many such examples).[43] The minority and majority are not necessarily conscious of themselves as such because their numbers are not readily discernible as being significantly different. In such a case, the introduction of instruments of violence by the government against the majority public seems absurd and would probably only serve to grow the majority public against the unpopular policy. Instead, *argumentation*, that which lies between the extremes of agreement and violence, must be integrated into the discursive processes that ultimately generate communicative power. That is to say, the minority public or the government should engage the opposing majority public in argument. To secure real power, they would need the voluntary and active conferral of the people. And those people, who act in concert to produce communicative power, must not do so without ongoing, critical consideration of multiple perspectives. Absolute unanimity is not the aim, but rather, as much agreement as possible. And this agreement must be communicatively produced (allowing for argumentation), not propagandized or otherwise coerced.

Arendt observes that there are serious dangers that follow from the proliferation of public opinion in the absence of argument. Opinions that have an extraordinarily wide appeal can spread throughout civil society like a germ, and agreement, in the ideal sense of communicative power, could be overthrown by the uncritical acceptance of popular opinions. Arendt points out that sometimes it is "because of the overwhelming power of the many that the voice of the few loses all strength and all plausibility. . . . This is the reason why the Founding Fathers tended to equate rule based on public opinion with tyranny; democracy in this sense was to them but a newfangled form of despotism."[44] There was a fear, she explains, that certain opinions could catch and spread, not by the strength of their reason, but by way of human passions. The U.S. Senate was created for the purpose of guarding against rule by impassioned opinion. In the late eighteenth century, the climate of European revolution, roused by the French Revolution, impressed upon the Founding Fathers a fear that public opinion could be hijacked and could lead to revolution. Hence, Arendt's shining example of the least problematic and the most vital public realm, the ancient Greek *polis*, which guided her discussion of the public and the private realm beginning with the second chapter of *The Human Condition*, remains, in the end, her preferred illustration of the idealized political action of the public realm.[45]

The term "communicative power" is ultimately redundant because, for Arendt, there is no other kind of power than communicative power.[46] Power is powerful precisely because of its ability to back or to contest authority. For a representative state to be in power, for example, it must be in agreement with the communicatively produced opinion of the people on whose behalf it claims to act. Such an institution of authority must change the laws and its own behavior to reflect this agreement, or else it must argue its case publicly in order to earn the conferral of public opinion, or it must give up representative pretensions and resort to some kind of tyranny.[47] Power, by definition, already in the moment of its formation, will either support or contradict existing authority publicly, and so the public discourses that culminate in power cannot help but expose the fitness of states and rulers to the position of the people.

In this way, the political public realm is the principal mechanism of any democratic, republican state in that it demonstrates or disputes the legitimacy of the representative claims of power-holders simply by forming. Of course, this also means that the public realm makes sense politically only in relation to a state that is somehow beholden to it. And let us not forget that the public realm is only imagined as an association of people acting in concert *and in person*. So for Arendt too, the power of the political public realm is understood as state-bounded, as consisting in the relationship between a people and their government.

Notes

1. I want to be clear here about what I mean by "first paradigmatic transition." I am speaking specifically about paradigms of scale, the national or the transnational paradigm of the public sphere (I am not referring to paradigms of composition here, bourgeois or subaltern, for example). As we shall see, it is typically held that the public sphere was first theorized as strictly national and only recently as transnational, whereas a study of Kant disproves this contention.

2. See chapter 9.

3. The example of Diogenes is cited in Michel Foucault's *History of Sexuality, Vol. 2*, and Michael Warner's *Publics and Counterpublics*.

4. One way to understand this is to say that all public spheres are formed in and of civil society (by the activity of a group), but that *not* all of civil society is in and of public spheres (some may be excluded from participation, or may not participate for other reasons such as lack of leisure time or sufficient education).

5. We begin with Immanuel Kant because he explicates specific political functions for public opinion and because he is a clear and influential predecessor to Hannah Arendt and Jürgen Habermas in theorizing the power of the public realm. In addition, Kant took up the question of a national or transnational political function for the public realm, now a major concern in contemporary political philosophy, yielding insights that we will revisit throughout this work.

6. Immanuel Kant, *Political Writings*, 137.

7. See Jean-Jacques Rousseau, *The Social Contract*, 64 for the meaning of being "forced to be free," and 83 for the "necessity of a lawgiver."

8. Ibid., 114.

9. See Taylor's essay "Invoking Civil Society" in his *Philosophical Arguments*. See also Michael Hardt's argument that Hegel first made this distinction in his essay "The Withering of Civil Society" in *Masses, Classes and the Public Sphere*.

10. See Kant, *Political Writings*, 58–60, for discussion of these points.

11. This feature of Kant's idea of public reasoning is important for a number of reasons. For public reasoning to be effective, it is often required to initiate a communicative event that we would otherwise consider private. That is, public reasoning *must not always address the general public* with an open invitation to everyone, but must often only address those to whom the address can be acted on constructively by specialists. And, as we shall see later, Arendt would have considered a critical speech given by a cleric to the clergy, made in a church after its doors have closed to the public, to be a private affair precisely because of its lack of openness. Yet, for Kant, while a congregation of people is being addressed by a cleric in a church, even when that congregation is open to anyone, the cleric is only acting privately. This tension regarding what constitutes public activity is one that we will return frequently throughout this work.

12. Kant, *Political Writings*, 58.

13. It is perhaps this contention, revived in light of the totalitarian and authoritarian regimes of the twentieth century, that underlies the recent distrust of revolution among political radicals today such as the Zapatistas, who are far more likely to call for the radical restructuring of existing political institutions instead of their seizure.

14. Kant, *Political Writings*, 56.

15. Ibid., 126.

16. Ibid., 11 and 113, respectively.

17. Ibid., 105.

18. Ibid., 105.

19. Ibid., 55.

20. These observations of Kant's following of the American and French Revolutions are cited in the postscript to his *Political Writings*, 261–62.

21. Ibid., 183.

22. Ibid., 123.

23. Ibid., 107–8.

24. For good discussion of these risks and their negotiation by rebellious slaves, see James C. Scott's *Domination and the Arts of Resistance: Hidden Transcripts* (New Haven, Conn./London: Yale University Press, 1990).

25. See chapter 4 in Nancy F. Cott's *The Grounding of Modern Feminism* (New Haven, Conn./London: Yale University Press, 1987).

26. See point #5 in Marx's *Critique of the Gotha Programme*.

27. It should be said that others, outside of the Frankfurt school, had already begun to develop theories of manipulable masses. Freud's work was formative of course. Also, notably, is Karl Mannheim's *Ideology and Utopia: An Introduction to the Sociology of Knowledge* (1936). In particular, see his remarks on false consciousness and the whole of chapter 4, "The Utopian Mentality."

28. See Theodor Adorno and Max Horkheimer, *Dialectic of Enlightenment*, 149–67, for a discussion of how fascism was being acculturated in advanced capitalist societies.

29. See in particular Mills' "Mass Media and Public Opinion" (1950), "Mass Society and Liberal Education" (1954), "On Knowledge and Power" (1955), and "The Cultural Apparatus" (1959).

30. In France, in the 1950s and 1960s, there were some notable theoretical and social movements that should be mentioned here. Writers such as Cornelius Castoriadis and Guy Debord, and the groups and journals they were associated with such as Socialisme ou Barbarie and the Situationist International, did preserve a vital interest in the potentialities of a contentious public sphere of sorts after World War II, but already in the 1940s and 1950s. The political theories of these figures ran contrary to the pessimism often characteristic of German Critical Theory. Unlike Mills, Castoriadis and Debord did not use the language of "the public" or "public opinion," and also, Arendt and Habermas did not cite their work in any foundational sense, as with Mills. Hence, these French theorists are only a footnote here. Still, it is important to acknowledge these traditions that did remain committed to an emancipatory politics in an era of mass media that relied in key ways on the proliferation of radical critique throughout civil society.

31. C. Wright Mills, "Mass Media and Public Opinion," 586.

32. See Adorno and Horkheimer's "The Culture Industry: Enlightenment as Mass Deception" in their *Dialectic of Enlightenment*.

33. The distinction between publics and masses is discussed in Mills' "Mass Society and Liberal Education," 355.

34. Notice here that there is no definitional requisite of collective communicative engagement for cultural publics, and that such publics therefore do not necessarily conform to our earlier definition of a "political public realm." That is, according to Mills, a cultural public can form and subsist in a collection of generally unassociated individuals who are only linked by their consumption of the same cultural products, by their watching of the same television shows.

35. Mills' discussion of cultural publics, cultural workmen, and the cultural establishment can be read in his "Cultural Apparatus," 409–22.

36. Hannah Arendt, *The Human Condition*, 50.

37. Seyla Benhabib, "Models of Public Space: Hannah Arendt, the Liberal Tradition, and Jürgen Habermas," 78, in Craig Calhoun's *Habermas and the Public Sphere*.

38. Ibid.

39. It is necessary to make a few qualifying remarks here about the term "communicative power" and our ensuing discussion. Indeed, this concept of power as a political cogency that emerges in the collective communication of a group of people, or a public, is Arendt's. However, our discussion of communicative power as such reenacts a previous practice of taking this concept out of Arendt's larger context. That is, Arendt discusses the idea of communicative power in chapter 2 of her study *On Violence* (1969). This chapter was reprinted in 1986 as if it were a standalone essay, under the imposed title of "Communicative Power" in *Power*, a reader edited by Steven Lukes. Before this (in 1977), and likely as a precedent for the reprinting, Habermas published an essay on Arendt's communications concept of power, which also appears in the 1986 volume. Following this, Arendt's concept of communicative power has been discussed as a theory unto itself. This practice is not wrong, as Arendt's con-

ception of power is rightly included in the volume and treated quite fairly by Habermas (though, as I shall explain in chapter 2, I don't fully agree with his treatment). Nevertheless, these qualifying remarks are necessary lest any reader should go searching Arendt's works for her theory of communicative power. As well, because of this, I admit that we begin already viewing the concept through the lens that Habermas would employ (see chapter 2). Finally, I want to remind the reader that our goal here is not to situate Arendt's concept of communicative power into a broader understanding of *her* philosophy, but rather to properly show how her thinking on the public realm precedes, lays the groundwork for, and influences later accounts.

40. Arendt, "Communicative Power," 64, in Steven Lukes' *Power*, a reprint of chapter 2 of Arendt's *On Violence*.

41. See Max Weber's *Politics as a Vocation* (1921).

42. Arendt, "Communicative Power," 62–63.

43. Public opinion polling, however, does not really poll public opinion. Rather, it accesses the privately held and privately expressed opinions of citizens who, as a group, are withdrawn from and unbeknownst to each other, and who may in fact never constitute a public together. In the Arendtian sense, public opinion is that opinion formed in and of a group, an actually existing public formed by real and voluntary communication, and this can never be bypassed or replaced with a calculation that merely adds up surveyed private opinions.

44. Arendt, *On Revolution*, 226.

45. "To be political, to live in a *polis*, meant that everything was decided through words and persuasion and not through force and violence. In Greek self-understanding, to force people by violence, to command rather than persuade, were prepolitical ways to deal with people characteristic of life outside the *polis*."In Arendt, *The Human Condition*, 26–27.

46. This follows from her separation in *On Violence* of the concept of power from the concepts of strength, force, authority, and violence.

47. To be clear, Arendt is not writing in these texts (*The Human Condition* and *On Violence*) about representation and democracy; concern about the legitimation of representative democracies is Habermas', not hers. Arendt is more interested in how power interacts with authority, and how these terms differ from strength, force, and violence. I interject with representation here in order to bring her concept of power to bear on it, and to segue to the following chapter.

2

A Prefigured
National Framework

Legitimation and the Public Sphere

Habermas on Communicative Power and
Legitimation: Addenda to Arendt's Basic Theory

In this chapter, I turn my attention to some of Habermas' central ideas and early arguments about the public sphere, specifically to those outside of his major work on the subject (Habermas' *Structural Transformation* will be the focus of chapter 3). Here, I consider his reflections on and criticisms of Arendt's basic theory of communicative power, his definition of discourse, and his idea of legitimation. I focus on these aspects of Habermas' theory in order (1) to segue from the prehistory of public sphere theory to the ideas of the classical account and (2) to break out the distinct theoretical signposts that provided the basis for concretizing the concept of the public sphere as an intrastate organ of democratic legitimation. Habermas' early public sphere theory is the most fixedly and explicitly national in its form and function, and in the present chapter we critically assess the moves that made it so.

As with chapter 1, chapter 2 serves a general contextual and a particular argumentative purpose. Generally, in the first section, I show how Habermas misinterprets Arendt's theory in certain ways, and yet expands it in important new directions.[1] But more specifically, and more critical to our overarching concerns, Habermas also extends Arendt's basic theory of communicative power through an introduction of two crucial terms: *discourse* and *legitimation*. I argue that it is precisely these terms and their explication in Habermas' early work that most inextricably tie the concept of the public sphere to a national framework and function. How does the public sphere, within the limits of discourse and legitimation, function? That question will be answered here. As well, I shall illustrate how rethinking the meaning of discourse and legitimation necessitates rethinking the political function of the public sphere in important ways.

Although I will show how the concept of the public sphere was unnecessarily fitted to a national framework in Habermas' account, its prefiguring as such must also be understood in a historical context that influenced thinking about civil societies and public spheres. Thus, the contextual aim of this chapter is linked to its argumentative one. I shall clarify the historical circumstances that supported a strictly national theorization of the political public sphere.

Mostly, Habermas works rather neatly within the parameters of Arendt's basic sketch of public and private realms and of the concept of communicative power, retaining most consistently the supposition that publics become political precisely in their relationship to states that purport to represent them.[2] However, when Habermas directly takes up Arendt's communications concept of power, he makes some important and critical provisos. As would become thematic in a more comprehensive and technical way in Habermas' later work, he focused in his early work on the general problems in the conditions of communication. When Arendt discussed the fear of the Founding Fathers that people's passions and desperations, that people's cultural proclivities and social position, might incline them toward dangerous and irrational opinions, she only began to consider the problems in the conditions of communication that Habermas made his focus.

Habermas insists that it is possible to explore these conditions more thoroughly, distinguishing the rational achievements of communication from misled and distorted outcomes. He argues that the rationality of a consensus can be determined by the conditions under which it was generated.[3] Here, I focus on Habermas' general problematization of the conditions of communication and his critique of Arendt's concept of communicative power. Habermas' concern with the conditions and quality of communication is rooted in a general apprehension about intervening biases and special interests. And his critique of Arendt's theory derives from a general distrust that states will be fair and reciprocal to the citizens they should represent. Such problems of distortion and reciprocity underwrite Habermas' larger concern with the quality of the one-to-one relationship between civil society and its correlated state; a public must be truly independent from biases and special interests, it must be rational and critical (undistorted) and assuming that it is, the state must be influenced by and representative of such a public (reciprocity).

Habermas answers the problems of distortion and reciprocity, respectively, with theories of discourse and legitimation. In turn, these theories of discourse and legitimation calcify the national framework as the logical framework for the public sphere in Habermas' early work. To explore these critical turns, I consider Habermas' essay on "Hannah Arendt's Communications Concept of Power" and his arguments about discursively generated rational will and representation in contemporary capitalist democracies (in his *Legitimation Crisis*).

In the course of these considerations, I shall also show how Habermas' critique of Arendt underestimates her understanding of the problematized public realm, presenting it as a naively romanticized picture. This picture does indeed emerge in Arendt's *The Human Condition* and *On Violence*, but is preserved only at the expense of ignoring central insights from her *Origins of Totalitarianism*. A brief consideration of some of the key themes from this latter book will serve to deepen our understanding of Arendt's view of the public realm as well as to defend against some of Habermas' criticisms of her concept of communicative power. Neglecting the picture of the public realm in *The Origins of Totalitarianism* is not just Habermas' oversight, since almost all contemporary public sphere theory, while acknowledging Arendt rather consistently, ignores this text. Paying it some attention serves another purpose as well. It links the start of contemporary discussions of the public sphere to the historical context Mills wrote in when he discussed mass publics, and it reminds us that Arendt too, for biographical as well as for intellectual reasons, was thinking in the aftermath and amidst the tumult and terror of the totalitarian movements of the twentieth century. Theorizing the public realm in this context, Arendt can be seen to have a far more complex and less optimistic view than is commonly attributed to her, yet still a view that situates the political public realm as an explicitly national arena. And all of this is a major part of our story: Totalitarianism demonstrated the horrifying dangers of manipulated publics within national contexts with such overwhelming clarity; Kant's cosmopolitanism may have never been more displaced than during the short twentieth century (1914–1989).

But let us begin by turning to Habermas' consideration of the communications concept of power. Habermas characteristically insists on a high standard for communication, one that is immediately at odds with our common sense idea of communication. Understanding precisely what constitutes communication for Habermas is essential for two reasons. First, communication is the primary (though not the final) activity of public spheres. And when Habermas speaks of the communicative generation of a collective will and opinion, he intentionally discounts a lot of what we might consider part of the communicative process— that is, the public sphere must not only take up topics, but must do so in a very specific way. Second, the major developments of this work ultimately require a refutation of Habermas' particular conception of discursive rationality, of ideal communication. As we shall see in chapter 3 and beyond, many people cannot speak and expect be heard while abiding Habermas' rules of communication. Rather, in order to enter the public sphere and to eventually participate in processes of rational-critical will- and opinion-formation, Habermas' rules of communication and discourse must be violated.

For Habermas, if a common will and opinion are communicatively produced then they are not, by definition, produced by the imposition of force and bias. The speech of the group must be illocutionary, not perlocutionary. Illocutionary speech discovers its endpoint only during the process of being spoken; it does not determine its conclusions before it begins. Illocutionary speech is that of a spirited genuine inquiry, where special interests and hypotheses may be stated, but where only an open collective investigation can settle them. In illocution, we can make arguments and disagree, but we understand that any new resolution will be the product of our communication, that new resolutions do not present themselves prior to the communicative process. Perlocutionary speech, on the other hand, engages others for the purpose of achieving agreement on or compliance with a particular resolution—a resolution not generated by the communication, but one that was favored prior to and imposed on communicative processes. In this, perlocution resembles the commonsense understanding of rhetoric in which language is used as an instrument to effectively and persuasively produce consequences taken by the speaker to be the goals of speaking prior to speaking with his target audience. With perlocution, then, communication is a pretense, or a formality, that may or may not be understood as such by participants in the conversation. As Socrates to the sophists, Habermas heralds illocution over perlocution. But even though they are clearly defined opposites, illocution and perlocution may look identical in practice.

Arendt's concept of communicative power rejects the instrumentalization of one's will by another, so Habermas points out that the communication of her concept must be illocutionary. Habermas agrees with Arendt that real power must not employ the instrumentalization of one's will by another, and that, if communication is indeed illocutionary, it will lead to the formation of a common will that could ultimately reveal problems of political legitimation (legitimation discussed below). Habermas contends that agreement is powerful because it is what grounds the common will in a rational-critical basis, a rationally and critically assessed set of premises. However, he is not convinced by the teleology of Arendt's argument in which communicative power checks the will of governments, ensuring that the common will is represented by states, simply by forming in the public realm without further mediation. Arendt presents communicative power too unproblematically as an end in itself, because in her account, communicative power reveals at once the standing of the state in relation to the public. Habermas, on the other hand, sees communicative power as a tool for "realizing goals," for "purposive-rational action," and thus argues that power, the mobilization of common interests, is required for democratization, for proactively challenging institutions that lack legitimacy.[4] Political opinion- and will-formations are necessary but insufficient first achievements. Asserting public power on governments through demands for accountability and reform, responsiveness and heightened representation are neither instantaneous nor inevitable, but are distinct and necessary tasks.

But, returning to the difficulty of identifying perlocution as such, how can we be sure that the public power is not manipulated and irrational? Habermas goes some distance toward answering this question by paying special attention to the problem of unimpeded communication, communication that is not distorted within the public realm. Distorted communication loses or simply never develops its rational-critical character. But Habermas also insists on considering how the public realm itself can be deformed (manipulated and/or exclusionary) and how, when this is the case, public discourse would then be distorted too (ruled by bias and/or special interest). Distorted communication may arise from exclusionary public realms as well as from perlocutionary speech. In either case, its distortion means that communication is neither sufficiently rational nor sufficiently critical to discover ethical-theoretical faults and logical shortcomings, or to assess such problems and identify reasonable and implementable solutions. So distorted communication undermines the public sphere as a rational-critical agent of legitimating power. And distorted communication is rarely an accident, because unimpeded communication does not always serve the interests of those who can seize it with perlocutionary interventions. In other words, powerholders often infiltrate the public sphere mobilizing its biases, influencing its will and opinion.

Part of the reason why Habermas does not fully answer the question of how we can be sure that the public power is not manipulated and irrational is because his definition of unimpeded illocutionary discourse presents discourse as an ideal form of communication that is difficult to imagine, let alone to assess empirically:

> Discourse can be understood as that form of communication
> that is removed from contexts of experience and action and
> whose structure assures us: that the bracketed validity claims
> of assertions, recommendations, or warnings are the exclusive
> object of discussion; that participants, themes and contribu-
> tions are not restricted except with reference to the goal of test-
> ing the validity claims in questions; that no force except that of
> the better argument is exercised; and that, as a result, all mo-
> tives except that of the cooperative search for truth are ex-
> cluded. If under these conditions a consensus about the
> recommendation to accept a norm arises argumentatively, that
> is, on the basis of hypothetically proposed, alternative justifi-
> cations, then this consensus expresses a "rational will."[5]

Discourse is thus a particular and ideal form of communication.
As Habermas defines it, discourse might seem flatly impossible,
especially when one thinks about the complex of interests, motivations and distinct dispositions among those who make it up,
and all of the perlocutionary efforts disguisable to its criteria.
The makers of discourse must withdraw their thinking from
their own subjective biases, refraining from making whole assertions, recommendations or warnings in order to analyze the
essential validity claims of each without partiality. The course of
discursive inquiry must be unbounded, guided and restrained
only by a collective aim to discover what claims are true. The cooperation of participants in discourse must supplant any competitive tendencies to dominate, leaving all participants equally
joined in inquiry toward what would thus be an entirely voluntary consensus that is not only general but also incontestably rational.

One cannot resist asking: Who could be capable of measur-
ing, let alone participating in, the communication of any group
of interlocutors to see if it qualifies as discourse as such? But it is
not Habermas' intention here to provide us with a means of
measurement that could be empirically put to use to determine
the quality of communication. Rather, he intends to define ideal-
typical discourse as an achievable (in principle) but unsurpassable guide for our communicative efforts, a guide that can help
us to recognize all of the points of entry for distortion in the

conditions of communication, and to critically evaluate what such impediments may be.

Given the two major contentions I have discussed, that (1) communicative power must be utilized beyond its formation for purposive-rational action and that (2) achieving unimpeded communication is an intricate problem in itself whose certainty cannot be presupposed, Habermas concludes that Arendt's arguments about power and the public realm are starkly misfit with the realities of any modern society. The idea that the communicatively produced will of the majority of civil society would be generally well represented in and by representative political institutions strikes Habermas as naïve. A legitimation crisis exists precisely where there are radical divergences between the publicized, discursively formed (rational) will of the people and an unresponsive public authority that fails to represent that rational will. Unless this authority is openly tyrannical, such divergences throw into question its representative legitimacy. Arendt's discussion of power does not account for radical divergences between rational-critical agreement in the public realm and the state, and if it did, the intrinsic power of communicative power would be greatly diminished.

When it comes to the second contention, Arendt seems to romanticize political discourse in the ancient Greek *polis*, failing to take into account just how deformed and distorted discourses in the public realm can be and often are.[6] Whereas Arendt maintains that communicative power will inevitably emerge in the agreement of an open and active public realm, Habermas see this agreement as only one possibility among others, maintaining that Arendt does not quite grasp how difficult an achievement communicative power is. Its development always faces obstinate challenges in the quality of the conditions of communication and against competing interests of influence on public opinion.

But this criticism will be overdrawn if we proceed from the conclusion that Arendt simply overlooked the problems of communication. Unfortunately, in the texts in which she writes most directly about the public realm and communicative power (*The Human Condition* and *On Violence*), Arendt does neglect the mobilization of biases and other problems of communication. Yet, in

The Origins of Totalitarianism, she offers a thoroughgoing analysis of the manipulability of mass publics, claiming in the end that even totalitarian regimes depend on public support. She points out that

> Hitler's rise to power was legal in terms of majority rule and neither he nor Stalin could have maintained the leadership of large populations, survived many interior and exterior crises, and braved the numerous dangers of relentless intraparty struggles if they had not had the confidence of the masses. . . . The widespread belief that Hitler was simply an agent of German industrialists and that Stalin was victorious in the succession struggle after Lenin's death only through a sinister conspiracy are both legends which can be refuted by many facts but above all by the leaders' indisputable popularity.[7]

Totalitarianism organizes masses of people using an extreme form of perlocution, propaganda. Yet totalitarian movements do this because, even in possession of tremendous military might, securing the esteem of public opinion remains necessary. Otherwise, totalitarian governments would appear to their own people as tyrannies and would not be able to implement policy with the confidence of the masses. Interior and exterior crises are survivable, in part, because such regimes have popular support. With this, it should already be clear that Arendt had an acute sense indeed of the dangers of perlocution and the manipulability of the public realm.

In fact, totalitarian governments did not only demolish democratic illusions, as is typically thought, but also appealed to them. They "made apparent what no other organ of public opinion had ever been able to show, namely, that democratic government had rested as much on the silent approbation and tolerance of the indifferent and inarticulate sections of the people as on the articulate and visible institutions and organizations of the country."[8] That is, totalitarian movements could justify their violence by claiming that the relative silence, tolerance and indifference within the public realm of civil society served as public justification of their actions. This was and is a popular refrain of democracies—that the lack of contestation coming from the public realm testifies, to a significant extent, to the success of the

democracy. Arendt indeed saw that, in contrast to the paradigmatic Greek *polis*, there were "masses," "mobs," and "elites" in
the twentieth century, complicating her idea of the illocutionary
communicative projects of political public realms. And Arendt
discussed masses, mobs, and elites at great length in *The Origins
of Totalitarianism*: "The totalitarian movements aim at and succeed in organizing masses—not classes, like the old interest parties of the Continental nation-states; not citizens with opinions
about, and interests in, the handling of public affairs, like the
parties of Anglo-Saxon countries."[9] And yet, "the totalitarian
regimes, so long as they are in power, and the totalitarian leaders, so long as they are alive, 'command and rest upon mass support' up to the end."[10] In this account, Arendt is clearly aware of
the historical crisis of the public realm brought about by totalitarianism, which reveals that she did in fact share many of the
critical insights observed by Adorno and Horkheimer that were
carried by Habermas into his own early work.

It is telling that claims to popularity made by the most
prominent liberal democracies have also been made by totalitarian regimes, for it highlights the vital role of the public realm
even when and where the means of its formation could not be
further from satisfying the criteria for ideal-typical discourse.
This underlines and expands the link between the public realm
and the legitimacy of established powerholders. Habermas con-
curs with this power of the public realm—a power formed in
public recognition, claiming that, "political rule can last only so
long as it is recognized as legitimate."[11] Political institutions
must be legitimate and their legitimacy is conferred by public
approval. Hence, although Habermas is specifically concerned
with democracies in a nontotalitarian world, historically, totalitarian governments have effectively demonstrated their legitimacy, for a time, in the conferral of propagandized and irrational
publics.

But what we must also notice here is that these conclusions
serve to link the public realm with special fixity to domestic politics and the legitimation of single states, totalitarian or liberal
democratic. The conferral of the public sphere is something that
powerholders of every kind fight for, whether such public approval has formed and functioned on its own, utilizing real

illocution, or whether it has been shaped by perlocutionary mobilizations of bias. Yet, in the end, it is the approval of the domestic public sphere that matters, that is, only the public on whose behalf the state purports to act. The story of public opinion manipulated by the totalitarian regimes of the twentieth century has driven theories in which the public sphere was understood as an intrastate formation with a state-bounded function.

Yet there are even more commonplace ways in which the problem of legitimacy afflicts present-day capitalist democracies. According to Habermas, wherever norms of democracy prevail a state apparatus must secure its legitimacy in the conferral of the public realm, and wherever there is conflict in democratic society, it should be negotiated discursively. This is the ideal, but in practice the serious legitimation problems facing present-day democracies are rarely addressed in such a way. One major problem comes from the very existence of formal democratic institutions and procedures, which often "stand-in" for actually occurring legitimation processes. The focus in democracies should not be on the formal existence of institutions and procedures, but on actual processes of public discourse and the ways in which their consensuses, or rational wills, are registered and incorporated at institutional levels.

Habermas points out that there is a difference between mass loyalty and active participation, and that the world's democracies often rely on the former instead of the latter: "The arrangement of formal democratic institutions and procedures permits administrative decisions to be made largely independently of specific motives of the citizens. This takes place through a legitimation process that elicits generalized motives—that is, diffuse mass loyalty—but avoids participation."[12] Mass loyalty, however, is not real legitimacy, no matter how often it is mistaken as such, and this mistaking it as such poses a serious problem to (by way of impeding, eroding, and diverting attention from) actively participatory and meaningful democratic legitimation processes. If the opinion and will of an active public realm is nowhere represented in and by institutions, there exists either (1) a failure of formal institutions and procedures or (2) a deliberately selective incorporation of public opinion as a functional feature of the system.

Thus, the active political public realm is the space in which the legitimation of states actually occurs. If there are legitimation crises, they have to do, in large part, with various problems of connectivity, reciprocity, and representation between civil society and the state. From totalitarian regimes to present-day capitalist democracies, the public realm of civil society, whether it is manipulated as a mass, or whether it is in the "classic democratic" or "synthesis" phase in Mills' account, plays a critical political role. As we have elaborated and explored this role, we have situated the political public realm more and more clearly within the Westphalian states to which they correlate, and we have defined their function as one that pertains specifically to the representative authorities they seek to influence. When we think of public opinion with a political function in Hitler's Germany, we think of the minds of the German people; when we think of democratization in any country, we think of the people of that country—politically, the cultural-valuational opinions of these internal populations are of utmost importance. The political role of the public realm has appeared to us to be increasingly state-bounded.

Narrowing the Focus, Role, and Understanding of Political Public Spheres

The historical development of theories of the public sphere, as outlined above, not only tells the story of how the concept has come to be better understood, but of how it has come to be misunderstood. Its better understanding is certainly a major part of the story, but efforts to refine the idea of the political public sphere for contemporary discussions have been made in the interest of answering very specific questions about its role in the catastrophes of the twentieth century. With the totalitarian movements of the twentieth century, and with World War II, the Cold War, and the ongoing evolution of mass media, theories of the public sphere have largely neglected important insights that were clear and present in the prehistory of the concept. In concluding this chapter, I will argue that some of these earlier insights not only remained relevant as they were being forgotten, but were only growing more relevant. In particular, Arendt and Habermas, as well as those who enlarged their discussions of the public sphere, have mainly misidentified the public sphere as a strictly state-bounded entity until around the early 1990s,[13] just after the end of the Cold War and the English translation (and thus, revitalization) of Habermas' *Structural Transformation*.[14]

Though thinking about international civil society and public spheres are today common currency, in large part due to the overwhelming impact and accessibility of media technologies, the ideas are at least datable to Kant, and were certainly employed and well understood by political movements such as the communists of the nineteenth century. 1989 inaugurates a sort of rediscovery of the concept of transboundary publics because it was then that thinking about distinct states, related through the Cold War, and seen to some degree as pitted against one another as members or potential members of tactical blocks, was largely replaced by thinking about globalization and the diminishing significance of national boundaries. Habermas notes that, "a consensus has emerged that the 'long' nineteenth century (1789–1914) is followed by a 'short' twentieth century (1914–1989). The outbreak of the First World War and the collapse of the Soviet Union thus frame an antagonism that stretches through both world wars and the Cold War."[15] And he points out that millennium begins with the world facing the clear fact that "expanded political alliances are a necessary condition if politics are to catch up with the forces of a globalized economy."[16]

Although Habermas is thinking chiefly of institutional alliances, the EU being his primary example, many of the most prominent social movements of the 1990s have given further resonance to the idea that transnational public spheres are an important part of the story. Some of these movements, such as the Zapatistas, as I will show in part III, demonstrate the deficiencies of *both* the national and the transnational frameworks for discussing public spheres. As I explained my general introduction, the overarching goal of this work is not to choose between the national or the transnational formulation, but to critically assess existing understandings of the boundaries of each framework, and ultimately, to transgress those boundaries. Yet, for now, I intend to show that analyzing the viability of each of these frameworks for specific contexts did not need to be, and should not have been, postponed in political theory until the preeminence of globalization (as the principal issue of early millennium) could no longer be ignored. This postponement, I argue, is explicable by the prefiguring of a national public sphere in the foundational literature reviewed thus far.

We should recall here that Kant did not neglect the transnational framework. In fact, he insisted that international right would ultimately call for a cosmopolitan, international state (*civitas gentium*) and that such a state, or world republic, would require public justification from some kind of global civil society.[17] Revisiting this now, we may locate the presentiments of Habermas' theory of the legitimacy of states in Kant's ideas of the public justification of existing national states and of possible transnational ones. The difference, however, is that for Kant it was not only single states that required legitimation by state-bounded publics. Kant maintained that as the interconnectedness of political realities grew more and more transnational, there would need to be a corollary transnational public sphere that could provide public justification of a just world republic.

But the public counterpart to transnational state building (that is, the simultaneous and corollary building of a transnational public sphere) has unfortunately been taken for granted, as is perhaps best evidenced by the story of the EU. We may begin the story with the European Economic Community (EEC) in 1958, implemented to reduce tariff barriers and promote trade among Western European countries, including Belgium, Luxembourg, the Netherlands, France, Italy, and West Germany. Then the European Community (EC) was established in 1967 to consolidate the European Economic Community, the European Coal and Steel Community, and the European Atomic Energy Community. Finally, members of the EC ratified the Maastricht Treaty in 1993 establishing the European Union (EU). Yet, notwithstanding the EU's actualization as a transnational state, there has only been a very slow and reluctant development of a European public sphere (in part this development is slow because the task of forming a European public sphere is not simple, and in part it is reluctant because national publics do not always want, for a variety of reasons, to rethink themselves as Europeans in any deep and abiding way).

In fact, following the idea of a political public in Kant, Mills, Arendt, and Habermas, it is difficult to say that there is much of a European public sphere at all. Major transformations in political identity are prerequisite for new developments in peoplehood and the self-understanding of a public. The development of the EU and the assertion of a European identity over the various national identities have been successful in some regards, but have also roused reversions to national chauvinisms within the respective national public spheres. Simply put, the French and the Germans, for example, may be reluctant to rethink themselves as "Europeans" out of a fear that a loss of national identity and culture is at stake in the "Europeanization" of their identities. National resistance to Europeanization is not a simple or typical example of patriotism or national pride in that it hinges more on the terms of preservation and continuance than it does on a sense of superiority or on a general aversion to internationalism.[18] In part II, we shall further consider how communitarianism, nationalism, and patriotism are typical responses to cosmopolitanism and globalization.

In the meantime, it remains difficult and heavily contentious for the EU to act as the representative body for a European public. It was one thing when the EEC and EC claimed to represent the agents of international trade and the coal, steel, and energy corporations, but it is quite another to represent "a people" who do not understand themselves as such. The purpose of raising this example here is to illustrate the claim that the importance of a legitimating public for single states exists as well for transnational state building and that Kant's understanding of this as an optimistic theory can actually be exemplified with major political undertakings today. For Kant, the "universal community" means a kind of international civil society that participates in a cosmopolitan public sphere that serves a similar political function as does the national public sphere in Arendt's and Habermas' accounts—to feed back to institutional representatives about the public opinion that will either uphold or contest them.

We may also take an example of a transnational public sphere that thrived throughout the long nineteenth century, and whose efforts to make itself political, through the efforts of a reading public, have not been assessed as such in the history of the development of the concept. I am thinking here of socialism, and particularly, of Marx's efforts to build a communist movement. The much-maligned *superstructure*, or realm of ideas, in Marx's writings was nevertheless the critical space in which the translation and distribution of his texts worked to expand the communist reading public around the globe. This reading public differed from those that Kant participated in as a "detached political observer" in that it aimed not only to share the information and experiences of a movement with the hope for solidarity or other affections, but to populate and mobilize a political movement with active participants. Marx's reading public was not to be an academic one. It is worth noting, of course, that it often ended up as such, notably and perhaps most ironically in the case of the Russian Revolution where the bourgeoisie had read his works widely to help them predict their own development and that of capitalism in Russia, while the revolutionist proletariat knew little to nothing about Marx until after the revolution.[19] Nevertheless, for Marx, an international communist reading public was the prerequisite for an international communist political movement.

To this end, Marx and Engels formed the Communist Correspondence Committee in 1846, with which they intended nothing other than the widening of the reading public for their political ideas, and by that, the metatopical organization of an international revolutionary class. Their base, an international class comprised of the proletariat in modern bourgeois societies, was not produced by their propaganda. Marx and Engels gave credit for the existence of the international proletariat to the movement of industrialization that drove capitalism around the globe establishing new industrial centers and new markets. Indeed, Marx's historical materialist account of the course of capitalism was one of the first theories of capitalist globalization and the necessity of globalizing a response to it. Moreover, it was a theory that predicted the eventual dissolution of national identities brought about by the synthesis of the opposing trends in globalization. Modern industrial labor, according to Marx, "the same in England as in France, in America as in Germany, has stripped him [the proletariat] of every trace of national character."[20]

All of this reinforces, with striking clarity, the claim that a political public sphere can only emerge within a broader civil society, and it envisions the radical rethinking of political community from the national to the transnational. Civil society can be defined differently than as a society of legal citizens with national political identities. For the communists, capitalism had produced an international civil society in its special product of the proletariat and through the spread of the bourgeoisie, both of which were understood as irreducibly international classes. But the world proletariat was not already politicized as such. The economic structure would create them and eventually disaffect them making their inexorable antagonism with capitalism clearer over time. But the job of the communists was to mobilize them as a class toward an unambiguous and comprehensible resolution, to rebut capitalist narratives, and to bring about the end of their exploitation with as much expedience and singleness of purpose as possible. These latter goals, those that would not be inevitably achieved by the necessary dialectic of history, were the first goals of the communists, and they sought to take them up in a republic of letters. Here, they would circulate arguments that clarified their positions against competing ones, they would refute the promises of the bourgeoisie, they would help give shape to a revolutionary consciousness and a revolutionary spirit, they would finalize an agenda and elucidate demands, and they would inspire hope in those who could bring about the revolution. And this republic of letters was designed to cross as many national boundaries as capitalism itself.

But as I mentioned above, the communists of the First International did believe in beginning their project within the nation. This seemed to them a practical necessity.[21] Nevertheless, the two most important addressees of the First International were capitalism (understood as a world system, never as a national system), and the world proletariat (never just that of a particular nation). For as long as communism was believed to be a still-vital opponent to capitalism, that is to say, nearly to the end of the short twentieth century, it was perceived even by its opponents to be a world system that required great international support for its success.[22] Marx knew that communism could only fail without a transnational framework that ultimately achieved global stature.

This is the reason why Marx famously indicted the German Worker's Party for what he saw to be an internationalist pretension. Marx argued that,

> the framework of the present-day national state, *e.g.*, the German empire, is itself in its turn economically within the framework of the world market, politically within the framework of the system of states. Every businessman knows that German trade is at the same time foreign trade, and the greatness of Herr Bismarck consists, to be sure, precisely in a kind of *international* policy.[23]

Single states, after the Industrial Revolution, were increasingly economically integrated into a vaster world market and, politically, they increasingly saw themselves as actors in a global system of opportunities. Indeed, as Marx himself pointed out, this fact was even better understood and more clearly acknowledged by every businessman and political leader than it was by many purported communists.

Today, the fluidity, freedom, and sheer size of the world market are greater than ever before, and the linkages of cooperation (i.e., economic interdependencies) between states have only multiplied throughout the twentieth century, often under catastrophic circumstances, and most rapidly at the close of the century. Media technologies have thickened all of these linkages, and have become increasingly accessible to a civil society that, by its active use of them, is becoming increasingly transboundary. Yet, despite all of this, I have shown in this chapter how conceptions of discourse (the activity of the public sphere) and legitimation (the function of the public sphere) has led to the formulation of publics as organs of single national states. In Arendt and Habermas, we saw how purportedly representative states were, by definition, directly beholden to a clearly defined citizenry. Civil society provides the terrain for public spheres, and when we say that these spheres become political, we mean precisely that they register their opinion and will with institutions established for public service and that public spheres can thereby reveal a crisis of legitimation in these corollary institutions. But we have also recovered some prominent conceptions of transnational public spheres that not only preceded but were also studied well by Arendt and Habermas. Given this, we must ask what happened to the theory of transnational political public spheres.

Following the conclusions of chapters 1 and 2, you may anticipate the answer to this question, as it has emerged in the historical analysis of the concept. It remains only to be frankly stated. We have reviewed some of the major reformulations of the concept of the political public sphere from Kant to Habermas and have found that a forward looking theory of international political publics was already an important part of Kant's work, and that the idea of transnational political reading publics was well developed and employed by the revolutions and revolutionary movements throughout the nineteenth century. And although these conceptions could have remained at the core of thinking about public spheres, they were ultimately obscured by the orientations of public sphere theory, from Mills to Arendt to Habermas, which were sensibly but shortsightedly anchored to the major events of the short twentieth century.

Habermas' ideas of discourse and legitimation laid the groundwork for a theory that tied the public sphere to the state. And such a model was already and inevitably being concretized by the conceptual dominance of the state as the most relevant unit of politics while communist states were differentiated from capitalist adversaries, during the rise of fascism, and after World War II in the opposition of national blocks presented by the overdrawn rhetoric of the Cold War. In all of these developments, dark lines demarcating states and their own domestic publics from other states and other publics elsewhere were emboldened, and linkages and alliances among states did little to subvert national boundaries or to positively collectivize a transnational public sphere with a political function. The resultant conceptual confinement of public spheres to their corollary states led to the bracketing and postponing of further serious exploration of the idea of transnational political public spheres.

In Mills, publics were not theorized in general because of the degree to which they were particularly distinguished by the cultural establishment of their nation, by a cultural mainstream that was strictly national. During Mills' time, countries in possession of a mass media politically defended their cultural mainstreams from penetration by external ideologies as a key component of the Cold War. Yet, because public opinion in each country was often delimited by the focus of the national mass media, Mills was able to offer a theory of manipulable masses. In Arendt, when taking stock of the role of the public in her *Origins of Totalitarianism*, we discovered the ultimate illustration of how agreement in the public realm and the consent of public opinion could empower even the most authoritarian and brutal governments. If in principle only the rule of tyranny could do without the support of communicative power, the totalitarian movements of the twentieth century proved that they still did require it. That is, the need to achieve popularity remained critical for even the most murderous and exploitative regimes, as it enabled them to demonstrate a degree of legitimacy. In Habermas, we turned to the self-identified democracies of liberal capitalist countries and saw that they too suffered from severe problems of legitimation.

In the end, we arrive at a picture in which the actually existing problems and the tangible tasks of the political public sphere all appear to be essentially state-bounded. Civil society is legally established by the parameters of state-conferred citizenship, and states have only their own citizens to represent. By extension, political publics cannot hope to register and to formalize their opinion and will with and in institutions that have no formal responsibility or obligation to them. This problematic was both realized and reinforced in the defining moments of the short twentieth century in which we saw states appropriating publics to such ruinous effect that all earlier theories that had elucidated the lines of transnational public spheres could be shelved as abstractions. And a focus on this particular problematic prefigured discussions of the public sphere as national, but more importantly, it postponed analysis of publics that had already been expanding beyond national boundaries (we consider some early transboundary public spheres in chapter 3).

Today, social scientists generally agree that among the most major problems of early millennium is that civil society, the long necessary counterpart to institutions of governance, has been outflanked by the expansion of a transnational political topography that leaves both citizens and states rethinking *how* to hold political sway (an explication of this topography and problematic will be the primary focus of chapter 4). In the context of an accelerated economic globalization of a greater scale than ever before, it has recently been argued that public spheres have remained of too small a scale and thus too far behind newer transboundary institutions whose legitimacy they might rightly contest (more on this in parts II and III).

On the grounds of these more recent contentions, public sphere theory has belatedly but resolutely turned to focus on transnational public spheres. This focus has characterized the conversation since the early 1990s. Decades of distance from the totalitarian movements, and the collapse of the Soviet Union, corresponded well with the English publication of Habermas' *Structural Transformation*, providing not only renewed interest for its topic but also a new context. On the occasion of the latter event, much conferencing and research coalesced around the book that originally introduced the term "public sphere" into academic debates, the book that presented the single most thorough study of the state-bounded political public sphere.

I now turn to investigate the accomplishments and shortcomings of Habermas' major study, and to argue that, in addition to problems of the national framework, the classical public sphere theory neglected the unique agency of nonbourgeois public spheres. The public spheres of "dangerous classes" were more radical and innovative than those of the bourgeoisie, and they effectively redefined the conception of discourse (as the standard activity) and legitimation (as the standard function) for the public sphere.

Notes

1. His misinterpretation, I contend, derives mainly from insufficient attention to Arendt's *Origins of Totalitarianism*.

2. Habermas works within the basic parameters delineated in the discussion of Arendt's work, not only in the texts studied here, but generally, in all of his works.

3. If we sought a highly detailed analysis of such conditions we would need to carefully study Habermas' major work, *The Theory of Communicative Action*.

4. Jürgen Habermas, "Hannah Arendt's Communications Concept of Power," 77 in Steven Lukes' *Power*.

5. Habermas, *Legitimation Crisis*, 107–8.

6. See Arendt, *The Human Condition*, chapter 2, section 4.

7. Arendt, *The Origins of Totalitarianism*, 306.

8. Ibid., 312.

9. Ibid., 308.

10. Ibid., 306.

11. Habermas, "Hannah Arendt's Communications Concept of Power," 88.

12. Habermas, *Legitimation Crisis*, 36

13. I will discuss some of the most influential theorists who have enlarged the debates in important ways in part II, chapter 5.

14. Upon the English translation of Habermas' *Structural Transformation*, many who had studied Habermas' more accessible works for decades discovered for the first time this major work. Not only was the work taken up as the theme of countless conferences, but also in the research of scholars across many disciplines. Habermas' book on the public sphere has become a part of the canon of media studies, and remains of critical interest to sociologists, historians, political scientists, and philosophers.

15. Habermas, *The Postnational Constellation*, 43.

16. Ibid., 53.

17. For a fuller discussion of Kant's idea of the *civitas gentium* and its public justification, see chapter 1.

18. Nationalism is certainly involved to some extent, but only very complexly. The example of the European Union and the emergence of a European public sphere will be taken up again in chapter 6, and is too complicated to treat here in any further detail.

19. See Antonio Gramsci, "The Revolution against *Capital*," 32–36 in *The Gramsci Reader*.

20. Karl Marx, "Manifesto of the Communist Party," 216 in *The Portable Karl Marx*.

21. This point foreshadows both the case of the Zapatistas and much of what I will say in chapter 9, the concluding chapter of this work. Specifically, I am referring here not only to the communists' insistence that only a transnational construction could work for them, but that the national locations of their politics could not simply be overlooked. Although the communists insisted on the necessarily transnational scale of their politics, they understood and acknowledged the necessity of the national framework.

22. To be clear, I agree with French socialists Cornelius Castoriadis and Guy Debord that, already after World War II, communism did not exist anywhere in the world. No ideal society in the imaginations of Marxists could be pointed to, and least of all in Stalin's Russia and the Russia thereafter. The so-called communism of the Soviet Union was by the end of Word War II a bureaucratic, state-centered capitalism in contrast to the free market capitalism of the United States (Castoriadis, 1947; Debord, 1967). Even so, within the superstructures of the world, and in the rhetoric of the Cold War, communism was perceived to be a real and vital threat to capitalist societies until the collapse of the Soviet Union.

23. Marx, *Critique of the Gotha Programme*, 13.

3

Habermas' Classical Theory in Light of Nonbourgeois Public Spheres

Bourgeois Public Spheres and How They Work

Central to Habermas' *Structural Transformation* is an effort to show that the public sphere is a historical category that emerged specifically in the development of bourgeois society and under liberal capitalism, and that it functions as a fourth estate, distinguished from the state, the marketplace, and the intimate and internal associations of the family. The genealogy of the bourgeois political public sphere excludes consideration of public spheres that assembled in the more "plebeian" sectors of civil society. That is, the public sphere as a critical historical category that performs the function of a fourth term was understood to be a sphere of the bourgeoisie, as an association among the more affluent members of society who enjoyed common leisure time, the best available education, and the literacy to engage in the most "high-minded" discourse of the day.

The preface to Habermas' study includes a proviso that he will not analyze the plebeian public sphere because it has been generally suppressed throughout history. Its suppression effectively prevented its development into a public sphere with a clear and vital political function, therefore excluding it, he says, does not deprive his study of significant insights into the concept of the political public sphere. He does cede that during the French Revolution a public sphere began to emerge that was not wholly populated by the educated and leisurely class, but maintains that "even this plebeian public sphere, whose continued but submerged existence manifested itself in the Chartist Movement and especially in the anarchist traditions of the workers' movement on the continent, remains oriented toward the intentions of the bourgeois public sphere."[1] In saying that these nonbourgeois public spheres were "oriented toward the intentions of the bourgeois public sphere," Habermas contends that even the proletarian anarchists, arguably those with the smallest amount of faith in reformism, sought nevertheless to win a relationship with the state such as the bourgeoisie maintained, and moreover, that they sought to *legitimate the state's authority* by compelling it to represent and to instate their opinion and will.

Now, I am not here interested in anarchism per se, but it is critical to note from the outset that this contention is rather shocking. If we are to take anarchist political history at the word of its makers, it is not possible to find much in it, if anything at all, that could be seen as seeking a "working relationship" with the states that it indicts as thoroughly corrupted and in need of being radically restructured or razed to the ground.[2] Indeed, the anarchists of the mid-nineteenth to the early twentieth century comprised a nonbourgeois public sphere whose orientation and intentions stood in stark contrast to those of the bourgeois public sphere.

I shall briefly review Habermas' classical public sphere theory, considering some of the criteria for a bourgeois public sphere in a national framework, and argue that nonbourgeois public spheres violated these criteria and have distinct comportments from those of bourgeois public spheres in critical ways. I argue that "plebeian" public spheres could not have had an effective political function by comporting themselves toward the state as the bourgeois public sphere did, and thus, they could only constitute a political function by other means, and by comporting themselves toward more responsive addressees.

I begin by presenting a general schema of my argument. As with all schemata, the following paragraphs lay out an inexhaustive and ultimately imprecise picture, but one that should provide a fair explanatory outline of the central argument. Any political public sphere has numerous important dimensions, but here I shall focus on three. Any given public sphere has a particular character or composition (C), that is, its active participants share certain collective traits and/or identities (class, nationality, "race," gender, sexuality, political affiliation or other self-understanding, etc.). Also, any given public sphere has, or at least strives to have, a particular function or orientation (F). For example, a suffragist public sphere is oriented toward expanding the right to vote. Finally, any given public sphere has some actual location in the world (L), that is, its active participants and members must communicate *someplace* (cafés, cyberspace, reading publics, etc.).

I intend to show that these three dimensions (C, F, and L) are embedded within and partially determine each another. For example, Habermas considered the model public sphere to be bourgeois (C), its function and orientation was legitimation (F), and its location was national, or state-bounded (L). I shall show why none of these things are independent variables, and how all of them are and may be affected by the others. The bourgeois public sphere was recognized and respected by the state, so it addressed itself to the state (within the state) making appeals for reciprocity and representation. In contrast to Habermas' contention that "plebeian" public spheres could be left unaccounted for because their aims and orientation were the same as those of the bourgeois public sphere, I argue that the character, function, and location of nonbourgeois public spheres were importantly different. Where C was "nonbourgeois," F was often "to challenge the state," and L was often "transnational" or "transgressive," or at least, F and L betrayed the presumption of a one-to-one reciprocity between the public sphere and the state.[3] Nonbourgeois public spheres needed to be more creative and contestatory (because of C), thus their function (F) and location (L) were fundamentally different than that of the bourgeois public sphere.

It is important here to make one methodological remark here. Throughout chapter 3, I employ the method of immanent critique. That is, rather than replacing Habermas' lexicon with my own—justifying the latter in reference to the former—I work with Habermas' terminology and conceptual framework in order to show that, ultimately, it cannot work. Generally, the specific cases I discuss serve a dual purpose; they serve to illustrate Habermas' conception of the public sphere, yet at the same time, they reveal the deep structural instability of the whole model.

Habermas understands the state, in liberal capitalist society, as a public institution and whatever offices are associated with it are understood to be the offices of public authority, regardless of how opened or closed they might be to members of civil society. This is because the institutions of liberal capitalist societies are established to serve the public, or the common welfare of the society at large. State institutions in this context are authoritative, preside over the satisfaction of social needs, and are identified as the formal addressees of a public in need of assistance. The term of generality (as in the general public) is reified here in that even if these institutions are off-limits to direct control *by civil society*, they exist *for civil society, for the general good*. This sense of public is at the heart of Habermas' concept of the bourgeois public sphere. The public sphere need not be open to and inclusive of everyone in society so long as it is oriented toward the common welfare of society at large.

The concept of private has two senses. First, private refers to special interests, that is to say, not necessarily in the interest of and not necessarily for the benefit of society at large, but rather, in the interest and for the benefit of a person or a group whose interests may or may not coincide with those of the society at large. Of course, we can speak about the special interest of a particular class of people, recognizing that self-interest may need to be restrained to some extent in the service of satisfying special interests. Second, private refers to a person's or a group's differentiation from the institutions of public authority. Hence, if a person becomes mayor or governor or president, they become official agents of public authority who have been elected or appointed for the purpose of serving the public, or the common welfare of the society at large. To the extent that they act *as mayor, as governor*, or *as president*, they are not private citizens. On the other hand, a company incorporated for the purpose of earning as much profit as possible is a private entity, no matter how many people it employs, no matter how big a role it plays in other arenas than the marketplace.

In light of this, Habermas defines the bourgeois public sphere as "the sphere of private people come together as a public."[4] Private individuals, here in the second sense, as those not acting as institutional representatives of the public or as elected officials, come together to form the public sphere. The public sphere is characterized as "bourgeois" for historical reasons, since, according to Habermas, it was bourgeois society that first conceived of itself as a society with openly divulged common interests that were voiced in public criticisms of society and of public authorities. The active participants in early political public spheres had to be members of the bourgeoisie because they had to be those citizens who could form an educated reading public in common leisure times; participants had to be citizens whose basic needs were well satisfied. Despite its exclusions, the bourgeois public sphere, according to Habermas, did effectively "put the state in touch with the needs of society."[5]

It is critical to clarify the difference between civil society and the public sphere. We understand civil society to mean a delimitable group of people bound by a collective identity. We understand public sphere to mean a discursive arena constituted in the active engagement in a particular discourse by members of civil society. Hence, civil society passively exists once it is established, say by citizenship, regardless of the activity or inactivity of its members. On the other hand, the public sphere forms only in the active participation of its members and dissolves wherever the binding discourse ceases to be engaged—so the public sphere is a subset of and within civil society.

Throughout part I, the collective identity that forms civil society is understood, conventionally, as a society of citizens who share a common legal standing *as citizens of the same country*. That is, the collective identity that defines civil society is typically national identity. In chapter 3, we shall begin to see the shortcomings of a legally delineated civil society as such and we shall ultimately use a far more open conception of collective identity in chapter 5 and thereafter. But whatever conception we use, civil society always refers to a generally shared space, and public sphere always refers to a more specialized common space within it, a common space constituted by engagement in a particular discourse.[6] Civil society may be defined and redefined according to different conceptions of collective identity, but wherever it is defined it is sustained as such without further activity. Following Arendt, public spheres cannot be sustained without the actively engaged discourses that give them their shape.

The public sphere had to be highly regarded, both by the state and by other parts of civil society, as a fair, rational-critical body, a body that could and would consider important matters with objectivity and without undue haste. A public sphere that was not regarded as such could not expect public authorities to look to it as an advisory council. And, if civil society did not hold the public sphere in high regard, this would cast doubt on the possibility that it could self-generate a mechanism of evaluation and judgment autonomous of state institutions. But the bourgeois public sphere of the eighteenth century was successful on both scores, because it not only communicated the needs of society to the state, but it also served as a testing ground for new ideas. Writers and academics of all kinds would submit their work first to the consideration of the public sphere, and only after would they pursue publication.

Recall the seemingly impossible criteria for discourse discussed in chapter 2, as it was defined in *Legitimation Crisis*. Recall the kind of bracketing of bias, experience, and action that discourse defined as such strives for so that the validity of assertions can be rigorously tested with a temporarily convened unimpeded objectivity. Well, the bourgeois public spheres of the eighteenth century appear, in Habermas' account, to have approached this ideal to as far an extent as possible. They engaged in discussion without internal bias or hierarchy, and with an honest and equal consideration of which argument possessed the inherent authority of being the better one. In terms of art and culture, as well as discussions of literature and philosophy, on matters where the questions were not to do with what is correct or incorrect, inquiry had to do with settling the meaning and the value of cultural products for the common good.

Clearly, Habermas seems to have romanticized this early public sphere, and indeed, much has been written about how such romanticization led Habermas to overlook many of the shortcomings of the bourgeois public sphere. Yet critics of Habermas, particularly on the issue of the exclusivity of the public sphere, often fail to acknowledge that, even with all his idealizations, he did not completely ignore its exclusive shortcomings. Habermas does acknowledge a fundamental mistake that the bourgeois public sphere makes in its purporting to represent common concern and its principle, not practice, of inclusion. He writes that

> [w]omen and dependents were factually and legally excluded from the political public sphere, whereas female readers as well as apprentices and servants often took a more active part in the literary public sphere than the owners of private property and family heads themselves. Yet in the educated classes the one form of public sphere was considered to be identical with the other; . . . *The fully developed bourgeois public sphere was based on the fictitious identity of the two roles assumed by the privatized individuals who came together to form a public: the role of property owners and the role of human beings pure and simple.*[7]

Habermas does two things here. He acknowledges the confusion in the self-understanding of the public sphere, and justifies it on other grounds. The public sphere conflated its position as a conference of "property owners" with that of a conference of "common human beings," and as such it was content to rest upon and to invoke principles of common humanity and inclusion rather than to see marginal and contradictory discourses outside of itself. But even though this was the case, Habermas nevertheless maintains that the public sphere "turned the principle of publicity against the established authorities" and worked toward "the political emancipation of civil society from mercantilist rule and from absolutistic regimentation in general."[8]

The early bourgeois public sphere was quite effective indeed and was understood as an important power formed in civil society and acting on its behalf. Governments were not accustomed to the circulation of fierce criticism directed at them and as early as the late seventeenth century the government "found itself compelled to issue proclamations that confronted the dangers bred by the coffee-house discussions. The coffee houses were considered seedbeds of political unrest."[9] There was something threatening about the formation of critical opinion that could be published widely as the opinion and will of a people independent of and in contrast to the pronouncements of the state. It was the public sphere that first made clear the fact that election results do not exhaustively map public opinion, and that even in a democracy secured and supervised by state power, the "sense of the people" could stand at odds to what is represented in an election.

Habermas cites Charles Fox's (a member of the British House of Commons in the late eighteenth century) reflections on the subject:

> It is certainly right and prudent to consult the public opinion. . . . If the public opinion did not happen to square with mine; if, after pointing out to them the danger, they did not see it in the same light with me, or if they conceived that another remedy was preferable to mine, I should consider it as my due to my king, due to my Country, due to my honour to retire, that they might persue the plan which they thought better, by a fit instrument, that is by a man who thought with them . . . but one thing is most clear, that I ought to give the public the means of forming an opinion.[10]

Public opinion interacted with Parliament in a number of ways, and Fox was largely responsible for elevating the status of public opinion from a more derogatory conception of it as common or vulgar and uneducated to something to which the state needed to look for approval if it was going to claim its own representative authority. Fox's contention underscores clearly the way in which public opinion was raised to having the status of an important political player, but only in direct correlation to the state, and only in the state's ascription of prestige and authority to public opinion. This delineates one genealogy, among others in other countries, of the way in which the public sphere can generate a rational critique of political policies and proposals with autonomy—outside of, and sometimes even against, the state.

The public spheres in France, Germany, Great Britain, and the United States retained a political function as such, with growing claims to power and for representation, until increasing state and corporate encroachment in societal affairs, during the nineteenth century, began to alter its comportment. This would be the beginning of what Habermas calls the public sphere's structural transformation. States, along with private corporations, in a consortium of public authorities and private business, began to identify public functions that could be transferred from the former to the latter. In all of the countries where a bourgeois public sphere flourished, states began to negotiate the transference of some of their decisionmaking and administrative duties to privately owned firms, thus privatizing, or turning over to the private sector, many formerly public functions.

This privatization of public authority confounded the distinct roles of the separate spheres (the public and the private) in that the private sector was here a constellation of business firms that were not formed for any expressly social purpose, or for the common good. Habermas wrote,

> state intervention in the sphere of society found its counterpart in the transfer of public functions to private corporate bodies. . . . Only this dialectic of a progressive "societalization" of the state simultaneously with an increasing "stateification" of society gradually destroyed the basis of the bourgeois public sphere—the separation of state and society.[11]

In other words, what is today commonly called "privatization" had an initial effect of obscuring and diminishing the hard won position of civil society observed by Kant, its position as a contestatory, independent power. And, despite an early optimism that this transference of public authority would lead to competition among private corporations thereby preventing the monopolization of power by one firm or office, it led to a contrary if not completely opposite outcome—the concentration of power into few private hands.

This situation caused a crisis for the political public sphere. For profit businesses became increasingly in charge of managing and providing housing options, the arts became increasingly organized by corporations, from concerts to theater productions, and education too became a domain of private industry. Care for the elderly and the homeless was outsourced from institutions of public authority to corporations, whose underlying and overarching aims were "private" according to the first sense of the term. A political public sphere must address itself to the appropriate body. However, when social welfare functions are entrusted to bodies that have neither a formal obligation to further social welfare nor a formal need for democratic legitimation, the public sphere faces its own depoliticization. For Habermas, the structural transformation of the public sphere is its depoliticization.

The erosion and loss of the public sphere's capacity to serve as a conduit of influence and pressure between civil society and the state is a transformation that must be understood as structural. The depoliticization of the public sphere is structural because it has been understood as a category with an essentially political function.[12] That is to say, we understand the political public sphere, by definition, through its political function; stripped of its function, the public sphere loses its structural comportment and its normative status. In the cessation of its structural function is, at the same time, the cessation of its normative status as an organ of democratic legitimation and the transformation of it into something else.

The history of the commercialization and privatization of public functions, which Habermas very carefully (if not exhaustively) traces, culminates in a near total transformation from a "culture-debating" to a "culture-consuming" in which "the people" become indistinguishable from "the market." Habermas calls this a transformation of the political public sphere into a "pseudopublic." It is in this part of the analysis, almost all of the second half of the book, that we see the still profound influence of Adorno and Horkheimer on the young Habermas. Indeed, images of the culture industry are unavoidable here. Civil society appeared in a new light, as a population of consumers who must tend to their own welfare within the marketplace. At bottom, earlier roles of consumers were transformed by an expanded market in which social welfare could be secured along with (and just like) the rest of purchasable goods, and the public sphere could no longer be distinguished as a fourth term from the state, the marketplace, and the family. One could say, rather, that the public sphere was assimilated into a changing marketplace.

The pseudopublic sphere works best wherever there is the smallest amount of critical discussion and public deliberation.

The prestige of an argument or opinion regarding political news and current events is not determined through the collective deliberation of a rational-critical body, but is rather assigned in advance to the authority of the speakers. Capitalist media is inscribed with prestige from the start and is presented to the public as an authoritative voice: "The public sphere becomes the court *before* whose public prestige can be displayed—rather than *in* which public critical debate is carried on."[13] Habermas saw this crisis of the public sphere more ominously after World War II, informed by the insights of the culture industry thesis. But as we shall see, while the bourgeois public sphere was being depoliticized, other public spheres, neglected by Habermas, followed a different historical and developmental model.

Yet before discussing nonbourgeois public spheres, their uniquely contestatory function, transnational (or transgressive) scale, and the socioeconomic reasons for both, I shall review the three structural criteria for Habermas' conception of the national public sphere.[14]

Criterion 1

The first criterion for a national public sphere has to do with the specific meaning of civil society. Civil society has been defined as the larger and delimitable group of people within which political publics take shape as a subset. I have stipulated that, conventionally, civil society consists of legally conferred citizens. Habermas follows the conventional stipulation of civil society as a society of citizens. That is, in all of his Kantianism, Habermas does not yet mean the more abstract Kantian notion of "world citizens" in a cosmopolitan sense, but those who have a specific citizenship status, a membership conferred by national (in a Westphalian sense) governments. In his early work Habermas thus defines the public sphere as a discursive arena formed within state-bounded and legally delimited civil societies.

According to this first criterion, broader conceptions of civil society as formed by imagined linkages, such as those that Benedict Anderson and Michael Warner argue for, or society in terms of diaspora, are neglected. In these broader conceptions, the term of collective identity, requisite for any definition of civil society, is preserved. However, these conceptions utilize a kind of collective identity that does not require legal or state conferral in order to be established. For Anderson, the central component of the creative forces that generate nationalisms is a personal and cultural feeling of belonging to a nation. In his view, a theory of imagined community is required to explain diaspora and/or to explain the sharing and spreading of feelings of ethnic, religious, and/or national belonging among people who are in many ways, through displacement or migrations, stateless. For Warner, who is largely concerned with reading publics, the imagined community is that of strangers for whom belonging is achieved through the taking up of the same texts; such a single public sphere may be gathered from civil societies all over the world, at least as far as a single read text may travel.[15]

So civil society as a legally determined society of citizens is not the only way to think of it. One way to understand the difference between Habermas' conventional conception of the civil society within which publics form, and the theories of Kant, Anderson, and Warner, for example, is to introduce Charles Taylor's discussion of "topical common space" and "metatopical common space." Indeed, introducing these terms will help us to understand the rest of the criteria as well.

Citizenship statuses, in the classical account, must be conferred by the state, and in their conferral the state identifies not only who its citizens are, but also *to whom* it is beholden itself. A legally delimited civil society has a clear purpose and can be seen firsthand in the places where its members come together. Taylor says that

> an intuitively understandable kind of common space is set up when people are assembled for some purpose, be it on an intimate level for conversation, or on a larger, more "public" scale for deliberative assembly, a ritual, a celebration, the enjoyment of a football match or an opera, and the like. Common space arising from assembly in some locale I want to call "topical common space."[16]

Recalling the salons and coffee houses in which the bourgeois public sphere took shape, topical common space has generally been the space in which state-bounded public spheres emerged. Geographically separated imagined communities and reading publics come together ideationally, not in the sense of physical assembly that Taylor invokes with the concept of topical common space.

Though Habermas was well aware of reading publics and of Kant's and Marx's theories, his understanding of the political function of public spheres remained focused in the more cohesive and material power of a physically assembled group.[17] Simply put, Habermas sought to understand public spheres as tangible and active groups organizing themselves and operating within a clear and defined civil society, which had a clear and defined addressee. To see public spheres strictly in topical common spaces is to see them more concretely ("metatopical common space" is defined below in a note).

Criterion 2

The second criterion for a national public sphere has to do with the content and form of its discourses. The public sphere must develop and then publicize its opinion and will, and these are anchored in a shared objective reality, a shared language, and shared social experiences. This is of course related to the first criterion, that the public sphere forms in the topical common spaces of a legally defined civil society. However, this criterion focuses more on the character of communication. If, by definition, the public sphere takes up issues of common concern, then its participants must be capable of identifying such common ground, and must be able to articulate feasible resolutions to a set of problems that a given collectivity face *as a collectivity*. Furthermore, print media and other literatures are conducted in a particular language and are of a particular national origin, and, therefore, do not work across boundaries nearly as effectively as they do domestically. Thus the character of communication consists of both its content and its form, and both of these are fitted best to topical common spaces. The discourses of a reading public sphere can only be as inclusive as they are accessible in terms of their content. The language and orientation of any given discourse is already necessarily exclusive, at least to some extent. And, even where language can be translated, experience and orientation often elude translation.

I'd like to try to make the above point of translatability by discussing some examples of fragmentation processes around the world. More specifically, I will simultaneously exemplify and problematize this second criterion by considering some cases that both flesh it out and demonstrate its instability. Let us take, for instance, crises in human development and human rights in sub-Saharan Africa. The following give some impression of crises that have been widely circulated to reading and viewing publics all over the world. During the 1990s, the number of people living in extreme poverty in sub-Saharan Africa rose from 242 million to 300 million people and per capita income shrank drastically throughout that whole decade. Twenty sub-Saharan countries were poorer in 2002 than they were in 1990, and twenty-three sub-Saharan countries were poorer in 2002 than they were in 1975. Beyond these issues of extreme poverty are a host of severe health problems related to poverty. Child immunization rates had fallen below 50 percent of the whole population of children in sub-Saharan Africa. And, by the end of the year 2000, over forty million people worldwide were living with HIV, and 75 percent of those infected lived in sub-Saharan Africa.[18]

From a comparative standpoint, certainly from the vantage point of the United States, it is fair to say that the economic and health crises that afflict sub-Saharan countries are extraordinarily more dire than those that afflict the American population, particularly in terms of scale, resources, and infrastructure. These crises, however, are translatable to some extent to those of us living in the relative calm of the more comfortable regions of the global north. By translatable, I mean understandable in terms of both an intellectual and an emotional sense of the problems. Simply put, impoverishment and catastrophic health crises can be imagined at a greater scale than we experience them ourselves, through an extrapolation of what we *do* know.

But even though the translatability of sub-Saharan crises may be high, our feelings about these crises consist primarily of our sympathies as strangers. Imagination can take us some distance, but it has some limits.[19] Our comportment toward a civil society afflicted with impoverishment and death in sub-Saharan countries is that of the sympathy of outsiders, and though we can imagine enough to feel our way closer to those crises, we cannot imagine our way into the civil society that actually suffers under such destitution and death. It is indeed a strain to say that we share the same issues of common concern, because as outsiders *we* must be given an occasion to sympathize, we must be given the data (for example, that I have listed above), for the topical common reality that the data describes is not our own. Now, this does not mean that we cannot understand enough to form or to join a public sphere with people far away (I think that we can)—only that even where understanding is achievable, problems in the translatability of experience and orientation may always serve to keep us somewhat estranged. This goes rather far to substantiate the meaning of the second criterion.

But solidarity can be formed and maintained on the basis of agreement on moral and political principles, and political solidarity and the collective action it gives rise to do not require total existential understanding in order to be meaningful. Remember the example of the French Revolution. In that case, the sympathies of outsiders who did not share the experience of the revolution did nevertheless take the shape of political solidarity. This political solidarity did not make members of a distant reading public into participants in the revolution itself, but it did lend the weight of international favor to the revolution. In the final analysis (part III), I shall argue that it is possible to invite outside membership in expressly national or subnational movements by rethinking the subject position of those who frame the political discourse from within their particular community or locale.

The Zapatistas, we shall see, retained a vigorous focus on locale, on the crises of the indigenous in relation to the Mexican state, and they did not abandon their focus on topical common space in organizing a political public sphere metatopically. Indeed, the Zapatista public sphere will vividly illustrate how political discourses can be situated outside of this dichotomy. That is to say, it will be necessary to think not just about the binary construct of topical common spaces versus metatopical common spaces, as Taylor does,[20] but also of the imbrications of these spaces. These themes will be explored more fully in parts II and III (in the discussions of cosmopolitanism and indigeneity, respectively), where we will see how transformations of political identity can in fact make geographically, ethnically, and culturally disparate participants in the metatopical common spaces of public spheres members of each others' movements.

Criterion 3

The final criterion for a national public sphere has to do with its political function: "The public sphere as a functional element in the political realm was given the normative status of an organ for the self-articulation of civil society with a state authority corresponding to its needs."[21] This criterion for a national public sphere is already well familiar to us, but I would like to cast it in a different light here. The public sphere has a need for a state to prevail upon, and the state has a need for public opinion to legitimate its rule. This reciprocally fixes the public sphere to a particular state. Yet, in what has been said about the second criterion of a national public sphere, we saw that in certain instances and regarding certain issues a political public sphere, such as a public sphere confronting the AIDS pandemic in sub-Saharan Africa, can be transnational. But the third criterion for a national public sphere poses a problem to this potentiality.

Even if the weight of outside pressure on the leader of a sub-Saharan country, such as Thabo Mbeki of South Africa, is mounted from public opinion funneling in from civil societies all over the world, something further is at stake if such opinion prevails. The paradigm of state-bounded public spheres has consistently represented that the state secures its legitimation through its corollary public. By extension then, most states will not be quick to acknowledge the opinion of civil societies elsewhere as that to which it must also be beholden. If a state responds to and works toward satisfying the appeals and pressures of public spheres in civil societies other than its own, then it shifts its need for democratic legitimation to rest on a larger citizenry than that of its own legal citizens. In other words, by seeking the conferral of a transnational public sphere, the conferral of a state's legitimacy is harder to secure, and its responsibility to its own citizens is diluted with responsibility to others.

One clear illustration of this point was made prominent in the rhetoric of George W. Bush's 2004 presidential campaign for reelection. That administration's military policy toward Afghanistan and Iraq between 2000 and 2004 was met with massive protest all over the globe. The Bush administration, however, has responded defiantly to all such criticisms. And, with regard to national allies in Europe and to transnational bodies such as the United Nations and the International Criminal Court (ICC), Bush has said that neither he nor his administration would be restrained by the opinions of outsiders, that is, other institutional bodies as well as other peoples. During the first presidential debate on September 30, 2004, in response to Senator John Kerry's remarks about how preemptive military action must pass a "global test," George W. Bush replied: "I just think trying to be popular, kind of, in the global sense, if it's not in our best interest makes no sense." About refusing to join the ICC, Bush said, "[a]nd I wouldn't join it. And I understand that in certain capitals around the world that that wasn't a popular move. But it's the right move not to join a foreign court that could— where our people could be prosecuted."[22] In this, Bush expressed clearly that the American state's legitimacy would be harder to secure, and its responsibility to its own citizens would be weakened if it were constrained to the judgment and opinion of others. Governments understand what is at stake in appealing to a larger community of interest and opinion, whether that community consists of other institutions of governance or of political public spheres. Thus, even if a transnational public sphere were formed, it would not necessarily be able to constitute its political function. If, for example, Mbeki and Bush refuse to be swayed by the opinion and will of a transnational public sphere, we must ask ourselves in what sense such public spheres are political.

States will not be eager to surrender or to transfer the means of their own legitimation to a transnational community. Indeed, regarding the war in Iraq, the publicity and circulation of oppositional voices, around the globe, was disregarded as opinion to which the U.S. and British governments were not beholden; this disregard, interestingly, was extended to the dispositions of each country's own civil society, particularly Great Britain's. Thus, the possibility for a transnational public sphere in principle does not mean that its political function will remain intact in actual practice. In short, a transnational public sphere can only achieve its political function if there are institutions seeking legitimacy in the conferral of that public.

Analytically, then, the national character of Habermas' early concept of the public sphere is determined as such by (1) the physical and/or legal space it occupies, zones of citizenship, (2) its issues and means of communication, rooted in a shared language and shared experience, and (3) who its responsive addressee is. These criteria enable us to understand concretely the national framework of political public spheres. For example, wherever the public sphere operates within a nation's civil society among its own legal citizens, wherever its issues and means of communication are shared in common social experience and language, and wherever it appeals to its official institutions of state for the satisfaction of its demands and the representation of its will, the public sphere is national in the classical sense. And, because each state is the ultimate authority to its corresponding public, at least for all matters raised in and by the public sphere, the classical theory assumes a Westphalian conception of the state. For Habermas, these criteria are implicit in what he takes to be an actually functioning and powerful public sphere. That is to say, he maintains throughout *Structural Transformation* that the most tangible and concrete public spheres will satisfy all three of these criteria.

Public spheres coalescing around issues of campaign finance reform, engaged in circulating and debating the political discourses of the American Democratic and Republican parties, those critically assessing most taxation issues (excluding the Tobin tax, for example), gun control, education reform, health care, minimum wage, and media reform, are all publics that mostly meet the three criteria above, and are therefore easiest to imagine as national publics. But let us think through these criteria a bit more carefully with the help of some examples.

A small, low budget newspaper assembled by three friends with a monthly press run of one thousand copies takes up a host of LGBTQ issues ranging from city development and local culture to state legislation on civil unions and same-gender marriage. The paper is circulated throughout the city in which its three editors live. The paper's editors see their work as having a modest but hopeful political function. They aim to address members of the LGBTQ community and others about social and political problems based on heterosexist discrimination, or prevailing cultural-valuational norms. They aim to impact the thinking of their readership on key issues, changing cultural-valuational norms, and to mobilize support. These are public sphere initiatives. Their efforts are focused toward the topical common space inhabited by a reading public in a clearly defined locale. The paper uses the main language spoken in the city, and it takes up many issues of common concern for those living there. Its reading public is a knowable population, folks who pick up the free monthly at cafés and shops within city limits. The editors admit that their loftier ideal is to motivate the paper's reading public to become politically active about these issues, that some of them might further populate existing efforts to influence elected officials, or work to restructure the political culture sufficiently to elect a better state government altogether. Whether or not it is successful, the public sphere engaged by this newspaper meets all of the criteria for a public sphere in the classical sense.

Yet, if we imagine a public sphere that does not meet *even one* of the criteria for a national public sphere, the certainty of its national character is thrown into question. Let us imagine the same newspaper. Now, however, its editors are posting each issue online, are buying advertisements for their paper in other presses with larger readerships, and are selling it to subscribers outside of the city. Essentially, the editors recognized that the paper's discursive content had wider appeal, and that with a slight shift in its orientation, deemphasizing its more parochial content, it could become a more ambitious enterprise. In their success, the paper's political function transcended the third criterion. Through online activity and subscriptions, the paper's reading public ultimately became international, winning readership in countries all over North America and in the United Kingdom. Thematically, the paper internationalized reader forum on the issue of legislation on same-gender marriage, appealing to activists outside of the state and the country. Of course, such organs and reading publics exist in the world.

This is precisely the kind of leverage animal rights groups have come to employ, inviting concerned publics all over the world to write letters to public authorities in other countries presiding over animal protection legislation. Because of this, it becomes immediately difficult to think of such public spheres as fitting the national framework. Animal rights activists populate a metatopical common space, a space in which people are linked up for a political function without physical assembly in a topical common space. The killing of dogs in South Korea for food and the poisoning of stray dogs and cats that wander the streets in Greece are issues that have mobilized public spheres that are neither South Korean nor Greek. Yet these public spheres are formed for the purpose of pressuring those countries' respective governments to uphold laws that ban such practices. When Marijo Gills, founder of an animal rights group in Greece who documented the poisoning of strays says to a transnational reading public, "[p]lease join me in conveying outrage and shock over the compassionless treatment of animals in Greece," he is engaging a public sphere that cannot rightly be thought of as national.[23] Though we cannot yet say what effectively makes a public sphere transnational, we can see that such public spheres are more or less unfit for dichotomous thinking about national and transnational frameworks, in that they keep the national state as their addressee (the South Korean or Greek state in these cases), but are transnational in other key regards.

I have argued (in chapter 2) that Habermas overlooked the transnational thinking of Marx. In *Structural Transformation* Habermas writes, "Marx denounced public opinion as false consciousness: it hid before itself its own true character as a mask of bourgeois class interests."[24] This is true, Marx did make such denouements, but he did not believe this completely. Marx surely saw public opinion as a problematic feature of the superstructure, but he did not think its manipulation was exhaustive and irreversible. In much of his own work, Marx took as a central aim the recalibration of consciousness toward a devalorization of capitalism and a more critical understanding of intractable class antagonisms. Indeed, public opinion, although not bourgeois public opinion in Marx's story, was assigned the key task of helping to foment, and to come to understand the historical materialist dialectic.

I have raised some examples in the preceding critique that demonstrate how easily cases that illustrate the features of a national public sphere can also illustrate its deep structural instability as such. But more important than destabilizing the national public sphere as such is the fact that nonbourgeois public spheres had to struggle for recognition and reciprocity. And in the course of this struggle, they were compelled to violate the three criteria of the national public sphere. Indeed, the so-called plebeian public sphere had many distinctive functions that cannot be accounted for by Habermas' classical theory.

In sum, for Habermas discourse (the activity that constitutes and sustains the public sphere) has a stringent and narrow definition. It is a particular and ideal kind of communication, which mainly consists of rational, critical, reciprocal, and unbiased collective deliberation—the format is discussion. And legitimation (the political function of the public sphere) is state-bounded. Every public sphere has a corollary state that it can address, a state that is structurally beholden to it. If a state claims to be a legitimate democratic representative, then it must be felicitous with and influenced by the publics it purports to represent. Otherwise, the state's democratic legitimacy is thrown into question, it faces a legitimation crisis, and the public sphere loses its political function. However, I shall now turn to argue that a consideration of nonbourgeois public spheres necessitates a rethinking of discourse and legitimation as such, as the activity and the purpose of the public sphere.

Nonbourgeois Public Spheres: Different Discourse, Different Aims

I would like now to return to Habermas' claim that the "plebeian public sphere . . . remains oriented toward the intentions of the bourgeois public sphere."[25] Evaluating this claim is integral because if Habermas is wrong that nonbourgeois public spheres aspire to the status and aims of the bourgeois public sphere, and I argue that he is wrong about this, then I must say why nonbourgeois public spheres matter—why they challenge the general theorization more seriously. I argue that nonbourgeois public spheres employ methodologies that are discounted in the general theory. As well, nonbourgeois public spheres draw on resources beyond what is at their disposal in their own national context, and thus work to transcend the national framework as much as is possible.

Nonbourgeois public spheres, neither automatically nor inevitably, provide the political function of the bourgeois public sphere (democratic legitimation). In order to constitute a political function, they not only employ other methods than the bourgeois public sphere, but also, they resort to metatopical common space. To get the state to listen, bourgeois public spheres had only to speak to it. Nonbourgeois public spheres, on the other hand, had to take other addresses than an unresponsive state and they had to do more than speak to make themselves political. Social movements and civil disobedience, for example, have often been the terrain of nonbourgeois public spheres, means for the generation of new public spheres and conduits of communication for existing ones.

Consideration of nonbourgeois public spheres, many of which formed and functioned concomitantly with and in juxtaposition to their bourgeois counterparts, not only reveals that there were other political publics than those represented in an by more dominant publics. More importantly, an assessment of nonbourgeois public spheres reveals that while some publics were national in terms of their membership and function, others struggled to transnationalize, that is, they fought to establish linkages, communications, and ultimately new collectivities beyond national boundaries. Accounting for such public spheres does more than suggest a historical corrective. For we consider not only the fact that "plebeian" public spheres have been unaccounted for, but that some such public spheres, for strategic reasons and/or for reasons of material necessity, have attempted to address other bodies besides their own state and beyond their own national boundaries. This essentially frees the political function of public spheres from their state-boundedness and raises the question of how far and wide they may have effect.[26] As we shall see in the example of the Zapatista public sphere, it is often the marginalized social position of nonbourgeois groups that makes a transnational, or transgressive construction favorable, necessary, or both.

But first, what do I mean by "nonbourgeois public sphere," and, if I am invoking Marxist signifiers to some extent, why not just say "proletarian public sphere" (as do Oskar Negt and Alexander Kluge, whom I will discuss shortly)? Or why not use the term "counterpublic" as Michael Warner does?

I do not want to call nonbourgeois public spheres proletarian because I do not want to inextricably tie them to the means of production. Women, for example, have constituted important nonbourgeois public spheres, even during the Industrial Revolution where they were marginalized in factory work and thus not considered the main subjects of proletarianization. In Marx, to be clear, exploitation applied to women as well, particularly in reference to prostitution, reproduction, and household divisions of labor. Marx was remarkably forward-thinking on these issues. However, the driving crux of exploitation entailed in proletarianization placed special emphasis on the industrial transformation of society and the mass scale of alienation from species being brought about by capitalist mass production, and this was envisioned as a mass of men. In addition to women, we may think also about indigenous communities living in the forests of the Amazon or in the mountains of Chiapas, whose modes of labor are still largely if not wholly oriented toward subsistence rather than toward capitalist development. It is awkward to think of indigenous peoples as a "massified" proletariat in a conventional sense (or, in an industrial or postindustrial sense), and is less problematic, within the context of their societies, to say that they are radically differentiated from the bourgeoisie, or from the dominant class.

I also do not want to call nonbourgeois public spheres counterpublics, although this term hews closely to mine. The idea of counterpublics is part of the idea of nonbourgeois public spheres, but the former cannot suffice as the whole definition of what I mean by nonbourgeois public spheres. What Michael Warner means by counterpublic is a public defined by its

> tension with a larger public. . . . Discussion within such a public is understood to contravene the rules obtaining in the world at large, being structured by alternative dispositions or protocols, making different assumptions about what can be said or

> what goes without saying . . . it maintains at some level, con-
> scious or not, an awareness of its subordinate status.[27]

So counterpublic does not mean "not public," but rather, it functions like the term counteract, which is *to act* but is *to act against*. I prefer to speak of nonbourgeois public spheres because this term does not imply differentiation from a larger, or triumphant public. In the first place, it is often the larger public that is subordinated in a hierarchy that favors a small ruling elite, as in the now proverbial wealthiest 1 percent. Secondly, I would like to leave open the possibility for nonbourgeois public spheres to win in cultural and political struggles, to emancipate themselves from being subordinate. Being subordinate is by no means a virtue and sometimes the best ideas prevail.

I define nonbourgeois public spheres diacritically: Belonging to the category "nonbourgeois public sphere" (used analytically here as a "catch all" category, and not to demarcate a singular, cohesive group that endures as such over time) are all those publics we can speak of *other than* the bourgeois public sphere that Habermas had in mind. But nonbourgeois public spheres must be defined according to what they are, not only according to what they are not. Indeed, nonbourgeois public spheres often *do* occupy a subordinate socioeconomic position than the bourgeoisie, their members do not have much common leisure time, and their basic material needs are not well satisfied. But by nonbourgeois public sphere I also mean to refer to public spheres distinguished from the dominant public sphere along other lines.

Nonbourgeois public spheres are often populated by people who understand their own citizenship as unstable or partial, by those who do not understand themselves and who are not understood by others as full-fledged members of society (we may think here of the marginalized positions of women, "racial" minorities, immigrants, gays and lesbians, indigenous people, and people with disabilities, just to name some). For example, when Habermas admits that, "women and dependents were factually and legally excluded from the political public sphere," he is acknowledging that their status as citizens was not fully formed.[28] Yet, despite these exclusions, women nevertheless gathered in and actively formed historically and politically important public spheres.

On the one hand, members of a nonbourgeois public sphere may be understood as subaltern or otherwise marginalized members of civil society. On the other hand, due to the content of the discourses of nonbourgeois public spheres, and not due to their membership, *their worldview* may be subordinate to the dominant worldview, and their opinions subaltern or marginal. By introducing these other ways to understand nonbourgeois public spheres, I de facto assign to the bourgeois public sphere the characteristic of "dominant"—it is the public sphere that underwrites prevailing hegemonies. It is also exclusive because its dominance derives from being able to point out others beneath it. More simply, where there are varying opinions, some will be those of a group that dominates attention with broad and effective publicity and that maintains reciprocity with powerholders, whereas other opinions will be those of a more marginalized sector of civil society, whose opinions are discounted, if not entirely disregarded, because they are subaltern or for some other reason. Nonbourgeois public spheres therefore are those that fight against exclusion, for inclusion, and for the capacity to hold sway in politics.

The crisis facing nonbourgeois public spheres has historically been a crisis of *becoming political*. It has not been the crisis of an already political public sphere facing its depoliticization, which is the story of the bourgeois public sphere in *Structural Transformation*. What nonbourgeois public spheres must do in order to *become political* and what is meant by their *being political* is what differentiates them markedly, indeed *structurally*, from bourgeois public spheres.

It is worth noting at this juncture, after some preliminary remarks about proletarian public spheres and counterpublics, that an influential history of a certain nonbourgeois public sphere, the English radical reading public of the nineteenth century, was written by E. P. Thompson and published in 1963—one year after the original German publication of Habermas' *Structural Transformation*. In Thompson's *Making of the English Working Class*, in his section on "Class Consciousness," he discusses not only the actual and cohesive existence of radical reading publics (circa early nineteenth-century England), but the ways in which such publics were both structurally different from their bourgeois counterparts *and* politically indispensable to the Chartist movement.[29] This in itself challenges Habermas' contention that nonbourgeois public spheres shared their orientation and aims with the bourgeois public sphere.

Beyond this, and contrary to the conception of reading publics fostered by Habermas' (and Kant's) theory, Thompson's account of an actually existing, influential nonbourgeois public sphere included the participation of illiterate and uneducated members who would travel great distances to hear radical orators, to attend sermons and meetings, and public readings of published letters and periodicals. This politically radical public was not "a single, undifferentiated 'reading public.' We may say that there were several different 'publics' impinging upon and overlapping each other, but nevertheless organized according to different principles."[30] This understanding, we shall see, although it was contemporaneous with Habermas' classical theory (in Thompson's work), becomes increasingly important to contemporary critiques of Habermas and to my own overarching arguments.

The most substantial criticism of Habermas' early national theory of the public sphere has proceeded on two separate tracks. Along the first track, the critique consists of accounts of nonbourgeois public spheres that Habermas declares he can unproblematically ignore in his preface. Along this track, Habermas' neglect of nonbourgeois public spheres is shown to be a problem with his social history of the public sphere, a problem that entails the omission of the political histories of marginalized groups. Along the second track, and only much more recently, is a critique that holds that the national framework is insufficient for dealing with the problems of our time.[31] It has not been shown, however, that there is a juncture at which these two tracks converge, that a consideration of the political function of nonbourgeois public spheres requires acknowledging a serious lack of fitness between neglected publics and the national framework. Simply put, states are unresponsive to nonbourgeois public spheres because they have little need for their own legitimation from neglected and marginalized publics. And when states determine little to no obligation to nonbourgeois public spheres, when states demonstrate no reciprocity with such publics, such public spheres find themselves situated on a different terrain than their bourgeois counterparts. It is on this different terrain that nonbourgeois public spheres discovered that appeals and invitations to publics and institutions elsewhere were essential to garnering the weight of the solidarity of other more respected and differently recognized bodies.

I shall begin our consideration of nonbourgeois public spheres by considering political discourses that were alive in public spheres, but excluded from the dominant public sphere. Women such as Frances (Fanny) Wright, Emma Goldman, Margaret Sanger, Charlotte Perkins Gilman, and Mother Jones, among many others, acted out of the bounds of their inscribed private spheres in an effort to infiltrate the public sphere. However, these women's ideas were only integrated into the dominant public sphere after decades of contestation, and even then, not all were. And after some feminist ideas were integrated into the dominant public sphere they still had further to go before they would negotiate changes at the level of the state. Yet, before calcification in the bourgeois public sphere, these women were already working in other public spheres, in nonbourgeois public spheres. It would be absurd to think that Emma Goldman's arguments about birth control were trapped in a kind of purgatory between private and public until some of them were accepted, popularized, and recognized with respect by the state. One must acknowledge a multiplicity of public spheres, and must acknowledge that nonbourgeois public spheres were not merely aspiring to be bourgeois public spheres, but that they were both opposing themselves to bourgeois public spheres *and* were politically important.

Geoff Eley revisits the historical period in which the idea of democratic public discourse really took hold, the period of the Enlightenment and the French Revolution. Eley claims that the public sphere of the eighteenth century was by no means as inclusive, not even in principle or in spirit, as Habermas characterized it in *Structural Transformation*. Indeed, the eighteenth-century public sphere barred women wholesale. This underlines my insistence on decoupling the term bourgeoisie from its more narrow meaning vis-à-vis economic class, for the bourgeois public sphere also defined its parameters of inclusion and exclusion according to overt sexism, and this exclusion was continued well into the nineteenth and twentieth centuries.

> Chartism in Britain . . . is a good example, because the famous Six Points for the democratization of the constitution drawn up in 1837–1838 expressly excluded votes for women. While individual Chartists raised the issue intermittently thereafter, the enduring consensus (shared by the movement's women no less than the men) was that female suffrage deserved a low priority.[32]

Eley thus insists that such public spheres as the suffragist public sphere were marginalized from and by the dominant public sphere and did not, by any means, seek what the bourgeois public sphere sought. With regard to sexism and female suffrage, Eley invokes Antonio Gramsci's language, claiming that the dominant public sphere represented the "hegemony" of public opinion. Feminist, nonbourgeois public spheres sought to erode that hegemony, and, also in Gramsci's terms, attempted to do so by fighting "wars of position" to restructure the existing structures of society, and not by fighting "wars of movement."[33] In other words, public opinion was the terrain on which feminists fought to restructure hegemonic thinking on their issues of common concern.

Eley points out that not only women, but also subordinate nationalities, and popular classes such as the poor, the working class and the peasantry were excluded from the dominant, bourgeois public sphere. There is, he insists, a far richer social history of the public sphere than the one that Habermas presents in *Structural Transformation*. Because of this, studies of the public sphere, at least if they intend to be more historically precise, must not be confined to consideration of the bourgeois category alone.

Oskar Negt and Alexander Kluge also make the case that political public spheres must be understood pluralistically in their 1972 work, *Public Sphere and Experience: Toward an Analysis of the Bourgeois and Proletarian Public Sphere*. This book is important for many reasons, largely because it was a major contribution to the German conversation about the public sphere that was developing without the attention of English-reading scholars. And, like *Structural Transformation*, Negt and Kluge's book was only published in English recently, in 1993, and has been given rather scarce attention outside of German scholarship.

Negt and Kluge insist that the public sphere must be understood as a plurality of public spheres because, besides the bourgeois public sphere, there are also various "public spheres of production" and "proletarian public spheres." The public spheres of production

> tend to incorporate private realms, in particular the production process and context of living. These new forms *seem* to people to be no less public than the traditional bourgeois public sphere. . . . Thus, the classical public sphere is originally rooted in the bourgeois context of living, yet separates itself from the latter and the production processes. By contrast, the new public spheres of production are a direct expression of the sphere of production.[34]

What Negt and Kluge mean by this is that the whole context of life, for those in nonbourgeois social positions, from within their homes to the realms of consumption to their work communities and the interaction of their families could and must be sharply distinguished from the context of life in which the bourgeoisie live. In the public spheres of production the issues of common concern are not the same as those taken up by the bourgeois public sphere.

Proletarian public spheres are distinguished rather faithfully along Marxian lines. The proletarian public sphere is the sphere in which the interests of the working class, as a class, are developed. Proletarian public spheres are populated by people whose self-understanding is that they are part of a class that is subordinated, by force of exploitation, to a ruling capitalist class. The proletarian public sphere is expressly political within the framework of class antagonisms, and it articulates its position, its needs, and it makes its demands as not only distinct from, but as mutually exclusive with those of the bourgeoisie. According to Negt and Kluge, the most potent seeds for revolutionary counterpublics reside in proletarian public spheres.

An important part of Negt and Kluge's theory is that it is not solely concerned with how public spheres influence states, but also with the ways in which they engage hegemony. Although I have mentioned Eley's contention that nonbourgeois public spheres engage hegemony, Negt and Kluge view engagement with political culture to be the main work of political public spheres. Public spheres need not always take a plaintive stance toward the state, but could be *productive* on their own—public spheres could produce their own media formats and even their own products and various components of their means of subsistence; they could be *circulatory* in that they can help proliferate their critiques to other publics using art and other creative forms of communication, and they could work on *reception*, negotiating readerships or viewing audiences toward the sympathetic receipt of unfamiliar discourses that might otherwise prompt reaction. Kluge is himself an award-winning filmmaker, a TV producer, and an editor and owner of the Development Company for Television Production and the Cairos Film Company, and he perceives all of his roles as such politically, toward the kind of *production, circulation,* and *reception* just mentioned.

Negt and Kluge thus conceive of the political function of public spheres as a kind of radical democracy. By radical democracy I mean processes of democratization that bypass or work outside of the conventional channels of formal mechanisms for hearing and responding to public opinion. The notion of radical democracy challenges election-centered notions of democracy, and does not refer to state sanctioned procedures, but rather to processes that challenge or point out the deficiencies of the official procedures of democracy. Nonbourgeois public spheres, for example, have had to *compel* or *provoke* consideration of the rationality of their vantage point, to counteract being misconstrued in the main as irrational and stripped of agency. Hence, nonbourgeois public spheres utilize radical democratic approaches, seeking to create stakes for powerholders, often situating themselves as oppositional to existing power structures, and not amenable to felicitous cooperation. From the standpoint of radical democracy, democratization is construed as making society as a whole more democratic, more inclusive and egalitarian, more broadly responsive to the needs of both the largest part *and* the least advantaged of civil society, in short, more oriented toward principles of social and economic justice in all contexts.

I want to be clear about how I perceive the role of the state vis-à-vis nonbourgeois public spheres and radical democracy.

The role of the state should not be neglected or downplayed here, even though highlighting its role is not my central concern. It is true that the substantive activities of radical democracy do not pass primarily through the state via formal channels of reciprocity, and that, in my conception, radical democracy has much to do with transforming dangerous cultural valuations, belief systems, and power relations typically reproduced in and by civil society (even if these valuations, systems, and relations are supported by powerholders). For example, consider the subordinating comportment of predominant publics toward gays and lesbians, transgender people, undocumented workers, or people with disabilities. Here, we expect emancipatory political discourses to take hold within the public sphere, and not only within the state, because we understand that these discourses can generate recognition and respect for historically despised and maltreated subsets of the population.

Of course, recognition and respect matter most for the greatest number of people when they are ultimately codified in enforceable law. Nonbourgeois public spheres understand this well, that new recognition and respect must be generated to underwrite legal and state-sanctioned measures that can grant and protect the full (or fuller) citizenship of marginalized members of society. However, working *with* the state must often remain a future possibility for a future state of affairs, only possible after a period of struggling *against* an existing state or state of affairs that is politically and culturally nonresponsive or reactionary, regressive, and protective of existing hierarchies and inequalities.

So, we inevitably arrive at considerations of unconventional politics, politics as it occurs outside of and in between institutional procedures and established conduits of reciprocity. Habermas disqualified social movements from an analysis of public spheres in *Structural Transformation*; in his more recent works, he does speak of the role of social movements, but this role is limited and such political action remains a devalued and degraded form of communication. I argue that new public spheres form around social movements, that social movements are a major component of the approach that distinguishes the nonbourgeois from the bourgeois public sphere.

Craig Calhoun, for example, claims that it is a major flaw of Habermas' account that he neglects social movements, which are an important part of understanding how public opinion and the public sphere are shaped. Calhoun points out that both

> public discourse and democratic politics, however, seem crucially influenced by social movements. . . . Moreover, social movements are occasions for the restructuring not just of issues but of identities. . . . The absence of social movements from Habermas's account thus also reflects an inattention to agency, to the struggles by which both the public sphere and its participants are actively made and remade.[35]

Social movements also have the virtue of being more clearly multifarious. If there exists a public sphere for each social movement, then we must acknowledge that societies contain many, often competing, public spheres.

Jean Cohen and Andrew Arato take the discussion of public spheres and social movements a step further to account for civil disobedience. They suppose in general that modern civil society needs to be democratized and needs to take the kind of radical democratization that I have discussed as its objective, and not revolution. Cohen and Arato have little faith in the concept of political revolution in the traditional sense of a war of maneuver. They maintain that reform does not need to mean cosmetic and/or minimal structural change, but rather, that it could mean more radical institutional reforms and cultural transformations, and that it is precisely such goals that new social movements are working toward. Social movements today are not trying to seize the state as much as they are working to democratize reluctant or unresponsive institutions that are run like private companies (and in some cases might be), and that affect our and others' lives. Social movements try to expand rights, which is not a regulative but a positive goal. Social movements are both *defensive* (i.e., protecting people from the actions of other bodies) and *offensive* (i.e., influencing and negotiating the expansion of rights).

Like public spheres, social movements are extra-institutional projects that assemble independent of and often contrary to the wishes of the state. Like public spheres, social movements emerge from and within civil society. Furthermore, social movements often form around the central aim of more widely distributing a subaltern political discourse. Social movements are primarily instruments of nonbourgeois public spheres, since the bourgeois public sphere hardly needs recourse to the streets, so to speak, to circulate its opinion. Bourgeois public spheres don't need to "speak" in such a way to garner respect and responsiveness from powerholders. Yet, when it comes to nonbourgeois public spheres, even social movements often fail to impel responsiveness from their addressee, so civil disobedience is often used to raise the stakes and make neglected discourses impossible to ignore.[36]

What is particularly interesting about civil disobedience is that it works in between insurrection and reform—it functions between civil war and civil society.

> A legal right to engage in civil disobedience is self-contradictory. But it does not thereby violate the principles of civil society. Rather, direct political action in the form of civil disobedience keeps the utopian horizon of a democratic and just civil society alive, for two reasons. First, civil disobedience is principled collective action that presupposes at least the partial institutionalization of rights and democracy; that is, it presupposes the rights that establish and protect civil society as well as a representative political system claiming democratic legitimacy (in the sense of representing and responding to citizens' opinions and interests) and providing for at least some political participation. Secondly, a fully democratic and just civil society is, of course, a utopia in the classical sense; it can never be fully realized or completed but operates as a regulative ideal that informs political projects. Civil societies can always become more just, more democratic.[37]

Civil disobedience thus simultaneously tests and challenges the political culture and degree of democratization in the society by taking risks on the borders of legality. There is always an array of political opinions and actions that are recognized as viable and reasonable. Over time, civil disobedience expands the inventory of what is considered politically reasonable. For instance, strikes, sit-ins, boycotts and mass demonstrations are common tactics today in politics, yet they were once illegal. It was civil disobedience that first employed these illegal strategies in the context of larger social movements, and through their enactment they were eventually calcified as rights, making liberal societies more liberal.[38]

One way to look at civil disobedience is to say that it raises directly one of the most important questions of democratic theory; in other words, it asks, "How liberal *is* this democracy?" And it asks this question by performing a test that necessitates the attention of legislators and those who uphold the law. Civil disobedience violates laws that are not particularly objectionable in order to make other claims, and because laws are violated in the process of this claim making, the claims, or at least the claim makers, cannot be left ignored. Of course, this does not mean that civil disobedience will provoke the response most desired by its participants, but whatever response follows civil disobedience will reveal the extent to which the democracy can be understood as liberal.

Civil disobedience does not only test how liberal the state is, but also how liberal civil society and its political culture are. A good deal of civil disobedience, Cohen and Arato contend, seeks to influence popular opinion in the dominant public sphere, despite the fact that civil disobedience is itself such a marginal behavior:

> Such action seeks to influence majority opinion outside the legislatures, within civil society, and bring it to bear on the legislative process. . . . It also presupposes that, ultimately, the principles of rights and of democratic legitimacy have their locus first and last in the public and private spaces of a vital civil society. . . . Civil disobedience is thus the litmus test of both democracy and liberalism.[39]

Because civil disobedience, in the context of a broader social movement, can be the event that succeeds in registering marginal opinion in the dominant public sphere, it is necessary to count civil disobedience as an important resource for nonbourgeois public spheres.

Cohen and Arato's argument serves one purpose in this chapter, to show that nonbourgeois public spheres function very differently, with different means (i.e., social movements and civil disobedience), different ends (various ends of radical democracy), and a different orientation (subaltern, generally neglected) than bourgeois public spheres. However, their argument will prove critical also to the larger aims of this work, as it is Cohen and Arato's theory that serves as the clearest point of entry for our discussion of the Mexican Zapatistas taken up in part III. Why? Because the Zapatistas too have always functioned in between insurrection and institutional politics, despite the fact that their uprising occurred during a time when Mexico could hardly be characterized as a liberal democratic society. Yet, even in their most insurrectionary moments, the Zapatistas were demanding negotiations with the Mexican state rather than attempting to overtake it. Cohen and Arato's discussion of civil disobedience is well illustrated by the case of the Zapatistas who could not have won the attention of the state and the favor of civil society were it not for the way in which their largely reformist agenda was first presented as a guerilla uprising. Indeed, the Zapatistas' position in between civil war and civil society was precisely what was needed to secure the serious attention and the responsiveness of their two addressees.

Now, let us return to the original thesis. This brief consideration of social movements and civil disobedience as means of publicizing marginalized critiques shows that nonbourgeois public spheres function very differently, with different means, also with different ends (i.e., radical democratic or revolutionary comportment rather than a reformist comportment, the inclusion of politically excluded discourses, building broader solidarities), and a different orientation (subaltern, generally neglected) than bourgeois public spheres. And, when the character and composition (C) of a public sphere is nonbourgeois, and its function (F) is radical democracy, then its location in the world (L) is also often different. But what is the location or the scale of a nonbourgeois public sphere with such a function?

What we have considered thus far suggests that there have been important nonbourgeois public spheres with discernible and viable political functions at least since the appearance of the first bourgeois public spheres. However, what has not been argued is that the national framework for political public spheres is too narrow to accommodate the discernable, distinctive, and viable political functions of nonbourgeois public spheres.

Nonbourgeois public spheres serve not only as a corrective to the singularity of the bourgeois public sphere, but also, they are often compelled to work outside of the bounds of the states in which they originate. Because such public spheres are typically denied equal access to the conventional democratic channels of a state, they often work beyond the bounds of their own states in order to transnationalize their political discourse and consolidate leverage. Following this latter point, we can see that in neither being adequately recognized by the state nor being structurally integrated into the state's political process, nonbourgeois public spheres are not officially state-bounded in the same way as the bourgeois public sphere. Because of this, we must acknowledge that nonbourgeois public spheres can be and often are more critical, more innovatively contestatory, and ultimately more transformative than their bourgeois counterparts. In acting as they must act in order to be heard, nonbourgeois public spheres give rise to new and redefine old paths of political action.

Subaltern and proletarian public spheres have been discussed by theorists in order to correct Habermas' social history and to demonstrate the critical importance of a multiplicity of public spheres for the internal democratization of states. Yet, because states historically ignored nonbourgeois public spheres the latter had to find ways to rouse serious attention. Early nonbourgeois public spheres discovered quickly that speaking to a state that wasn't listening was not an effective course of action. For nonbourgeois public spheres, consolidation with international public opinion was frequently the prerequisite for the effective constitution of a political function. In the concluding pages of chapter 3, I shall argue that the general relationship of reciprocity between a democratic state and its dominant public sphere does not accurately define the scale and function of the public sphere as a concept for political philosophy.

To show the insufficiency of the national framework for nonbourgeois public spheres we need only consider how mismatched they are to Habermas' criteria for his early national conception of the public sphere. Nonbourgeois public spheres violated all of the criteria of the national framework. Nonbourgeois public spheres took other addressees than the state. In terms of physical space and zones of citizenship, nonbourgeois public spheres sought to occupy metatopical common spaces with more of an eye toward solidarity than citizenship. In terms of the communicability of shared experiences and issues of common concern, nonbourgeois public spheres were certainly limited, but they worked to generalize their experiences and concerns as much as possible.[40] Habermas' early notion of the public sphere relied on "thick," intimate and interpersonal social bonds within a directly shared culture and experience, whereas nonbourgeois public spheres tried to loose themselves from this "thick," intracommunity prerequisite. Transnational public spheres depend on "thin," conceptually established (shared principles, for example) social bonds. Public spheres may either emerge from "thick" or from "thin," or they may begin "thick" and then expand, crossing boundaries by way of the proliferation of "thinner" linkages.[41]

To illustrate the lack of fitness of nonbourgeois public spheres with the state-bounded public sphere, I return to the case of feminism and the suffragist movement. In 1907, a national suffragist organization was founded in the United States called the Equality League of Self-Supporting Women. This group was successful in enlarging its membership from two hundred to twenty thousand within the first year and a half of its existence. Its members were Americans, though not drawn from the bourgeoisie.[42] That is to say, its membership was mainly drawn from unions, radical teachers, socialists and radical students. And many were women who, as we know, were barred from the bourgeois public sphere as such. Members of the organization may have enjoyed economic comfort, but their political discourses proffered an opinion and will in serious contrast to dominant public opinion. Many of these people did not believe that a felicitous relationship with the state would yield the kind of changes they sought, and the American government had only an increasing interest in suppressing socialist tendencies in the years before World War I. And because female suffrage was asking states to recognize women as part of an already-existing electorate, it required rethinking the position and status of women in society, and loosening the monopoly over formal political power by men, at least to some extent. Thus, public spheres populated by the members of the Equality League of Self-Supporting Women knew better than to expect the state to listen and respond to them.[43]

In the years before World War I, universal suffrage was an issue of international discourse and national organizations understood themselves as participants in an international movement.

The feminist and female suffrage movements, and especially movements for universal suffrage, needed to fight a war of position on a large scale. Such movements sought to organize themselves internationally in order to demonstrate that their demands were considered reasonable and viable internationally.

> Reciprocal influence between women in the U.S. suffrage movement and their counterparts in Britain and Europe reached a peak in the decade before World War I, as illustrated by the founding of the International Woman Suffrage Alliance in 1904 and its subsequent biennial conventions in European capitals until war broke out. Woman suffrage was indeed an international movement, in all the industrialized countries, especially the protestant ones. When Finland in 1906 became the first European nation to grant women unrestricted suffrage, campaigners in surrounding countries intensified their endeavors. Socialist networks as well as the International Woman Suffrage Alliance served as international couriers after the Congress of the Second International in 1907 issued a directive for member parties to undertake campaigns for universal suffrage.[44]

Recasting national suffrage in the context of universal suffrage made it impossible to conceive of the political discourse nationally. Yet the international discourse substantially aided national efforts that remained focused on winning suffrage domestically. When Finland granted suffrage to its women, suffragists in other nations were able to characterize their own national states as being less developed socially. Beyond this, the case of Finland demonstrated to other national states that suffrage could be granted without inviting other kinds of dangerous contestation— that is, that women given the right to vote could still be kept in subordinate roles.

The internationalist character of the suffragist movement prior to World War I demonstrated the critical potentiality for a political public sphere to exceed national boundaries without surrendering its national objectives. Indeed, the international character of what we could call the "universal suffrage public sphere" only made its national initiatives more realizable. And it is important to point out that even on a transnational scale, the universal suffrage public sphere remained distinctly nonbourgeois, according to the terms I used to characterize the American movement, for many years to come.

So we can discuss public spheres that retain or constitute their political function without conformity to the criteria for a national public sphere. In more recent works (*Between Facts and Norms* and *The Postnational Constellation*, for example), Habermas consistently grants this. What is not found there, however, is acknowledgment that marginalized publics throughout the nineteenth century did transnationalize both their constituencies and their political discourses (through the help of international reading publics) well before the current phase of globalization, and that they did this precisely because their socioeconomic position in stratified societies made such outreach a requirement. As well, feminism did not employ the same communicative paradigm that was used by the bourgeois public sphere. Feminists, as is true for most if not all nonbourgeois public spheres, would have been ignored for too long if they restricted their political activism to reading publics. Feminist public spheres utilized contentious social movements to produce, circulate, and to improve the reception of their ideas.

Take, for example, the Pankhursts (a small subgroup of suffrage activists following the methods of Emmeline and daughter Christabel Pankhurst prior to World War I), who engaged in direct action and civil disobedience so effectively that they often launched themselves into international headlines. Protests, boycotts, pamphleteering, even smashing windows, property destruction, arson, disrupting male politicians' meetings, withholding taxes, and heckling members of parliament were some of the tactics used by the Pankhursts, which they claimed to have learned from Irish nationalists: "The staging of sensational events, the use of nonviolent civil disobedience, and the disruption of government as usual that came to be called militance in the woman suffrage movement were tactics adopted from an inventory available in working-class, socialist, and nationalist politics."[45] It was only with the help of these and other, more conventional, protest demonstration techniques, that the political discourses of suffrage activists infiltrated the political discourses of the bourgeois public sphere.

When the state can secure its democratic legitimacy in the affirmation of the bourgeois public sphere, it can ignore, devalue, and disqualify the discourses of nonbourgeois public spheres. So nonbourgeois public spheres must discover other ways to accumulate leverage than speaking to reluctant interlocutors as if the latter had agreed to a felicitous conversation. In the classical model, the bourgeois public sphere does not need to struggle for recognition from the state. Nonbourgeois public spheres must struggle for recognition and reciprocity through mounting pressure and creating stakes. To do this, nonbourgeois public spheres often generalize (transnationalize) their discourse to create additional points of entry for popular traction.

As universal suffrage illustrates, transnationalizing the principle of the movement by recasting the suffragist political discourse as that of a transnational cause for all women proved effective. The goal of universal suffrage was, in part, to make the cause of suffrage in Germany the cause of suffragists in America. Indeed, the goals of universal suffrage were seen as unfulfilled by those who fought for and won it in Finland. Women in Finland who could vote remained active in the movement for universal suffrage, and this and the progressive stature of the Finnish government added weight to women's movements in other countries. It was not until suffrage was won in states other than Finland that the mounting example of some states to others would begin to hold more sway.

Nonbourgeois public spheres have existed and do exist and they possess a vital political function even in the absence of any established conduit of reciprocity between them and the state. According to Habermas' account, nonbourgeois public spheres are merely in want of precisely that status and relationship that gives the bourgeois public sphere its political function, but in actual fact nonbourgeois public spheres can succeed and have succeeded in locating a political function for themselves in other ways (i.e., a radical democratic or revolutionary destabilization of power[46] instead of striving to create more effective inroads for reformist influence that are wholly compatible with existing bureaucracies, their hierarchies and exclusions, and the codification of the state through legitimation processes.[47] Also, nonbourgeois public spheres work for the inclusion of historically excluded actors), and critically, by addressing other publics and states than their own local and official registries for political communication.

As we have seen, nonbourgeois public spheres often use social movements and civil disobedience, two means of communication that are not readily comprehended as conversational. To regard what appears to be an insurrection as a discussion entails a significant revision of conventional thinking. Demanding is not the same thing as discussing. Habermas held that the two were incompatible. He wrote in *Structural Transformation* that "[l]aws passed under the 'pressure of the street' [*dem Druck der Strasse*] could hardly be understood any longer as embodying the reasonable consensus of publicly debating private persons."[48] Discourse, as defined in *Legitimation Crisis* is clearly undermined by making demands and hoping to have them satisfied through the use of punitive force or under the pressure of ultimatums.

As Warren Montag points out in his essay "The Pressure of the Street: Habermas's Fear of the Masses," Habermas consistently maintains that "if any force other than the mere force of reason is brought to bear in the public sphere, rational debate ceases, the universal is lost and the necessarily violent rule of the particular is established, with the certainty that one particularism will soon be replaced by others."[49] In this claim Habermas' argument hews closely to Kant's in that they both represent a fear that positions will change due to coercion rather than due to a reasoned reevaluation of validity claims. And, it is worth recalling Kant's warning that moving from discussing to demanding opens the door to the possibility that the winning position will be won by whoever employs the greatest brute force.[50] But there is a normative defense against the appropriation of my argument for a "might makes right" interpretation: The public sphere's function has always coupled legitimation with democratization. If the public sphere deepens its commitments to the latter via radical democracy and transnationalization (as I suggest), then it necessarily enlarges its commitments to openness, inclusion, and deliberation. In this light, brute force appears unacceptable in principle.

For now, we shall keep Kant's warning in mind, and return to Habermas; his conception of the political function of the public sphere and what constitutes discourse necessarily holds that taking to the streets generally shifts communicative processes away from authentic discourse and toward a more hostile mode of contestation with undertones or overtones of coercion and violence. The street, for Habermas, is thus essentially outside of the public sphere. Nonbourgeois public spheres that take to the streets create a space for airing grievances, not a space for a rational exchange and in this way, the public sphere stands opposed to the street.

But we may take a broader view of discourse and publicity that does not pit social movements and civil disobedience against rational deliberation.[51] In fact, we must take this broader view unless we want to say that nonbourgeois public spheres act irrationally. For they often act precisely in these ways, in ways that do not ask for deliberation but demand or provoke it. The long struggle of suffrage for women, racial minorities, and poor people always contained at its basis the principles of social equality that are today widely recognized as rational and politically right. And the production, circulation and reception of these principles did not come about through a felicitous discussion between civil society and an attentive state, but as the result of a kind of radical democratic speaking—of subordinated social groups finding ways to get the attention and reciprocity of reluctant interlocutors.

Boycotts, strikes, and civil disobedience are distinguished from more conventional discursive efforts (spoken or textual) to appeal to the rational deliberation of a willing interlocutor. Nevertheless, nonbourgeois public spheres that apply the "pressure of the street" do raise issues *for* rational deliberation even if not *by* or *through* rational deliberation. Social movements and civil disobedience (for example, the more confrontational strains of feminism, or the Zapatista rebellion), neither impede nor preempt discursive processes of rational-critical deliberation, but generally encourage such deliberation where it would not otherwise occur.

Public spheres that must struggle for recognition—to become political—often address foreign states and publics before their own. They must accumulate and consolidate support elsewhere if it is not at first realizable domestically. What it means for nonbourgeois public spheres to speak in a radical democratic way is that they use different discourse, fix on different targets, and have different overall aims than their more privileged, already recognized, and respected counterparts. They have a different character, function, and location, and a politics that does not utilize existing political terrains as much as it aims to restructure them and to forge new, unexpected inroads.

I now turn to analyze the concept of the transnational public sphere. Many theorists present the transnational public sphere as a solution to the problems of the nationally framed public sphere, as well as to many contemporary political problems. It is in the following part that we shall discover the insufficiencies of the transnational framework and the need for a third conceptual framework, the latter of which will be developed in the third and final part.

Notes

1. Jürgen Habermas, *The Structural Transformation of the Public Sphere: An Inquiry into a Category of Bourgeois Society*, xviii.
2. A mixed bag on anarchism would likely contain the philosophy of Pierre-Joseph Proudhon, Michael Bakunin's antagonisms with Marx in the First International, Nestor Makhno's armed contingent during the Bolshevik Revolution, the philosophies of Peter Kropotkin and Rudolph Rocker, anarchist activism in the United States and the United Kingdom before World War I, and anarchist involvement in the Spanish Civil War. How any of these could be construed as oriented toward the interests of the bourgeoisie would require a good deal of historical interpretation and gymnastics that Habermas does not pretend to do.
3. I cannot get further into my theory of transgression at this point. However, it is crucial to point out that when (L) is transgressive, (C) and (F) change. Alternatively, when (C) is partly national and partly transnational, inclusive and heterogeneous, when (F) is to challenge or legitimate multiple states, publics, and transboundary institutions, then (L) is transgressive. Simply put, when (L) is transgressive, so are (C) and (F).
4. Habermas, *Structural Transformation*, 27.
5. Ibid., 31.
6. There will be more on the malleability of this idea of common space below (particularly, in the discussion of topical and metatopical common space).
7. Havermas, *Structural Transformation*, 56.
8. Ibid.

9. Ibid., 59.

10. Charles Fox, cited in Habermas, *Structural Transformation*, 65–66.

11. Ibid., 142.

12. This has also been explored in part I in the context of Hannah Arendt and C. Wright Mills, in addition to Habermas' *Legitimation Crisis*. With Arendt, we saw how totalitarian regimes eliminated some of the basic premises of communicative power by appropriating the formative processes of public opinion with propaganda. And with Mills, we saw how publics could be manipulated as and into masses, thereby being stripped of their publicist function—their function of forming critical public opinion and publicizing it. The function of forming critical public opinion is a structural function of the political public sphere, so the loss of the former means the structural transformation of the latter. We will revisit Mills' discussion of masses toward the conclusion of our analysis of Habermas' *Structural Transformation*.

13. Habermas, *Structural Transformation*, 201.

14. Nancy Fraser, in her essay "Transnationalizing the Public Sphere," identifies six tacit presuppositions of Habermas' commitment to a national public sphere that are more particular than the broad categories I discuss here. However, Fraser's six presuppositions are not incompatible with my criteria, and her six presuppositions could be arranged as subcategories within my three, more general categories as follows. Her presuppositions 1 and 2 are part of what I discuss as the "responsive addressee" criteria below. Her presupposition 3 is part of what I discuss as the "zones of citizenship" criteria below. And her presuppositions 4 and 5 are part of what I discuss as the "means of communication" criteria below. Her discussion of presupposition 5 is also a part of my "zones of citizenship" criteria. See my discussion above and pages 4 and 5 in Fraser's essay.

15. See Benedict Anderson's *Imagined Communities* and Michael Warner's *Publics and Counterpublics*.

16. Charles Taylor, "Liberal Politics and the Public Sphere," 263 in *Philosophical Arguments*.

17. Emphasis on the material political power of a physically assembled group is essentially a Marxist emphasis, and I do not mean to say that Habermas is forgetting Marx in making this emphasis himself. What I mean by invoking Marx here is that his conception of politics could not have been restricted to a national framework, and also that his propaganda work was aimed always at an international reading public.

18. *UN Human Development Report 2002: Deepening Democracy in a Fragmented World*, 10–11.

19. In the debates on cosmopolitanism contained in Martha Nussbaum's *For Love of Country?*, Elaine Scarry makes this point rather convincingly. In her contribution, "The Difficulty of Imagining Other People," Scarry argues that cosmopolitanism depends on "generous imaginings" of strangers, which, she points out, might actually be emotionally and psychologically impossible. Her point is well-taken: The possibility for seeing other people as members of one's own community or family requires our being able to imagine them and their

lives with sufficient feeling. While I cannot explore this further here, I do agree that Scarry points out a difficulty—but a difficulty is not an impasse, and the possibility for cosmopolitanism strikes me as both viable and vital (explored further in part III).

20. Taylor says the following of the metatopical public sphere: "It transcends topical spaces. We might say that it knits together a plurality of such spaces into one larger space of nonassembly. . . . I want to call this larger kind of non-local common space 'metatopical.'" —*Philosophical Arguments*, 263.

21. Habermas, *Structural Transformation*, 74.

22. Text from the transcript of the presidential debate cited from *The Washington Post*'s website at http://www.washingtonpost.com (still readable at National Public Radio's website at http://www.npr.org—search for "presidential debate").

23. Cited on In Defense of Animals' website at http://www.indefenseof animals.org during the 2004 Olympics, which were held in Athens and which occasioned a new initiative to rid the streets of stray animals.

24. Habermas, *Structural Transformation*, 124.

25. Habermas, *Structural Transformation*, xviii.

26. I explore the normative implications of this later. For now, it will have to suffice to say that the scale and function of such plebeian public spheres entails an expansive definition of democracy qua radical democracy and deeper commitments to inclusion and pluralism than are present in the classical public sphere theory.

27. Michael Warner, *Publics and Counterpublics*, 56.

28. Habermas, *Structural Transformation*, 56.

29. E. P. Thompson, *The Essential E. P. Thompson*, 74–75.

30. Ibid., 80.

31. For criticisms on the first track see Craig Calhoun (1992), Geoff Eley (1992), Nancy Fraser (1997), and Michael Warner (2002). For criticisms on the second track see James Bohman (1997); Martin Köhler (1998); John A. Guidry, Michael D. Kennedy, and Mayer N. Zald (2000)? and Nancy Fraser (2002, mimeo). Habermas has himself revoked his early nationalist conception of the public sphere and has become a foremost critic of state-bounded public spheres (2001 and after). The second track criticisms as well as what is meant by "the problems of our time" will be discussed in part II.

32. Geoff Eley, (1992) "Nations, Publics and Political Cultures: Placing Habermas in the Nineteenth Century," 313, in *Habermas and the Public Sphere*, Calhoun (ed.), 1992.

33. *War of maneuver* (or of war of movement) and *war of position* are military terms used in relation to World War I and mean, respectively, a war of rapid movement with a series of frontal assaults, and trench warfare backed up by supplies, munitions and reserve soldiers waiting behind the lines. The first, the *war of maneuver*, is intended to describe matters of the state, whereas the second, the *war of position* is intended to describe matters of civil society. A war of maneuver would be like that of Lenin's in 1917, an attack on the state resulting in the rapid transition from one order of things to another order of things. The

war of position, on the other hand, is more closely linked to the concept of hegemony, referring to more ideational types of political action that take place within a civil society. The spreading of ideology through journalism, for example, employs the strategy Gramsci means by war of position. See (2000) *The Gramsci Reader: Selected Writings 1916–1935*, New York: New York University Press.

34. Oskar Negt and Alexander Kluge, *Public Sphere and Experience: Toward an Analysis of the Bourgeois and Proletarian Public Sphere*, 13.

35. Craig Calhoun, "Habermas and the Public Sphere," 36–37.

36. The formulation of social movements and civil disobedience as mechanisms for radical democracy lays important groundwork for our discussion of the Zapatistas in part III.

37. Jean Cohen and Andrew Arato, *Civil Society and Political Theory*, 566–67.

38. In this case and in the following paragraphs I mean by "liberal" tolerant or permissive of disagreement and contestation and open to changing one's position in light of an adversary's.

39. Cohen and Arato, *Civil Society and Political Theory*, 603–4.

40. In sum, the criteria for a national public sphere are (1) that it has a national addressee, the state, (2) that it has a national location, a legal society of citizens that associates in topical common space, and (3) a national set of issues, formulated in a common language about shared experiences.

41. This conceptual rubric of thick and thin comes from Michael Walzer's *Thick and Thin: Moral Argument at Home and Abroad* (Notre Dame, Ind.: University of Notre Dame, 1994). What I ultimately argue is that a political discourse can transgress this duality by linking "thick" solidarities to the proliferation of "thin" ones.

42. Here, I mean bourgeoisie in the particularized sense defined above.

43. Nancy Cott, *The Grounding of Modern Feminism*, 25.

44. Ibid.

45. Ibid., 26.

46. When I say "power" in this passage, while I do mean state power in material and ideological terms, I also mean power in Michel Foucault's sense, power relations outside of the state, in the family, in the society, maintained in and by the political culture (see, for example, Foucault's interview in part 6 of *Power/Knowledge: Selected Interviews and Other Writings, 1972–1977*, Pantheon Books).

47. To be clear, Habermas' legitimation theory does not simply suggest that the public sphere should seek to legitimate its corollary state. His idea is more complex; it does allow for contentious politics and for what he has called a siege model of communicative power (see p. 486 in the 1998 edition of *Between Facts and Norms: Contributions to a Discourse Theory of Law and Democracy*, MIT Press). Still, no matter how complex and contentious, Habermas conceives of legitimation crisis in terms of identifying democratic deficits, and suggesting communicative means of working to resolve them as an alternative to traditional revolution. Nonbourgeois publics do not need to identify democratic deficits in any abstract terms because they suffer those deficits subjectively, and

they often recognize that the political system will neither voluntarily nor effectively resolve these problems because of the costs of such a resolution to the state and its partners (we may think here of indigenous peoples' claims to land against the interests of powerholders in Bolivia, the United States, and Mexico, for example). Hence, any complex legitimation process that stops short of deep structural change will not ameliorate certain crises addressed in nonbourgeois public spheres.

48. Habermas, *Strukturwandel der Offentlichkeit* (Neuwied: Hermann Luchterhand Verlag, 1962), 147.

49. Warren Montag, "The Pressure of the Street: Habermas's Fear of the Masses," 133, in Mike Hill and Warren Montag's (2000) *Masses, Classes, and the Public Sphere.*

50. See Kant's comment on revolution in his essay "An Answer to the Question: 'What is Enlightenment?'" Specifically, see 55 in Kant's *Political Writings.* Cambridge: Cambridge University Press.

51. Ernesto Laclau and Chantal Mouffe, in their *Hegemony and Socialist Strategy: Towards a Radical Democratic Politics* (Verso, 1985) do define discourse so broadly as to include things such as social movements and civil disobedience. However, Laclau and Mouffe wholly exclude consideration of the public sphere as a specific and important discursive mechanism, whereas, I maintain that the public sphere is an enduring concept essential to understanding what people in civil society can do to hold sway; we need to rethink the public sphere (its function and its scale) in accordance with any deeper, more unconventional view of discourse. More on Laclau and Mouffe in chapter 9.

II

PUBLIC SPHERES AND THE TRANSNATIONAL FRAMEWORK

Introduction to Part II

In part II, I assess some of the more fully developed theories of transnational political public spheres, which have been proposed in response to the insufficiencies of the national framework. The concept of the transnational public sphere is developed and discussed in light of both what we have said so far and the recent and rising prominence of what could be called and is regarded a transnational political problematic (understanding this problematic will be the task of chapter 4). After three chapters devoted to public spheres and the national framework, it is necessary to turn to the topic of public spheres and the transnational framework and to address contemporary questions of globalization. But first, I shall briefly restate the major conclusions of part I.

We analyzed the historical-theoretical development of the concept of the political public sphere, and saw how particular accounts and emphases, to the exclusion of others, fitted the concept of the public sphere rigidly to a national framework. We then turned our attention to the classical theory of the bourgeois public sphere and its structural transformation in Habermas' major work on the subject. There, we worked through an immanent critique of the theory drawing on examples of public spheres from subaltern political histories. We did this in order to show how an account of nonbourgeois public spheres entails considering various ways to expand the substantive activities and the function of the bourgeois public sphere, and to exceed national boundaries. It has, therefore, already been shown that accounts of the public sphere as strictly state-bounded mechanisms of legitimation are inadequate and that public spheres have often worked transnationally.

In the present chapters, then, we arrive squarely at the task of a critical assessment of the concept of transnational public spheres—of public spheres whose occupied spaces and political functions are understood as transnational. To what extent is the transnational public sphere a sufficient compensatory antidote to the problems of the national public sphere, if not completely? Or does the transnational public sphere only introduce new problems and inadequacies, and what are they?[1] These may be taken as the overarching questions of part II that bind chapters 4, 5, and 6 together.

I will not argue on behalf of the transnational public sphere as a satisfactory compensatory antidote to the inadequacies of the national public sphere. This statement should confound common sense at first, to which the transnational framework is perceived as the only alternative to the national framework—if not a national or a transnational public sphere, then what? The main problem regards how the transnational public sphere has been theorized in relation to the national public sphere—dichotomously, as an either/or choice. I argue that the ways in which a transnational framework for thinking about politics has been theorized have relied on and strengthened dichotomous thinking about the national and the transnational. Indeed, a recurring allegation in theories of the transnational public sphere has been (sometimes open and sometimes implicit) that the transnational public sphere can only exist as an antithesis to its national precursor. Treating these conceptual frameworks as competing, distinct zones fails to take account of actual political action that betrays dichotomous thinking about the national and transnational frameworks. You may readily observe that social scientists and political theorists typically make such dichotomous stipulations, always clarifying whether they are discussing a national or a transnational context. The fact that politics does not abide by this analytical rubric appears to elude analysts in all fields concerned with questions of globalization. It is in the over-looked potentialities and unique comportments of actually existing political action that a new theoretical framework must be discovered.

I will look ultimately (in chapter 6) to an actual political public sphere (that of the Indian rights movement in Latin America) that has been directly engaged in confronting the preeminent problematic that will be outlined in chapter 4 in order to show that public spheres do not always function in accordance with theorists' efforts to understand them. I will ultimately point out the possibility for a new theoretical framework that neither relies on nor reproduces false dichotomies and false antipathies between the national and transnational frameworks.

Public sphere theory, as well as the social sciences in general, has increasingly turned toward considering transnational problems, for reasons that will be explicated in chapters 4 and 5. But I must define from the outset what is the difference between the terms "international," "transnational," and "postnational," since these are often used interchangeably, and will appear without qualification or consistency in the texts studied in part II.

By "international," I mean *between or among* national states. International is rightly synonymous with multinational, in that both terms assume wholly intact state powers that are united or regrouped for particular occasions or purposes (however, multinational, technically, "of multiple nations," is commonly and misleadingly used to refer to transnational corporations). Most simply, any agreement that is made between nations is an international agreement. A good example of an international institutional structure is the United Nations, a structure that is comprised by a membership of multiple states.

By "transnational," I mean *beyond* national states. Transnational is rightly synonymous with supranational. Both terms may or may not assume wholly intact state powers because they refer to structures that exist beyond, rather than among or between, states. The World Trade Organization, for example and many (but not all) social movements are not about reorganizing states into multinational powers but about working in a larger-than-national framework that is not comprised of states themselves. The anticapitalist globalization movement and the World

Social Forum, for example, are generally and correctly seen as transnational.

"Postnational" is the only one of these terms that not only demarcates a scale, but also implies an historical moment. Postnational means *after* national states, or more specifically, after the diminution of their sovereignty or the surpassing of their jurisdiction with regard to particular issues. Postnational is Habermas' term and I will use it mostly in the context of his own work. It implies transnational, but with the qualification of transnational *after* the diminishment of state sovereignty and jurisdiction.

We have already seen how public spheres have exceeded and may exceed national boundaries. And we have seen that they have done so for two basic reasons: (1) Public spheres often form transnationally in order to address issues that exceed national boundaries; (2) Public spheres often work transnationally to accumulate solidarity and support to add weight to national or subnational initiatives. Today, there is new occasion to transnationalize the public sphere. Relatively recent international policies such as GATT, NAFTA, FTAA, and CAFTA, the establishment of the UN, the ICC, and the EU, and the eminence of transnational consortiums of bankers, investors, and neoliberal economists, such as the WTO, the IMF, and World Bank have loudly signaled the hastening prominence of a transboundary institutional, policy, juridical, regulatory, and political-economic world system. All of this was accelerated by the collapse of the Soviet Union, the collapse of historic "boundary" obstacles to the flow of capital and free trade. Political public spheres are everywhere today engaged in forming opinions about, forming a collective will about, and evaluating and contesting, this newer transboundary system. These developments have substantially shaped and redirected the attention of social scientists, making the Westphalian public sphere appear particularly outflanked and insufficient.

Hence, many theorists have been working on the conceptual development of the kind of response that they believe this new regime of transboundary problems calls for. Recommendations have an institutional and noninstitutional component. On the institutional side the European Union seems to have inspired the most reflection, leading theorists to creatively assess ways that the existing system of states could reorganize itself in order to become an effective regulatory force on the terrain of transnational politics. On the noninstitutional side, theorists are working to rethink civil society, community, and political identity such that a transnational populace body could be formed and made strong enough for various ambitious tasks, including the democratization of the transboundary system. In both the institutional and noninstitutional components, the role of a political public sphere is implicit: Institutions need democratic legitimacy, and a transnational populace body needs to form a collective will and opinion to bring to bear on institutions. I agree with the need for political development on both of these fronts, and, in general, I too maintain that the national framework for political action has only been increasingly outflanked by a recently emergent regime of transboundary actors and problems that escape the sovereignty and jurisdiction of national states.

However, I will argue, particularly in chapters 5 and 6, against two inaccurate yet characteristic tendencies in new theorizations on the subject, both of which render the new theories incapable of grasping important insights about politics today. These problematic tendencies in the existing literature crop up in various ways. They are the problems of (1) assuming a national/transnational dichotomy and of (2) assuming an antipathy between the national and transnational frameworks. The assumption of a national/transnational dichotomy is based on mistaking a heuristic distinction between the national and transnational as actual fact. That is, theorists tend to speak as if political action is either national or transnational, as if political action may only move from being national to being transnational, and that, even if it does so erratically, it still inhabits one or the other framework at any given time.

Those theorists who make the second mistake, that of assuming an antipathy between the national and transnational frameworks, tend also to make the first mistake. But those who assume the antipathy further maintain that the national framework for political action, for civil society, community, and political identity represents an impediment to the development of a strong transnational politics capable of engaging the newer transnational problematic.[2] They see reversion to nationalist models, and all efforts to continue to work with and within single states as if states are still-vital units of power (especially in the context of transnational politics), as insufficient and misguided, or at worse, as a dangerous ethnonationalist kind of resistance. Those who assume this antipathy see the national and transnational as pitted against one another, and they argue for the supplanting of the former with the latter. This tendency can be observed throughout social science today, wherever discussions about globalization and transnational politics treat the national framework as something to surpass.

I argue that these assumptions are false, that the heuristic distinction that is useful for analytical and rhetorical purposes must not be taken too seriously, and that there need not be an antipathy between the national and transnational frameworks. The danger in these assumptions is that they separate our theoretical understanding from actually existing political action that does not map out over such distinctions. More importantly, I will argue here as well as in part III that it is precisely the political action that confuses our dichotomous thinking about the national and transnational frameworks in which a new theoretical framework must be discovered. This new theoretical framework will not rely on false dichotomies and false antipathies and will point out new ways of thinking about as well as doing politics. The contours of this third paradigm could have been viewed much earlier (in Marxism, for example), or in the history of the struggles of colonized peoples against their colonizers, or against imperialism. In these cases the necessity of addressing the national (or subnational) predicament *within* the transnational (or international) predicament was well understood. Indeed it is only now, when dichotomous thinking has prevailed, that the relevance of a third framework that is neither national nor transnational calls out for theoretical development.

It is important to note that much of my project requires rethinking political identity, or identity politics. Identity is often regarded as made up of the thick, cultural linkages of topical common spaces, and identity politics is, therefore, not given a particularly large role in discussions about transnational politics and global justice. That is, the most substantive and thick senses of political identity are taken to be on the side of the national

(Walzer, Thompson, Habermas) and so identity appears such that it must either be radically expanded (as will be seen in some discussions of cosmopolitanism) or largely avoided. But strong and deeply meaningful political identities can and do form out of the supposedly thin linkages that bind people in metatopical common spaces. Identities such as these destabilize our national self-understandings, yet they do not simply lead to a transnational self-understanding. In other words, a consideration of complex political identity will go far to reveal why political action and political actors cannot always be seen as fitting into the national or the transnational framework.

In chapter 4, I explore what I've been referring to as a new topography, or the present-day occasion for rethinking the public sphere transnationally. There, I argue that globalization is not a new phenomenon, but that there has been a new phase of globalization—international, transnational, and postnational political developments (and economic and cultural developments)—that effectively evades many of the regulatory powers of the national state and the influence of national public spheres.

Following this, in chapter 5, I assess the concept of a transnational public sphere, critically evaluating cosmopolitan theories. There, I argue that the most influential new public sphere theories (including Habermas' own) posit an either/or choice between national and transnational frameworks and problematically call for a transition from the former to the latter.

Finally, I argue in chapter 6 that recasting public spheres transnationally, as a response to the insufficiencies of the national framework, is ultimately inadequate to redress such insufficiencies. We have thus far looked at how the public sphere has overflowed national boundaries throughout its earlier historical development, particularly in the case of nonbourgeois public spheres. But today, the need to rethink public spheres transnationally is different in important ways.

In chapter 5, I review some initiatives to understand and develop the theory of transnational public spheres by way of cosmopolitanism and other efforts. Cosmopolitanism provides an ideal focus for our inquiry because all cosmopolitan theorists believe in making politics transnational (both in terms of political institutions and in terms of political community and our sense of citizenship), yet there is deep confusion about how to regard the national state, state-bounded political process, and national identity. Some theorists insist on the need of both frameworks for varying issues, rather than turning against or away from the national framework entirely. But turning to a model of transnational public spheres in the stead of or even in addition and juxtaposition to the national sphere runs the risk of reproducing the weaknesses of the national model outlined in the previous chapters. That is to say, the communicative circuitry that makes public spheres work does not always originate and flow unidirectionally. In actual practice, national and transnational are not necessarily distinct zones and these zones may be simultaneously occupied by a single public or by multiple publics (indeed, this is the basis of my own theoretical contribution, explored and developed in part III).

Later in chapter 5, we return to Habermas to analyze his more recent reformulations of the public sphere, which contradict his classical theory in two key regards. First, Habermas no longer believes in the totality of the structural transformation thesis, maintaining that even now, decades after the original theory, the public sphere is still a vital part of politics and that it could in fact be the most important part. Second, he turns sharply away from the national public sphere, and he strongly asserts both the national/transnational dichotomy and the antipathy between frameworks that I intend to refute. In Habermas' new account, not only is a transnational political public sphere possible, something that will have to be explained given all that has been said about legitimation, but it is also something that must largely supplant the national public sphere.

By the end of chapter 5, we will understand the contours and the content of transnational public spheres. However, what I will ultimately show in chapter 6 is that the various juxtapositions, along with the assumed dichotomy and antipathy between the national and the transnational, are not so consistently borne out in practice as they are assumed in theory. I look to the Indian rights movement in Latin America to exemplify this pragmatic point. That is, I look to an actual political public sphere that is specifically engaged in confronting the problems of the topography outlined in chapter 4 and find that the public sphere does not act in ways felicitous with the ways theorists attempt to speak about them. The most innovative political public spheres neither choose between national and transnational frameworks nor do they inhabit always one or the other. It will be the overarching task of the chapters in part III to formulate a third way, outside of the national/transnational dichotomy, to speak about such public spheres.

Notes

1. It is important to note from the start that when I discuss problems of the public sphere and their potential solutions I am first and foremost speaking about conceptual problems and conceptual solutions for theorists thinking about public spheres. But I am also always thinking about problems of political action and their potential solutions (as I believe a good theorist should). At times here, but more so in part III, I do not want to make any exacting choice between analysis and advocacy. Rather, I fully intend to acknowledge the points of entry for advocacy in my analysis and to make recommendations for political action at fitting junctures.

2. In the present chapters, particularly in chapters 5 and 6, I argue that Jürgen Habermas is the most influential representative of this dichotomous thinking, although he is certainly not alone; many other theorists, including Janna Thompson, Nancy Fraser, and Martha Nussbaum, also draw such a sharp distinction between the national and transnational frameworks.

4

"Globalization"

A New Topography
for the Public Sphere?

I have briefly mentioned that there have been recent shifts in politics that occasion a new theorization of public spheres transnationally. I would like to explore this new political topography and to show that, indeed, there are recently emergent and concrete problems that cannot be addressed by the channels of influence between society and state as we have discussed them thus far. In this chapter, I will flesh out the problematic that is typically referred to as "the problematic of globalization," and I will show some of the ways in which features of this problematic do in fact escape the regulatory powers of the national state and the national public sphere. Understanding what is meant by globalization is an essential part of understanding the larger aims of this work because it is under the rubric of and in response to globalization that the national framework has paled in comparison to the transnational framework; the discourse on globalization has provided all of the major reasons for surpassing the national framework.

It is also critical to begin with a thorough understanding of globalization because globalization is the axis on which social science in general has turned to centralize questions of transnational politics and global justice. It is only with a strong working definition of globalization that we can discuss the problems it engenders and the most fitting responses. I will, however, insist

127

throughout that globalization is not a new phenomenon, but that globalization is only new in terms of a relatively recent and collective acceleration and intensification of processes that, on their own, have long histories. In light of the Industrial Revolution, we must remember, Marx already had a highly developed theory of globalization by the middle of the nineteenth century.

John A. Guidry, Michael D. Kennedy, and Mayer N. Zald sum up how globalization is defined in current writing:

> Recent transformations in transportation and communications technologies have altered our sense of distance, radically compressing time and space (Harvey 1989; Giddens 1990, 1994). Territorial states have apparently lost some of their capacities to establish order or mediate change within their borders (Sassen 1996). The number and power of intergovernmental institutions and multinational corporations have grown remarkably (Smith et al. 1997; Keck and Sikkink 1998; Risse-Kappen 1995). The communications media are increasingly global in both their reference and their reach, and the media also help provide resources in the building of transnational epistemic communities of immigrants or like-minded activists (Appadurai 1996).[1]

David Held sums up that,

> Globalization today implies at least two distinct phenomena. First, it suggests that many chains of political, economic and social activity are becoming interregional or intercontinental in scope and, secondly, it suggests that there has been an intensification of levels of interaction and interconnectedness within and between states and societies. . . . It is best thought of as a multidimensional phenomenon involving diverse domains of activity and interaction, including the economic, political, technological, military, legal, cultural and environmental.[2]

Held agrees that globalization is neither a new thing, nor something that makes the national state obsolete. Each of the processes of globalization that we may discuss could be traced back in history, at least to the beginnings of interregional trade and finance, transnational corporations (think of the East India Company of the middle of the eighteenth century), early communications technologies as basic as the printing press that internationalized aspects of culture as well as debates, the onset of the first environmental problems, and questions of international law and security, which Kant and others had thought about carefully during the enlightenment (referring here, by the term enlightenment, to the philosophical movements of the eighteenth century). So globalization processes are by no means new and have developed alongside the development and the strengthening of nation-states. Globalization does not negate the importance or the power of national governments, and there remains a long list of problems today that can be as effectively negotiated on the national level as they ever could have been in the past.

Nevertheless, it must be recognized that globalization processes have restructured the needs for democracy, have challenged and outflanked the power of national governments regarding many issues, and have placed civil societies, as well as governments, in various positions of disempowerment. It cannot simply be assumed that national governments possess the effective political power, at least not on their own, to negotiate and resolve the major political crises of our day.

Communities of fate whose members see themselves as facing the same crises are often not state-bounded. "Community of fate" refers to a collectivity of people who identify with and who take up the same issues as issues of common concern and who approach the resolution of problems from a similar vantage point, their commitments and actions rooted in a kind of solidarity, regardless of potential differences in stakes and lived experience. Communities facing environmental pollution or global warming, for example, or suffering from AIDS, or jeopardized by the proliferation of weapons of mass destruction are communities of fate that are situated beyond national boundaries. Yet there are no institutions with a formal responsibility to legitimate themselves and their actions in the opinion and will of these communities of fate. We may speak of moral imperatives as Kant did in "Perpetual Peace," but by "formal responsibility" I mean that without applicable and enforceable laws or institutions established to serve transnational communities of fate, such communities lack addressees who are obligated to intervene on their behalf. National states have lost a degree of autonomy and sovereignty, such that even if they could have once held sway on certain issues, they no longer can. Examples of this abound in instances of privatization. It is not that it is impossible in principle for states to manage with full authority their water resources, forests, health care, or social security, but once the management of these things is privatized, states cannot simply exercise the regulatory powers they once did—and moreover when the behavior of corporations is increasingly deregulated.

Held does well to outline some of the problems that elude national jurisdiction without overdrawing the story of globalization. He returns us, for example, to the AIDS pandemic, which I briefly discussed in chapter 3. AIDS is a transnational problem in that it does not reside in any one nation. And, as we have seen, even where it may exist to a further extent in a particular region, such as in Africa, it is never confined to national boundaries. AIDS is also a problem that cannot be addressed under the jurisdiction of any one state.[3] Wherever there is a means to control it, to stay its spreading, to treat HIV to prevent it from worsening, these means are most effectively wielded by international effort. And the flow of financial resources, the business of transnational corporations, organizations such as the World Bank and IMF, have done quite a bit to move the workings of the economy beyond the reach of national governments.

Yet there are citizens all over the world asking their governments to do something about these matters. And the political function of the public sphere instructs us to employ just such a paradigm—that of making our demands and concerns known to the government that represents us. But what if the government that represents us is incapable of intervening and solving the problems at hand? What does this mean for the relevance of the national state and the health of democracy? Indeed, one of the central problems of globalization is that existing channels and procedures for democratic influence have remained restricted to the national state while some of the issues most urgently in need of democratic steering have not.

Because of this, the questions of who should be accountable, to whom, and on what basis are not easy to answer. To illustrate this point consider again health problems such as AIDS and Bovine Spongiform Encephalopathy (BSE), consider the use of nuclear energy, global warming, the deforestation of rainforests, the abuse of nonrenewable resources, the volatility and instability of global financial markets, and complex issues of economic regulation and resource depletion as well as any other instance of environmental degradation (i.e., water and agribusiness pollution). What body or bodies do we hold accountable for the responsible treatment or regulation of each of these matters, who is the "we" that attempts to hold those bodies accountable, and why would those bodies respond to us anyway? In other words, if it is a corporation, a consortium of investors, an international coalition of governments, or some other body, who is the constituency that confers their legitimacy and delimits their jurisdiction? Do corporations and capitalists even seek democratic legitimation? There are many people who care about these issues, and they belong to a community that exceeds national boundaries, yet there is no formal mechanism in place for this community to democratically control the issues of their concern:

> In the liberal democracies, consent to government and legitimacy for governmental action are dependent on electoral politics and the ballot box. Yet the notion that consent legitimates government, and that the ballot box is the appropriate mechanism whereby the citizen body as a whole periodically confers authority on government to enact the law and regulate economic and social life, becomes problematic as soon as the nature of "relevant community" is contested.[4]

The relevant community, in the case of many of the issues associated with globalization, is always larger than any single voting community.

Existing mechanisms for democratic input, steering, and legitimation fall short in their capacities to regulate transnational problems in three ways. First, the relevant community with a collective opinion and will, with clear demands and with something at stake, is not state-bounded and does not constitute a single electorate. Second, many of the problems I have mentioned are not problems that even a willing state could intervene in effectively. And third, the business of capitalists has been increasingly decoupled from democratic steering since World War II, and most markedly since the end of the Cold War, so business increasingly transcends and escapes democratic process. This poses a new problem to the public sphere. Public discourse on the harvesting of rain forests has been widely circulated. It could be said that there is a single community that speaks with a collective voice against the deforestation of rain forests, not a community of people who share a citizenship status, but a community of fate. So it seems that we can reconstruct one part of the public sphere, but perhaps not the most important part, not the part that makes it political. Even if a public sphere forms transnationally, it does not necessarily or automatically bring its political function with it—that is, it does not necessarily end up addressing sympathetic and responsive powerholders and institutions of governance that seek their legitimation in the transnational public sphere.[5]

But for many who consider the problems associated with globalization, concern over a public sphere seems a superfluous, or at the very best, a secondary concern. Held, for example, does not articulate the slightest need for a public sphere to facilitate the solution of such problems as those we have mentioned. The problems of globalization are big and the stakes are often fatal and irreversible, so what is needed are new institutional commitments, new institutional efforts. Held outlines an array of short-term and long-term institutional features that would have to be developed in order to fill what he sees as a dangerous democratic deficit. He recommends, for example, reforming the United Nations to give developing countries more say, a global parliamentary system, an accountable international military force, the development of a global legal system, among many other interesting and rather persuasive ideas.[6]

However, it is difficult to forget for even a moment the public sphere, because it is difficult to imagine that any of these short-term or long-term institutional goals are going to become the commitments of institutions just because they make sense to liberal theorists. If we ask the question of how Held's institutional suggestions could become the actual goals of institutions, I do not think we can avoid invoking the role of public spheres. Institutions form and reform in light of peoples' needs and demands, and in light of the self-interest of powerholders. It is, therefore, imperative that peoples' needs and demands are brought to bear on institutions, or that stakes are created for institutions, for them to be compelled to form new organizations or to reform old ones. Beyond this more immediately pragmatic role, I mentioned in chapter 2 (and we will see more fully in chapters 5 and 6) how problematic it has been for the European Union that there is no strong European public sphere. In other words, wherever there *are* transnational institutions, their democratic legitimacy will be in question unless or until a corollary transnational public sphere forms and confers it.[7]

We should recall that the public sphere is always a means, never an end in itself.[8] Habermas argued that participants in a public sphere mustn't stop at the rational-critical development of a collective opinion and will, but must also work hard to bring them to bear on states (see my discussion in chapter 2). Furthermore, we saw in chapter 3 that certain public spheres have been historically ignored—neither recognized nor respected as vital and worthy claimants. Nonbourgeois public spheres, for example, were certainly never ends in themselves, for they had to struggle for recognition, reciprocity, and political influence long after coming together as publics. We should recall all of this here because the same is true of the public sphere on a transnational scale, that it is a means of legitimation and contestation, of the circulation of political discourses, and ultimately (as we shall see in part III) of the formation of new political identities. And the problems of struggling for recognition, reciprocity, and political influence do not go away either, but often become more difficult to surmount. Thus, new transnational political developments and institutions, just as their national counterparts, may be challenged by, associated with, or in need of strong political public spheres. But even though the function and orientation (F) of transnational public spheres may remain the same as that of the national publics discussed in part I, their character and composition (C) and their location in the world (L) are importantly different.

Habermas has had to reformulate his thinking about the public sphere in light of the basic problems raised by the globalization processes we've discussed. One point worth noting from the outset is that the bourgeois public sphere does not maintain the same position today as in the classical theory. The liberal, bourgeois public sphere, which once enjoyed a felicitous, reciprocal relationship with the state, today speaks to a state that can no longer act on behalf of its own internal populations, nor outwardly, with regard to many transboundary problems that the public sphere might want it to address. Hence, the bourgeois public sphere, like its nonbourgeois counterpart has had to do throughout history, must now transnationalize too and must attempt to reconstitute its political function on a larger scale.[9] Still, today the bourgeois public sphere continues to be unmistakably more effective than the nonbourgeois public sphere. For example, the trend of deregulation since GATT and the ideological ascendancy of neoliberalism in politics and culture have been supported in and by the bourgeois public sphere.

In chapter 5, I will analyze Habermas' updated theory of the public sphere more fully. For now, though, I will draw on his insights about globalization and the problems it engenders. Habermas' elucidation of the historical and the conceptual problems of globalization will help to bring into focus the most relevant details of the problematic for our purposes, that is, how it transforms the terrain for and the political function of public spheres.

Habermas uses the concept of globalization

> to describe a process, not an end-state. It characterizes the increasing scope and intensity of commercial, communicative, and exchange relations beyond national borders. . . . Timelines show globalization tendencies running in many dimensions. The term is just as applicable to the intercontinental dissemination of telecommunications, mass tourism, or mass culture as it is to the border-crossing risks of high technology and arms trafficking, the global side-effects of overburdened ecosystems, or the supranational collective network of governmental or non-governmental organizations.[10]

Habermas looks at globalizing trends rather holistically. He believes it is possible to speak of a world society and of a global context largely because of the impact of communications technologies and the transboundary accomplishments of the economic system. The transnationalization of politics, he maintains, has only actually happened since communicative and economic systems have been established across national boundaries. The world market has ensured that the world society is stratified, because increased productivity is accompanied by increased impoverishment and because development is accompanied with underdevelopment. On the other hand, people all over the world, through their engagement with each other in transnational communications systems, are beginning to see themselves as members of various transnational communities of fate. The result of these trends is that people are simultaneously becoming increasingly united (via communications) and increasingly divided (via stratifications). The communities of fate I am speaking of here, it should be stressed, can be found on both the winning and the losing sides of stratification. On the winning side, successful businesspeople and corporations are, all over the world, increasingly interdependent on each other and are bound together in a community of shared opportunity. On the losing side, impoverished and jobless people, for example, are all over the world facing neoliberal economic policies with similar dispositions and related stakes, and so they too are bound together in a community of shared risk.

Habermas is convinced of two of the strongest theses of globalization—the decomposition of the relative homogeneity that has been preserved within states and the substantial disempowerment of the national government. Wherever we look in his more recent writing on the subject, national states not only appear to be radically outflanked by the major problems of our day, but are also fragmented and weakened in their traditional self-understandings and traditional functions.

> The trends summed up in the word "globalization" are not only jeopardizing, internally, the comparatively homogenous makeup of national populations—the prepolitical basis for the integration of citizens into a nation-state—by prompting immigration and cultural stratification; even more tellingly, a state that is increasingly entangled in the interdependencies between the global economy and global society is seeing its autonomy, capacity for action, and democratic substance diminish.[11]

Internally, a homogeneous sense of national identity is complicated by immigration and the reorganization of societies as multicultural, diasporic, and ethnically heterogeneous. While these things are happening internally, communications systems are linking people all over the world. The nation-state no longer retains the self-understanding of a society of a particular kind of citizens. So on the one hand, there is a diminished sense of a nation as a single community of people, and on the other hand is the fact that the political capacity of states is diminished.

Habermas sees three general ways in which state power has been eroded. First, there is the decline of the state's capacity to control the various forces of globalization, whether those forces are in the market, the communications industries, or in the initiatives and the identities of communities of fate.

Second are growing democratic deficits in states' internal processes of their own legitimation. We know from chapters 2 and 3 that Habermas does not believe that states can secure their legitimation through the utilization of formal electoral processes alone. The temporal distance between elections, the lack of participation in them when they do occur, and the confusion of generalized motives and mass loyalty with active participation are all factors that have always separated the decisionmaking processes of states from the specific motives of citizens. But globalization further compounds this problem in the breaking down of the homogenous makeup of national populations. The diversification of societies has pluralized its will and opinion exponentially, making it difficult, wherever it is even possible, to locate emphatic and uncontested support for decisions, policies, and actions.

Finally, and related to both of the above problems, is "an increasing inability to perform the kinds of steering and organizational functions that help secure legitimacy."[12] That is to say, in light of the fact that single states do not hold sway with regard to many of the problems of globalization and the fact that their own populations are made up of multiple communities of fate that include others elsewhere, states cannot mobilize the opinion and will of those to whom they are beholden as widely or as effectively as in the past. People soon come to realize what states already know—that states cannot sufficiently shield their own populations from the effects of globalization.

The detrimental effects of globalization are thus compounded by the problem of how to restore or to compensate for the functional losses of national states. The problem, Habermas insists, cannot be solved by politics at the national level, and we cannot hope to rein in the global market to make it subordinate to national states. The state is by definition a unit of fixed scale, corresponding in the degree to which it is federated or united with other such units. But the global market has achieved a level of freedom from the scale of states that cannot simply be revoked—neither in principle nor in practice. In principle, the political will is not there. The predominance of neoliberal ideology (coupled with real economic consequences such as embargos, sanctions, and the refusal of loans) has convinced governments to deregulate and privatize. In practice, if states try to restore their capacity to subject capital to regulation, the behavior of transnational corporations, indeed the very infrastructure of international business, would have to be transformed. But following Habermas, political power, traditionally embodied in states, must find new ways to catch up with globalization if the detrimental effects of the latter are ever to be effectively resolved. The more particular conclusion here (also following Habermas) is that the political power of the state cannot be sufficiently augmented or enlarged, and so state power must be supplanted with a new supranational power organized beyond the existing power of national governments. It is here, in Habermas' analysis of globalization, that we first see not just a distinction but also an oppositional tension between the national and transnational frameworks (a tension that I will ultimately reject).

For Habermas, an understanding of these developments could not have been grasped prior to the second half of the twentieth century (remember that Habermas refers to the short twentieth century, 1914–1989). In Habermas' account, the end of the twentieth century, that is to say, the collapse of the Soviet Union, marked the real moment of the intense acceleration of globalization forces:

> The end of the twentieth century was marked by a structural threat to the welfarist domestication of capitalism, and by the revival of a socially reckless form of neoliberalism. . . . Even the old problems—peacekeeping and international security, economic disparities between North and South, the risks of ecological catastrophe—were already global ones. But today these problems have all been sharpened by a newly emerging problem that supercedes the old challenges.[13]

So to understand the genesis of the new transnational problems is to understand an acceleration of preexisting processes and an enlargement of the scale of the problems. For Habermas, the problems of globalization cannot be accurately regarded either as "brand new" or as "always there." There is indeed something very new about globalization, he insists, which could not have been studied until now, but he underlines the fact that each of the constitutive parts of globalization has a longer history.

We can see here why Habermas ultimately chooses to speak of the postnational. If you accept the strong thesis of globalization, that the power of national governments is outstripped to so far an extent that the national level of politics has become conclusively inadequate, then you are not just speaking of going beyond the power of the nation, you are dealing with an historical surpassing of the nation itself.

Institutionally, Habermas agrees in general with Held, that new transnational institutions, policies, and processes are the only things that will effectively address and potentially resolve transnational problems. But Habermas chooses the European Union as the most exemplary paradigm for what needs to be done on an institutional level. Supranational authorities need to be created, but also single states need to transfer social welfare functions to them. What Habermas calls the postnational constellation, that is, the whole constellation of fragmented actors and organizational bodies with political functions or political interests and identities having to do with or to deal with the outstripped national realm of politics, must work together to recuperate and rebuild democracy on an appropriate transnational scale. The postnational constellation needs to organize itself for the creation and the strengthening of political powers capable of engaging the challenges of globalization on more equal footing. And the European Union can be a model for postnational democracy, Habermas ultimately argues, an argument we will return to more fully in chapter 5.

In Habermas' account, we find the idea that globalization is driven by global capitalism and there is a kind of anticapitalist logic that underwrites his call for effective regulation. Habermas' critique of capitalism, from *Structural Transformation* to the present, is anchored largely to his concern for democracy, as he sees democracy being jeopardized both historically and by the current spread of capitalism. Habermas understands by "democratic constitutional state" a political order formed by the people and always subordinated to their opinion and will, since these are what legitimates the political order. This is, more or less, the kind of logic we expect democracies to abide by; yet "because capitalism follows a logic of its own, it is unable to conform to these demanding premises by itself: politics must see to it that the social conditions for public and private autonomy are met. Otherwise an essential condition for the legitimacy of democracy is endangered."[14] This is not particularly surprising, but it is important.

The idea that there is a kind of necessary antagonism between social welfare and capitalism was seen in Habermas' earlier discussion of the depoliticization of the bourgeois public sphere. It was precisely the overtaking of the means of communication by capitalist interests that depoliticized a public sphere that was a major democratic force while it was intact. Today, Habermas rejects the logic of neoliberalism that insists on the compatibility of, even a causal relationship between, capitalism and social welfare. He does not accept that the success of capitalism in increasing production, wealth, and development will necessitate upward economic movement for those who suffer impoverishment, and he does not accept that a free market will make governments and cultures more liberal.[15] This tone in Habermas is less pronounced elsewhere in his writing, where he seems to say that the divergent logics of democracy and of capitalism are malleable enough to not entail the cessation of one for the other.[16]

What I am interested in here is the way that engaging capitalism in its present, global mode of production, necessitates also the globalization of its opponent. It has long been understood that any antagonistic response to capitalism, that the response of any opponent, would have to be at least as transnational as capitalism (remember, for example, Marx's insistence that communism could not work within a national framework because capitalism did not work within those limited bounds). Globalization is certainly *not* a new topography for the nonbourgeois public sphere, since public spheres without legitimating power have always sought to globalize themselves in their struggle to accumulate influence. Whereas nonbourgeois public spheres have always been driven to transnationalize, for structural and material reasons, bourgeois public spheres have not shared the same impetuses. Today, the enduring tension is represented by the fact that bourgeois public spheres have supported capitalist globalization whereas nonbourgeois public spheres remain at the losing end of these processes. But across class lines, the loss of democratic procedures for controlling capital is a loss for everyone committed to democracy.

To illustrate this point, let us return to the British East India Company, which I mentioned in passing above. The East India Company was an early kind of transnational corporation, a British corporation operating in many parts of India, but particularly in Bengal. Agents of the company were accused of torturing, raping, and mutilating Indians, of being involved in acts of plundering land resources and extortion, and all under the supervision of Warren Hastings. Hastings was a British statesman serving as governor-general of Bengal during the period of Britain's imperial rule in India. Edmund Burke, a political philosopher and member of the British parliament for thirty years, used reports of these atrocities as the basis of impeachment trials of Hastings, which he led in the British parliament. Burke kept up a campaign to rein in and to regulate the East India Company for almost ten years.[17]

What is critical to note in this story is that while the East India Company was functioning entirely outside of Great Britain, it was, nevertheless, subjected to the regulatory powers of the British government. Burke, although he was a member of parliament, represented the widespread opinion of a liberal, bourgeois public sphere in civil society, which was concerned about the behavior of British companies in India. Many who learned of the East India Company felt that the company's abuses must be stopped and that Hastings should be punished for allowing the crimes committed there. If Burke's movement succeeded, the British government would have acted beyond its own borders to regulate the behavior of a company with bases of operation in another country. Today, however, the transnational corporation is protected against such intervention by international trade legislation,[18] and movements that ask states to perform regulative functions such as Burke asked in parliament in the 1780s, must realize that no single state retains such a capacity to regulate transnational companies, even if they do retain some.

To conclude this discussion of globalization, I would like now to consider some of the new problems of political identity associated with it. Let us return to Habermas' account of the breakdown of national identity. The breaking down of homogeneous national identity makes public spheres more susceptible and open to recasting their self-understandings along lines other than nationality. There is, however, a reactionary movement that problematizes this openness. Habermas points out: "Our own prosperous societies are witnessing a rise of ethnocentric reaction against anything foreign—hatred and violence against foreigners, against other faiths and races; also against marginalized groups, the handicapped and—once again—Jews."[19] I will later argue that nationalisms mustn't always take the form of dangerous ethnonationalisms, but that they can be defended on grounds that are both productive and in the interest of reversing social inequalities (in chapter 6 below, and throughout part III).

Some feel that certain national identities are being eroded by the proliferation of new identities overwhelmingly produced through a movement of what is called "Americanization." A lopsided flow of cultural goods sees the wealthier Western countries sending out far more cultural products to greater cultural effect than it receives from elsewhere. Mass communication and global markets have served as pipelines through which Western cultural products are disseminated and circulated around the world. Everything from fashion to television shows and movies, to music and books, and even to language is under the pressure of standardization by the global flow of prevailing cultural products. Many traditional cultures find their ways of life under siege by this flow. But this mass circulation of cultural products affects national identity everywhere: "The clocks of Western civilization keep the tempo for the compulsory simultaneity of the nonsimultaneous. This commodified, homogenous culture doesn't just impose itself on distant lands, of course; in the West too, it levels out even the strongest national differences, and weakens even the strongest local traditions."[20]

However, bracketing the drawbacks for the moment, now that discursive processes of opinion- and will-formation cross national boundaries with such great fluidity and speed (instantaneous in fact), it appears possible to form a collective political understanding, an actual collectivity that sees itself as sharing risks, and is made up of complete strangers who may never meet but who may nevertheless come together and act together. Habermas imagines how to make such a common political community more concrete. This involves shifting the basis of solidarity from specific historical geneses and the practices of particular cultures "onto the more abstract foundation of a 'constitutional patriotism.'" In other words, institutions would have to draw up a constitution that unifies people by cutting through the thick cultural contexts into which they were born (and in which they live) to very basic principles that resonate cross-culturally, such as principles regarding human rights. Political identity would have to, therefore, cease to be a nationalist identity, and instead be a more inclusive identity, inclusive enough for the multicultural and diasporic internal populations of states, as well as for their transnational linkages.

We are thus left with a picture of a new topography for political public spheres that *is* new, but only in certain regards. We may speak of a host of major political crises that have escaped the jurisdictions of national governments, a host of problems that may have long histories but have seen a rapid acceleration and enlargement of scale toward the end of the short twentieth century. This acceleration of transnational problems has made what were once undeveloped and potential stakes more present, starker, and more probable, and the situation certainly does require a response on equal footing. The problems associated with global warming, AIDS, increasing impoverishment, and a greater distance than ever before between the wealthiest and the poorest parts of the world population can only be addressed under the rubric of transnational politics and global justice.

The solidarities that underlie political action must be expanded from those of national political action and national identity and culture to those of broader and more resonant principles. A loosening of national identities and national cultures is well underway, in part due to globalization itself, but what forms in their place remains to be seen. As ethnocentrism struggles for traction on the one hand, and Westernization creates volatile tensions in its production of a new cultural homogenization, there are other, more pluralistic movements, normatively committed to democracy and to the reduction of social and economic inequality. And although we will explore some of the key ways in which these "other" efforts can help to resolve the problems discussed above, we will also see the various ways they overextend imprecise claims and assumptions about the national and transnational frameworks, indigenousness, political culture and identity, and civil society.

Notes

1. John A. Guidry, Michael D. Kennedy, and Mayer N. Zald, *Globalizations and Social Movements: Culture, Power, and the Transnational Public Sphere*, 1.
2. David Held, "Democracy and Globalization," 13 in *Re-imagining Political Community: Studies in Cosmopolitan Democracy*.
3. Ibid., 12, 22.
4. Ibid., 22.
5. This problem of the political function of a transnational public sphere will be taken up more constructively in chapters 5 and 6.
6. Held, "Democracy and Globalization," 25.
7. It is worth pointing out that the European Union confuses the working definitions I have given of international and transnational. In some sense, the European Union is a union *between and among* intact states, yet in another sense, it intends to move beyond these states, transferring political authority to a European institutional structure. I will call it a transnational institution primarily because of the public sphere it is in want of. A European public sphere is clearly transnational because it is rooted in a political identity beyond national identity.
8. Here, I am openly disagreeing with Arendt who maintained that the public sphere *was* an end in itself, at least inasmuch as the "public" was an organ for the generation of power; power, for Arendt, can never be instrumental (see my discussion in chapter 1).
9. I do not mean to suggest that the distinction between bourgeois and nonbourgeois public spheres can be collapsed. To the contrary, within states some public spheres still do occupy a clearly dominant position while others are marginal and subordinated. The point here is that, in moving to a transnational terrain, the bourgeois public sphere does not carry over *all* of its privilege because it is not empowered as a legitimater of political institutions and power-holders beyond its state-bounded jurisdiction.
10. Jürgen Habermas, *The Postnational Constellation: Political Essays*, 65–66.
11. Habermas, "The European Nation-State and the Pressures of Globalization," 219–20 in *Global Justice and Transnational Politics*.

12. Ibid., 220.

13. Habermas, *The Postnational Constellation*, 48–49.

14. Ibid., 65.

15. See ibid., 65 and 90–103.

16. Compare the above cited passages to Habermas' arguments about Westernization and democratization in his essay "On Legitimation through Human Rights," 197–214 in *Global Justice and Transnational Politics*.

17. See Edmund Burke's "Speech on Fox's East India Bill" (1783) and "Speech in Opening the Impeachment of Warren Hastings" (1788) for my sources of Burke's ideas on the East India Company and Warren Hastings. Both speeches are published in Burke's *On Empire, Liberty, and Reform: Speeches and Letters*, edited by David Bromwich (2000).

18. I would like to be a bit more specific about what exactly international trade legislation does to protect transnational corporations. Briefly, I shall cite some examples that highlight the impact of developments such as the GATT (General Agreement on Tariffs and Trade), NAFTA (North American Free Trade Agreement), and the WTO (World Trade Organization). These mechanisms have very clear bearing on international trade, inaugurating "the authority to prevent, overrule, or dilute the environmental, social, consumer, and labor laws of any nation. . . . Should a country refuse to change its laws when a WTO panel so dictates, GATT can impose international trade sanctions, depriving the resistant country of needed markets and materials" (see 32 in Michael Parenti's *Against Empire*, 1995). The WTO, for example, prohibits discriminating against a product on the basis of its method of production. That is, if a nation objects to the manner in which a product was produced, it cannot, on those grounds, oppose importation without violating a WTO rule. And this applies even to the most powerful countries, including the United States, which was taken to the GATT for refusing to accept Mexican tuna caught in nets that killed millions of dolphins; a similar action was taken against the United States when it attempted to block shrimp imports that entailed capturing and drowning one hundred fifty thousand sea turtles annually (see 16 and 132 in Kevin Danaher and Roger Burbach's, eds., *Globalize This!*, 2000). As Mark Malloch Brown wrote in the foreword to the *1999 United Nations Human Development Report*, "Markets need institutions and rules—and too frequently in the global setting they are not yet adequately subjected to the control of either." This is largely due to the effects of the trade legislation I mention here, which protects the transnational corporation by placing it beyond the jurisdiction of states and the reach of their policies.

19. Habermas, *The Postnational Constellation*, 72.

20. Ibid., 75.

5

Transnational Cosmopolitan Public Spheres and a Turn Against the National Framework

Cosmopolitanism and Other Efforts to Theorize Transnational Public Spheres

I will now consider cosmopolitanism and other efforts to rethink political organization, action, and identity transnationally, in both institutional and noninstitutional terms. Although few cosmopolitan theorists explicitly consider the role of the public sphere,[1] it is nevertheless necessary for thinking through the implementation of institutional recommendations (as, for example, I suggested above regarding Held's recommendations).

This chapter provides a critical review of some of the major ways the public sphere has been theorized transnationally. I discuss various accounts, critique them, and sum up persistent errors repeatedly made by theorists. My overarching aim is twofold: First, I want to make clear various important ways that transnational public spheres have been theorized. Why is the transnational public sphere so important and how can it actually be formed? Second, I shall raise some serious problems pertaining to the juxtaposition of national and transnational frameworks—problems that emerge from a critique of contemporary theories. As well, I point out problems that arise from theorists assuming a dichotomy between the national framework and the

145

transnational framework, and suggesting that we ought to choose (both as theorists and actors) the latter over the former.

Dichotomizing these frameworks is not, as it might appear at first, a simple oversight, a mere difference of focus among theorists, or a surface-level problem. Rather, it represents a deeper normative problem in contemporary thinking about the advantage and necessity of different constructions of political self-understanding and the scale of political action. Today, choosing a national (or subnational) framework signifies a more provincial kind of politics—often, it signals an ethnonationalist or patriotic sense of superiority and exclusivity. Whereas choosing a transnational framework signifies a broader concern, purportedly better suited to addressing current problems of globalization; choosing a transnational scale and self-understanding signals an antinationalist, more cosmopolitan orientation. I argue that these significations are not only imprecise but that either choice is inadvisable wherever important struggles remain state-bounded in key ways, wherever the nationalist side of the debate is on the side of fighting *for* inclusion, pluralism, and more democracy (and *against* various forms of exclusion, imperialism, fundamentalism, or neocolonialism), and wherever state-bounded, national orientations are understood in a transnational context, in community and solidarity with others elsewhere, and in conflict with certain global trends in politics and economics. Wherever there are such imbrications of the national and transnational (and I shall show that these are common), choosing between a national or transnational framework is not merely an oversight or theoretical focus; it is objectionable on normative grounds.

I begin this chapter with Michael Walzer's *Thick and Thin: Moral Argument at Home and Abroad* because his discussion of the concepts of thick and thin underwrite and run through all of the subsequent discussions of this chapter and later chapters. Walzer's ideas serve to introduce and to frame the underlying philosophical principles and problems of cosmopolitanism.

I then turn to a consideration of cosmopolitanism in the works of Janna Thompson, Daniele Archibugi, Martin Köhler, and James Bohman. Because there is a growing and virtually endless list of influential theorists who have written about

cosmopolitanism, something must be said about the selections
I've made. I have tried to choose the smallest number of texts
that cover the widest range of central issues taken up by cosmopolitan theorists, and that explicitly address the public sphere.
Thompson's essay, for example, emphasizes cosmopolitan identity. She focuses more on the need for the cosmopolitan self-
understanding of peoples than on the need for cosmopolitan
institutions of governance. Archibugi, on the other hand, acknowledges the need for cosmopolitan identity, but focuses instead on what is needed in terms of political institutions and
new democratic mechanisms. He argues for cosmopolitan institutions of governance and the idea of cosmopolitical democracy.
Having a sense of both the noninstitutional and the institutional
components necessary for creating cosmopolitanism, we turn to
Köhler and Bohman who discuss cosmopolitan political public
spheres. Indeed, theirs are the only cosmopolitan theories (besides Habermas', considered in later in this chapter) that explicitly address the role of a cosmopolitan public sphere. In these
accounts, as is always true of accounts of the political public
sphere, the institutional and noninstitutional sides of cosmopolitanism are brought together in order to imagine channels of influence and reciprocity between society and state.

Finally, we turn to Nancy Fraser and John A. Guidry and
Mark Q. Sawyer to represent what I have designated "other efforts to transnationalize the public sphere." Fraser represents a
critical theory standpoint here, exploring the basic structural reasons why the public sphere of the classical account must be
made transnational. She argues that the concept of the public
sphere can only retain a political function if it is transnational-
ized, but that it could still serve a vital function if it is reconstituted on a larger scale. Guidry and Sawyer situate the
transnational public sphere within a theory of "contentious pluralism," which invites us to return to a serious consideration of
social movements.

What ties together all of the theorists considered here is that
they accept the basic premises of globalization outlined in chapter 4 and they try to formulate a response. In this regard, they are
all a part of the general turn of attention in political science and
philosophy that has shifted the focus from a national to a

transnational framework. In the first part of this chapter, I critically evaluate these important efforts to transition from the national framework to the transnational framework, illustrating the shortcomings of each theory, and ultimately revealing a deep confusion about how to regard the national framework. In the second part of this chapter, I turn to Habermas' theory of a transnational public sphere.

I have invoked Michael Walzer's ideas of thick and thin on numerous occasions, but they now call for fuller consideration. Walzer's *Thick and Thin: Moral Argument at Home and Abroad* includes some very important ideas about the resonance of moral arguments and moral principles across cultures and national boundaries. Of all of the authors in this chapter, Walzer is the furthest from engaging directly the debates I am taking up. However, his discussion of thick and thin is useful to the thinking in my project, and particularly instructive is his insistence on the basic compatibility of thick and thin (although I ultimately use this compatibility to make a case that Walzer would object to). As we shall see, the thick is typically associated with the national, topical community, or subnational community, and the thin is typically associated with the transnational, metatopical community. But what is meant by thick and thin?

Walzer uses thin to refer to moral minimalism and thick to refer to moral maximalism. Moral minimalism means highly abstracted and minimally specified or minimally qualified moral or political principles. When you think of "justice" or "equality" without thinking about competing definitions of each idea, you are still left with concepts that have some generalized moral and political meaning. You can say something of what it is without saying enough to close out particularized conceptions. A minimalist formulation of equality, for example, the belief that people should be treated as equals, is an idea that can easily generate mass agreement. As such, it lacks important layers of definition and meaning. But thinly formulated, this version of equality can be expected to provide a basis for more solidarity than could be expected from a thicker, more specified version of the concept. As we "thicken" the meaning of equality, making it more maximal, more specified, there is more complexity and, therefore, more negotiation, more compromise, and less agreement.

The standard philosophical view of moral minimalism is that "it is everyone's morality because it is no one's in particular; subjective interest and cultural expression have been avoided or cut away."[2]

However, the temptation to think of moral minimalism as flimsy and not at all substantive or as emotionally shallow must be avoided. In fact, moral minimalism is *deeper* than moral maximalism in a very important sense. That is, it cuts through all of the cultural complexities and reaches to the core of the idea, to the most universally felt center of moral feeling. In a sense, moral minimalism gets to the root of morality.

Although Walzer agrees, he insists that maximalism (thick) precedes minimalism (thin). The thin is abstracted from our thicker experience. A minimalist formulation of morals only makes sense to us because of our maximalist experiences. In other words, we have a deep understanding of our own moral sensibility, a sensibility that was formed from birth by the mores and the practices in our own culture. Nevertheless, certain moral ideas (say, the idea that one ought to tell the truth, or honesty) in such a minimalist formulation will be found to hold sway all over the world. Yet telling the truth has limits when you get down to a thicker, cultural understanding. In some cultures, for example, you are expected to answer honestly when asked by a friend if he or she is gaining weight. In others, the moral sense is that you should know better than to tell the truth. The thin formulation is always abstracted from the thick. Moreover, it is only the thick that is foundational of cultural community. Walzer makes this a strong point: "We have in fact no knowledge of the stone; we begin with the finished statue; maximalist in style, ancient, carved by many hands. And then, in moments of crisis, we hastily construct an abstract version, a stick figure, a cartoon, that only alludes to the complexity of the original. . . . Minimalism is not foundational."[3] One can see here why Walzer is often considered a communitarian.

But it is precisely this part of Walzer's argument that is unconvincing, particularly when we think about certain transnational public spheres (cosmopolitanism, as well as our discussion of the Zapatista public sphere in chapter 7, will bear this out). Transnational public spheres and cosmopolitanism are usually founded on minimalism, and it is the "abstract version" that brings them into existence. Transnational communities have cultural dimensions. Minimalism can be so foundational in fact that new political identities can be rooted in it, as is also the case with the beckon call of a European identity and any cosmopolitan sense of being a world citizen. These examples, and others explored below, contest Walzer's insistence on the order of things as starting from thick and moving to thin when necessary. To be clear, I do not mean to deny that we begin life in the thickness of our cultural and familial communities, nor that our morality is first acclimated to the maximal principles of these communities. Rather, I am suggesting that transnational communities and a cosmopolitan political identity (for example) are not only founded on minimalism, but that they do not need to remain thin, that what begins thin can be thickened, and even that some aspects of life can have both thick and thin dimensions (these suggestions will be argued more fully in part III).

One thing that minimalism does is enable and enliven solidarity among geographically disparate people, which can then be used as the basis for various kinds of pressure coming from metatopical communities and through public spheres. Moral or political solidarity, if it is to span far distances, indeed, cannot be too thick. The more we specify the demands and the more we qualify highly resonant principles in highly particularized contexts, the more we will bring into relief divergent historical, religious, political, and cultural contingencies, and the further we will be from agreement. Walzer exemplifies this point by talking about the ideal of democracy in China. Thinly, we may all agree on democracy and democratization, but Chinese democracy will be Chinese in important ways, and so democratic theorists outside of China cannot rightly hope to inform it in its thicker forms. Walzer explains that if he were to give a seminar in China on democracy, he would be clear about his views as a democratic theorist, but he would have to insist at every juncture that democracy in China will have to be Chinese, and that fleshing out the meaning of Chinese democracy is not something that could be done by anyone other than the Chinese.[4]

Walzer makes some important points that pertain to my overarching interest in indigenous rights politics in the context of globalization. Moral minimalism in international politics, he says, often employs the principle of self-determination. This principle invokes the idea of rights in and for a particular local community, rights to its own continuation and self-modification, rights to preserve and determine the thickness of its culture. Thus, self-determination is a minimalist principle that implies the preservation of maximalist culture. But, how does the principle of self-determination fare today, in the context of recently emergent multicultural communities and other imagined communities? Walzer says:

> This value is not compromised, it seems to me, by the post-modern discovery that communities are social constructions: imagined, invented, put together out of a great variety of cultural and political materials. Constructed communities are the only communities there are, and so they can't be less real or less authentic than some other kind. . . . *They ought to be allowed to govern themselves* (in accordance with their own political ideas)—insofar as they can decently do that, given their local entanglements.[5]

Walzer is specifically thinking here of cultural communities on the national or subnational level. But as we shall see with cosmopolitanism, the Zapatistas, and my own theory of transgression, communities can also be bounded by a broader common commitment. So what happens to thick and thin in the context of cosmopolitanism and other efforts to rethink the public sphere transnationally? One thing is that the thick gets tied to the side of the national (as in the maximal meaning of Chinese democracy) and the thin gets tied to the side of the transnational (as in the minimal principles of democracy in general). In terms of identity, we will see that the thin is generally pitted against the thick, as if one will inevitably win out in the end. But what we are ultimately after in this work are the ways in which thick and thin are *not* antagonistic, the ways in which these antipathies are proven evitable. For example, as we shall see more extensively below, cosmopolitan public spheres begin already within single national states, as multiculturalism and diaspora link state-bounded public spheres to public spheres elsewhere. Of course, we may not want to say that these public spheres are state-bounded in any strict sense, because of their transnational linkages, but there is certainly a sense in which cosmopolitan public spheres do exist and understand themselves within a national framework.

We thus arrive squarely at the arguments of cosmopolitans and the concept of cosmopolitan public spheres. Cosmopolitan theories problematize Walzer's account in numerous ways, mainly due to the fact that they prioritize and promote more minimalist ties that bind communities across boundaries rather than maximalist ones. But there are two further reasons why we will periodically return to Walzer's conceptual rubric of thick and thin throughout this work. First, contemporary transnational theories tend to neglect the enduring political significance of moral maximalism, largely identifying it as the stuff of provincial resistances to cosmopolitanism. Second, and more importantly, I intend to increasingly observe and emphasize the complementarity of thick and thin in developing my own theory of transgression and transgressive public spheres.

The most rudimentary idea of cosmopolitanism is that the self-understanding of citizens *as world citizens* in the community of human beings must take moral precedence over any more parochial kind of self-understanding. That is, cosmopolitanism rejects any essentialist valuation of one people over another writ large—it rejects chauvinistic patriotism and decentralizes nationalist political identity, insisting instead on the primacy of a more egalitarian valuation of human beings within the multifarious lifeways of the world, as well as one's own membership within that larger community. Cosmopolitanism is always transnational, but that which is transnational is not always cosmopolitan. Capitalism, for example, is transnational, but rarely is it abiding cosmopolitan ideals. The subordination, more so than the elimination, of national identity to a cosmopolitan identity is much of the crux of the concept. But what I have just said is hardly the whole thing, because this much makes cosmopolitanism sound like it is wholly achieved within civil society.[6] The proper picture of cosmopolitanism is more complex. Indeed, many, if not most cosmopolitan theorists prioritize institutional efforts to transcend limiting national identities and inadequate national political powers. They argue that cosmopolitan institutional initiatives can lead the way for cosmopolitan transformations in civil society. So, for example, cosmopolitan education is discussed, as are cosmopolitan institutions that encourage the development of world citizenship. Cosmopolitan theorists have varying positions about the prioritization of the institutional or the noninstitutional components of the cosmopolitan project.

Janna Thompson makes some critical contributions as well as some dire missteps in thinking through the community identity and world citizenship part of the problem. She argues that the best conception of identity will not only acknowledge that people can identify with multiple religious, ethnic, political, and social communities, but that it will promote such identifications. She considers the identity of peoples first, and then uses that as a basis for institutional transformations. Thompson argues for what she calls complex identity because she sees it as a way to subvert and to supplant unnecessary divisiveness, and she argues that original, familial, more maximal identities are treated with too much reverence and with a fear of their destabilization and fragmentation. But there is, according to Thompson, the more pragmatic and uneasily surmountable fact that most people "identify much more closely with their family, their friends, their religious group, etc., than they do with their political society."[7] In general, Thompson claims, peoples' political identities are less important to them than their familial, thick, cultural ones.[8] This would appear a problem for national identity, let alone for cosmopolitan identity.

People are born into communities, and it is in these communities of birth that they acquire their first sense of identity. These are not chosen communities. Over time, many people grow critical of their communities of birth and choose to enter other types of communities. These other types of communities, communities of choice, sometimes end up more important to people than their communities of birth. Community is, therefore, not a fixed thing and it is rather common that one's community of birth is to some degree replaced by a community of choice that seems a better, more tailored fit. This shows that identity is malleable. This malleability is often the very thing that enables us to make identifications that are more meaningful to us, beyond those that we inherited at birth and in the stead of those we shed in the development of our personalities and political self-understanding.

For Thompson, cosmopolitanism needs to work with some such conception of identity because it depends ultimately on the creation of a new political identity. World citizenship requires that people find broader, thinner, more transnational identities that are ultimately preferable (more meaningful) to all of the more parochial ones that they might choose. For Thompson, this is the basis of the idea of cosmopolitan identity. It is not a matter of replacement, but of priority.

But cosmopolitan identity, because it is a complex identity, one that complicates self-understanding, is not something that people will simply seek. Indeed, Thompson acknowledges that cosmopolitan identity will be less attractive in many ways than competing, thicker, political identities. Because of this, the case needs to be made everywhere for the virtues of a cosmopolitan identity by theorists, activists, and institutions that seek the development of cosmopolitanism.

> Individuals with a complex social identity will never be at one with themselves and their social world or free from conflicts of loyalty, but this is a reasonable price to pay for the expansion of moral consciousness and the opportunities of choice that complexity provides. A complex identity is not only compatible with cosmopolitanism. It is conducive to the establishment of procedures for resolving conflicts between communities. People who regard membership in a number of communities as important to their lives will be motivated to search for and abide by such procedures.[9]

Even making the case for complex identity, we can see how literally risky it is to take up. That is, an effective cosmopolitan identity represents a decisive willingness to understand oneself as sharing in a greater number of the risks of life. We begin in one community of shared risk, yet cosmopolitan identity asks us to join others for their as well as, ultimately, for the world's benefit.

Theoretically, Thompson's argument follows a clear and sensible reasoning, even if we are left unconvinced of the likelihood of complex, cosmopolitan identities taking root on a large scale. Yet, there is a line running through Thompson's argument that is deeply problematic and indicative of a kind of error that will be of central concern to us throughout this chapter (and the rest of this work). That is, from what has been said already, we can see that Thompson sets up cosmopolitan identity as *versus* all others in a contest of ranking for first place. While other identities are *included in* complex identity, complex identity as such must compete with each one individually. Following this, Thompson positions thicker cultural identities and, explicitly, indigenousness, as impediments standing in the way of the development of cosmopolitanism. She maintains that among the many backlashes against cosmopolitanism, and one of the major visceral resistances to it, is the resurgence of a defensive cultural identity and indigenous community in the face of neoliberalism.[10]

Referring to the resistances of indigenous peoples to the advancements of neoliberalism, Thompson says, "these developments not only impede cosmopolitan programmes, as they are usually defined. They also present a philosophical challenge to cosmopolitan ideas."[11] While Thompson wants to resolve (and not to accept) this problematic, the juxtaposition is simply false. What is so interesting, to the contrary, is how the resistant assertions of indigenous peoples have managed to take on a staunchly cosmopolitan disposition. One of the things that the case of the Zapatistas demonstrates is that movements for self-determination, of which indigenous rights groups are a major part, work with principles that are fundamentally compatible with cosmopolitanism. As we will see with the Zapatistas, for example, indigenous rights was cast far and wide as an objective for people and organizations around the world who took it up in a politics of cosmopolitanism, a politics that inspired a series of large demonstrations a few years later in wealthy, "first world" countries (such as in Seattle, Washington, in 1999 and Genoa, Italy, in 2001). These demonstrations in particular were largely about the welfare of people other than those participating in them, and were reliant on a kind of cosmopolitan thinking. Notably, the political movements and the plight of indigenous peoples made up a good deal of the concern about the detrimental effects of globalization processes. In fact, a logical compatibility between community identity and local interests with cosmopolitanism has been made clear in critical responses to capitalist globalization.

Despite this, in a table mapping out different theories of justice, Thompson maintains an opposition between cosmopolitanism and communitarianism (in her model, we may think of any subnational or state-bounded political community, such as indigenous communities and politics, in order to instantiate the idea of communitarian identity).[12] Thompson argues that according to communitarianism and community identity the "meaning and possibility of justice depends on the identification of individuals with their community and its values."[13] She charges that this community identity is antithetical to cosmopolitan identity adding that, "the communitarian challenge to cosmopolitanism is likely to be favored by those who insist on the value of *their* community and want to defend it from economic and political forces, including programmes for a cosmopolitan world order."[14] Indeed, the Zapatistas (as we shall further explore in part III) *do* insist on the value of indigenous lifeways and they do want to defend themselves from encroaching economic and political forces. However, within the Zapatistas' orientation and political discourse, indigenous communities and their political programs did not find an opponent but rather an ally in cosmopolitan programs. Community identity and local cultural-valuational notions can be enlarged. Thus communitarian identities and the concept of world citizenship should by no means be considered necessarily at odds, for they can in fact be mutually supportive. Still, in Thompson's account, supposed antagonisms between cosmopolitanism and indigenousness have been confused and to some significant effect. In this work, what we are after is, precisely, what is to be learned from the confusion about (and potential dissolvability of) these antagonisms.

But cosmopolitanism does not always focus on transformations in political identity. Many cosmopolitan theorists are thinking of ways to remake political institutions (such as was briefly seen in Held's call for institutional changes). Daniele Archibugi has worked to develop a theory of "cosmopolitics," yet he does not focus on the political identity and the self-understanding of civil societies. His primary concern is the formation of cosmopolitan institutions with functional democratic mechanisms. He certainly agrees that civil society does and must continue to play an important role in the development of cosmopolitanism, and he refers periodically to social movements, but even then, he understands the reciprocity and influence between society and state as mediated by formal democratic processes. If cosmopolitan democracy is to be achieved, he maintains, institutions of governance must make their dispositions and their democratic input mechanisms more cosmopolitan.

Archibugi calls his conception "cosmopolitical democracy." The basic idea of cosmopolitical democracy is to focus on making the formal mechanisms of politics and democracy more cosmopolitan, ultimately extending the scope of democracy to regulate problems beyond the jurisdiction of the state: "Cosmopolitical democracy is based on the assumption that important objectives—control of the use of force, respect for human rights, self-determination—will be obtained only through the extension and development of democracy."[15] But cosmopolitical democracy is not a call for the replacement of states with some form of world government or with some kind of massive federated power. What Archibugi means by cosmopolitical democracy is, in large part, the rethinking of war policies and international law. For example, cosmopolitan states would not pursue war or economic sanctions as if the related suffering of populations could be justified as "collateral damage." The language of lawmakers, institutions of governance and their spokespeople, would refer to other peoples beyond their own national borders as fellow citizens. Regarded as such, sanctions could only be justifiably imposed on those who violated laws, not on those who live under the rule of those who violated laws.

At first, such cosmopolitan aspirations might seem like the utopian dreams of progressive theorists. However, it is worth considering the official and popular discourses of states, particularly of those that do indeed impose or support the imposition of sanctions. Doing so reveals the extent to which the ideal of cosmopolitanism is already recognized by existing institutions. Wherever it is asked, most will readily admit a clear distinction between any people and its government. Take, for example, the war in Iraq. In this example, the most fervent supporters of the war, even in the face of a growing Iraqi insurgency, insisted at least rhetorically that the Iraqi people were clear and distinct from the tyranny of Saddam Hussein. That is, those who speak most unflinchingly on behalf of the war insist that the war effort has been made to free the Iraqi people from the rule of tyranny, to assist the transition to democracy, and to work toward these ends with as little as possible negative impact on the civilians and their lives.[16] None of this is, of course, tantamount to calling the Iraqi people "fellow citizens" but it is rhetorically inclined toward such a view. The reality of war, however, even if the stated intentions of the U.S. and British governments went undoubted (which has not been the case), is that Iraqi civilians are neither treated nor represented as fellow citizens undeserving of the carnage and physical desolation that their country has been subjected to. Collateral damage is regularly justified by the administrations, and we see everywhere, most unswervingly in mainstream American media, that U.S. and British casualties are sharply distinguished from Iraqi casualties, that the former are categorically less acceptable than the latter.[17] Hence, cosmopolitanism has idealist resonance even though it has not been transposed in material terms to the world of law, policy, and action.

Regarding this description, one could reply that this is simply the necessary course of war, but Archibugi and fellow cosmopolitans would disagree. They would insist that the underlying rhetoric, which already incorporates a tone of cosmopolitanism, could be made stronger and more concrete. The basic principles of the cosmopolitan ideal are already well integrated into the public presentations of those who violate it in practice. What this means for Archibugi is that cosmopolitanism already has a high normative status in the opinion of the general public, that states are sensitive to this fact, but that its development is lacking in terms of policy and practice.

Beyond all of this, Archibugi thinks also about existing transnational nonstate institutions, such as the WTO and the IMF and World Bank. Currently, there are no sufficient avenues for the democratic steering of such transnational bodies by a relevant transnational community. Because of institutions like these, and the democratic deficit in their steering, democracy cannot remain a state-based affair. One of the major criticisms of these institutions repeatedly made at protests against the WTO, the IMF, and the World Bank is that they are not open to democratic steering. States' elections, no matter how their populations feel about the behavior of these institutions, cannot lead to their effective regulation. So democracy needs to be extended. Otherwise, it risks being hollowed out by globalization processes.

The democratization of states, then, even as more states are transitioning toward democracy, is a positive development but it does not address the problems of globalization. This brings us to a major part of Archibugi's argument. Archibugi disagrees with John Rawls and others (see, for example, the United Nations Human Development Report for 2002: *Deepening Democracy in a Fragmented World*) who believe that the extension of democracy beyond national boundaries is achievable by making more and more states democratic: "A set of democratic states does not generate a democratic globe, any more than a set of democratically elected town councils generates a democratic nation-state. . . . It is necessary to add a level of political representation to those [democratic states] that already exist."[18] It is for this reason that not only democracy but also cosmopolitical democracy must be stressed. In addition to democratic states with a cosmopolitan disposition, and certainly not in replacement of them, there must also be a level of power established beyond national power. There must be institutional bodies that function beyond national borders that are steered by the input of a transnational community, bodies that can monitor and change the course of globalization processes with appropriate scale and regulatory force.

What is particularly refreshing about Archibugi's account is that it does not present us with a choice between the two frameworks; his account retains the importance of the national framework for democracy, insists on the importance of single states with a cosmopolitan disposition, yet also insists on a transnational framework for new institutional developments. But Archibugi does not blur the line between national and transnational frameworks. To the contrary, he sees the national and transnational in the context of a division of labor—some jobs should be left to individual states, while others will require the attention of transnational cosmopolitical institutions. Although it is a step in the right direction to posit these frameworks as cooperative rather than as antagonistic, we will soon see (in chapter 6) that the distinction between them is nevertheless overdrawn.

Our review thus far represents some of the basic suggestions of cosmopolitanism for civil society and political identity (Thompson) and for political institutions (Archibugi), but up to this point the public sphere has been merely implicit at best. For Thompson, it is implicit that people with a cosmopolitan identity will act together for the furtherance of cosmopolitanism, and for Archibugi, it is implicit that there will be some constituency of people feeding back on the input side of cosmopolitical institutions. However, it is important to think about the specific role of the public sphere in the development of cosmopolitanism. In part, this is because cosmopolitanism gives us a way to see a political function for public spheres beyond that of the classical relationship between a particular public and its representative state. Thus, bringing together cosmopolitanism with the concept of the public sphere helps to outline some of the ways in which a transnational public sphere may play a role in addressing problems of globalization.

Martin Köhler develops the idea of the public sphere from the standpoint of cosmopolitanism in his essay, "From the National to the Cosmopolitan Public Sphere."[19] Although his argument resituates the critical importance of the public sphere for the cosmopolitan project it ultimately stands in stark contrast to my own argument, which I will further delineate here in discussing Köhler's position.

Köhler maintains that there is indeed a need for a transnational public sphere in light of current problems of globalization. He uses the term Civil Society Organization (CSO) to refer to the whole range of organizations and organized events that start in and of civil society and work toward social and political change. CSOs are mobile. They have travel delegations of spokespeople that can attend intergovernmental conferences and try, with other like-minded CSOs, to influence the dispositions of their own and other governments. Among CSOs are reputable NGOs that have an established history of access to meetings that are not open to the general public. But even where this is the case, even where CSOs have access to exclusive meetings and conferences, Köhler maintains that they are organizations of the public sphere. This is because CSOs operate outside of the supervision of governments and they serve as active critics, interlocutors, and distributors of the more marginal discourses within civil society. Activist organizations that have a more antagonistic relationship with state institutions, such as Direct Action Network (DAN) and Peoples' Global Action (PGA), which organized much of the 1999 protest in Seattle against the WTO, are also counted as CSOs even though they do not have a seat at intergovernmental conferences or a felicitous relationship with policy-makers.[20]

CSOs are, more or less, the well-organized assemblages of public spheres, they are open to participation but have some bureaucratic structure in place. CSOs often utilize a network format, meaning that they speak and act together with other CSOs in order to consolidate influence. This network format is transnational. And, inasmuch as it entails that CSOs see each other's issues and risks as shared, it is well disposed toward cosmopolitanism. Following this, Köhler sees the emergence of a transnational cosmopolitan public sphere in the networking of CSOs:

> Though they have received no formal mandate from any political community or authority, CSOs and their transnational networks are increasingly recognized by governments as legitimate representatives of a global sphere of public interest which acts on its own behalf. For former UN Secretary-General Boutros-Ghali they are "a basic form of popular representation in the present-day world. Their participation in international relations is, in a way, a guarantee of the political legitimacy of those international organisations." . . . These examples support the claim that a transnational public sphere is emerging through which social interest groups are able to participate in international affairs beyond the traditional limits of state-confined politics.[21]

Notwithstanding the ways in which CSOs have reorganized themselves into a transnational public power, Köhler maintains that the public sphere is still essentially state-bounded. The civil society organizations that make up the transnational public sphere actively move across boundaries and address foreign states, but structurally, they only have a guaranteed, officially responsible addressee in their own national states (this reaffirms

Habermas' idea of the public sphere's structurally state-bounded legitimation function). And the transnational institutions that CSOs do address, such as the address made by the PGA and the DAN to the WTO, have no formal obligation to CSOs, so the latter are often just ignored.[22] For example, many of the most important institutions functioning transnationally, such as the UN Security Council and the WTO, are rather strictly off-limits to CSO participation. CSOs have made some progress on this front, demanding that the Bretton Woods institutions open themselves up to input from civil society, but it cannot yet be said that the transnational public sphere of CSOs has a responsive target with any obligation to consider its input.

The public sphere of CSOs remains essentially national in another sense too. CSOs are, after all, centrally concerned with influencing their own governments and raising their own level of legitimacy and status domestically (that is, even though they act transnationally in networks, they do so in order to accumulate and consolidate leverage for national projects). This does not simply strip CSOs in a network format of their transnational achievements. Logistically, however, CSOs have more success competing for a close and reciprocal relationship with their own governments than when they compete for attention on the world stage, where CSOs all over the globe speak en masse to the same transnational bodies, of which there are far fewer than states.

Another way to say this is that, for Köhler, the cosmopolitan public sphere is comprised of national public spheres. National public spheres work to preserve and deepen the circuitry of influence they have achieved with and within their own states. But they will occasionally come together in the format of a transnational cosmopolitan public sphere, comprised of a cooperative coalition of CSOs, instead of competing for influence on the world stage. Environmentalist CSOs do this. CSOs that work primarily with a national function, checking and pressuring state policies that impact on the issues of their concern, have come together in UN-sponsored intergovernmental conferences, such as in Rio on the environment, in Vienna on human rights, in Copenhagen on social development, in Cairo on population policy, in Beijing on women, and in Istanbul on urban habitats.[23] All of these issues, in these forums, are taken up from a cosmopolitan standpoint, from the standpoint that the environment, human rights, social development, population policy, women, and urban habitats are not state-bounded issues. The cosmopolitan public sphere of CSOs is ultimately a mechanism through which national public spheres can move beyond the national framework strategically, sharing stories and solidarity with like-minded and sympathetic publics elsewhere, whenever necessary or whenever a forum for such a public exists.

I would like to raise three major shortcomings of Köhler's argument for moving from the national to the cosmopolitan public sphere. First, even though CSOs are technically open to volunteerism and participation, which CSOs actually get to sit at intergovernmental conferences at the end of the day? The more contestatory the organization, such as Peoples' Global Action (PGA), the less they will be invited to participate. And social movements, which are technically CSOs according to Köhler, are left almost wholly ignored as his analysis develops. The more radical the CSO, the more excluded it will be. The public sphere of CSOs is, therefore, not as rich, diverse, and contestatory a public sphere as earlier accounts have allowed. For example, Köhler is silent on the means of circulating political discourses utilized by nonbourgeois public spheres. That is, the cosmopolitan public sphere of CSOs favors and focuses on less contestatory organizations, virtually discounting social movements, civil disobedience, and other innovative forms of contestation, which many contend play a critical democratizing role (i.e., Calhoun, Cohen and Arato, Negt and Kluge, and, just below, Guidry and Sawyer).

Second, and related to the first point, Köhler does not conceive of any alternate channels through which institutions could access those marginalized and more contestatory discourses, thus he repeats the central inadequacy of Habermas' classical theory. That is, his idea of an effective cosmopolitan public sphere consists of an elite cohort of CSOs that enjoy a distinguished status. It ends up excluding more unconventional and controversial political discourses and political action as if these belonged to the plebeian sector in Habermas' *Structural Transformation*. To sum up these two shortcomings, one could say that both in actual practice (the first point), as well as in Köhler's theorization of an effective cosmopolitan public sphere (the second point), important critical discourses are excluded.

Finally, Köhler's cosmopolitan public sphere depends on the opportunism of CSOs with regularly national programs that find occasion to join with other CSOs in a coalition format. Stated differently, the CSOs of the cosmopolitan public sphere have their own agendas tailor fitted to make the most sense at home, and only transnationalize their discourses and activities at the invitation to bring them to Rio or Beijing or to some other forum.[24] The problem with this aspect of Köhler's model is that it instrumentalizes cosmopolitanism, keeping transnational programs subordinate to national ones—it works transnationally only by way of proliferating preexisting national concerns. It does not function for or toward cosmopolitanism itself. But as we shall see, the indigenous rights movement, generally presumed to oppose cosmopolitanism, was able to establish a transnational cosmopolitan public sphere that included many people for whom no version of indigenous crises existed. The indigenous rights movement worked and continues to work to transnationalize concern over issues that were and still are not present everywhere in the world. Political action at the transnational level does not need to be made only in the occasional reassembly of existing national organizations, for it has greater productive capabilities. Political action can create new political community, new identifications, and new discourses where they did not previously exist. In fact, this more productive and creative aim is the very heart of cosmopolitanism, yet Köhler's cosmopolitan public sphere does not require it. All that is required is that the most privileged and cooperative part of the cosmopolitan public sphere of CSOs serves an advisory function to existing institutions on a semiregular basis.

James Bohman provides a different and more satisfying account of the cosmopolitan public sphere in his "Public Spheres of the World Citizen." There, Bohman builds on Kant's ideas of cosmopolitanism his own notion of a cosmopolitan public sphere that is more inclusive, more pluralistic, and more open to diversity of opinion than Kant envisioned. He follows Kant's arguments in "Perpetual Peace: A Philosophical Sketch." Bohman imagines a public sphere that is formally singular yet pluralistic and heterogeneous internally. He agrees with Habermas that the primary function of the political public sphere is to consider problems, deliberate on their solutions, and to register these solutions with institutions, thereby deepening institutional obligation to be responsive and representative. But Bohman does not see any reason to think of the public sphere as comprised of highly qualified actors such as the reputable CSOs of Köhler's account. Bohman provides a more open view of the participatory bodies that make up the public sphere, and he makes recommendations for the cosmopolitan transformation of civil society as well as for the cosmopolitan transformation of political institutions. He argues that a public sphere of world citizens must and will play a major role in facilitating these transformations. However, Bohman believes that the initiatives of civil society must nevertheless follow the lead of political institutions, and thus he ultimately limits, like Köhler does, the public sphere's contestatory status and steering capacity.

Bohman places a lot of faith in the power of the opinion of cosmopolitan world citizens to regulate and to influence the behavior of states. He argues, for example, "it is primarily the force of the opinions of world citizens, like the opinions of republican citizens in the state, that will bring about the limitations of military power necessary for peace."[25] He maintains that there is always an important dialogue occurring between public spheres and institutions. He calls the public sphere's power, following Kant's idea of the public use of reason, the power of a critical public. Bohman argues that state-bounded public spheres exist, and that a transnational civil society, and then a transnational public sphere, could be achieved through a federation of existing republican institutions, existing publics, and existing political identities. By federating already existing bodies, the conditions for a transnational civil society and a cosmopolitan public sphere can be created. For Bohman, the best way to make the public sphere transnational is by federating distinct publics.

Bohman believes that the first federation must be that of national states. Such an institutional transformation, coupled with intrastate processes of multiculturalism, would help to foster a strong cosmopolitan public sphere. Bohman argues "that this federation creates the conditions for an international civil society of nongovernmental organizations and a cosmopolitan public sphere, both of which can shape and ultimately reorganize existing republican institutions and political identities."[26] We may imagine that a cosmopolitan federation of political institutions precedes the cosmopolitan public sphere much like the European Union has preceded a European public sphere. Indeed, much of Bohman's argument seems to map out over the case of the European Union, yet he does not mention it, perhaps because the European Union has *not* led to a European public sphere with sufficient cohesion and unity of group interest.

Aside from his insistence on the order of things, Bohman takes seriously other critical processes that would accompany and facilitate both federation and the emergence of a cosmopolitan public sphere, processes that are well underway. Particularly important is the process of diminishing homogeneity *within states* as states diversify as a result of expanding multiculturalism, linguistic, and religious difference. In this multiculturalism, a kind of cosmopolitanism, one could say its principal attitude in the best scenario, is already being fostered within states. Migrations, multiculturalism, and a cosmopolitan disposition lay the groundwork for a transnational public sphere. Today, strangers, legal immigrants, and other noncitizens come together in the public spaces of the cities and states they settle in, and often, they are integrated into a national or subnational public sphere of some sort. Because these state-bounded public spheres are not homogenous in terms of a national identity, but are increasingly multinational in the sense of diaspora, they retain myriad cultural and international linkages to other state-bounded publics elsewhere. Hence the national public sphere, besides the fact that its members cohabitate in the common topical space of a single country, is stripped of much of its national meaning. In this observation, Bohman modifies Kant's notion of a universal community understood as a single community formed by assent to universal principles and universal right. Kant's notion of "one people" becomes "many people," understood as a single group of many groups (or a national sphere of multiple nationalities).

So cosmopolitan public spheres begin within single states as multiculturalism and diaspora create public spheres within nations that have a transnational disposition and transnational linkages to other nations and other public spheres. This warrants special attention because it complicates the assumption that cosmopolitan public spheres are transnational. In other words, it shows to the contrary that cosmopolitan public spheres can form within nations, are integrated into national communities, and even share to some extent in the country's national identity. It is the moral orientation, multicultural self-understanding, and diasporic linkages of the national public sphere that makes it cosmopolitan (the national public sphere can achieve cosmopolitanism if it develops a cosmopolitan disposition). So even if tied by other means to the national framework, the cosmopolitan public sphere exceeds that framework on an ideological terrain and implicates a more complex political identity.

Members of a multicultural or diasporic society may be deeply connected to the nation they live in, but these are not the only connections they have, and such societies must develop a more pluralistic self-understanding, a more complex political identity. If they do not do this, they risk losing any coherent sense of being one society. A serious consideration of such complex political identities is critical to our overarching purpose because it reveals with force and clarity that the national and transnational dichotomy is terribly inadequate. In other words, there is a sense in which a multicultural and/or diasporic cosmopolitan society is concretely and simultaneously both national and transnational. And on a deeper level the members of these societies, especially those who have taken a cosmopolitan disposition as world citizens, while they do not see themselves as being without a nation, nevertheless see themselves both within and beyond national borders. If we cannot understand people as always fitting within one or the other framework, then we cannot understand politics that way. Without getting too far ahead, let us just note here that the national and transnational are often overlapping and imbricated, rather than clear and distinct or at odds.

A major problem with Bohman's argument thus far, which we have seen in other theories as well (Held, Archibugi, and Köhler), is that the transnational public sphere is presented as something that must emerge following the exemplary lead of noble political institutions. Thinking about public spheres in this way is terribly problematic. It not only clashes with the classical conception of the public sphere, but also, it takes for granted the place of indignant antagonisms and noncooperation. That is, rather than assuming fierce disagreement between the public sphere and its addressee, disagreement in which institutions are on the side of reactionary resistances to the critical and forward-thinking opinions of the public sphere, Bohman puts the public sphere on the side of needing to be cultivated toward cosmopolitanism under the tutelage of a critical and forward-thinking institution. The position and methods of nonbourgeois public spheres cannot continue to be neglected. As we have seen, history consists of the stories of excluded and despised groups leveling harsh criticism and demands in public against reluctant and sometimes repressive institutions. Understanding the development of the public sphere as always following the lead of trailblazing institutions neglects the important roles that social movements and public spheres have played in leading the way for institutions.

Bohman says: "Federalism provides world citizens with the institutional means both to make civil society international and to promote effective public opinion."[27] While this is convincing, it is only a part of the story.[28] After all, what the public sphere has shown us is that institutions grow up under the guidance of critical publics, that public spheres may form in imagined communities, and that civil society can be recast outside of the legal parameters of citizenship.

Despite the primacy of institutional leadership, Bohman does admit the power of civil society's public spheres in leading institutions to restructure themselves. That is to say, he does not simply and categorically deny the productive capabilities of the public sphere. The one example he refers to is the civil rights movement and the associated movements that carried public opinion from the streets into the courtrooms and institutional forums for social policy. But to *become* transnational is a different kind of project that must, by definition, precede the possibility for a public sphere to *act* transnationally. Only after it becomes transnational can the public sphere reclaim its function of leading existing institutions and working to create new ones on a transnational terrain. Although institutional leadership will hold the most sway in this transformative process, Bohman contends that, "the public sphere itself will very often be both the terrain and the target of much of their political deliberation."[29] That public spheres may simultaneously address states and other publics as well as their own constituency is essential for the fostering of a complex political identity, of a cosmopolitan self-understanding. Still, for Bohman, without the encouragement of institutions and without invitations to participate, the transnational public sphere will not effectively exist as such, whatever its disposition may be.

I will now turn to a couple of discussions of the transnational public sphere outside of the discussions of cosmopolitanism. We will consider an argument for the transnational public sphere from the standpoint of the concept's viability in critical theory, as well as an argument that reintroduces the importance of social movements. These will represent what I have called "other efforts to transnationalize the public sphere" and will raise some important issues not raised by cosmopolitan theorists. Specifically, we draw from these the structural and other empirical impetuses for rethinking the public sphere transnationally. And yet we will see that a deep confusion regarding the national and transnational frameworks is not only endemic to cosmopolitanism.

Nancy Fraser, in her essay "Transnationalizing the Public Sphere," argues for the need to rethink the national public sphere and to consider the prospects for transnationalizing it. Hers is a critique of the national commitments of Habermas' classical theory. She makes the case that we need to rethink the public sphere transnationally and that we should try to salvage the concept, despite the fact that the original formulation was structurally bound to the national state, and that the public sphere as such cannot be used to address the present manifold of transnational problems. Empirically, she argues, the national framework is being surpassed, and so the public sphere will simply be disempowered unless it is reconstituted on a different scale. In this short essay, Fraser takes up a rather modest task, and so we must be cautious to not overdraw her conclusions. She intends to accomplish two things: (1) to critique the national framework and (2) to begin to imagine what a transnational public sphere might look like.

Interlocutors today communicate across national boundaries and are not members of the same political citizenry from a legal or national standpoint. How do we assess public opinion that is not that of a state-bounded political citizenry? Moreover, why should states be beholden to publics located beyond their national jurisdictions? These questions and concerns are some of the challenges to theorizing a transnational public sphere. Hence, Fraser does not simply assume that public spheres are now transnational, but only that they perhaps could be.

It should be observed from the outset, however, that Fraser frames the problematic in precisely the way that I will contest: "These developments force us to face the hard question: is the concept of the public sphere so thoroughly nationalist in its deep conceptual structure as to be unsalvageable as a critical tool for theorizing the present? Or can the concept be reconstructed within a transnational frame?"[30] She thus presents the national and transnational as alternate frameworks, and, as we shall see, she treats the national framework as an outflanked arena for public spheres in light of transnational crises. Fraser does not deny that single states still represent a level of sovereignty and that they have important functions and powers, but she argues that a new, multilevel structure of sovereignty is emerging that makes the national public sphere clearly insufficient.

She begins by challenging the tacit presuppositions of the national framework in Habermas' early formulation of the public sphere that tied him to seeing the public sphere as strictly state-bounded. She concludes that in the "classical" theory the public sphere was national because it was a "project of modern nation-state democratization."[31] In other words, the national public sphere has been a critical mechanism in the development of intranational democratization and it has expanded to account for the claims and activities of propertyless workers, women, racial minorities, and the poor. The processes of democratization that have integrated these marginalized views into the public sphere have not been wholly triumphant. Even today, the public opinion that weighs most heavily on state decisionmaking is not that of those groups who are still, even if to varying and changing degrees, marginalized within their own national contexts, those who are still struggling for inclusion.

Fraser's problematization of the national framework is achieved through demonstrating how each of classical public sphere theory's national presuppositions no longer holds true. Sovereignty has been reconfigured such that we can no longer think of sovereign power throughout the world as inhering in national governments alone. State sovereignty is still effective regarding many issues of critical importance. However, many of the key mechanisms of the economy are now in the hands of transnational bodies such as the World Bank, IMF, and World Economic Forum, and the economy plays a major role in determining the demographic of stratified societies. Citizenry presents another problem, Fraser explains, since we can no longer just assume that citizenship is national. Increased mobility, migrations, dual citizenships, and multiple residencies, all problematize the assumption that citizenship is national. Also, new technologies increasingly problematize assumptions of a national infrastructure for communication, literature, and language, since the mediums of these now function on a "world scale."

For Fraser, these changes necessitate that we rethink the public sphere as a possible means to compensate for "mismatches in scale" between Westphalian-type states and corporate powers, between nationally bound civil societies and shared international predicaments. If transnational publics could influence multiple states to collectively regulate the corporate powers that exceed them individually, if transnational publics could imagine themselves as members of a world community in solidarity with groups abroad, then these mismatches of scale might be balanced out by institutions in which transnational public opinion gets registered and represented. In these ways, the transnational public sphere could both be imagined and imagined to have emancipatory power.

But in the end, Fraser has no grandiose delusions about the public sphere. She maintains, along with most others, that theorizing and ultimately even forming a transnational public sphere will have its insufficiencies because the public sphere's political function, just as it was the case with the national public sphere, requires reciprocity with institutions of governance. Fraser agrees with Habermas that forming a public sphere is only the first step, for it would then need to bring its will and opinion to bear on institutions and powerholders. Moreover, Fraser has always emphasized the importance of the subaltern public spheres that Habermas has largely neglected.[32] The democratization of transnational politics will, therefore, also depend on the more antagonistic and the more marginal forms of contestation of detrimental globalization processes.

In many ways, I agree with Fraser's analysis of the public sphere. She accurately identifies the nationalist conceptualization of classical public sphere theory and convincingly demonstrates the ways in which such a public sphere has been outflanked by "world scale" problems. As well, Fraser remains critical of both the possibility and the efficacy of a transnational public sphere because she rightly comprehends the difficulty of constituting a clear political function for it. But Fraser frames the problem of the public sphere as the problem of a nationally oriented body with a historically intrastate democratization function. This public sphere, she claims, must face the question of its capacity to transnationalize or else it will face its irrelevancy and obsolescence. But framing the problem in this way overlooks the transnational dimensions of past public spheres, of nonbourgeois public spheres of the past that were simultaneously national and transnational in defining ways (discussed in chapter 3). Beyond this, the transgressive theory that I shall develop ultimately contests the claim that transnationalizing the public sphere is the right answer at all, on strategic and normative grounds, to the problem of an outflanked national public. Rather, the national must be imbricated with the transnational, and the transnational must always consist of compatible national and subnational politics, and, therefore, the whole dichotomy must be abandoned.

Moving on to resolutely evaluate the role of the more antagonistic and more marginal political responses to globalization, let's consider John A. Guidry and Mark Q. Sawyer's theory of "contentious pluralism." Their theory of contentious pluralism is helpful in many ways because it resituates the public sphere uniquely in democratic theory, reinvigorating the normative force of the concepts of the public sphere, of democracy, and of pluralism. In their essay, "Contentious Pluralism: The Public Sphere and Democracy," they make two major conceptual suggestions for our thinking about democracy.

First, they refuse to view democracy and democratization as two separate things, as if democratization is the means to democracy, where the latter is assumed an actually achievable end-state. Democracy, they insist, is *never* finished, so there exists no place on earth where further democratization is no longer possible or no longer necessary: "No democracy in modern times has emerged as a fully inclusionary polity, but democracies as we know them have roots in predemocratic (and even authoritarian) transitional practices. And just as important, no democracy is a finished work."[33]

The second conceptual suggestion they make is that we think about democratizing forces that can be called "contentious pluralism." But what is contentious pluralism? The "contentious" part of the term refers to the means by which nonstate actors contest or dispute ideas, policies, official positions of states, and particular ideologies. Contention, according to Guidry and Sawyer, should be very widely conceived of as all of the ways in which people make demands on authorities, including everything from violent revolution to reasoned debate. The "pluralism" part of the term is what gives the concept its normative commitments. Specifically, contentious pluralism, because it is pluralistic, refers only to contention that contests exclusionary and intolerant practices, and so fascist or sexist or religious fundamentalist politics, in that they oppose pluralism, could not qualify as contentious pluralism.

The definition of contentious pluralism hews closely to the classical conception of a political public sphere in that it refers to efforts emerging from civil society, efforts that are open to all (in principle) and that stress inclusion, to influence and to steer institutions of governance and popular opinion. Guidry and Sawyer point out that contentious pluralism lies "at the heart of the process by which ideas and practices are uprooted and social imaginations extended."[34] It is always concerned with enlarging inclusivity and diminishing exclusivity. Hence, contentious pluralism does, in many ways, precisely what is done by the political public sphere, and it affirms the same principles of inclusion and openness that have always characterized ideal-typical formulations of the public sphere. However, contentious pluralism covers a broader range of activity than takes place within any conventional public spheres in that the former could account for (at least in principle) violent revolutions aimed toward greater inclusion. In this way, contentious pluralism has more in common with nonbourgeois than with bourgeois public spheres.

In light of this and my discussion of nonbourgeois public spheres in chapter 3, the limits of communicative action, in conformity with Habermas' early definition of discourse, clearly exclude any act that could be construed as outside of reasoned debate and possibly coercive. There are many methods for the circulation of political discourses, for the enlivening of new public spheres. Although Guidry and Sawyer consider radical politics, their theory of contentious pluralism is not particularly focused on problems of scale, that is, on the special need for *transnational* contentious pluralism. Three out of four of the cases they consider are very clearly anchored to strictly national democratization processes (poor peoples' movements in England in the eighteenth century, reconstruction in Richmond, Virginia, and the politicization of maternal identity in Argentina).

The only examples they discuss of transnational contentious pluralism are those of the Seattle protest and of the relatively recent meetings of the World Social Forum (WSF). The authors agree that not all of contentious pluralism occurs in the public sphere, but that wherever its primary aim is to circulate discourses, the public sphere is its vehicle. The 1999 Seattle protest against the WTO, for example, made demands that the WTO could not accommodate, especially the demand to open up that institution as a space in which the full gamut of debate could be allowed. The World Social Forum first met in January 2001 in Pôrto Alegre, Brazil. Over fifty thousand people traveled there, from NGOs to activists, to prominent intellectuals, to create the kind of public forum for debate that the WTO could not provide: "When the Seattle protestors were locked out of the WTO meetings, the WSF provided an oppositional space for debate."[35] Alternative spaces are created in which the discussions, participants and participation that have been locked out of major forums can take place. These spaces are both the terrain of public spheres and instances of contentious pluralism—they make a communicative engagement that contests the exclusivity of the official proceedings of their addressees. And this further illustrates why Köhler's public spheres of CSOs is much too narrowly conceived.

Earlier in this chapter we asked *how* transnational public spheres could play the role of democratization and legitimation as the national public spheres of the classical account had. The problem of legitimation on a transnational scale, in terms of the democratic legitimation of transnational institutions that have no formal obligation to transnational publics, has appeared to us largely insurmountable.

But Guidry and Sawyer suggest a way to answer this problem in the context of their broadened understanding of democratization processes. For them, there is no such thing as a political institution that is simply legitimated by favorable public opinion. Institutions can always be more deeply legitimated or further democratized—not all states that we agree to call democratic enjoy the same degree of conferral by public opinion. According to the theory of contentious pluralism and the idea of democracy as a process rather than an end-state, there will always be important exclusions worth contesting wherever one lives in the world. The public disputation and contestation of exclusionary practices, of antidemocratic processes and of unresponsive institutions, brings all of these things under the light of public criticism, furthers deliberation on them inside and outside of designated forums, and is thus an indispensable part of democratization. Inasmuch as institutions take up and respond constructively to the contentious pluralism of the public sphere, they are conferred a corollary degree of legitimation. This holds true no less on the transnational than on the national scale. Hence, the scrutiny of public spheres carries a function in and of itself—it reveals problems and considers solutions, bringing attention to political problems heretofore unnoticed.

In light of the foregoing discussion of cosmopolitanism and other efforts to transnationalize the public sphere, I shall sum up what we have learned about transnational publics and the structure of a politics ample enough and able to effectively address the problems of globalization outlined in chapter 4. First is a point about political identity and community. We have seen that the material of local and national political solidarities, the stuff that both binds and rouses state-bounded public spheres to collective action—the thick stuff (in Walzer's terms)—can often be abstracted. It can be boiled down to more minimalist principles and utilized as the basis for political solidarity transnationally. Our feeling of a common political identity can work across boundaries, and the moral principles that underwrite local struggles can also underwrite a larger sense of struggling together with others who we may never meet in person. Living in multicultural and diasporic societies, bolstered by a sense of sharing the risks of a globalizing world, can lead to a pluralistic self-understanding. The emergence of such a "complex identity," as Thompson calls it, is a critical part of any political project that seeks to bring us closer to cosmopolitanism. The more we come to view people who live radically different lives and who live in other parts of the world as our fellow citizens, the more we create the basis for a transnational civil society, and the more viable is the transnational public sphere.

Second is a point about political institutions. Governments manage only the aspects of the economy that they retain jurisdiction over—managing deficits, national budgets, spending on social programs, and taxation. But so much of the economic activity that has the farthest-reaching effect takes place beyond the regulatory powers of any one state. Existing institutions cannot hope to reign in what is called the global economy, to regulate its agents, to constrain it to the political will of people unless they reform themselves transnationally or are subsidized by the powers of new transnational institutions. And this is not only true for the economy. Dealing effectively with environmental crises and the AIDS pandemic, for example, also calls for the attention of transnational political institutions. The accounts we have read emphasize how important it is that institutions have a cosmopolitan disposition, how important it is that they are beholden to the communities they affect transnationally, or to those they seek to represent and shield. In fact, the most detrimental effects of globalization processes stem from too sharp a differentiation between peoples, subordinating the interests of "others" to (rather than reconciling them with) the interests of powerholders. Some of the authors we have read believe that new cosmopolitan transnational institutions are so important that much needed cosmopolitan transnational political identities and political communities will only emerge following the lead and the comportment of institutions.

Whether a transnational public sphere forms first or forms later on, it is always a necessary development. Cosmopolitanism, together with the work of Fraser, and Guidry and Sawyer, presents us with the raw material for a picture of a transnational public sphere made up of multifarious efforts and organizations, evolving from civil societies all over the world. Public spheres circulate debates wherever forums exist for their input (Köhler), and wherever such forums don't exist, public spheres find ways to create alternative spaces to give voice to their opinion and will (Guidry and Sawyer).[36] Wherever the transnational public sphere has been seen, its political function has been harder to see, largely because it has been harder to find an addressee obligated to represent and respond to it. The transnational public sphere has seemed sometimes weak and insufficient, and mainly as a *potentially* vital means by which legitimation and democratization could occur in the world of transnational politics (Bohman, Fraser).

Finally is a point about what now appears to us a clearly inadequate national framework (Thompson, Archibugi, Bohman, Fraser). The national framework as we have discussed it is simply not enough, and whether or not it takes place through cosmopolitanism or by some other means, a transnational politics must be developed in order to effectively interact with and regulate globalization. But what does that mean for the national public sphere and the national framework for political action? None of the theorists have said that the national framework must be categorically supplanted, as it remains the central arena for so many important political struggles. However, when it comes to today's regime of transnational problems, there is no consensus on what role, if any, the national framework still plays. In addition to this confusion, the national/transnational dichotomy has been retained rather consistently throughout. That is, all of the varying arguments fundamentally agree that there are two separate zones for political action. Even where it has been argued that both are necessary, the national and transnational frameworks have been reified as clear and distinct. Other times, they have been pitted against each other.

On the whole, it is fair to say that there is serious uncertainty and doubt about whether or not the national public sphere in particular and the national framework in general could play any part in negotiating transnational crises. Habermas too has come to grapple with these issues and has chosen to abandon the nationalist conceptual structure of his original public sphere theory. Instead, he has made numerous efforts to illustrate and to argue for a transnational public sphere anchored in what he calls "cosmopolitan solidarity." Yet, perhaps more than anyone else, Habermas has taken the route of assuming the national/transnational dichotomy *and* a bitter antipathy between the two frameworks. I will now explore his new position and its failings.

Habermas' Transnational Public Sphere: A Turn Against the National Framework

Habermas has revised his early notion of the public sphere. Here, I assess his more recent formulations of the public sphere in a number of key texts, and specifically, his conception of the transnational public sphere in *The Postnational Constellation: Political Essays*. In this section, I will show that and how Habermas brings all of the implicit and/or decentered assumptions we have considered about the national/transnational dichotomy into sharp relief. His new theorization on the public sphere both underlines and emphasizes a heuristic distinction between the national and transnational frameworks as if it were an actual matter of fact. Furthermore, Habermas makes the antipathy between thick and thin a deeper and more central concern. He thus enacts what I refer to as "a turn against the national framework," a turn that places all referential discussions of his new work, as well as his work itself, rather far out of the reach of achieving a much needed and thoroughly different understanding of the national and transnational frameworks. Such a rethinking of these frameworks, I will argue, is both better suited to actually existing politics and necessary for any satisfying political response to the problems we have been grappling with.

How does Habermas answer the question of whether or not there is any role for the national public sphere and the national framework in a new era of transnational politics? In short, he argues that the national framework for political action, and the resiliency of national public spheres are among the greatest impediments to transnationalizing politics, to bringing politics up to scale with the global market, so that the two may once again intersect. Habermas makes both of the theoretical turns I want to reject. First, he insists on seeing and sharpening a national/transnational dichotomy, and second, he argues that the national framework is antagonistically related to the transnational framework and that the former must be supplanted by the latter. To these two turns I will argue that Habermas treats a useful heuristic distinction between the national and transnational frameworks as a distinction that actually exists in the world, and that he maintains a false antithesis of the transnational to the national.[37] This is significant because these turns effectively preempt explanation of a wide range of actually existing political action (some of which will be discussed in chapter 6, and more of which will be discussed in part III). And in the end, Habermas' theory, because it insists on this false dichotomy and antipathy, obstructs the development of a new theorization based on the insights of a politics that defies both.

Habermas remains committed to the basic ideas of the public sphere discussed in chapters 2 and 3, in particular that political public spheres are a means of democratic legitimation. Even where they appear to be unlikely and weak, they at least retain that critical potentiality. Ideally, public spheres do more than determine the democratic legitimacy of the state; their communicative power would be channeled ongoing into institutions, influencing decision and law making, guiding powerholders in practice. In order to work with these commitments today, Habermas must retract his 1962 conclusion that a culture-debating has been completely depoliticized into a culture-consuming. He has made this retraction himself:

> In fine, my diagnosis of a unilinear development from a politically active public to one withdrawn into a bad privacy, from a "culture-debating to a culture-consuming public," is too simplistic. At the time, I was too pessimistic about the resisting power and above all the critical potential of a pluralistic,

internally much differentiated mass public whose cultural us-
ages have begun to shake off the constraints of class.[38]

Habermas now maintains that "consuming" publics still
possess a vital legitimating and democratizing potentiality
whether or not it is ever realized. So, the first important distinction of Habermas' new public sphere theory is that it rejects the
culminating argument about the structural transformation.

Mike Hill and Warren Montag, in their essay "What Was,
What Is, the Public Sphere? Post–Cold War Reflections," make
some very concise and clear summations of the major shifts in
Habermas' thinking. They point out that discussion of the public sphere in the 1990s, after the end of the Cold War and the fall
of the Berlin Wall, is necessarily different. Regarding Habermas'
ideas about the national and transnational frameworks, Hill and
Montag summarize that

> while Habermas initially saw the public sphere as a "national"
> phenomenon, both belonging to and helping to define distinct
> national cultures, he has followed the argument to its logical
> conclusion and posited the existence of an international public
> sphere, the global totality not simply of national public
> spheres, themselves composed of multiple spheres, but also of
> transnational public spheres. Globalization, whatever its chal-
> lenges, is therefore the bearer of a genuine universalism that
> insofar as it is communicative in its essence transcends the
> merely material differences between nations. Indeed, the fall of
> the Soviet Union has ended the atmosphere of permanent civil
> war that characterized international politics for most of the
> twentieth century.[39]

This serves as a fair and succinct preface to the following, more
careful analysis of Habermas' transnational public sphere.

In *Between Facts and Norms*, Habermas does not yet develop
a theory of transnational public spheres, but he outlines the viability of the concept beyond national borders. In chapter 8 of that
book, he updates his conceptions of civil society and the political public sphere in light of criticism and current events. He
maintains that if we take the state apparatus as our basic unit of
political power, then the political public sphere is on the "input"
side of political process. Whatever the state apparatus does with

this input is the "output" side of political process. This is essentially a restatement of the original relationship between society and state, as negotiated through the public sphere. The input can come in different modes, by way of siege or sluice. In siege mode, the public sphere forcibly and antagonistically makes its demands, argues with the state, attempts to overwhelm it, to pressure it to comply. In sluice mode, the public sphere works more felicitously and cooperatively with the state, taking advantage of any open channels for feeding back that are available to it.[40] For Habermas, the sluice model is more tactical and creative than the siege model, as it must work hard to frame and thematize problems strategically and effectively. The siege model on the other hand resorts to shaming powerholders, or vigorous protest, things that may be effective but that are anchored in a kind of desperation. Siege is not a sincere attempt to initiate an orderly dialogue—it is, according to Habermas, less communicative. Although Habermas' preference is (like Held's, Archibugi's, and Köhler's) for the sluice model, it is at least refreshing that the siege mode is here acknowledged as a way that the public sphere functions, despite its relative distance from ideal-typical discourse.

Transnationally, Habermas explains, only relatively weak publics can exist. Their ties are implicit, or they lie in a potential solidarity that must be made more and more tangible. But because communication among strangers *does* take place over great distances, Habermas accepts that public spheres are linked by transnational communicative connections. In agreement with Walzer's arguments, the national public sphere is presented as bound by thicker principles and relationships, whereas the transnational public sphere is presented as bound by thinner ones. Thick or thin, the capacity of any public sphere to solve problems must never be overdrawn, Habermas cautions. Even transnationally, a public sphere may have important functions on the "input side" of the political system, but it is ultimately up to the system to act on this input. The public sphere's primary function is a kind of warning mechanism that must

> amplify the pressure of problems, that is, not only detect and identify problems but also convincingly and *influentially* thematize them, furnish them with possible solutions, and

dramatize them in such a way that they are taken up and dealt with by parliamentary complexes. Besides the "signal" function, there must be an effective problematization.[41]

Even though Habermas begins to articulate the contours of public spheres abstracted from physical assembly, he continues to emphasize the kind of topical common space that was so important in the salons and coffee houses of the early bourgeois public sphere. Concrete assembly in particular locales, actual physical gathering, is always important for Habermas because the kind of unmediated communicative action possible in topical common spaces promises to be more nuanced and, in general, more conducive for the production of ideal-typical discourse. One can see Habermas' continued emphasis on locale even in his consideration of transnational public spheres with thinner linkages. He maintains that effective political public spheres must develop "out of the communication taking place among *those who are potentially affected*."[42]

This claim is interesting because the qualification of "potentially affected" is stressed (italics are Habermas') and yet it is left without any further definition. But does Habermas really mean for the qualification of "potentially affected" to stress locale and topical common space? According to cosmopolitanism, those who think of themselves as world citizens are "potentially affected" by issues of grave concern to others. And Habermas, as we shall see below, is indeed a cosmopolitan. By insisting on the significance of the "potentially affected," Habermas wants to preserve the meaning and importance of identifying communities of shared risk, and not to abstract the public sphere from the actual problems people face.

That we can congregate and communicate outside of physical assembly, in a virtual community of "scattered readers, listeners, or viewers linked by public media"[43] is an ever-increasing reality that must be taken into account. *Between Facts and Norms*, originally published in 1992, saw just the early stages of an electronic communications technology that made it possible for scattered readers, listeners, and viewers to respond to each other in real time. Such communications technologies have only been improved and made more accessible since then. Media and communications technologies have always been a major focus for Habermas. And even though he retracted the conclusion that commercial media has led to the depoliticization of the public sphere, he maintains that mass communication has transformed and continues to transform the public sphere.

Much of this transformation has been toward the transnationalization of the public sphere. After the Cold War, technological communication networks, assisted by the satellite technology of the mid-1980s, managed to produce a "reading" or "viewing" public televisionally. This has mostly had the effect of weakening existing public spheres worldwide, but ironically, it has established a new world public sphere, even if not one formed by its own initiative.

Even under these less-than-ideal conditions, Habermas now maintains that there are limits to the extent to which public spheres can be manipulated. The pessimism of *Structural Transformation* has been left behind. While public opinion can certainly be manipulated, Habermas insists that it cannot be bought or blackmailed. A public sphere cannot be manufactured. It produces a collective will and opinion only and always *"out of itself,"* and though it may be subjected to influence and bias, it has sufficient internal checks and balances to keep it, more or less, on a rational-critical course.[44] None of this is to say that the public sphere is not mobilized by biases—or that it is not infiltrated by outside interests that seek to manipulate it. It is only to say that the totalizing kind of control that was characteristic of Adorno and Horkheimer's culture industry thesis, a thesis that held great sway in *Structural Transformation* is rejected here. Public opinion can neither be so easily nor so wholly usurped. If it is eroded and misdirected, it will regain its own bearing soon enough. Habermas maintains this position largely because there has been a growing mass media aimed at a greater mobilization of bias, which has nevertheless failed to eliminate the public's harsh criticism of the powerholders who wield such influence.

So, Habermas now acknowledges, public spheres do exist transnationally and they retain a vital political function (even if this function remains underdeveloped at a given time and place). Habermas ultimately redefines the public sphere more abstractly: "It represents a highly complex network that branches out into a multitude of overlapping international, national, regional, local, and subcultural arenas."[45] In this short statement Habermas admits that the public sphere of public spheres includes national and transnational public spheres and even, presumably, those subcultural ones that were excluded from his earlier study. He wants to speak now of varying levels of public sphere:

> Moreover, the public sphere is differentiated into levels according to the density of communication, organizational complexity, and range—from the *episodic* publics found in taverns, coffee houses, or on the streets, through the *occasional* or "arranged" publics of particular presentations and events, such as theater performances, rock concerts, party assemblies, or church congresses; up to the *abstract* public sphere of isolated readers, listeners, and viewers scattered across large geographic areas, or even around the globe, and brought together only through the mass media.[46]

What is immediately notable about these three levels of public sphere is that the *episodic* and *occasional* are more firmly situated in topical common space, whereas the *abstract* is the only one inclined to characteristically cross boundaries with ease and efficiency. The *abstract*, transnational public sphere depends on the mass media. Thus, the mass media appears in a new light. We have seen throughout the historical development of the concept of the public sphere that the mass media was the advancement most likely to undermine the public sphere. From Mills and Arendt on the use of media technologies in World War II to Habermas' association of the growth of commercial media with the depoliticization of the public sphere, it has appeared to us as something that, without regulation, could take over the public sphere in the most destructive ways. Today, the mass media is one of the key means by which public spheres can form beyond the jurisdiction of nations.

Whether *episodic, occasional*, or *abstract*, if they are to have any political function, public spheres still require responsive institutions. That is, "public influence is transformed into communicative power only after it passes through the filters of the institutionalized *procedures* of democratic opinion- and will-formation and enters through parliamentary debates into legitimate lawmaking."[47] Indeed, the concepts of legitimation and legitimation crisis can ultimately be transferred to the transnational stage. A public sphere that forms transnationally must find an institution or institutions to address in order to become political. And for a transnational public sphere to be successful, the institutions that it addresses must incorporate the public sphere's opinion and will into their decisionmaking. This part has perhaps been obvious enough, but it is more important to notice that the flipside of this classical model also remains true: If powerholders functioning at the transnational level, whether they are corporations, courts, federations, or financial institutions, are not legitimated by the approval of public opinion, and if they are seen to be part of a transboundary political system, then "the political system is pulled into a whirlpool of legitimation deficits and steering deficits that reinforce one another."[48]

Habermas' thinking about the transnational public sphere has since evolved under the guidance of his own cosmopolitanism. In his essay "Kant's Idea of Perpetual Peace, with the Benefit of Two Hundred Years' Hindsight" he returns, as Bohman did, to Kant's essay on "Perpetual Peace." Habermas attempts to reformulate Kant's ideas on cosmopolitanism and transboundary politics for the present era. He finds in Kant an idea for a transnational, cosmopolitan public sphere, which with the benefit of two hundred years' hindsight, is crucial for thinking through the problems of our time. Of course, Kant's ideas on the matter were no less available to Habermas in 1962 when *Structural Transformation* came out. This would appear an insubstantial quip were it not for the fact that it underlines the argument I made in part I, not merely that this part of Kant's thinking was left wholly out of *Structural Transformation*, but that Habermas worked to develop a strictly national public sphere to the exclusion of contrary historical and theoretical developments (transnational nonbourgeois public spheres provided evidence of contrary historical development, and Kant's cosmopolitan position represents a contrary theoretical development).

In fact, Habermas notes that the concept of a transnational cosmopolitan public sphere was, already in Kant, identified as one of three major components in the project of building a cosmopolitan order: "Kant identifies three naturally occurring tendencies which meet reason halfway and which explain why a federation of nations could be in the enlightened self-interest of states: the peaceful nature of republics, the power of world trade to create communal ties, and the function of the political public sphere."[49] A cosmopolitan federation of nations is an ideal goal, and for Kant (and Habermas agrees) it requires as a precondition the development of a functional political public sphere on a global scale. Habermas hews closely to Bohman here, following Kant, and taking the federation of nations to be the institutional aim of a cosmopolitan politics. Habermas speaks of how pre-scient Kant's thinking was, in that he was unable to anticipate electronic mass media, and yet was able to imagine a global public sphere. In fact, Habermas suggests that it is probably because of what Kant could *not* have known about the future course of human communication that made it possible for him to so optimistically envision a global public sphere that is finally, over two hundred years later, actually emergent in the world.

Still, I contend that it is not tenable to say that transnational public spheres are only now becoming visible. Habermas disagrees, maintaining that the "first events that actually drew the attention of the world public sphere, and polarized its opinion on a global scale, were the wars in Vietnam and the Persian Gulf."[50] We have seen, however, that woman and universal suffrage movements, as well as communism (also examples such as the abolition of slavery and the French Revolution) not only drew the attention of a world public sphere, but also were highly polarizing issues. Yet Habermas insists, which would justify his postponement of any consideration of the transnational public sphere, that it is only recently emergent and can be seen most clearly in the UN conferences, which he calls "world summits," that try to pressure governments by appealing to world opinion.

The summits Habermas is speaking of are of the variety we have called *occasional*. Still, there is no transnational public sphere that vigorously sustains itself and that applies ongoing pressure in between such scheduled special events. That is, the most politically effective transnational public spheres do not yet exist in and of themselves, but only in particular forums and of smaller bodies.

One should not overlook the fact that this temporary public attention is still issue-specific and channeled through the established structures of national public spheres. Supporting structures are needed to stabilize communication between spatially distant participants, who exchange contributions at the same times on the same themes with equal relevance. In this sense there is not yet a global public sphere, let alone a European one, as urgently needed as it is.[51]

This marks an interesting juncture in Habermas' thinking about a transnational public sphere. *Abstract* public spheres have not managed to sustain themselves or to secure official channels of influence outside the context of world summits. As it was in Köhler's account, national public spheres come together in transnational forums, but retain their national agendas and their national support structures.

Habermas differs from Köhler though, because he is more critical of opportunistically constructing and then disassembling the transnational public sphere for special occasions. As such, the transnational public sphere is not really an *actor* in itself, but more a kind of *activity* of national public spheres. Public spheres that form transnationally retain a vital political potentiality, but they have no structure in place for a continual presence and ongoing activity. The circuitry of communication utilized by national public spheres sometimes takes place on a transnational terrain, but that does not mean that a properly transnational, functionally political public sphere has been formed.

Habermas seems to take for granted the *abstract* public spheres that work in tandem with the *occasional* and *episodic* ones. In between UN-led world summits, for example, political discourse on the issues discussed in those forums continues to circulate, and even ends up at he basis of more grassroots political action and social movements. In between occasions for sluice input, discussion continues and input by siege is attempted. New communications technologies and the increased ease of distributing and maintaining correspondences worldwide have effectively placed a good deal of the exchange of arguments, planning, and organization beyond national borders. These conduits of communication *are* support structures, and the transnational public sphere depends on their effective use. This is easier said than done (more on this difficulty in chapter 9). Habermas emphasizes the need for these communicative and other institutional support structures that are in no way rooted in the national framework. He maintains that a coalition of national public spheres, essentially Köhler's idea of a cosmopolitan transnational public sphere, is guaranteed to be insufficient. In this, we see the very beginnings of what I am calling Habermas' abandonment of the national framework.

The impetus for this turn is exacerbated by the fact that nationalisms flare up in the face of efforts to build a support structure beyond the national framework. These "flare-ups" are rooted in reactionary and ethnonationalist feelings about having to lose a sense of national belonging, national identity, and even patriotism. Efforts to move from an international (among nations) to a transnational (beyond nations) scale appear hostile to nationalist thinking: "The contemporary world situation can be understood in the best-case scenario as a period of transition from international to cosmopolitan law, but many other indications seem to support a regression to nationalism."[52] This reveals the first premise of a tautology between a bad kind of nationalism and all resistant senses of connectivity to locale and contestations of trends that globalize political culture and political identity. "Regression to nationalism" ends up characterizing all clinging to national political projects and identities in the face of the problems of globalization. Thus, the national framework appears a stubborn and dangerous impediment that must be overcome.

In the spirit of cosmopolitanism, Habermas favors thinning our more maximal moral and political solidarities—as Thompson has argued, doing so is necessary for cosmopolitanism. Our thick political and moral communities cannot be sufficiently cosmopolitan. These communities must shift their self-understanding to thinner political and moral principles, and only then can a transnational public sphere be created. Thus, the thick (the stuff of national solidarities) and the thin (the stuff of transnational solidarities) appear to be at odds with each other. Moreover, because of a conflated association of the national with the ethnonational, the thick appears to thrive in an irrational, emotional, and uncritical state, in a reactionary pride in one's community of birth. On the other hand, the thin appears to thrive in rational-critical deliberation about shared risks and political solidarity. One might imagine a patriotic, national chauvinism rooted in a communitarian identity (like that mentioned in our discussion of Thompson's essay) defending against a reasonable and measured call to transition from rootedness in an exclusive and narrow regional identity toward a more inclusive cosmopolitan identity. In the most exaggerated picture, the national/transnational dichotomy looks like the dichotomy between irrationality and reason.

Habermas repeats the common commitment of liberal philosophy to the ideal of having large and inclusive political units. Indeed, Habermas maintains what leftists have generally believed throughout history, "that larger and more inclusive political units were always better. So many nations had lived together in peace under imperial rule: why couldn't they continue to live together under the aegis of social democracy?"[53] Habermas concludes by saying that the politics of human rights can only prevail "through the cosmopolitan transformation of the state of nature among states into a legal order."[54] Invoking Kant's idea of the state of nature among states, Habermas suggests a larger state of states. He is not thinking of a summit of states here, but more along the lines of the European Union, of a new political institution whose scale is not *of* but is *beyond* states.

Habermas maintains that human rights could serve as the axis of leverage between a transnational public sphere and emergent or already existing transnational institutions. Taken up by the public sphere, the definition of and demand for human rights could provide a critical means of the legitimation of institutions of governance. Habermas recommends that a constitutional commitment to a universal declaration of human rights could provide the basis for the legitimacy of the authority of states.

In his essay, "On Legitimation through Human Rights," Habermas argues for the cross-cultural viability of human rights against recurring questions about the imposition of Western morality and political conceptions on the ancient and tribal cultures of Asia and Africa, and in light of the challenges posed by fundamentalist resistances to modernization. This antagonism,

Habermas maintains, will ultimately be dissolved by the modernization of these regions. He argues that social modernization processes around the world will inevitably lead other, non-Western cultures and countries toward formulating principles of human rights in the same way they were originally formulated in Europe. In other words, the principles of human rights were not formulated in Europe because they were European ideas. They were formulated in Europe for the same reason they were formulated in other Western countries—because of a high level of social modernization and economic development. The argument seems to be that the principles of human rights are as cross-cultural and universalizable as other cultures and countries are open to and prepared for them—that a human rights discourse grows in proportion to a peoples' evolution from tribal life to more integrated, larger, and more modern social coexistence.

At least one problem with Habermas' argument here is that he situates all resistances to a more transnational political order (in this case a constitutional democracy with a foundational commitment to a declaration of human rights) as being tied to various conditions of underdevelopment and the fundamentalisms of outdated and dangerous cultural and tribal traditions. This argument is frighteningly overdrawn and bears a precarious resemblance to colonialist thinking. Not only is it too categorical a characterization of such cultures and traditions, but also even where it is not so overdrawn, resistances to a more transnational order are often rooted in other, less malignant reasoning. It is important to remember, for example, that social modernization often means "Westernization," and that with Westernization many aspects of the lifeways of traditional cultures are placed in jeopardy, some of these lifeways are actually worth fighting to preserve, and many aspects of modernization may be worth fighting to stave off.[55]

Although we can now see why Habermas pushes so resolutely for a move beyond the thickness and resiliency of locale, I have not yet fully explicated the heart of the problem. The very heart of the matter is to be found in his essay on "The European Nation-State and the Pressures of Globalization," as well as in his *The Postnational Constellation: Political Essays*. There we see more clearly how Habermas overextends and presses too hard on the heuristic distinction between the national and transnational frameworks.

As we saw in chapter 4, Habermas is convinced that globalization has outflanked political power as it is embodied within the national framework. He maintains that there are essentially two ways to respond to resultant legitimation crises. First, there is the *defensive* response. The defensive response is sort of like "damage control" against the detrimental impacts of capitalist globalization. National governments, as well as the CSOs within them, may defend a rainforest and other natural resources, may defend land and even values against the threatening encroachments of globalization. This kind of work, even if done to its utmost limits, will not reverse any of the globalization processes it defends against, though it may stave off some of the undesirable impacts. Second, there is the *offensive* response. An offensive response attempts to expand the scale of the political action of institutions as well as of civil societies (i.e., the action of public spheres) to a transnational scale—to extend political powers beyond national borders into a network of supranational regulatory force that could subordinate an increasingly unfettered global capitalism to the fetters of principles of social and economic justice. Habermas prefers the offensive route, however necessary defensive action may be in the meantime.

And I would agree with Habermas that the nation-state is simply not an effective power in the present era of globalization (as that era has been defined in chapter 4).

> The attempt to resolve the dilemma between disarming welfare-state democracy or rearming the nation-state, however, leads us to look to larger political units and transnational systems that could compensate for the nation-state's functional losses in a way that need not snap the chain of democratic legitimation. . . . Politics will succeed in "catching up" with globalized markets only if it eventually becomes possible to create an infrastructure capable of sustaining a global domestic politics without uncoupling it from democratic processes of legitimation.[56]

Habermas invokes the European Union paradigmatically, as an exemplary structural achievement. The European Union's two shortcomings are that it *does not* engage globalized markets with nearly enough regulative force and that there is no European public sphere making such demands for it to do so. At bottom, it is struggling with its own legitimation crisis. However, the example of the European Union illustrates one way to create an offensive mode of engagement with globalization processes, to compensate for the difference in scale that now separates politics from the activity of globalized markets.

The European Union is only potentially exemplary for Habermas because it has far too weak a commitment to social and economic justice, its redistributive aims ranging from nonexistent to grossly inadequate. A transnational European public sphere comes into play in answering the question, how could the European Union come to act more forcefully on issues of social and economic justice? Habermas believes that a strong, cosmopolitan European public sphere, something that does not exist as of yet, *would* make the European Union a stronger and more cosmopolitan institution. Indeed, in analyzing the weaknesses of the European Union, Habermas continually returns to the concept of the public sphere, calling for a European solidarity and public sphere that does not exist. The European Union needs the kind of legitimacy and the kind of political pressure that could only come from a strong public sphere. Neoliberals are much more satisfied with the European Union. I outlined in chapter 2 the economic policies and international trade agreements that were the precursors to the European Union. The softening of national border impediments within Europe to the flow of capital represents a welcome development to neoliberals. But for progressives and cosmopolitans the European Union represents only a vital potentiality. In it lies the basic structure of a strong transnational counterpower to the unrestrained powers of global capitalism.

Habermas maintains in *The Postnational Constellation* that

> the economic problems besetting affluent societies can be explained by a structural transformation of the world economic system, a transformation characterized by the term "globalization" . . . this transformation so radically reduces nation-states' capacity for action that the options remaining open to them are not sufficient to shield their populations from the undesired social and political consequences of a transnational economy.[57]

Not only is the nation-state's jurisdiction and sovereignty outflanked, but also the possibilities for sufficiently enlarging its capacity as such are not very hopeful. The fact that the traditional unit of political power has been so markedly superseded by globalization underwrites the meaning of the term "postnational." In other words, we now see the emergence of a whole problematic that makes it possible for us to speak of a historical period and a score of corollary problems *after* the sovereign role of Westphalian states.

The concept of "postnational," in fact, requires Habermas to abandon the national framework, and if not totally, at least to some significant degree. As I explained in the introduction to part II, postnational not only implies a scale beyond the national framework, but also a world-historical moment in time when a new era can accurately be described as the one that follows the era marked by the sovereignty of nation-states. In discussing a postnational world Habermas must, by the internal logic of the concept, turn away from the outflanked national framework. It is worth noting here that Marx was the first to observe a world-historical triumph over nationalism in the Industrial Revolution and free trade. Yet for Marx, while capitalism and bourgeois society appeared as harbingers of a *substantively* postnational era, *formally*, political contests still made sense within the national framework. For Habermas, the transition to a politics beyond the national framework must be both formal and substantive.

The European Union's failure to lead civil society to displace its national identifications with transnational European identifications has demonstrated to Habermas a plain fact that Bohman should not have failed to observe: Transnational institutions will by no means simply lead the way. On the contrary, Habermas insists that institutions will have to follow the lead, under the pressure, of a demanding civil society, of hardworking CSOs, and of activists and social movements. Institutions can only create the shell of a supranational political power (formal), but in addition to their need for democratic legitimacy, they also need to be led by the will and opinion of the society they act on behalf of (substantive). Civil societies cannot be expected to follow the lead of institutions, and institutions established for reasons other than ensuring social and economic justice cannot be expected to act as if they were, at least not without pressure and leadership from outside.

For Habermas, bringing politics up to scale for an offensive engagement with global capitalism has much to do with the political consciousness, self-understanding, and solidarity of peoples.

> Thus the decisive question is whether the civil society and the political public sphere of increasingly large regimes can foster the consciousness of an obligatory cosmopolitan solidarity. Only the transformed consciousness of citizens, as it imposes itself in areas of domestic policy, can pressure global actors to change their own self-understanding sufficiently to begin to see themselves as members of an international community who are compelled to cooperate with one another, and hence to take one another's interests into account. And this change in perspective from "international relations" to a world domestic policy cannot be expected from ruling elites until the population itself, on the basis of its own understanding of its own best interests, rewards them for it.[58]

Here we see not only a clear political function for a transnational political public sphere, but also a leadership role. The public sphere must work to rework the self-understandings of civil society and of ruling elites, must work to rework political consciousness, must work to rework the way people and governments understand the detrimental effects of globalization in communities we do and do not live in.

Ultimately, the forces that Habermas has traditionally neglected are finally assigned a major role in the most pressing political project of the millennium. NGOs and social movements are here acknowledged as key mechanisms of fostering cosmopolitan self-consciousness and cosmopolitan solidarity, of bringing the interests of other people into view. Institutions that purport democratic legitimacy are more likely to pass the policies, write the laws, and follow the initiatives that resonate widely with their populations: "Thus the first addressees for this 'project' are not governments. They are social movements and nongovernmental organizations; the active members of a civil society that stretches beyond national borders."[59] It is a rare but revealing occasion for Habermas to single out the special importance of social movements and NGOs in creating an offensive and ultimately institutional supranational power. But because the European Union has remained mainly a shell of potentiality for the kind of normative political response to globalization that is called for, Habermas acknowledges the importance of the political action of civil society beyond national borders.

This provides a good piece of the picture of what transnational democratization processes could look like. To make transnational politics more democratic, to create means of democratic legitimation for transnational institutions, we must rethink democracy outside of the conventional electoral models used in single states. Globalization processes produce a democratic deficit because they take place beyond democracy as it occurs as a state-bounded process. Yet the various actions in the sluice and siege modes of bringing opinion and will to bear on transnational institutions and on communities around the world, along with transformations in political self-understandings, are, taken together, very much of the activity of democratization in the realm of transnational politics.

But there are resistances to this progress, Habermas argues. Nationalism has flared up, for example, under the development of a federated Europe and in the face of more cosmopolitan political self-understandings, and this nationalist reaction gets in the way of European citizens learning "to mutually recognize one another as members of a common political existence beyond national borders . . . redistribution policies must be borne by a Europe-wide will-formation, and this cannot happen without a basis of solidarity."[60] Hence, the solidarity required to form a strong European public sphere faces an intensification of nationalist feeling that was more latent and dissipated beforehand. National identity is being rigorously challenged by migrations and the subsequent emergences of multicultural societies. Anger and distrust of anything foreign, of other faiths and "races," of marginalized groups—all of this has seen resurgence even in prosperous societies and sometimes takes a violent turn. All kinds of ethnonational hostility, previously less visible, bubbles again into full view.[61] The national public sphere, understood classically as a relatively homogenous collective of political civil society of national citizens, is now bitterly contested by an increasingly heterogeneous internal population formed by migrations and multiple citizenships. The prospects for a postnational cosmopolitan public sphere, already forming in the cosmopolitanism of domestic populations, appear an irreconcilable antithesis to the national public sphere of the classical account. The postnational cosmopolitan public sphere calls for an antinationalist and radical pluralist politics, whereas the national public sphere remains, among other things, the defensive domain of chauvinistic nationalism.

Habermas does not simply laud the internal fragmentation of domestically homogenous civil societies. The breakup of cultural homogeneity within states has both a positive and a negative side.

> Even if the majority of emigrants never even reach the borders of OECD societies, these countries have already witnessed a considerable change in the ethnic, religious, and cultural composition of their populations, through migrations desired, migrations tolerated, or migrations unsuccessfully resisted. Nor is it just traditional immigration countries such as the United States or the old colonial nations like Britain or France that are affected by patterns of migration. Despite harsh regulations on immigration arrayed as a protective cordon around Fortress Europe (in violation of basic constitutional rights, in the case of the Federal Republic of Germany), all European nations now find themselves on the path toward a multicultural society. Naturally, this pluralization of life forms will not be without frictions.[62]

The positive side of this we have already stressed, that multiculturalism can loosen up the population toward a cosmopolitan disposition and create an international constituency already within the borders of a single nation (as Bohman illustrated best), increasing our capacity to see ourselves in community with "others." But this fragmentation has a negative side too, which has to do with one of the major causes of the breakup of cultural homogeneity—globalization. True, globalization has weakened and fragmented national identity and homogenous political culture even in the face of reaction, but it often does so by introducing a new homogenization. Mass consumption, mass communication, and mass tourism send the cultural products of a mass culture all over the globe. The breakup of cultural homogeneity in light of mass culture does mean a cross-cultural infiltration to some extent, but it also often means the supplanting of an old homogeneity with a new one.

In the end, Habermas returns to the idea of cosmopolitan solidarity, which he thinks can negotiate all of the deep tensions of culture and globalization we have discussed. Simply put, solidarity with strangers is the starting point for all of the transformations Habermas argues for. National consciousness and national civic solidarity, Habermas points out, originally evolved among strangers, and so there is no reason why it cannot also be formed among strangers transnationally. Cosmopolitan solidarity binds us by thin over thick and is the prerequisite for a transnational public sphere. Yet, despite Habermas' concluding emphases on NGOs, social movements, and the solidarity of peoples, we must never lose sight of the fact that, for him, it is ultimately the behavior and comportment of decisionmaking institutions that will matter the most. Even with a

> functioning public sphere, the quality of discussion, accessibility, and the discursive structure of opinion- and will-formation: all of these could never entirely replace conventional procedures for decision-making and political representation. But they do tip the balance, from the concrete embodiments of sovereign will in persons, votes, and collectives to the procedural demands of communicative and decision-making processes.[63]

In the final analysis, then, the political function of a transnational public sphere, as it was with the national one, is still to be achieved in a regular and dependable relationship of influence between the public sphere and institutions of governance.

What is seemingly intractable in Habermas' updated notion of the public sphere is that national public spheres, strengthened by nationalisms, are pitted against the transnational, that they serve as impediments to cosmopolitan solidarity, and therefore must be superceded by a broader public opinion and a broader civic solidarity, explicitly in the European case, but implicitly for any other case too. Habermas argues that even national solidarity had to be learned in a kind of emerging consciousness, so "why should it be impossible to extend this learning process beyond national borders?"[64] He gives hope to the prospects for cosmopolitan solidarity, and subsequently, for a transnational political public sphere. And again, the internal logic of the notion of a postnational era makes the transnational framework a necessary antithesis to the national, and it appears as one that must prevail—if we are indeed beyond the sovereignty of states, then we are beyond the efficacy of any state-bounded politics. The dichotomy between the national and transnational frameworks is compounded in Habermas' account by the contention that there is a vigorous antipathy between them. Habermas takes a heuristic distinction between the two frameworks too seriously, arguing that one can only prevail at the expense of the other, all of which results in an apparent "choice" between them.

I shall now turn to a preliminary effort to problematize and to move our own discussion beyond the national/transnational dichotomy. In chapter 6, I controvert the false dichotomy and antipathy resultant of Habermas' mistaking the heuristic distinction between the national and the transnational as actually existing. In addition to this, and as a preliminary effort to preface a longer discussion of the case of the Zapatista public sphere, I will consider some examples of public spheres in Latin American that empirically complicate the national/transnational dichotomy and the assumption of an antipathy between the two frameworks.

Notes

1. James Bohman, Martin Köhler, and Jürgen Habermas are the notable exceptions.
2. Michael Walzer, *Thick and Thin: Moral Argument at Home and Abroad*, 7.
3. Ibid., 18.
4. For Walzer's discussion of Chinese democracy and the role of foreign democratic theory, see ibid., 59–61.
5. Ibid., 68.
6. Here, when I say, "cosmopolitanism wholly achieved within civil society," I understand that this confuses our previous definition of civil society as a

clearly state-bounded legally conferred society of citizens. Although I will soon revise this earlier definition in order to discuss the concept of "global" or "transnational" civil society, it is important to note that cosmopolitanism *can* in fact emerge in a state-bounded civil society. This is possible because cosmopolitanism first and foremost entails an orientation toward others elsewhere, and so it can be fostered in any one group, and, to some extent, it entails the one group's geographic differentiation from the others elsewhere toward which it is comported.

7. Janna Thompson, "Community Identity and World Citizenship," 188 in *Re-imagining Political Community: Studies in Cosmopolitan Democracy*.

8. See ibid. To be clear, this represents Thompson's contention, not mine. We may contrast to this the fact that political identity *is* cultural identity in some instances, in indigenous rights politics for example, and that peoples' political identity is sometimes the one they are willing to die for.

9. Ibid., 187.

10. Other theorists do the same thing. Besides Habermas and Thompson, notably, is Richard Falk's argument in his *Predatory Globalization: A Critique*. There, in section III, chapter 9, he argues that a backlash to the idea of global civil society comes from indigenous groups (see 142).

11. Thompson, "Community Identity and World Citizenship," 179.

12. Ibid., 181.

13. Ibid.

14. Ibid., 180.

15. Daniele Archibugi, "Cosmopolitical Democracy," 7 in *Debating Cosmopolitics*.

16. We may take perhaps the most obvious example, George W. Bush's comments about the war in Iraq in the text from the transcript of his September 30, 2004, presidential debate with John Kerry (still readable at National Public Radio's website at http://www.npr.org—search for "presidential debate"). There, Bush staunchly defends the war in Iraq, and at the same time consistently expresses a primary concern for the people of Iraq, insisting that the people should be free from tyranny and that they should in no way be confused with the government of Saddam Hussein.

17. Evidence of the disparity of concern over U.S. and British versus Iraqi casualties has been widespread in print, Internet, and television media since the start of the war. One group of researchers, Iraq Body Count (http://iraqbody count.net) has committed itself to cataloging Iraqi civilian casualties on the premise that no major news outlet is or will be concerned with doing so. Indeed, the BBC reminded its readers on June 6, 2005, (http://news.bbc.co.uk) of the view famously expressed by U.S. general Tommy Franks that "we don't do body counts." This statement, the BBC article continues, "still resonates in government circles." The sentiment stems from the fact that Iraqi casualties are counted as an unfortunate but necessary toll in the liberation of Iraq from the tyranny of Saddam Hussein (a position harder to defend after Hussein's capture). Yet U.S. casualties are by no means treated in the same manner. Countless major papers and news outlets have published biographical profiles for

and personal stories about U.S. casualties in Iraq, treating each one with individual care (see, for example, *The Washington Post* at http://www.washingtonpost.com where they maintain a running database called "Faces of the Fallen," which pays proud homage to U.S. military casualties while categorically ignoring civilian casualties). *The Washington Post* and other major news sources that run such features have not presented any similar picture of Iraqi civilian deaths, no doubt because such attention would be considered inappropriate, inflammatory, and an affront to the costs and aims of "Operation Enduring Freedom." Beyond this, researchers such as those at Iraq Body Count have had their findings flatly ignored by major presses time and again (see, for example, Lila Guterman's article in *Chronicle of Higher Education*, January 27, 2005, "Researchers Who Rushed into Print a Study of Iraqi Civilian Deaths Now Wonder Why It Was Ignored").

18. Archibugi, "Demos and Cosmopolis," 263–64 in *Debating Cosmopolitics*.

19. It is worth noting that the title of Köhler's essay presupposes that the national is not cosmopolitan, hence having to move from one to the other. This is representative of a common assumption in cosmopolitanism that I will revisit and problematize throughout this work.

20. Köhler appears to place more of his faith, or, at the very least, his focus, on CSOs that have a higher status and a more amicable relationship with government institutions.

21. Martin Köhler, "From the National to the Cosmopolitan Public Sphere," 232 in *Re-imagining Political Community: Studies in Cosmopolitan Democracy*.

22. See PGA's website at http://www.agp.org for more information about Peoples' Global Action and their involvement in organizing the 1999 Seattle protest against the World Trade Organization.

23. Köhler, "From the National to the Cosmopolitan Public Sphere," 232.

24. Köhler says that "CSOs, in fact, are primarily concerned with influencing their own governments and, by fostering close relations with state officials, with increasing the domestic importance of their organization." In Köhler, "From the National to the Cosmopolitan Public Sphere," 232.

25. James Bohman, "The Public Spheres of the World Citizen," 180 in *Perpetual Peace: Essays on Kant's Cosmopolitan Ideal*.

26. Ibid., 181.

27. Ibid., 182.

28. This is about half of Kant's story. Kant's idea of enlightenment (recall my analysis in chapter 1) does entail that competent and mature institutions lead the public toward its own competency and maturity. Yes, but Kant also insists that civil society must convince and/or provoke political institutions to transform by critiquing them with the public use of reason.

29. Bohman, "The Public Spheres of the World Citizen," 189.

30. Nancy Fraser, "Transnationalizing the Public Sphere," 3.

31. Ibid., 6.

32. See chapters 3 and 4 in Fraser's *Justice Interruptus: Critical Reflections on the "Postsocialist" Condition*.

33. John A. Guidry and Mark Q. Sawyer, "Contentious Pluralism: The Public Sphere and Democracy," 275 in *Perspectives on Politics*, June 2003, Vol. 1, No. 2, 247–472.

34. Ibid., 277.

35. Ibid., 283.

36. James C. Scott also argues this convincingly in his *Domination and the Arts of Resistance: Hidden Transcripts* (1990, Yale University Press).

37. The term "postnational" (which Habermas employs in *The Postnational Constellation: Political Essays*) both foreshadows and logically commits Habermas to an opposition of the transnational to the national. In other words, the term "postnational" implies that moving *beyond the national* is not just a spatial but also a temporal-historical moment (post) demarcating a moment *after the national* itself.

38. Jürgen Habermas, "Further Reflections on the Public Sphere," 438 in *Habermas and the Public Sphere*.

39. Mike Hill and Warren Montag, "What Was, What Is, the Public Sphere? Post–Cold War Reflections," 4 in *Masses, Classes, and the Public Sphere*.

40. See Habermas' discussion of "siege" and "sluice" in appendix I of *Between Facts and Norms: Contributions to a Discourse Theory of Law and Democracy*.

41. Habermas, *Between Facts and Norms: Contributions to a Discourse Theory of Law and Democracy*, 359. It is worth observing here that despite Habermas' preference for the sluice model, we shall see how remarkably well the Zapatistas' uses of poetry, mysterious anonymity, and political theater resonate with Habermas' favorable view of influential thematizations and effective dramatizations. Indeed, the primary function of the public sphere, as Habermas outlines it above, is well realized in the siege models of many social movements.

42. Ibid., 365.

43. Ibid., 361.

44. Ibid., 364.

45. Ibid., 373.

46. Ibid., 374.

47. Ibid., 371.

48. Ibid., 386.

49. Habermas, "Kant's Idea of Perpetual Peace, with the Benefit of Two Hundred Years' Hindsight," 119 in *Perpetual Peace: Essays on Kant's Cosmopolitan Ideal*.

50. Ibid., 124.

51. Ibid., 125.

52. Ibid., 130.

53. This quotation is by Walzer, *Thick and Thin*, 64–65.

54. Habermas, "Kant's Idea of Perpetual Peace, with the Benefit of Two Hundred Years' Hindsight," 149.

55. Ultimately, I will argue that keeping this in mind means rejecting the idea of a transition from the national to the transnational and means supporting a more transgressive approach to the national/transnational dichotomy instead.

56. Habermas, "The European Nation-State and the Pressures of Globalization," 226.

57. Habermas, *The Postnational Constellation: Political Essays*, 51.

58. Ibid., 55–56.

59. Ibid., 57.

60. Ibid., 99.

61. It must be acknowledged here that this claim of resurgent nationalisms is rather underspecified in my analysis and that the reader may want to know what examples or evidence I have for this claim. I am working mainly with two materials here: First, I am working with the conceptual antipathy between "nationalism" and "transnationalism." This antipathy has been fleshed out by definition and explication of the concepts. Second, I am working with Habermas' own acceptance of this antipathy, despite the fact that concrete examples for it are scarce and underspecified in his own work. Indeed, I am not myself convinced of the proposed antagonism between nationalism and transnationalism. Nevertheless, the "flare-ups" I refer to here are references to actual historical and current events. For more specific references of such nationalist resurgences please see the following discussions: Habermas' remarks about ethnocentric reaction to foreigners, the movement of Italy's Northern league, and Germany (*The Postnational Constellation: Political Essays*, 72); Habermas' remarks about the absence of a European public sphere and a regression to nationalism ("Kant's Idea of Perpetual Peace, with the Benefit of Two hundred Year's Hindsight," 125 and 130, respectively); Craig Calhoun's remarks about Nazi Germany and Slobodan Milosevic's Serbian nationalism ("Constitutional Patriotism and the Public Sphere: Interests, Identity, and Solidarity in the Integration of Europe," 278–79).

62. Habermas, *The Postnational Constellation*, 73.

63. Ibid., 110–11.

64. Habermas, "The European Nation-State and the Pressures of Globalization," 231.

6

Beyond the National/ Transnational Dichotomy

Moving Toward a Theory of Transgressive Public Spheres

In this chapter, I set out to accomplish two tasks. First, I will fully elaborate a refutation of the divide between national and transnational as actually existing. In this, I will demonstrate what is problematic and dangerous about the turn away from the national public sphere and the national framework. I will make clear the theoretical failings of this turn, showing instead that it is more precise and more constructive to consider the productive capacities of both national and transnational political action, and to see that in fact the lines separating the two frameworks are neither clearly delineated nor abided by in practice.

After having done this, I will finally turn to the part of my discussion that claims that the treatment of these frameworks as clear and distinct zones, as we have seen them treated in chapter 5, is not compatible with the comportment of actual political action that works transnationally. Throughout this work, I have made numerous promissory notes for a discussion of the Mexican Zapatistas, maintaining throughout that a careful consideration of the Zapatistas and their public sphere (and the implications of indigenous identity) will offer much to political theory, and particularly to public sphere theory. Namely, I have invoked in passing that the Zapatista public sphere is a *kind* of public sphere that exemplifies the inherent problems of an analytical rubric that takes the heuristic distinction between national and transnational too seriously. Yet I have not defined the Zapatista public sphere, what kind of a public sphere it is, and how it is misfit with both the national and transnational frameworks.

In this chapter, I make a preliminary start at this discussion, but I provide only a preface for my theory of transgressive public spheres. The development of a theory of transgressive public spheres will be the central focus of the next and last part of this book. For now, I am primarily concerned with a problematization of transnational public sphere theory. I look briefly at the Indian rights movement in Latin America, and, particularly, at precursors to the Zapatistas in Mexico. Mainly, our preliminary consideration of the Indian rights movement in Mexico will demonstrate that and how it is possible to speak of a politics that does not fluctuate between the two frameworks, but is always somehow beyond them and in them both at once. This discovery prefaces the need for a different framework altogether. But why do I choose the example of Indian rights in the first place? An answer to this question cannot be postponed any longer.

The indigenous rights and democratization movements in Latin America, just prior to the Zapatista uprising, cut across many of the cleavages in the debates that I have considered. Nearly all of the theoretical questions that are raised by globalization can be empirically illustrated within the context of indigenous rights politics.[1] The questions of legitimation, of thick and thin, of the national versus the transnational, of political identity and political community, of self-determination, of the environment, of human rights, and of free trade and the global market are all characteristically and centrally engaged by discussions of Indian rights in Latin American politics. Furthermore, Latin America gives us an example that elucidates Guidry and Sawyer's theorization of democratization as a never-ending process that can be studied in nondemocratic or predemocratic situations. The issues I examine in this concluding chapter of part II set the stage for the discussion of the Mexican Zapatistas in part III. In short, Latin American politics concerning indigenous rights and democracy prior to and including the uprising of the Zapatistas provides us with empirical cases that simultaneously illustrate and complicate all of the theoretical discussions we have evaluated thus far with poignancy and clarity.

It is fair to regard the innovative political action of indigenous rights struggles in Mexico in the 1990s as the motor that
drives my theorization of a new kind of public sphere. We will
see why it is theoretically problematic to treat the heuristic distinction between the national and transnational as concrete and
will begin to understand empirically that political public spheres
can and do violate the supposed dichotomy and betray the antipathy between national and transnational frameworks. We
thus lay the groundwork for moving our own discussion beyond
the national/transnational dichotomy and pointing the way toward a new framework.

Part II has been devoted to assessing the *transnational* framework and public sphere. Chapter 6 presents my culminating critique of transnational public sphere theory and the national/
transnational dichotomy. Hence, this chapter is properly a part
of my problematization of contemporary public sphere theory.[2]
The reader has surely observed that, throughout this work, I
have never hermetically sealed off discussion of the national
from the transnational from the transgressive public sphere, in
part because such a clinical separation is really not possible. I
shall, therefore, bring in my idea of the transgressive public
sphere in a preliminary way here, but only in order to conclude
my critique of the transnational.

Craig Calhoun's essay, "Constitutional Patriotism and the
Public Sphere: Interests, Identity, and Solidarity in the Integration of Europe," goes far to illustrate the problems associated
with an apparent choice between the national and transnational
frameworks in a way that will link us rather clearly to the discussion of indigenous rights movements. Calhoun provides a
critique of the national/transnational dichotomy as it crops up
throughout public sphere theory, and particularly in Habermas.
Calhoun insists on the importance of a kind of national framework. He discusses the case of European unification too, but he
speaks at length about interests, identity, solidarity, and culture.

Calhoun notes that Habermas has abandoned his early cele-
bration of the ideal national political public sphere, and has ar-
rived at a kind of vilification of nationalism writ large, seeming,
along with others, to view nationalism only as a kind of "ethnic
nationalism." This turn, Calhoun admits, has some justification

in history. National identity was once learned and formed, whereas today it is largely inherited. Because of this, national political identity is largely and to some extent rightly understood as intrinsically prejudiced, as inherited at birth rather than founded on rational-critical discourses. Calhoun agrees with the negative characterization of such "ethnic nationalisms," as they are indeed exclusionary in a way that makes it impossible for nonmembers to achieve equal standing. But Calhoun argues that not all nationalisms must be inherited identities as such, and that it is possible for certain nationalisms to strengthen the prospects for a transnational public sphere. This is counterintuitive. The example Calhoun gives of a "nonethnic" national identity is that of the American founding and early constitutionalism. Colonists, he explains, turned into nationalists *without* a primary appeal to any ethnic identity, but rather by taking the nation to be a common project rooted in a collective interest in forging a legal constitution and a new culture.

This example illustrates a different way to negotiate the problem Habermas identifies as the lack of European "peoplehood." In Habermas' polarization of "inherited identity" (nationalism) to "rational discursive identity" (transnational peoplehood based in cosmopolitan solidarity), he sharply separates the national from the transnational. According to Calhoun, it is possible to foster nationalisms as common projects rooted in a collective interest in forging a new culture of cosmopolitanism.[3] In the case of the European Union and a European public sphere, at least something like this is intended. That is to say, European peoplehood does not have to imply the decimation of the national public spheres of Europe, and it does not have to signify the replacement of national identities with transnational European identities. Rather, it is possible for the national public spheres of Europe to understand themselves still, and importantly, as single bodies—but bodies whose own projects entail, at least in part, enjoining other nations and other national public spheres in a common project rooted in a collective interest in forging a new European peoplehood.

Calhoun speaks in terms of "imaginaries," much in the same sense of Benedict Anderson's idea of imagined communities I referred to in chapter 3. Nationalist imaginaries, Calhoun admits, have been developed and have been used to resist various trends in globalization. In trying to grasp, organize, and even to resist the ideas and cultural products flowing in through the global market, and the global flows of people, the nationalist imaginary has been strengthened. Efforts to transnationalize the public sphere must, therefore, negotiate nationalist imaginaries that may be hostile to perceived attempts to supersede nationalism with a broader framework for understanding and doing politics. It is precisely for this reason, Calhoun says, that Habermas construes all nationalism as an opponent to transnationalism that must be contested and defeated. It is the European Union, once again, that bears this out. The countries of the union have continually asserted their distinctive nationalities in opposition to the liquidation of their national culture, which many fear is implicit in the European Union.

Calhoun thinks it is problematic to oppose the national to the transnational for many reasons, but first and foremost because transnationalism can never simply defeat nationalism. Our lives and our identities are complex, made up of some national and some transnational identifications and understandings, so moving beyond the nation does not need to mean contesting it:

> If nationalism is to give way to some postnational organization
> of social life, it will not be simply a matter of new formal or-
> ganization, but of new ways of imaginatively constituting iden-
> tity, interests, and solidarity. . . . Can shared participation in the
> public sphere anchor a form of social solidarity in which the na-
> ture of life together is chosen as it is constructed?[4]

Calhoun believes that the answer to this question is yes (and this is precisely what will be demonstrated by the Zapatistas). But such transformations should not entail any posthaste push beyond nationalism to transnationalism, which for Calhoun, might undermine the strength of existing collective identities, might weaken and fragment existing publics, inadvertently weakening the prospects for solidarity between them. Transnational coalitions or regroupings of national bodies cannot take place if those national bodies are deteriorated or abandoned. Simply put, if existing groups are destabilized, then solidarity among them loses its meaning.

Often in Habermas' recent work, the national public sphere has been associated with thick cultural ties (and irrationality) while the transnational public sphere has been associated with thin cultural ties (and rational-critical discourse). Calhoun is not convinced that these associations are accurate:

> To treat nationalism as a relic of an earlier order, a sort of irrational expression, or a kind of moral mistake is to fail to see both the continuing power of nationalism as a discursive formation and the work—sometimes positive—that nationalist solidarities continue to do in the world. As a result, nationalism is not easily abandoned even if its myths, contents, and excesses are easily debunked. Not only this, the attempt to equate nationalism with problematic ethnonationalism sometimes ends up placing all "thick" understandings of culture and the cultural constitution of political practices, forms, and identities on the nationalist side of the classification. Only quite thin notions of political culture are retained on the attractive postnationalist side.[5]

This equation of thick and thin to national and postnational implies a tautology, particularly in Habermas' account, of all nationalism with ethnonationalism. This tautology strengthens, deepens, and intensifies the antipathy between the national and transnational frameworks; it situates them as frameworks for opponent political ideologies. But Calhoun insists that it is neither true empirically nor theoretically to say that all nationalisms are of a dangerous ethnonationalist variety, that they are all either already ethnonationalisms, or potentially ethnonationalisms.

His key example remains the founding of America and American constitutionalism. As mentioned above, the constitutional patriotism that grew up in early America was not based mainly on an appeal to ethnic identity. Rather, it was an identity borne of public discourse, and one that took real shape during the American Revolution. The nation, in this context, was a common project, it was something made in political discourse and revolution, and it was not an inherited identity. Indigenous rights movements have taken on a nationalist tone in a similar way, as implied for example in the name, "Zapatista Army for National Liberation." Although the Zapatistas employ a nationalist rhetoric, their idea of national liberation has to do with the common political project of fighting to preserve the self-determination of particular cultures and practices. Remember that self-determination is a political ideal that Walzer maintained as the minimalist principle that could found a new international-ism, and yet, within this principle, is a link to locale that often finds its discursive expression in what we would call a good na-tionalism. I would add that, in postcolonial studies, even eth-nonationalism is understood as having played an emancipatory role and does not always appear as an opposition to cosmopoli-tanism or some other reasonable international program. In India and Algiers, for example, the opponents were imperialism and colonialism, military occupation by a foreign power, and even though these things represent a kind of international thinking, they have no normative resonance with cosmopolitanism.

Habermas' turn against the national framework does not leave room for such considerations. Habermas works, says Cal-houn, "with an overly sharp dichotomy between inherited iden-tity and rational discourse."[6] Nationalism is exhaustively perceived as an expression of inherited identity, and is therefore necessarily exclusive. But deep agreement and thick cultural ties are also made in social interaction, and are not only ever inher-ited. Rational discourse can lead, whether within or beyond na-tional borders, to thick cultural ties between people. It is, therefore, misleading to speak of a choice between thick (qua ir-rational and inherited) and thin (qua rationally assessed and vol-untarily produced), because identity, culture, solidarity, and interests do not map out over this dichotomy.

Identity is made and remade in complicated ways. Our in-herited identities are often retained after and in light of rational-critical deliberation, and identities other than those we inherited are often chosen without much rational thought at all. Moreover, it is possible to create new and different identities, even an iden-tification as a member of a community of choice (rather than of birth) whose members may never meet, but who have thick cul-tural ties nonetheless. Many subcultures, such as the punk rock subculture for example, are this way. No one is born a punk, be-cause punk is a community of choice, and yet, wherever you go, there will be thick cultural practices and traditions, ranging from diet to dress to values to political and moral dispositions shared by punks. These shared sensibilities run through to the core of daily life and are not all simply minimalist agreements on generalized moral principles. It is possible to voluntarily enter a transnational community that is bound by deep cultural and political identifications.

"Engagement in public life establishes social solidarity partly through enhancing the significance of particular categorical identities and partly through facilitating the creation of direct social relations."[7] In other words, *categorical identities* (more abstract and complex identities indicating membership in a defined group—by "race," nationality, sex, class, or anything else), as well as *direct social relations* (our lived experiences with people we engage with in topical common space), are both critical to participation in a public sphere. And sometimes our categorical identities can be thicker and more deeply meaningful than our direct social relations, which can be rather thinly held together by the sole fact that we share a lived experience. What this means is that a political public sphere can be national and thin (i.e., new immigrants, undocumented workers), national and thick (i.e., committed patriots), transnational and thin (i.e., humanitarians or moderate cosmopolitans), or transnational and thick (i.e., members of various diasporas or committed cosmopolitans whose self-understanding as such shapes their political consciousness and community), and thus the equation of thick and thin to national and transnational, respectively, is demonstrably false.

Addressing the lack of a European public sphere, Calhoun points out that the focus on unification as an economic strategy, as a means of competition against Asian countries and the United States, has been a major part of the problem. For Calhoun, the European Union would have done better to follow the paradigm of the historical role and development of good nationalisms. In other words, there is just not enough of a sense of a common project in terms of European culture, identity, interests and solidarity, and so it is not surprising that there is no European public sphere. If Europe is centrally regarded as an economic project with an already decided direction and purpose, there is not much of an invitation to a European public sphere. The European Union did not effectively present itself as a common project for European civil society and it therefore faces a legitimation crisis.

John A. Guidry, Michael D. Kennedy, and Mayer N. Zald, in their essay "Globalizations and Social Movements," provide a definition of the transnational public sphere that gets further to the heart of the problem of the false antipathy between the national and transnational frameworks. They define the transnational public sphere as "a space in which both residents of distinct places (states or localities) and members of transnational entities (organizations or firms) elaborate discourses and practices whose consumption moves beyond national boundaries."[8] The political action of the transnational public sphere is what the authors refer to as "action at a distance."[9] What this means is that political action originates in some locale, then proceeds through various channels to be taken up by an audience whose membership makes it transnational, and then the discourses and practices that move beyond national boundaries have some measurable effect in particular places.

Guidry, Kennedy, and Zald insist that the transnational is not pitted against the national. They argue that the transnational public sphere is only heuristically distinct, and that this must not be forgotten. They are right. Analyzing the transnational public sphere entails always considering national more localized discourses and practices. Guidry, Kennedy, and Zald recognize that originally local responses can be globalized by the transnational public sphere and thereby lose some sense of what it means to call them local; yet, we cannot neglect that the localized space in which the political action originated is still its root source, providing the transnational public sphere with its discursive matter. And of course, concrete locales are ultimately where most problems get resolved. The national public sphere feeds the transnational public sphere with political discourses and practices, that is, it informs and shapes the transnational public sphere.[10] The transnational public sphere globalizes the political discourses and practices of national public spheres, carrying advocacy, pressure, solidarity, and influence beyond national borders. In short, "the transnational public sphere renders the global and local mutually transformative."[11] Each framework is in fact fluidly related to the other, so oppositional rhetoric regarding an antipathy between them should never be taken too seriously.[12]

An overemphasis on the significance of the local and localities in globalization risks missing the importance of those transnational modular forms that organize our recognition of particular places. Privileging the global, on the other hand, leads us to recognize the deviant only as aberrant or temporary rather than as a moment in which the global could potentially be refigured locally.[13]

Those who discuss the national and transnational frameworks as distinct overlook important ways in which each one structures the shape of the other.

Guidry, Kennedy, and Zald come very close to a workable analysis of transnational public spheres, but for one major conflation. The authors use the terms transnational social movement and transnational public sphere interchangeably.[14] But these two have very different meanings and we must be careful not to dull the differences discussed in chapter 3.

Social movements serve as one means of proliferating a particular political discourse to wider audiences or targets or of bringing an already-formed opinion and will to bear on some addressee. Public spheres are the spaces in which the opinion and will of a collectivity takes shape and becomes decisive as the opinion and will of that group. Social movements, civil disobedience, letter writing, published articles, radio broadcasts, community forums, even rebellion may all be means of publicity from the standpoint of public sphere theory. While the public sphere is itself a mechanism of influence, it utilizes a multiplicity of instruments, of which social movements are one. Social movements are one means of publicity among others. Social movements often target public spheres, so that the deliberative, rational-critical assessment of what they have to say can be taken up elsewhere and at other times. Both social movements and public spheres are formed and enlivened by the voluntary collective action of civil society (however defined), but we must not confuse them because of this.

Margaret E. Keck and Kathryn Sikkink, in their *Activists Beyond Borders: Advocacy Networks in International Politics*, offer some additional insights for how to think about the national and the transnational frameworks. Most importantly, their concept of the "boomerang effect" will provide segue to understanding why the Indian rights movement invalidates the supposed antipathy between the national and transnational.

Keck and Sikkink speak of transnational advocacy networks (TANs). TANs are essentially CSOs that have a more decisively transnational comportment, rather than simply participating occasionally in transnational forums. Network means communicative structure here. TANs participate in domestic and international political affairs, often reaching outside of their own state to enlist or to invite the assistance of other actors. Broadly conceived, TANs are made up of NGOs, social movements, citizens' groups, and other networks of communication. The goal of TANs "is to change the behavior of states and of international organizations. Simultaneously principled and strategic actors, they 'frame' issues to make them comprehensible to target audiences, to attract attention and encourage action, and to 'fit' with favorable institutional venues."[15] TANs function much like public spheres in that they introduce and circulate new ideas, norms, and discourses, and they provide alternative sources of information and testimony. Because TANs do not have conventional political power, Keck and Sikkink maintain that they must rely on the power of their information and ideas to be widely resonant and to win popular traction, as has often been the case for public spheres.

For Keck and Sikkink, TANs are mechanisms of reform. In other words, they are always discussed along the lines of effecting policy changes, in contrast to effecting revolution, radical democracy, or the deep restructuring of political identity. However, there is a method that TANs employ that I would like to reformulate for public spheres. That method, the "boomerang effect," refers to national movements' appeals to political actors outside their own borders in order to bolster and bring back leverage.

> When channels between the state and its domestic actors are blocked, the boomerang pattern of influence characteristic of transnational networks may occur: domestic NGOs bypass their state and directly search out international allies to try to bring pressure on their states from outside. . . . On other issues where governments are inaccessible or deaf to groups whose claims may nonetheless resonate elsewhere, international contacts can amplify the demands of domestic groups, pry open space for new issues, and then echo back these demands into the domestic arena.[16]

As we shall see, the boomerang effect is and has been central to the efficacy of the political action of Indian rights movements in Latin America, and has been taken to a new extreme by the Zapatistas. With groups that employ the boomerang effect, the national/transnational dichotomy is *crossed* but not *transgressed*. That is to say, the lines are not effective boundaries but they are treated as apparent and are ideationally reified.

TANs are enlivened today about the issues of neoliberalism, capitalist globalization, and human rights. However, transnational advocacy has not just been invented. Many political issues and actions have used the method of the boomerang effect and have functioned like TANs. The anti–female circumcision, anti-footbinding, antislavery, and woman and universal suffrage movements all adopted both national and transnational comportments. But like other TANs that Keck and Sikkink discuss, these took on "dual comportments" that crossed national boundaries without problematizing the national/transnational dichotomy itself.

According to Keck and Sikkink TANs employ four different kinds of strategy: First, they use *information politics*, or the politics of circulating alternative sources of information. Second, they use *symbolic politics*, or the politics of attaching particular explanations to powerful and symbolic events. Imagine, for example, competing explanations of the attacks of 9/11. Third, they use *leverage politics*, or the politics of employing material or moral leverage to efforts to pressure targets (i.e., boycotts or shaming, respectively). Finally, they use *accountability politics*, or the politics of holding institutions accountable for principles that they have publicly committed themselves to upholding. Political public spheres, it is fair to say, also employ these four kinds of strategy. They share with TANs the goals of issue-creation, agenda setting, influencing the discourses of their targets, and influencing institutional procedures and policies.

Keck and Sikkink insist on the characteristic capacity of political activism to fluidly cross boundaries, but in the end, their own theory remains subordinated to the national/transnational dichotomy. The boomerang effect, which is used by public spheres as well as by TANs, requires constant border crossing. But it does not raise any deeper questions about the dichotomy of these borders itself because what is missing from this inventory of political strategies (information, symbolic, leverage, and accountability politics) is *identity politics*.[17] It is generally assumed that political identity is so firmly tied to the thick and maximal bases of specific cultures that identity will forever be too thick to work well transnationally. But we have discussed the importance of complex identities that prevent a wholly national or a wholly transnational self-understanding, and we have shown that identifications with transnational community can indeed be anchored in rather thick and maximal culture. Keck and Sikkink neglect the ways in which domestic political actors uproot their national subject position to better appeal to others elsewhere, to increase membership and participation and the leverage of the boomerang effect, to strip themselves enough of nationalist identifications to accomplish these ends, but not enough to thoroughly subvert national identifications and an orientation toward local problem solving. Identity politics are not only critical here, but they are a critical component in the transgression we will further explore in part III.

But do the struggles of indigenous peoples and for democracy in Latin America confront this dichotomy and address the question of identity politics any better? The answer is yes, and I will draw this chapter to a close showing why. What I discuss here is not yet the fully formed Zapatista public sphere. I begin with an incomplete consideration of the situations that preceded that public sphere in order to see why it does not make sense to fit certain kinds of political action into the theoretical frameworks that we presently have at our disposal.

Let us begin with some general remarks about the Indian rights movement in Latin America. Alison Brysk's essay, "Acting Globally: Indian Rights and International Politics in Latin America," explains well how various Indian rights movements in Latin America transformed themselves into international movements without abandoning a commitment to their local crises. This ultimately came about through the use of the boomerang effect. Indian rights movements have brought about national reforms through an effective utilization of linkages to public spheres elsewhere, NGOs, and TANs.

Brysk tells us that there are forty million Indians in Latin America, and they are easily the hemisphere's most marginalized people. But the indigenous rights movements had, by 1992, led to the clear demarcation of Indian lands in Brazil, Ecuador, and Nicaragua. It became clear by then, in those countries, where the indigenous populations lived and what land they wanted protected. Moreover, the Indian rights movements of Latin America have effectively linked themselves to one another, to many reputable NGOs, and have won widespread recognition in the United Nations. By Indian rights we mean the rights of Indians in all of the countries of Latin America, yet we mean at the same time the varying particular crises that face each population in each country. Inasmuch as indigenous rights movements have placed the issue of the rights of Indians on multiple agendas and in multiple forums, it is fair to say that some major strides have been made.

At the same time, Indian rights movements have illustrated the limits of state-bounded political action. Without the use of the boomerang effect, the demands of indigenous peoples would not travel very far and would have to rely solely on their own undervalued weight. Existing channels of communication from civil society to the state within each country have been essentially closed off to Indian populations. This should remind us of what has been said about nonbourgeois public spheres in chapter 3. The desperate and neglected social position of marginal groups requires them to reach beyond national boundaries in a struggle to accumulate the leverage needed to make their addressee(s) responsive.

Specifically in the Indian rights movement, indigenous groups discursively situated themselves within the larger environmentalism movement. This enabled the political discourse of Indian rights to embed itself in a more resonant political discourse, to be bound up with preexisting norms and a regime of international influence that had already picked up a good deal of popular traction throughout the 1980s. The incorporation of Indian rights politics into environmentalism was also desirable to the environmentalist movement. What it did for environmentalism was to thicken its links to human rights. Hence, an environmentalist–Indian rights coalition was formed, and it was this coalition more than anything else that bolstered the efficacy of Indian rights politics. The Rainforest Foundation explains the power of this coalition: "The rain forest card is stronger than the indigenous card. They [indigenous people] know that, and we [advocates] know that—and without that, indigenous people wouldn't have a chance in hell."[18] Today, the World Bank, Inter-American Development Bank, Congressional Human Rights Caucus, and other groups simply list indigenous rights issues as environmental issues.

Indigenous rights politics, as others in the history of non-bourgeois public spheres, reached outside of the nation-state precisely because it lacked political access at home:

> The initial demands of local indigenous groups were reactive to a range of specific threats, though generally connected to land rights, relief from human rights abuses, and preservation of native languages and cultural practices. The diverse needs of a pan-American movement eventually coalesced around the concepts of self-determination and "ethnodevelopment": informed self-management of cultural and social change.[19]

It is important to stress here that as transboundary as the political action was, all of the issues and their resolutions were not only anchored to specific locales. But also, they had to do precisely with the preservation of particular cultures, the protection of the lifeways and lands of specific subnational communities, and often they had to do with defense against the threat of transboundary encroachments. Yet, for indigenous people marginalized within their own states, without political influence, the international system has been the only way to ensure their survival. Hence, there is a formal transnationalization of national struggles that remain, in terms of their content, not at all abstracted from the particular problems of particular locales, most of which have to do with the commitments of their own national states. Movements discursively disconnect from the exclusivity of citizenship and from the narrowness of their state's political process, linking themselves instead to norms and identifications that have more resonance abroad. But in Latin America the implications of this for political identity were not yet borne out, and would not be until years later after the uprising of the Zapatistas in 1994.[20]

Indian rights movements seek to settle domestic matters domestically, and incorporate a transnational component in order to garner solidarity that can be turned into pressure, increasing the negotiability of their national agendas. This is a utilization of both frameworks that illustrates Keck and Sikkink's ideas of boomerang effect.

The one great difference, which has not yet been sufficiently elaborated, is the fact that "indigenous" is an open, pan-American term that simultaneously demarcates national and transnational identifications—not one or the other given the time and place, but both all of the time and everywhere. Under the rubric of indigenous rights politics, the national and transnational frameworks are occupied simultaneously in order to keep accumulating pressure on the one hand, and to keep applying it on the other. What must be emphasized most about this is that it illustrates that a conception of a choice between frameworks is fundamentally misled. In the case of Indian rights, choosing one framework over the other is tantamount to losing. Double occupancy in both frameworks simultaneously is the necessary structure of the movement, this double occupancy is decided by the internal logic of indigeneity, and it is the reason why we will speak of the transgression of borders rather than their crossing. In all of this, there is a crucial interplay between indigenousness, identity, and transgression; coming to understand this interplay more fully will be largely the task of part III.

At this point in our analysis, however, we understand only that the nationally situated political struggles of indigenous peoples in Latin America must be recast transnationally, and embedded within a larger political movement, in order to take full and necessary advantage of the boomerang effect. The discussion of Indian rights in Brysk's account is correct, but only as far as it goes. Because the topic of political identity and indigenousness has not yet been brought to its fruition, we do not yet have a deeper problematization of the whole lexicon with which we speak of politics as national and transnational.

Breaking up the exclusive ethnocentric position of indigenous political identity, without losing the specificity of its purpose within the national context is a difficult and highly contentious endeavor for good historical reasons. Julio C. Tresierra, in his "Mexico: Indigenous Peoples and the Nation-State," focuses on the domestic situation of indigenous rights in Mexico and argues for the importance of seeing the movement in a national framework, rather than seeking to transnationalize it in various ways.

Tresierra frames his discussion by the terms "indigenismo" and "indianismo." Indigenismo refers to the official policy of the Mexican government toward its indigenous communities. The official policy has been one of paternalism and assimilation, and in its best guise, has been welfare-oriented. Under indigenismo, the Mexican government assumes the posture of a caretaker and encourages indigenous people to "modernize" and leave their marginal communities. Indianismo, on the other hand, refers to the political philosophy, or the worldview of the indigenous people themselves. Indianismo argues against the pressures of indigenismo by demanding more decisionmaking power, cultural preservation, and self-determination. On these three fronts, indianismo contests the paternalistic, assimilationist, and welfare-orientated comportment of indigenismo. Indianismo has functioned as both a defense against and a positive response to indigenismo.

Since its inception as an aggressive government initiative, indigenismo has taken on a more covert form and in turn, perhaps a more sinister disposition. In other words, indigenismo was originally a set of open policies that the Mexican government enacted in the 1940s to pressure integration, miscegenation, and assimilation with the ultimate aim of bringing about the complete disappearance of the Indian. These remain the hidden hopes of many in the Mexican government today, for in the 1980s and 1990s, those more belligerent policies were softened into a more liberal ethnophagous strategy:

> Ethnophagia thus expresses the overall process whereby the culture of domination seeks to swallow up or devour the many popular cultures, mainly by virtue of the weight that the "national" patterns exercise over the ethnic communities. It does not seek to destroy through absolute denial of or violent attack on other identities, but rather is aimed at gradual dissolution through attraction, seduction, and self-transformation.[21]

It is critical to notice here that the loosening up and subsequent transformation of the identities of ethnic communities does not imply any kind of benevolent achievement of complex identity such as that recommended by cosmopolitans. In fact, ethnophagia retains at bottom the same objectives as the aggressive assimilationist policies of the 1940s, that is, the disappearance of the Indian as such.

The liberal rhetoric of and under the rubric of ethnophagia did not convince the indigenous people. Thus, indianismo responded by deepening its resistances and becoming increasingly strategic in the defense of indigenous culture and indigenous identity. From these tensions, a strong ethnicist version of indianismo that "promotes an inward-oriented ethnocentrism" developed.[22] Ongoing aggression between indigenismo and indianismo has, therefore, turned a more staunchly insular ethnic political identity into an effective political stance from which to confront ethnophagia. Because of this, Tresierra insists that the plight of indigenous people in Mexico, despite transnational recasting for the boomerang effect, lies wholly within the boundaries of the Mexican state, where the real battle is being fought, however covertly.

If we are persuaded that the plight of Indian rights movements, as Brysk maintains, depends on their being situated in an international regime, within the broader and more resonant politics of environmentalism, and yet that the most substantive struggle for Indian rights consists of a conflict between indigenismo and indianismo internally, then how exactly does Indian rights politics fit with the national and transnational frameworks? If we take both authors' points seriously, then simultaneous emphases on both the national *and* the transnational frameworks for thinking about and doing politics are indispensable. Indian rights activists do not try to move between frameworks from one time and place to the next, but rather to occupy both spaces all of the time.

But I am stretching this analysis a bit beyond the conflicts in Latin America as we have introduced them thus far. I have done this so that I may underline the direction that indianismo in Mexico takes with the Zapatista movement. The Zapatistas have tried to introduce a third term to the conflict between indianismo and indigenismo: "Zapatismo." Zapatismo is essentially a response to the intensified ethnocentrism of indianismo. Zapatismo poses that the worldview of Indians can, at least in principle, also be that of others, and that the sharing and espousal of such a worldview actually enables a kind of *membership though identification* in the movement of the indigenous itself. Zapatismo tries to deconstruct the ethnocentrism of indianismo while retaining and strengthening a contestatory stance toward ethnophagia. Zapatismo makes an invitation to complex identity that not only uproots the ethnocentrism of indianismo, of political identities traditionally understood as inherited at birth. It also works to break down the national/transnational dichotomy. With Zapatismo, we shall see that actually existing political action, and even actually existing political actors, work so fluidly across and simultaneously within both the national and transnational frameworks, that these frameworks can barely be said to demarcate any boundaries at all.

If this is true about the structure of the political action of Indian rights movements, it is most firmly exemplified by the associated public spheres. Public spheres are always discursively formed, whether topically or metatopically. Their capacity to circulate political discourses across perceived and real boundaries has always been high, and has taken place since the earliest transnational reading publics. The destabilization and the opening up of exclusive political identities and the recasting of the subject position of political actors works to further disintegrate the national/transnational dichotomy, because in addition to increasing participation in political movements that are anchored to a particular locale, the participants are actually able to become members of those distant communities (via the construction of complex identities).

Because it is possible to speak of a politics that does not move between the two frameworks, but is always somehow beyond them and within them at once, it is more sensible to speak of a different framework altogether. That is, if it is simply inaccurate to characterize a particular public sphere as either national or transnational, then there is something about it that eludes our existing lexicon. A third framework, my recommendation to political theory grappling with the problems of globalization, will be the topic of the final chapters.

Notes

1. At this point, I will sometimes say Indian rights and other times say indigenous rights. There is, however, a distinction that will become more important later on when we see that the Indian rights movement *is* an indigenous rights movement, but that indigenousness can be abstracted from the lives and the political demands of Indians. In other words, while both terms here refer to the political movements of indigenous communities, indigenousness will ultimately be expanded and abstracted from the lived experience of the Indians about whom we are presently speaking.

2. Likewise, chapter 3, the concluding chapter of part I, presented my culminating critique of Habermas' classical bourgeois public sphere. Although I discussed the transnational dimensions of nonbourgeois public spheres in that chapter, I did so only in the context of my problematization of the national framework.

3. It is worth noting here that Calhoun's view of "nonethnic" national identities accords well with Bohman's concept of post-Westphalian national publics. In fact, multicultural diasporic publics could serve as more contemporary examples of what Calhoun means by nations as a new common projects.

4. Craig Calhoun, "Constitutional Patriotism and the Public Sphere: Interests, Identity, and Solidarity in the Integration of Europe," 277 in *Global Justice and Transnational Politics*.

5. Ibid., 279.

6. Ibid., 283.

7. Ibid., 289.

8. John A. Guidry, Michael D. Kennedy, and Mayer N. Zald, *Globalizations and Social Movements: Culture, Power, and the Transnational Public Sphere*, 6.

9. "Action at a distance" is originally Anthony Giddens' term (1994, 4), and was actually used to describe how globalization acts.

10. We may recall here the example of universal suffrage in which the discourses and practices of intrastate struggles fed, informed, and shaped a transnational movement—a movement whose successes were nevertheless achieved in one state and then the next, and so on.

11. Guidry, Kennedy, and Zald, *Globalizations and Social Movements*, 12.

12. In this and the preceding paragraph, it may appear that Guidry, Kennedy, and Zald make the same argument that I intend to make. Certainly, their position (and Calhoun's for that matter) is much closer to mine than Habermas' or the other cosmopolitan thinkers discussed in chapter 5. However, Guidry, Kennedy, and Zald demonstrate that the national and transnational frameworks cannot really be disaggregated, that the transnational public sphere globalizes the local and localizes the global, and that the national framework should not be discounted. But these claims only provide the grounding for my own argument; I maintain that beyond the national and transnational is a transgressive public sphere, indeed a third scale of politics that is normatively and strategically distinct. I shall further clarify this position in light of the

Latin American example discussed later in this chapter, and bring it into starkest relief in part III.

13. Guidry, Kennedy, and Zald, *Globalizations and Social Movements*, 30.

14. See the discussion on the top of ibid., 14 for an example of this.

15. Margaret E. Keck and Kathryn Sikkink, *Activists Beyond Borders: Advocacy Networks in International Politics*, 2–3.

16. Ibid., 12–13.

17. In chapter 8, which is focused on questions of political identity, I explain how identity politics is indeed a kind of strategy with normative advantages, and how it is an indispensable part of transgressing the boundaries between national and transnational.

18. As cited in Alison Brysk, "Acting Globally: Indian Rights and International Politics in Latin America," 36 in *Indigenous Peoples and Democracy in Latin America*.

19. Ibid., 33.

20. More on this in chapters 7 and 8.

21. Díaz-Polanco, as cited in Julio C. Tresierra, "Mexico: Indigenous Peoples and the Nation-State," 200 in *Indigenous Peoples and Democracy in Latin America*.

22. Ibid., 201.

III

TRANSGRESSIVE
PUBLIC SPHERES

Introduction to Part III

We begin here at the end of a series of inquiries into the political public sphere whose function has been assessed in a national framework (part I) and a transnational framework (part II).[1] We have learned in previous chapters of historical and ongoing efforts within political theory to use national or transnational conceptual frameworks to specify the scale of the public sphere and its problematic. Beyond analytical and heuristic invocations of one or the other framework, we have discussed the more substantive assumptions that tie the public sphere to one context or the other. In the classical account, for example, the public sphere has a functional role as a conduit of public opinion and will from civil society to its corollary beholden state. Yet, historically, many public spheres have exceeded this strict functionality for strategic reasons or for reasons of material necessity.

Today, theorists are trying to reconfigure the sense of the membership, location, and scale of public spheres, so that they can be a means of providing some cohesion to the concept of global civil society, and so that they could serve a political function of feeding back, as in the classical account, but now to multiple states and transnational institutions. Recent efforts to transnationalize the public sphere, as we have seen in part II, have initiated too hard a turn away from the national framework, and this turn has led to some hopeful but often vaporous

discussions about a cosmopolitan politics. In these recent formulations, I have argued, a critical potentiality of the national
framework is ultimately overlooked and something of the concreteness of the classical public sphere is lost, making the public
sphere a kind of ideal for which it is difficult to imagine any clear
instantiation.

Thus, it might be tempting to abandon speaking of the public sphere altogether as having a clear political role in what occupies the attention of many social scientists today—issues of
global politics and transnational justice. As an intrastate force for
democratization, perhaps the public sphere can fulfill its historic
role nationally or must remain confined to it. To the contrary, I
argue in part III that certain public spheres, both in terms of their
organizational form and discursive content, can confuse dichotomous efforts to understand them precisely as they must in
order to retain ongoing emancipatory potential.

I argue that there can be a third kind of public sphere, here illustrated in form and content by the case of the Zapatistas, that retains and deepens the normative commitments of the concept (i.e.,
democracy, inclusion, cosmopolitanism) as they have been elucidated in the works of Kant, Arendt, and Habermas. Understanding the atypical construction of the Zapatista public sphere will
help us to speak more generally about a different kind of public
sphere, neither national nor transnational, that can put us past the
impasses of previous chapters' conclusions. And with this new
construction, which I name the "transgressive public sphere," we
shall arrive in the end at a conception of a still vital public realm.

These general remarks disguise two deeper problems. First,
a transformation of political identity is implicated in transgressive public spheres, such that the identity of participants also
must have a transgressive character. That is, transgression entails that if actors see themselves committed to a national project
of some sort, perhaps even with some kind of "good" nationalism, they must (in order to achieve transgressive identity) simultaneously understand themselves as engaged in a larger
politics taking place beyond the bounds of their state and regional concerns, as world citizens with meaningful roots in particular places. Indigenous identity does well to illustrate this
imbricated self-understanding (chapter 8).

Second, much of what I say about the strategic advantages of transgression appears as if it presents an instrumental model that could be as well utilized by radical democrats as by proponents of Wahhabism or neo-Nazism. Yet this is not at all true. A public sphere that works for increasing exclusions and for the centralization of political power in the hands of an unaccountable class is a contradiction in terms. I will show why it is in fact necessary for a transgressive public sphere to be normatively committed to increasing inclusion and deepening democracy (chapter 9). To do so, I will discuss the ways in which transgressive public spheres reproduce, reinforce, and substantially deepen the commitments of Kant's and Habermas' classical and cosmopolitan theories. Indeed, I propose the theory of transgression as grounding for a more radical point of view, one that is in line with socialist and radical democratic politics.

Part III proceeds in three chapters that bring us from an elucidation of the transgressive public sphere of the Zapatistas (chapter 7), to a discussion of the transgressive subject position entailed by indigenous identity (chapter 8), to an argument for transgressive public spheres as a continuation of the politics of inclusion, democratization, contestation, and legitimation historically associated with public spheres (chapter 9).

But first, some further qualifications about the term "transgression" are necessary. The concept of transgression has a genealogical meaning, and a newer meaning in political science, both of which I do not intend. In the most basic formulation, transgression means to go beyond or over a limit or a boundary, to exceed or to overstep. This is part of the meaning I preserve. However, transgression derives from a religious lexicon in which it meant to act in violation of the law or to commit an offense by violating a command; these laws and commands being those of God, and so transgression, in this context, is a sin, certainly not something to encourage.[2] In my account, transgression is still understood in relation to a disobedience to boundaries, an exceeding of limits, but I do not carry over the evaluative connotation.[3] In other words, I recommend transgression.

I am not the first to detach "transgression" from its fourteenth-century religious etymology. Recently and influentially, Doug McAdam, Sidney Tarrow, and Charles Tilly have recast the term for political scientists in their *Dynamics of Contention.* They use the term to discuss a particular type of contention, as do I, but my usage must be distinguished from theirs. McAdam, Tarrow, and Tilly understand contentious politics to be collective political struggle that "is episodic rather than continuous, occurs in public, involves interaction between makers of claims and others, is recognized by those others as bearing on their interests, and brings in government as mediator, target, or claimant."[4] For sure, much of this definition has pertained to the kinds of politics we have discussed, and certainly describes well the politics of the Zapatistas. McAdam, Tarrow, and Tilly call some contentious politics "contained" whereas others are "transgressive." Contained contention is that of already-established political actors using preexisting means of claim making, whereas transgressive contention requires that some parties to the conflict are newly self-identified actors and/or that the kind of collective action is in some important way innovative. As we shall see, this criterion for transgression is well met by the Zapatistas who, in moving from peasant politics to indigenous politics introduced newly self-identified actors and whose mode of action, often a kind of political theater, utilized innovative means. Certainly, according to McAdam, Tarrow, and Tilly's definition, the case of the Zapatistas qualifies as a case of transgressive contention.

For McAdam, Tarrow, and Tilly, transgression refers to transgression of the conventions of contained politics; that is, it is transgressive because it surprises what we expect to see in the realm of collective action. Collective action that takes place outside of the sanctioned political processes established by the state for civil society to make use of is transgressive in McAdam, Tarrow, and Tilly's account. Indeed, public spheres (particularly nonbourgeois public spheres) also form and function outside of the sanctioned spaces and well-worn paths of conventional political processes. In fact, instances of political violence have been and can be included in the public sphere. An armed rebellion, for example, can effectively enter historically suppressed and excluded political discourses into the public sphere. But our two senses of transgression are only similar up to this point.

I specifically use the term transgressive to mean beyond the boundaries or in violation of the dichotomy of the national and transnational frameworks. What is different, in my account, is *what* is being transgressed. The case of the Zapatistas just so happens to satisfy the criteria for transgression in both accounts, in McAdam, Tarrow, and Tilly's and in mine; for our purposes, if a transgressive public sphere also qualifies as transgressive contention it does so by secondary traits. McAdam, Tarrow, and Tilly's conception of transgressive contention is compatible with my conception of a transgressive public sphere, but their argument does not pertain to the scale and function of public spheres, or, for that matter, to theories of the public sphere at all. What transgression goes beyond in my account is the concept of a public sphere *either* with an exclusively national *or* an exclusively transnational political function—it violates this analytical rubric. The kind of transgression I define is not at all a part of McAdam, Tarrow, and Tilly's definition, particularly because they choose cases of transgressive contention that they explicitly understand as state-bounded examples.[5]

A transgressive public sphere is a public sphere with a set of clear functions and concrete goals both within the context of and regarding the state of a particular nation *and* within the context of transnational politics and regarding multiple states or transnational institutions. Transgression as I define it does not subvert, undermine, or destabilize the distinction of the national scale as such or the distinction of the transnational scale as such. Rather, it problematizes the dichotomy of these scales, challenging claims of their mutual exclusivity and competitive comportment toward each other.

Transgression does not entail the deconstruction and elimination of national political identities and projects.[6] To the contrary, transgression entails understanding national political identities and projects as distinctive and even sharpening these identifications and projects, but only in a transformative way. That is, transgression does not imply that Americans or Mexicans should not understand themselves and their political terrain as "American" or "Mexican," but that this self-understanding does not and should not preclude a simultaneous, compatible, complicating, and ultimately necessary transnationalization of national political identity and projects. Transgression is transformative in that it produces a new kind of "complex identity,"[7] that is to say, a composite identity consisting of multiple levels of political identification (i.e., a person who sees herself as a socialist, a cosmopolitan, indigenous, and feminist). As we shall see, transgressive complex identity is neither that of cosmopolitanism nor that of nationalism, but neither is it one in which the terms of nationalism and cosmopolitanism are altogether dissolved. Transgression holds that both nationalism and cosmopolitanism can be cooperatively reconstructed and that a choice between them is an unnecessary and dangerous proposition for political theory and practice.

It is right to notice that there are components of both analysis and advocacy in my discussion of the transgressive public sphere. Indeed, I intend to move beyond the introduction of the transgressive framework to advocate for its advantages over previously considered frameworks. To this end, I will discuss potentially-but-not-yet-transgressive public spheres. I do not do this, however, with the assumption that any public sphere that so wishes can simply choose and achieve a transgressive construction. We shall see that transgression is a hard won achievement and that it is dependent on a number of variables beyond its own making. Understanding the concept and possibility of transgression, for both analysts and actors, is the major contribution of this work. Without this first achievement, regardless of the favorable salience and support of dependent variables, we cannot expect transgression to become the conscious objective of political actors. As well, without this first step, analysts will continue to employ a false dichotomy; public spheres, such as that of the Zapatistas, actually exist, and without a third approach to theorizing them, they will not be properly understood.

A transgressive public sphere has a national and a transnational set of functions and goals—it cannot be properly understood through any analysis that focuses on one set of functions and goals to the exclusion of the other. This construction matters because neither the national nor transnational framework is taken for granted, nor is one framework necessarily subordinated to the other (although each framework on its own is subordinated to the ideal of transgression). A public sphere's transgressive character is achieved precisely in its inextricable linking and discursive imbrication of both sets of functions and goals. This is a difficult point that will be sharpened in the following chapters. For now, it must suffice to say that a transgressive public sphere is established in and by the achievement of an irreducible dual comportment—that it is a public sphere in which the political identity of its participants also takes on a transgressive character as they refuse to preclude national identifications for cosmopolitan ones.

Simply put, transgression refers precisely to a public sphere and political identity that require an ongoing understanding of their double-occupancy in both national and transnational frameworks in order to be properly understood. Transgressive public spheres, apparently paradoxically, can have a nationalist and a cosmopolitan self-understanding.

The Zapatistas and the public spheres in which they operate encourage us to more closely study the national and the transnational as inseparable overlapping zones. In order to explore the Zapatistas as such a test case, I ask if the case of the Zapatistas adds anything new to what a public sphere is and/or can be. Initially, the Zapatistas demarcated a specific state-bounded public with an expressly local and national indigenous rights agenda that soon grew to play a productive role in shaping transboundary public spheres. I argue that the Zapatistas ultimately serve as an example of the overlapping fluidity of the national and transnational frameworks, of a cooperative rather than an antithetical relationship between these arenas, and of the inadequacy of dichotomous thinking about the national and the transnational. The Zapatista public sphere transgresses the boundaries between the national and the transnational, and increases its political leverage as a result of this transgression. Because of this, it serves as an example that both actors and analysts can learn from.

The Zapatista public sphere is not the only "boundary-transgressive" case that bears such features. Environmentalists and feminists (see the Rainforest Action Network and the Beijing + 5 meeting and declaration, for examples) have often articulated their work as being comprised of (1) immediate objectives in localized contexts, *and* (2) constructive objectives in shaping culture and changing laws internationally, both of which are presented as inextricably linked. (Note that I am only speaking here about what constitutes simple "boundary-transgression." In actual fact, as we will explore more in chapter 9, the transgressive public sphere *cannot* be produced by boundary-transgression alone, for it also requires a normative commitment to the ideals of inclusion and pluralism and to the deepening of democracy.) Other examples, such as German or French "Europeanness," *are* simultaneously national and transnational, but these refer to identities that are fitted to institutionally delineated spaces, whereas the identities of those populating Zapatista public spheres emerge within their public spheres as their own innovation and product. That is, "Europeanness" develops following (lagging quite a bit behind) the development of the European Union, and the European Union even requires the flourishing of "Europeanness" for its own strength and legitimation. "Zapatismo," on the other hand, emerges as a contestatory product of civil society that does not inhabit a state-sanctioned social space, and it is generally unwelcome by all of the states it addresses (thus, its formation and activity is, in principle, more contestatory).

It is in light of this last point that we may understand the lessons of the Zapatista public sphere as a contribution to socialist political theory. The case made by the Zapatista public sphere is not that we should try to achieve transgression in order to advance programs that are wholly compatible with existing capitalist societies. Rather, transgression appears here as a mechanism for challenging, radically restructuring, or categorically rejecting certain tenets of capitalism today. The transgression of the Zapatista public sphere, which both defends indigenous peoples where they live and raises a transnational critique of neoliberalism, is normatively at odds with any conception of unbounded capitalism—unbounded publics are thus presented as a kind of antithesis.

This returns us to the schemata I introduced in chapter 3 about the particular character or composition (C), particular function or orientation (F), and actual location in the world (L) of the public sphere. The Zapatista public sphere recalls and supports my argument that the character, function, and location of nonbourgeois public spheres are significantly different. Where (C) is "nonbourgeois," (F) is often "to *challenge* the state," and (L) is "transnational" or, in this case, "transgressive." What will be crucial to show is that when (L) is transgressive, (C) and (F) change. With transgression, (C) is partly national and partly transnational, it is inclusive and heterogeneous and reflects a pluralistic collectivity that combines compatible features of nationalism with cosmopolitanism. And (F), for a transgressive public sphere, is to challenge multiple states, international publics, and transboundary institutions. This is what happens to the character and function of public spheres when they become transgressive. When (L) is transgressive, (C) and (F) are too.[8]

As explored in chapter 4, some of the central debates about globalization concern environmental issues, outflanked democratic institutions, processes of political economy that exceed the jurisdiction of states, cultural hegemony led by a disproportionate flow of cultural products from rich countries to poor ones, and increasing disparities of wealth. All of these issues affect specific populations in very specific ways, and yet they all spill over the national boundaries in which the affected populations live. Discourses that make such issues their focus tend to construct themselves in transgressive terms. For example, it is always possible to frame the defense of a rainforest as both a local human rights issue for the people whose lives depend directly upon it, and simultaneously, as a global warming issue in a broader global framework. In general, choosing one framing to the exclusion of the other serves to diminish the leverage of the claim that the rainforest *ought to be defended*.

This basic insight underlies the organization of the Zapatistas as well. "Indigenous identity" (much like one's identification as an environmentalist) is never only local because it always implies community with other indigenous groups, yet indigenous rights demands are always asserted against trends that place the specificity of lifeways (particular values, practices, traditions, norms) in jeopardy.[9]

Most of the various globalization issues concern indigenous peoples in different ways. But something interesting has happened to indigenous identity since the early 1990s. "Indigenous rights" movements are not just populated by indigenous peoples but increasingly by those who proclaim their solidarity with the self-determination of indigenous peoples and, more generally, those who take a contestatory stance toward neoliberalism and capitalist globalization. Recent indigenous rights discourses have had a transformative effect on an indigenous rights public sphere that has historically been an exclusive ethnonationalist movement (see my discussion of Mexican "indianismo" in chapter 6). The Zapatista public sphere recasts historic indigenous rights discourses and transgresses the boundaries between national and transnational. Not all discourses can or do constitute such transgressive publics or can or do shape such transgressive political identities, hence some discourses are better than others in securing public affirmation at home and abroad.

By the conclusion of part III, I will have presented to the reader a new public sphere theory. According to this theory, national self-understandings do not preclude the simultaneous and ultimately necessary transnational self-understandings of people and movements today. And strategically, transgression provides the means for public spheres to bolster their political leverage. But my most central and overarching aim is to develop a normative political philosophy with stronger commitments to inclusion and pluralism than previous and prevailing theories of the public sphere, and to demonstrate the enduring importance of the concept for any emancipatory politics.

Notes

1. A qualification is needed regarding my use of the definite article "the," which often appears before "public sphere." It is important to know why I have not chosen to speak uniformly about "a public sphere," or "the public sphere" or "public spheres." A qualification regarding this matter is important at this juncture, at the beginning of part III, because I am no longer using the conventions of other authors. I have found it necessary to use all of these formulations variously. This is mainly because we are increasingly juxtaposing "types" of public spheres (the national, transnational, and now the transgressive type). I use the definite article to invoke with emphasis one type of public sphere in relation to another, or to invoke "the public sphere" as a concept, in a similar way that I have spoken about "the national framework," even though there are many such frameworks. On the other hand, the indefinite article, or the plural formulation are used when I want to invoke with emphasis the always possible multiplicity of public spheres in general or of a specific kind. To be clear, then, I never intend to suggest that there is only one public sphere of public

spheres in general or of a specific kind. Always, there may be a multiplicity of public spheres, but in some instances I want to emphasize one type of public sphere, or the singular conception, while in other instances I want to emphasize the potential or realized multiplicity of public spheres.

2. This definition of "transgression" from *Webster's Ninth New Collegiate Dictionary* and *The Random House College Dictionary*.

3. If I were to retain the religious, evaluative connotations of transgression, I would have to associate the state with God (as, for example, Hegel has done) and the boundaries of the state with unsurpassable, righteous limits. But this is by no means my intention.

4. Doug McAdam, Sidney Tarrow, and Charles Tilly, *Dynamics of Contention*, 5.

5. They say: "For further simplification, our sustained examples come chiefly from episodes in which national states were direct participants or significant parties to the claims being made. This focus on national, as opposed to local or regional, contention springs primarily from practical concerns." Ibid., 8.

6. The transnationalism of transgression does not reject nationalism. Nationalism within civil societies, as discussed in chapter 6 with reference to Craig Calhoun (and as it will be discussed in reference to the Zapatistas in chapter 7 and essays by Charles Taylor and Kwame Anthony Appiah in chapter 9) could still be a good and even necessary mechanism of democratization. Nationalism, for example, could emerge within a political community and bind with solidarity a common project that sincerely invokes universalistic democratic principles and that aligns itself with republican ideals.

7. See the discussion of complex identity in chapter 5 in reference to Janna Thompson.

8. Likewise, when (C) is transgressive, (L) and (F) are, and when (F) is transgressive, (C) and (L) are.

9. What exactly indigenous identity is will be much of the focus of chapter 8. For now, it can be said that indigenous identity generally *stems* from a sense of "native inhabitance" according to which a group of people identify as sharing particular lifeways that are somehow anchored to their place of birth, to the historic and geographic residency of the continuation of their cultural practices.

7

A Different Kind of Public Sphere

The Zapatistas' Transgressive Public Sphere

In this chapter, I try to understand both what is the Zapatista public sphere and what kind of public sphere it is. I do this to introduce and to explore a kind of public sphere that must be understood as transgressive, or else not understood at all. A transgressive public sphere is a public sphere that has an emphatic national, sometimes even nationalist, orientation, but which, at the same time, challenges its state-boundedness by seeking to cast itself, both discursively and organizationally, as a transnational public sphere. Analyzing a transgressive public sphere solely by its transnational features, let us say, as you would analyze a cosmopolitan public sphere in terms of its cosmopolitanism, leads to a misunderstanding of such a public sphere. Likewise, analyzing a transgressive public sphere solely by its intrastate demands and strategic orientation, let us say, as a national or nationalist movement, also leads to a misunderstanding of such a public sphere.

To be sure, transgressive public spheres do have these analyzable features and we can of course talk about them. But a transgressive public sphere, once it is developed as such, is not a national public sphere with a transnational feature, nor is it a transnational public sphere with a national feature. Its transgressive character is achieved precisely in its centralization of a dual comportment, a double-occupancy, and a dual orientation.

The dual comportment of transgressive public spheres becomes irreducible whenever the fates of its national and transnational initiatives are necessarily bound up in each other. This transgression of the national and transnational frameworks is also achieved through reshaping the self-understandings of the people who populate transgressive public spheres, that is, through the production of new political identities (this latter point, regarding identity, will be explored further in chapter 8).

The foremost aim of chapter 7 is to argue, through the consideration of an extended example, that certain public spheres cannot be accurately characterized as exclusively national or exclusively transnational in terms of their character or composition (C), particular function or orientation (F), and actual location in the world (L). Such publics, I argue, must be understood under the rubric of a third conceptual framework.

I must be clear from the beginning that what we will discover in the present chapter is the picture of and the possibility for transgressive public spheres in general. Although I will go into some detail in the following discussion of the Zapatistas, I am not doing so for the purpose of making claims about *them*. My guiding aim is to explicate the possibility for a kind of public sphere that is neither national nor transnational, but only ever both. Readers looking for a detailed account of the Zapatista rebellion, precursors to the uprising, and how it fits in Mexican history, should look elsewhere. Many such accounts have already been written and it is not my aim to present here what is far better and far more fully explained in other books.[1]

Parts of the Story

While I do not intend to retell the story of the Mexican Zapatistas, it will nevertheless be necessary to provide some picture of the uprising, and to further flesh it out where fitting. Indeed, the transgressive public sphere of the Zapatistas emerges from the history of indigenous rights politics in Mexico.[2]

In Mexico, one political party, the Institutional Revolutionary Party (PRI), took power as the ruling party in 1929 and remained as such throughout the rest of the century. Though there has been only one party in government, much has changed in Mexican politics and society under PRI leadership. Some of the developments have been deadly, particularly for the peasant communities to whom the PRI has been a consistent antagonist.[3] I have already discussed the two general tendencies of the antagonism between "indianismo" and "indigenismo" (see chapter 6). But it is important to acknowledge that the PRI government has also been rather successful in some notable ways especially since World War II. For example, John Womack, Jr., points out that

> infant mortality has declined sixfold, the population has nearly quadrupled, the urban population sextupled, society is more and more open and mobile, literacy has increased from 50 to 90 percent, the real national income per capita has tripled, and the government has functioned well enough through its Institutional Revolutionary Party (the PRI), so that no would-be military dictator has even tried to seize power.[4]

These developments, which must be noted as major accomplishments, might not be so clearly credited to PRI leadership by other critics or by the Mexican peasants living in Chiapas or elsewhere, but they do illustrate an important dimension in twentieth-century Mexican politics: Mexican civil society, publics outside of Mexico, and political analysts would not everywhere unanimously find a clear cut example of tyranny in Mexico since the Mexican Revolution of 1910. Despite this, it is objectively true that Mexico's massive peasant population has remained at the crux of ongoing tensions and would variously strive for political recognition, political power, and the accrual of influence on the state.

Mexico's national project since the Mexican Revolution has been modeled on that of the United States in an effort to forge a unified national identity out of a large population of multiethnic indigenous groups. One of Mexico's founding fathers wrote: "All of our steps have followed the model of that happy republic, the United States of America."[5] Yet, living in the multiethnic makeup of much of the population, resided a large cache of resistant, distinguished communities by no means eager to reconceive of themselves as Mexican nationals assimilating into a homogenous civil society. I have already discussed the assimilation and miscegenation policies of indigenismo (chapter 6), but it is worth underlining that these policies were at the heart of Mexico's national project. And so, opponents of this project living in Mexico would have to conceive of an alternative national project, one that was indeed national, but which contested the homogenizing aims of the founders. The possibility for such an alternative national project, as we shall see, was the precursor to a transgressive construction of political identity and political struggle that would take shape in the historical politicization of Mexico's peasants into indigenous peoples.

As a result of the tension between two incompatible visions for a national project, two opposing views of Mexico emerged: There was "imaginary" or "fictitious Mexico," on the one hand, and "deep Mexico" on the other. "Fictitious Mexico" refers to the Mexico of the founders' aspirations, a Mexico with a binding national identity that unifies and assimilates all of the different ethnic communities into a single mainstream polity. "Deep Mexico," on the other hand, refers to the Mexico that really exists, a Mexico made up of many different peoples who understand themselves as distinct groups, who do not want to lose their identities, nor their lifeways, to a national project.[6]

But notice that fictitious Mexico implies an actual project, whereas deep Mexico simply refers to the Mexico that already exists and that the latter merely invokes some sense of the preservation of cultures and the rights of their members. Because deep Mexico, as a basic idea of the country, does not clearly explicate a project, its proponents have always had to articulate a rival political project in the face of the policies of indigenismo and other efforts to make imaginary Mexico a reality. Proponents of deep Mexico have variously articulated a politics of protection, recognition, rights, and inclusion for the many multiethnic indigenous peoples. So even in its earliest forms, this politics has had to draw its strength from solidarity with other marginalized ethnic communities living in Mexico. The solidarity needed by proponents of deep Mexico would be accumulated and consolidated through the discursive generalizing of the basic predicament of the many indigenous peoples, a kind of generalized discontent. But simultaneous with this discursive generality, the politics of deep Mexico also always had to emphasize the importance of the specificity of particular communal identities.[7]

The "Mexican civil society" sought by proponents of deep Mexico would consist of, without assimilating, each distinctive community in the country. The kind of politics associated with deep Mexico has had to define itself against the pressures of the politics of fictitious Mexico, and the antagonism between the two has never gone away. The indigenous peoples of Mexico inherit the task of articulating such a politics from generation to generation, yet the contexts in which a politics of deep Mexico must be articulated are always changing. For example, deep Mexico today does not simply perceive some form of state indigenismo as their antagonist, but rather, economic globalization has become a central focus. To some extent, economic development has always been a threat to deep Mexico, but it has not always been understood as something driven largely from the outside, as a set of aggressive economic initiatives that have subordinated the Mexican state as an instrumental conduit for neoliberalism.

To be clear, the Mexican state is still seen to hold sway on issues of the rights to land and the rights of culture and cultural practice for its indigenous people, on the issues of negotiation and conference with dissident groups, social movements, and the demands of Mexican civil society. But in geopolitical affairs, the larger pressures and objectives of capitalist globalization and the initiatives of free trade in North America are seen to have weakened the sovereignty of the Mexican state on a good deal of major economic matters.[8] In light of this, the articulated politics of and from deep Mexico has had to shift its comportment toward a larger addressee—in addition to the Mexican state, they must think of other states, particularly the United States, civil societies elsewhere, and other indigenous peoples who are also facing the threats of neoliberalism to appropriate land and natural resources and to reorganize, or "modernize," cultures to the degree that indigenous lifeways could become extinct.

The first thing to notice here is that, politically, "the indigenous" is an international category despite the fact that indigenous communities are so deeply rooted in specific rural locales, languages, and lifeways. But also, perhaps the most fundamental question is how such an international class can hold and assert democratic influence over the decisionmaking processes that put the lives and lifeways of indigenous peoples in jeopardy.

In the first place, proponents of and from deep Mexico have had to change the comportment of indigenous politics: "Operating within the framework of the nation-state and formal democracy, it constantly challenges and transcends them: it adopts them only as an appropriate structure for the transition to a new form of society and democracy."[9] In other words, indigenous politics does not often place much faith in the possibilities for influence within the national framework, yet it must utilize all existing national and formal channels of influence at the same time as it criticizes and attempts to transcend them. In this way, the critical and transcendent efforts of indigenous politics could result in the reformation of, or the opening up of, existing political space for indigenous peoples within the national framework. This insight, it should be stressed, would lie at the basis of the politics of the Mexican Zapatistas, who resolutely, and with more widespread public audibility than ever before, proclaimed the national project of deep Mexico as a part of a larger transnational project. This basic insight and basic structure would eventually lead to the emergence of a transgressive public sphere, whose participants would increasingly understand themselves as having a transgressive political identity. These are indeed the ingredients of a transgressive politics, which, when combined and developed, necessitate a simultaneous emphasis on inclusion and openness on the one hand *and* distinctive lifeways and crises on the other.

The organization of the Zapatista Army for National Liberation (EZLN) began to take shape in the mountains of Chiapas upon the arrival of a small group of revolutionary intellectuals and activists to the Lacandón Jungle in 1983. These neo-Marxist intellectuals and activists moved to the jungle to organize the peasant communities, but ended up living in and learning from native communities from their arrival onward, adjusting their theoretical suppositions in light of local insights, experiences, and histories. Even so, the organizing impetuses of the EZLN came into Chiapas with the immigration of radicals. Because of this, it has always been acknowledged that at least some of the organizational form and discursive content of the Zapatista rebellion also came from outside of Chiapas, from Mexico City, and from the university. The Zapatistas were themselves, therefore, from the very beginning, formed at least in part by foreigners: "All of the accounts, however, recognize the hybrid nature of the Zapatista movement. Indians and mestizos from different parts of Chiapas and Mexico who came together to discuss their experiences allowed for the expression of multiple worldviews and political and religious ideologies."[10] One of the most characteristic proclivities of the Zapatistas was to invite outsider involvement and to even accept as "indigenous" those who were not born into particular indigenous communities.[11]

In the 1980s, the international media paid no attention to the problems of Mexico's Mayan population,[12] and the details of the struggles of deep Mexico were not accessible to a large public sphere. Because of this dearth of publicity, any transboundary aspirations of indigenous politics went largely unrealized. But in 1994, after the Zapatista rebellion, media publics were made aware of the Zapatistas through the heavy bias of the Mexican government. Subcomandante Marcos extended an invitation to the people of the United States, to those who had learned of their movement and wondered how they, living in the country whose government heralded NAFTA, could respond constructively to the uprising: "We need people in the United States to create counterpropaganda to that of the Mexican federal government, and get out the truth, against the lie of Salinas."[13]

"Getting out the truth" was taken to be a major part of the Zapatistas' struggle. Most of what the world has received from the Zapatistas, most of what they have been able to give to others, is explanations—explanations of who they are, what they want, and why they are doing what they are doing. And after the 1994 rebellion, these explanations served far more than propagandistic purposes. If the Zapatistas were successfully characterized as violent terrorists to international public opinion, as President Salinas first attempted to do, then the Mexican government would have the moral mandate to deal with them by any means. If, on the other hand, the Zapatistas' uprising could not be effectively reduced to an image of terrorist violence, but could be seen on the side of right and dignity, then international public opinion and that of governments abroad would loosely but collectively comprise a critical monitor of the behavior of the Mexican government. In other words, for the Mexican state, international public opinion could confer or contest the legitimacy of their reactions to the Zapatistas—international public opinion could find the state's reactions on the side of right or wrong depending on how the Zapatistas were perceived.

So the public sphere was not merely a philosopher's abstraction to the Zapatistas, who relied on public opinion not only to win good favor, but political solidarity and safety. We see this also, for example, with antagonisms between Israelis and Palestinians, or in the war on Iraq, that it matters greatly how each side is perceived in domestic and international public spheres. In a post-9/11 United States, for example, an understanding of Palestinian resistance as terrorist violence, the invocation of a terrorist trope, goes far to situate public opinion favorably toward any attempt to stop such terrorism no matter how violent the response. Thus, groups fight for public opinion in the public sphere wherever they can, because whether or not they will be received as right and dignified hangs in the balance.

Expanding Publicity: From the Local to the National to the Global

Although the EZLN understood these realities and dynamics, they would not try to move from a national forum to a transnational forum right away. Importantly, their first aim was to enlarge the concerns of indigenous peoples from a local scale to a national scale.[14] This is often the first step in the politicization of rural Indian communities. They are so far removed from the national arena of society and politics, that they are not yet even national in scale. This is important because it illustrates another reason why we must be careful to not forsake the national project for the transnational one. Simply put, for indigenous politics, registering the will and opinion of Indian communities with the national public sphere is a major accomplishment, and often even a step toward transnationalization. The unignorable placement of an indigenous rights agenda on a national scale was the first goal and achievement of the EZLN uprising.

And the Zapatistas' achievement of domestic popularity must be appreciated in its context, for the EZLN started off as a minority even among peasants. On January 1, 1994, the day of the Zapatista uprising, the majority of the rural poor did not join the rebellion. They were invited by the EZLN, many of them were in solidarity with the EZLN, and many were furious with the PRI and wanted to see a revolutionary change in Mexico, but it was mostly only those who had joined the EZLN who participated in the rebellion. This was ultimately a conscious decision, not one caused by class, ethnic, social, religious, or political differences. It was not, therefore, that the EZLN was simply more courageous: "It was principally in the choice made between rival strategies of struggle for 'a life worth living.' It was in practice a difference of organization—and not between the only locally organized and the Zapatistas, but between other regional organizations of struggle and the EZLN."[15] After the uprising, many other peasant communities did join in. "Zapatismo" (defined and discussed more below), was used to generate and to mobilize political solidarity abroad, but it was first used to mine for solidarity domestically.

Some descriptions of the Zapatistas have depicted them as a classical national public sphere, a bourgeois public sphere like those analyzed in Habermas' *Structural Transformation*. Most notable, are the observations of Octavio Paz:

> Although the political texts of the rebels are principally destined for the masses, they seem well thought out and written to seduce or irritate an elite—that middle class that flocks to literary cafes, reads cultural supplements, goes to exhibitions and lectures, loves rock and Mozart, takes part in avant-garde spectacles and attends marches. Thanks to his rhetoric and undeniable theatrical talent, Subcommandant Marcos has won the opinion battle. In this, not in a supposed "postmodernity," rests the secret of his popularity among intellectuals and among the vast sectors of the middle class in Mexico City.[16]

Paz thus observes that the popularity of the Zapatistas within Mexico has to do, not with the fact that they represent some kind of new postmodern revolution, but that they have fought a battle for public opinion and have largely won it. The Zapatistas utilized a national public sphere to win this battle, and it was even populated by a similar demographic to that of the bourgeois public sphere of Habermas' account: A middle class of intellectuals with lots of leisure time, those who discussed the rebellion in cafes, listened to others discuss it in lectures, and read about it in print media, were the ones in Mexico who devoted the most critical attention the communicative efforts of the Zapatistas. Hence, despite the greater hopes of the Zapatistas to resonate their agenda across cultures and classes, and across national boundaries, the national public sphere was an indispensable terrain. The enlargement of the Zapatista public sphere, the establishment of a communicative reciprocity with other publics than a relatively educated middle class in Mexico, would only be the result of ongoing and innovative efforts to generalize appeal, understanding, and solidarity.

One of the discursive links that the Zapatistas always had to other publics in metatopical common space was that, from the beginning, NAFTA was a central issue. NAFTA was described by the Zapatistas as "the death certificate for the ethnic people of Mexico."[17] So even while the EZLN was speaking to the Mexican state and Mexican civil society, inasmuch as their discourses were circulated outside of Mexico, they were also presenting an opposing picture of what the ever-increasing freedom of capital brings with it. This discursive focus on neoliberalism and capitalist globalization would ultimately presage pro-Zapatista demonstrations in the United States and Western Europe in February 1995.[18] Bolstering this discourse became increasingly important to the Zapatistas after they saw how far international solidarity could go to shield them from their own state (the bolstering of this discourse was a major function of the International Encuentros, discussed more below).[19]

So what is the Zapatista public sphere? First of all, it is a *political* public sphere, so while it is a place for the formation of will and opinion it is also committed to the broadcasting of already-formed opinion and will to other publics and to powerholders. The Zapatista public sphere is comprised of the collective realm of discussion and discussants within Mexican civil society and other civil societies in which the questions and demands of indigenous politics are engaged as they have been framed by the

Zapatistas. The Zapatista public sphere understands itself *as a collectivity* whose political commitments and solidarities overlap with and support those of the Zapatistas. And again, because it is a political public sphere, the Zapatista public sphere demarcates a collectivity that understands its own discursive activity as a way to proliferate its opinion and will (a particular worldview and critique) to wider publics. Of course, there are other publics that know of, think of, and talk about the Zapatistas, but depending upon their politics, these may or may not be part of the Zapatista public sphere.

The Zapatista public sphere has transformed since its early formation when Mexican civil society first began to listen to, read, and discuss the Zapatistas' publicized political discourses. At first, the most enlivened public was drawn from Mexican civil society, consisting of those who poured out into the streets in enormous gatherings in support of the Zapatistas and of those who were indecisive, intrigued, or opposed to them, who were inundated with news about the uprising and its demands on TV, radio, and in newspapers. Of this larger public sphere, the first concrete Zapatista public sphere was comprised by the Mexican reading and viewing public that was compelled to reconsider and debate the country's historical and ongoing regard for its large Indian population: "After being glued to screens and radios and newspaper headlines during the first dozen days of January, the nation inhaled deeply and wondered about the whys of rebellion. Why had Mexico treated its Indians so badly that they were driven into repeated rebellion? The bottom line was a sort of national sense of guilt about the 'Indian problem.'"[20] This sphere of enlivened public concern and discussion was in many ways the most important of all the EZLN's battlefields. Indeed, the public sphere as a political instrument for the EZLN became more central and better honed as the Zapatistas started to see how far and wide their political discourses could resonate.

Electronic communications and the Internet became a fast friend of the Zapatistas, expanding the reach of their political discourses beyond any of their early expectations. Soon after the rebellion, it became difficult to maintain that the public sphere of those considering the situation of the Zapatistas and taking a side on the matter was national.

> The communiqués were like a brilliant running commentary on Mexican life and their defiant, playful tone struck a nerve throughout the country—and the world—as, one by one, La Jornada, El Financiero (for a short while), and the opposition weekly Proceso circulated the epistles to a wider and wider audience. National and international diffusion was sped along by a press corps that numbered a thousand in the first 23 days of the war. Activists in El Paso were already translating the communiqués and posting them daily on the Internet.[21]

It is worth pointing out that there was a critical element of chance and of eloquence that favored the expansion of the Zapatista public sphere. By 1994, there was already massive competition in mass communications for the attention of publics everywhere. News media, multiplied and proliferated by Internet and satellite technologies, had already created a situation where the reading and viewing publics of the world could hardly learn about all the countless "speakers" appealing for their attention. In Mexico, the national media made it nearly impossible to not know about the uprising. But the fact that a large public sphere outside of Mexico did learn of the rebellion and did take it very seriously is not only due to that fact there was a good deal of international press.

Largely responsible for their wide publicity and resonance was the surprising quality of the uprising, the "look" of the Zapatistas, their appeal to mystery and to mythology, and a general interest in the poetic style of the communiqués. The Zapatistas were different, interesting, and even entertaining. In an era where the attention of civil societies is hotly competed for by a growing number of media, a rebellion has to be different, interesting, and entertaining to win international attention—it has to strategically navigate the proclivities of publics inundated by a mass entertainment industry. This is not a small point, and indeed echoes Habermas' demand of the public sphere to "not only detect and identify problems but also convincingly and *influentially* thematize them, furnish them with possible solutions, and dramatize them in such a way that they are taken up and dealt with by parliamentary complexes."[22] But the prerequisite of effective dramatization is not something that a political public sphere can simply plan to satisfy, for the conditions for a wider resonance lie outside of itself, in what else is already happening in the world, in what is occupying the attention of publics everywhere.

The Zapatista uprising never only aimed to demand rights and political power for the indigenous peoples of Mexico, but also to express an opposition to neoliberalism on the inauguration of NAFTA.[23] After the uprising, the Zapatistas began to hone more and more influence on and garner support from international solidarity groups. This development took organized form in what are called the *Encuentros for Humanity and against Neoliberalism*.[24] The encuentros are intercontinental meetings that invite people all over the globe who are in solidarity with the Zapatistas to meet for the purpose of organizing new and sustaining preexisting local movements *under the rubric* of a global movement against neoliberalism (the more recent World Social Forum is an example of another gathering like the encuentros). In the encuentros, politics is oriented to take up indigenous, region-specific issues that are ideologically and politically linked to other region-specific issues around the world. The discourse of these encuentros, which continues electronically in between each meeting, expands and constitutes a Zapatista public sphere comprised of multiple publics that is, rather concretely, small-scale and localized *and* global simultaneously. As Courtney Jung points out:

> The EZLN was also instrumental in developing links between the indigenous rights agenda and other elements of a global oppositional dialogue. . . . The Zapatista Internet listserv, which has been maintained continuously since 1994, regularly sends EZLN communiqués and newsclips to tens of thousands of sympathizers worldwide. Most of those who have signed onto the listserv would count themselves part of a global opposition, a multisonorous voice of dissent against persisting hierarchies and exclusions. Through these links, Mexico's rural poor have asserted their voice in global politics.[25]

And Mexico's rural poor have, largely because of bolstered leverage secured through global support and solidarity, asserted their voice in Mexican politics too. The Mexican state is acutely aware of the added weight a global community contributes to the Zapatista's demands.

Words as Weapons: The
Guerilla Seizure of Reading Publics

As Jung points out above, the Internet was a major tool in the development of the Zapatista public sphere. Harry Cleaver has said, "This has been a war of words, images, imagination, and organization. . . . Vital to this continuing struggle has been the pro-Zapatista use of computer communications."[26] The idea that words can be weapons, or, outside military language, that they can be used to bring about social and political change is indeed reminiscent of Kant's idea of the public use of reason. And despite new communication technologies, the Zapatista public sphere was essentially that of a reading public. Discussion in topical common spaces was rarely had with the Zapatistas themselves (aside from during brief and infrequent encuentros), but rather, with and about their texts:

> El Sup had a rifle, yes, but he hardly used it. His bullets took the form of faxes and e-mails, cluster bombs in the shape of communiqués, and nonstop e-mail midrashim through the Internet. He wrote in a torrent, producing hundreds of texts, disproving Hannah Arendt's claim that "under conditions of tyranny it is far easier to act than to think." In less than twelve months, during sleepless sessions on the word processor in the midst of fighting a war, El Sup generated enough text for a 300-page volume.[27]

Hence, Kant's public use of reason had much to do with the formation and the transnational growth of the Zapatista public sphere, a fact that is far from obvious in characterizations of a guerilla uprising.

But I must be cautious here, because a characterization of the Zapatistas as utilizing a public sphere as their primary terrain, as fighting a "war of words," can be seen as derisive. There were some, for example, who saw in the Zapatistas evidence that revolutionary possibilities are still alive today. To such observers, as well as to critics, an argument that understands the Zapatistas as an innovative and rebellious discursive project, a lively engagement with national and transnational public spheres, is an argument that ultimately denies the Zapatistas their revolutionary importance.[28]

To some extent, this latter view is accurate. I maintain that the Zapatistas do not represent a new kind of old revolutionary project, and that they have redefined their political function toward a more radical reformism—that the Zapatistas are situated somewhere in between reform and revolution. Theirs is what we have called a radical democratic politics, which we have discussed in the context of Cohen and Arato's theory and will revisit in chapter 9 in the context of the theory of Ernesto Laclau and Chantal Mouffe. The Zapatistas have never had much faith in existing democratic inroads of democratic influence in Mexico, particularly because such inroads were blockaded to indigenous peoples. At the same time, it became clear to the Zapatistas shortly after they began that a seizure of state power was a far less hopeful path than a contestatory politics consisting mainly of the circulation of political discourses. To be clear, this does not represent a rejection or a turning away from revolution. Rather, it is a recasting of the meaning of revolution, which is in fact not entirely new; it is about time that theorists and political movements caught up with Foucault in understanding that revolutions need not always culminate in a takeover of the state.[29] With the circulation of political discourses and the pressure of the public sphere, the Zapatistas could expand, deepen, open up access to, and create new inroads of political influence.

By singling out the public sphere I do not mean to diminish and deride the efforts of the Zapatistas. I do not regard the public sphere as an intellectual game consisting of playing around with words, no matter how playfully and artfully cast the language. And therefore, I do not agree that the Zapatistas need to be defended against the charge that their politics consists of a daring, high-risk infiltration of the public sphere (as their defenders have done). For example, Manuel Callahan has responded to Octavio Paz's and Jorge G. Castañeda's characterizations of the Zapatistas as "the cause of little spilt blood but much flowing ink" and as "armed reformists," respectively, by calling such analyses dismissive.[30] However, it seems to me that Paz's and Castañeda's characterizations are quite right and that they need not be understood as dismissive. A part of the problem for Callahan and other hopeful observers is that the EZLN introduced itself in a guerilla uprising, so when it was finally transformed into a public sphere it seemed that the movement of the Zapatistas might not be as revolutionary as it first appeared, that they might "just" be fighting a war of words. However, a war of words can be indispensably effective in restructuring political culture and I will substantiate this claim, in part, by showing just how much the Zapatista public sphere did in fact create new political possibilities, change the political reality of Mexico's indigenous, and make the nation, both the society and the state, address indigenous peoples' concerns and indigenous rights with seriousness.

A war of words has always been at the heart of the Zapatistas' politics, and it has been rightly acknowledged that the circulation of texts to reading publics was a far greater help to the Zapatistas than their militarism. Weinberg points out that these

> "post-modern" guerillas have been remarkably nonviolent and anti-authoritarian, effecting their advances less through military than moral means. Their rifles—and they have never had enough rifles to go around, as evidenced by the young rebel troops of January 1994 marching into battle with sticks symbolically shaped like rifles—have, to an extent, been props in a highly effective political theater.[31]

The EZLN's farthest-reaching cultural effect and the resonance of their struggle abroad has clearly come from the dissemination of their arguments, and so it has been the terrain of the public sphere, and not really a military terrain, that they have fought on. In Gramscian terms, the Zapatistas have been fighting a war of position more than a war of maneuver, yet by way of their theatrical seizure of the public sphere they have done the former under the guise of the latter—they have, that is, dramatized the presentation of their arguments in a risky and even deadly way, which has been a part of the novelty and appeal of the Zapatistas.[32]

So this characterization is not intended to be trite or belittling. A political organization that introduces itself with arms in a guerilla rebellion, no matter how many of those arms are later discovered to have been props, and no matter how much poetry is spoken, is a dangerous and potentially disastrous endeavor. And, again recalling Foucault, we should not cling to the bravado of the classical model of revolution so steadfastly that we are unable to identify new forms of revolt. Saul Landau has accurately described the Zapatista uprising as "armed theater."[33] The Zapatistas were not going to ask any longer to have their issues taken up and placed on the table by an irresponsive government. Theirs was far from a peaceable invitation to reciprocal dialogue that would have satisfied Habermas' definition of discourse (discussed in chapter 2). But it was, nevertheless, a sincere invitation for real reciprocity, for reflection in the public sphere, and for challenging the Mexican state.

The Zapatistas acted in the manner of the nonbourgeois public spheres we discussed in chapter 3 in that they registered their arguments and claims, creatively and resourcefully, by means of civil disobedience. In this way, the Zapatistas can be better described by Cohen and Arato's theory than by Habermas'. The Zapatista public sphere formed and functioned very differently than Habermas' ideal-typical bourgeois public sphere. Their rebellion seemed at first to be another event in the history of armed struggle in Latin America aimed to seize state power. But ultimately, the Zapatistas' militarism was employed primarily to enter the national Mexican public sphere by force, rather than by peaceably asking. Thereafter, their most powerful weapons were communiqués to reading publics at home and abroad.

Zapatismo Cultivates Transgression

After the rebellion, the Zapatista public sphere appeared to function as a conventional public sphere, but with clear and pointed discourses for both national and international reading publics. However, the political function of the Zapatista public sphere was not always clear. In 1996, the EZLN's Fourth Declaration from the Lacandón Jungle had three explicit addressees: It was addressed to the people of Mexico, and to the peoples and governments of the world.[34] Notably, the Mexican government was simply not addressed. By not addressing the Mexican state directly, the Zapatistas undermine the classical conception of a political public sphere, which by definition engages the national government that is beholden to it in principle.

The Zapatistas acknowledged that political solidarity, protection, and ultimately even achievements of democratization could be better won with the help of other bodies than their own government. In addition to the "governments of the world," the Zapatistas continued to address civil society, and they continued to distinguish Mexican civil society from world civil society. This illustrates that the Zapatistas saw clearly differentiated national and transnational frameworks, but that each had to be expressly and simultaneously engaged. The Zapatistas maintained a thoroughgoing commitment to the national struggle of Mexico's indigenous peoples, while understanding the instrumental role of the solidarity of others; but this role was never only instrumental. In the Zapatista public sphere, "others" elsewhere were not merely addressed for the purpose of assisting the struggle of Mexico's indigenous people—rather, it was supposed that involvement in a broader discussion about economic globalization could, in the best case, lead to a critical global response to it.

This leads us to a discussion of Zapatismo and to the heart of the meaning of a transgressive public sphere. Zapatismo, defined very loosely, refers to the contagious spirit of the Zapatista uprising, the contagious spirit of a serious yet exciting and innovative questioning of global capitalism and the dangers associated with it. Zapatismo refers to the high mobility and popular traction of Zapatista political discourses across national boundaries as the basis for widespread solidarity. But more specifically, Zapatismo is the idea that the Zapatistas, although they are situated as a very particular historical struggle for clear and concrete needs in Mexico, are a *representative* phenomenon. What I mean by this is that Zapatismo posits the Zapatistas as one expression of a more extensive kind of disaffection that could be expressed in other ways and places. The root disaffection refers primarily to that felt by other indigenous peoples, but it is also so loosely defined so as to be able to, at least in principle, include those who assume a similarly critical comportment toward economic globalization and neoliberalism.

Subcomandante Marcos and Yvon Le Bot, in a famous interview, try to get at just what Zapatismo is. They acknowledge that Zapatismo has a national and a transnational component, each one capable of being analytically distinguished from the other. However, Marcos insists that these two components are holistically unified in and by Zapatismo:

Zapatismo is the common point, or the pretext for converging. Each one has his own logic, but recognizes himself in certain very general propositions of Zapatismo. I see no resemblance at all among the Basque, Catalán, Greek, Kurdish, Swedish, Japanese Zapatistas, except that they all come here and each has its idea of Zapatismo or of what it should be. In any case it's a phenomenon that exists, and beyond the solidarity with the Indian movement, it aims more and more to retrieve a series of universal values that can serve as well for Australians, Japanese, Greeks, Kurds, Cataláns, Chicanos, Indians from Ecuador, for example, or the Mapuche [Indians in Chile]. . . . For the communities, you have to understand that the contact with this "international Zapatismo" represents especially a protection that allows them to resist. This protection is more effective than the EZLN, the civilian organization, or national Zapatismo, because in the logic of Mexican neoliberalism, the international image is an enormous stake.[35]

This passage is of critical importance because, firstly, Marcos speaks of both a national and an international Zapatismo. International Zapatismo, which did not exist at the time of the uprising in 1994, has become a prerequisite for the continuance of the national struggle. That is, it does not simply bolster the national project, but it insures it against repressive interventions from the Mexican state.

Marcos does not express hostility toward the inclination of other people elsewhere to appropriate the moniker of "Zapatista." That Zapatismo could provide a pretext for convergence, that it could represent an international effort to discover a common solidarity on the basis of certain general values, is potentially a good thing for others than the Zapatistas. Indigeneity is not a requirement for Zapatismo, but solidarity with indigenous struggle is. In this way, Zapatismo underlines the unique connotation of the term "Zapatista" itself, which never intended to suggest that the new Mexican Zapatistas were seeking the same kind of revolution sought by Emiliano Zapata in the early part of the twentieth century. Instead of this, the name "Zapatista" was intended to indicate something in the spirit of what that national hero did. The Zapatistas were doing *something else* for sure, but in the liberatory spirit of Zapata. Thus, the Zapatistas did not only represent a struggle for the inclusion of Mexico's indigenous peoples into the Mexican political public sphere and later, into other public spheres, but they also represented a deeper kind of inclusionary project in which they could make sincere invitations for participation, and not just for support.

We might recall at this point, the "indianismo versus indigenismo" debate discussed in chapter 6. In posing Zapatismo to and against both indianismo and indigenismo, the Zapatistas managed to severely recast the debate.[36] Zapatismo dissolves the exclusive, ethnic comportment of indianismo, a comportment that the government's indigenismo policies always hoped to dissolve in a different way (through miscegenation and assimilation). Zapatismo suggests that indigenous groups can struggle for their preservation, their self-determination, and their inclusion in political process, but that this struggle does not need to be theirs alone.

In August of 1996, in La Realidad, Mexico, at the first encuentro, Subcomandante Marcos said:

> Who can say in what precise locale, and at what exact hour and date this Intercontinental Encounter for Humanity and Against Neoliberalism began? We don't know. But we do know who initiated it. All the rebels around the world started it. Here, we are only a small part of those rebels, it's true. But to all the many walls that all the rebels of the world break every day, you have added one more rupture—that of the wall around the Zapatista Reality.[37]

Now, it is worth noting that this flowering language was characteristic of Zapatista communiqués, and that it must be parsed with some scrutiny if we want to consider its substantive content with measure. But what we derive from this pronouncement is a picture of an oppositional foment that will find ways to manifest itself, a picture in which the Zapatistas are one such manifestation. Marcos explains, as well, that the reality of the Zapatistas has been insulated in the mountains of Chiapas, that they have been walled off from other rebels who could not have previously joined them, until now.

One way to look at the Zapatistas is to see that and how they have recast a local struggle first nationally, then transnationally. But another way, which is suggested in the Zapatista encuentro, is that they are not recasting their struggle so much as overcoming impediments to seeing and working with those who are already with them. In other words, the struggles of indigenous Mexicans would, already in principle, place them in transnational community with other rebels challenging economic globalization and neoliberalism in different ways. According to this view, the achievement of the Zapatistas is not that they have created new streams of communication and coordination, but that they have cleared away blockages in preexisting streams that have kept the indigenous communities of Chiapas in a vacuum, marginalized and insulated within the walls of the country. As we shall see, both the generation of new linkages and political self-understandings *and* the superseding of communicative impediments must be considered in order to understand the case of the Zapatistas fully.

This was the question posed by Zapatismo (openly posed by the Zapatistas at the first encuentro): "How does the power against which we rebel affect you?"[38] The question acknowledges that various peoples are variously affected by economic globalization and neoliberalism, and that it is important to understand other peoples' disposition cooperatively instead of competitively. In terms of content, political identifications and experiences will be wildly diverse, but formally, myriad groups around the globe may frame a common politics. Habermas argued, "the political public sphere can fulfill its function of perceiving and thematizing encompassing social problems only insofar as it develops out of the communication taking place among *those who are potentially affected*."[39] For the Zapatistas, those who are potentially affected are very broadly conceived, and through the communicative linkages of the Zapatista public sphere, they are brought together into a single collectivity that does not necessarily displace their membership in other collectivities.

Indeed, Callahan has pointed out that, by the late 1990s, the Zapatistas were very concretely linked to other movements against economic globalization and neoliberalism, and, in particular, to the organizing bodies involved in the large demonstrations in Seattle in 1999 against the World Trade Organization (WTO) and in Genoa in 2001 against the G8.[40] Callahan explains that many of the organizations involved in planning the major events in Seattle, such as Peoples' Global Action (PGA), Direct Action Network (DAN), Independent Media Center, Black Bloc, and Global Exchange, had direct links to the Zapatistas, links of express solidarity, active communication, and of having met and conversed with them in the topical common spaces of the encuentros. Callahan suggests that even though the Zapatistas were themselves not in Seattle,

> Zapatistas and Zapatismo animated the street battles and solidarity during the "birth of a global citizen's movement for a global democratic economy." . . . In Seattle, paliacates covered the faces of anarchists, autonomists, and environmentalists linked with a variety of affinity groups, as well as other activists long associated with the conflict in Chiapas who claim Zapatismo as a politics and Zapatista as an identity. The awesome series of global actions, including Seattle, emerged, in part, as a consequence of a series of critical *encuentros* or encounters and *consultas* or plebiscites with civil society that the Zapatistas convened as part of their strategy to defeat neoliberalism.[41]

In this passage, Callahan affirms that Zapatismo can be and has been claimed as a politics by people outside of Mexico who are in solidarity with the Zapatistas. As well, Callahan observes that, by appropriating some of the style and content of the Zapatistas' political discourses, by invoking and reenacting their masked anonymity, "Zapatista" could be claimed as a political identity.

Innovative (specifically, transgressive) constructions of political identity will be the focus of chapter 8. So at this juncture, I would like only to make the following clarification: Claiming a Zapatista political identity does not imply *becoming* a member of an indigenous community living in another country. It is not an identity that links one to a homogenous group of people who share the same extant lifeways, and even within Mexico it could not have such an implication. To the contrary, Zapatismo affirms and recognizes the radical differentiation of groups against a politics of assimilation. But neither is Zapatismo merely solidarity. Through the activity of reciprocal communication between sectors of civil societies all over the world, political solidarity is transformed into binding relationships and new political identities are created. And, as we shall explore more fully in chapter 8, this is critical for political identity because it ultimately challenges *constitutive* theories of identity by suggesting the possibility for the self-conscious *construction* of new identities.

It is useful to stress that claiming a Zapatista political identity and Zapatismo politics may no longer be worth doing today. A political community needs to be active and actively contestatory, and it needs to be prominently present in the public sphere if it will have any chance of winning the serious attention and consideration of people, to reveal and to create stakes, and to influence or challenge powerholders. If these things no longer describe the Zapatistas today, then it will not make sense politically to claim Zapatista identity even if we are able to do so. To be clear, I am interested here in *what kind of political public sphere* the Zapatista public sphere is, not, strictly speaking, in the Zapatistas themselves.

The Zapatista public sphere reveals the conditions for the possibility of the construction of transgressive public spheres, not that Zapatista identity and Zapatismo politics in particular will remain useful and/or necessary, nor that they have been categorically successful. What we find in the Zapatistas is that where there is a contestatory group in need of solidarity and political community domestically *and* abroad, a transgressive public sphere will be paradigmatically superior to a classically constructed national public sphere or a cosmopolitan public sphere in a transnational framework. But understanding this is not yet a full understanding of a transgressive public sphere. We must remember that the normative commitments of indianismo had to be uprooted by the altogether different normativity of Zapatismo. That is, the Zapatista public sphere achieved transgression largely because it sought to expand, deepen, and open up access to existing inroads of democratic influence in Mexico, and because it opened itself up to outside identifications (rejecting ethnonationalism), participation, and even membership (more on these points in chapters 8 and 9). For the Zapatistas, transgression required a normative commitment to radical inclusion.

Zapatismo and the Zapatista public sphere work to assemble a political community amongst geographically disparate people. Zapatismo implies that if we understand ourselves as members of a community and that community acknowledges and affirms our membership as such, then such a community is as real as any other, even if wildly dissimilar people make it up. Communities are created in various ways, but their maintenance is rather typically achieved through the satisfaction of this kind of criteria (self-understanding and community conferral). The cosmopolitanism we explored in chapter 5 agrees with these criteria, and even depends upon them. Cosmopolitanism, remember, suggested that we ultimately reject political identifications such as national identities that serve to wall us off from other communities of which we could understand ourselves a part. But Zapatismo and the Zapatista public sphere fostered a strong cosmopolitan political identity without rejecting national identity as an impediment. Indeed, both national political identity and cosmopolitan political identity proved indispensable and inextricably linked in the Zapatista public sphere. And this is because the Zapatista public sphere is neither national nor transnational, but transgressive.

From the Particular to the General: The Transgressive Public Sphere

At this point, the claim that the Zapatista public sphere is neither exclusively national nor exclusively transnational has been shown in our analysis of its dual comportment. But it is important to flesh out more fully the "transgressiveness" of the Zapatista public sphere so that we might better understand this conceptual framework as one that can be abstracted from the present case selection and applied to other cases.

Carlo Manzo considers Zapatismo to emerge from the indigenous worldview, a worldview that contains a very particular critique that can be and is in fact shared by many others than the conventionally indigenous:

> We can re-establish the whole combination of possible relationships among ourselves, in the individual, communitarian, national and international spheres. We can respect, recognize and reproduce the sphere of community without diminishing, perhaps, individual and private rights. We could, finally, construct the groundwork for the next seven generations to build a world that contains many worlds.[42]

The idea of one world containing many worlds, or, for our purposes, of one public sphere containing many public spheres, is an idea that fundamentally emphasizes both the larger sphere of spheres as well as the smaller constituent spheres. It is in this imaginary that we can find the picture of a public sphere that is necessarily transgressive.

Let us continue to imagine, then, a large sphere that we are calling the Zapatista public sphere. In the very center of this sphere is a smaller circle that represents a smaller public sphere, let us say, it is the public sphere in Mexican civil society that has learned of, discussed, and become an advocate of indigenous rights as framed by the Zapatistas. Also within the larger sphere are many other smaller spheres, representing the public spheres that, collectively, comprise the Zapatista public sphere—the largest sphere is made by a line that encircles all of them. Each smaller sphere considers itself and is mutually considered by the others to be a part of the larger sphere. They are more or less aware of themselves and each other as such. This self-awareness and group conferral is constitutive. But each one has a very concrete site of contestation. That is, each one discursively engages a problematic *somewhere* in the world; each one has some localized project. Yet the more localized project is never the entire scope of their project, at least not as long as they have a self-conscious and externally affirmed membership in the larger sphere. These smaller spheres are moving parts of a larger body, they function where they are but, collectively, they enliven a larger body with a larger collective purpose.

The smaller spheres, let us now stipulate, are all situated in different countries around the globe, are all engaged in some state-bounded project, and may even understand this project as a national project and invoke a national group identity. The smaller spheres that make up the larger sphere insist on their double-occupancy in their own smaller sphere and in the larger sphere. And the larger encompassing one, the transnational public sphere, is not quite beyond the national framework, as the term would imply, for it consists of national projects and sometimes even nationalist political identifications, that at the same time see themselves as constitutive of a transnational sphere. Because of this, such a sphere of spheres could not be clearly or correctly said to fit more within the national or the transnational framework—thus, such a sphere of spheres is a transgressive public sphere, and the smaller spheres that make it up also take on a transgressive self-understanding.

Yet it remains to be said why it should matter that the Zapatista public sphere, rather than the human rights public sphere or the environmentalist public sphere is the larger sphere in my picture. The answer is that, at least among these, it does not matter much at all.[43] Indeed, since the Zapatistas have largely fallen out of the attention of publics worldwide, it might be better to discuss other public spheres that presently command more interest. But the more prominent political discourses of today are not necessarily those of tomorrow, and I do not intend to tie my analysis to a single public sphere on the grounds of its temporal popularity. The Zapatista public sphere has far more illustrative value for my project than other cases that could also help us to see the basic picture of transgression (some other cases are briefly discussed below).

The Zapatista public sphere grew out of a rethinking of a very particular subject position and a very particular struggle (indigeneity and indigenous rights) and has been uniquely situated in and anchored to Mexico's political development. The prehistory of the innovatively inclusive Zapatismo lies in the exclusive, intrinsically ethnic indianismo. And the Zapatistas' rhetorical employment of national liberation embodies precisely what has made the national framework so distasteful to cosmopolitan theorists, and most notably, to Habermas. So, I have chosen to discuss the Zapatista public sphere because it exemplifies with particularly acute poignancy why the dichotomous account of national and transnational frameworks is problematic by appropriating and recasting those features of a national politics that *should be* impediments to a transnational politics and utilizing them in the development of the latter.[44]

A national liberation movement (however ironically titled as such), led by indigenous communities from the mountains of Chiapas, *should have* reinforced more than anything the fear of an ethnonationalist reactionary politics flaring up in the face of globalization. But instead, the Zapatista public sphere has fostered the antithesis to this fear because it has positioned itself against both globalization *and* ethnonationalist reaction. And yet, it is not simply a cosmopolitan political public sphere either. Why not? The Zapatista public sphere retained a nationalist political orientation, framed continuously through its conjuring of

Emiliano Zapata, Pancho Villa, and the Mexican Revolution, and it retained a commitment to the plight of Mexico's indigenous peoples, arguing and negotiating most concretely and to greatest effect with the Mexican government and Mexican civil society. Because of this, the Zapatistas' transgressive public sphere problematizes with special clarity the structural assumptions underlying the analytical rubric that sees national and transnational public spheres as distinct arenas of scale. The Zapatistas' imbrication of two frameworks that have been discussed in many regards as mutually exclusive underlines the particular relevance of the Zapatista public sphere as, at least for our purposes, the larger encompassing circle.

Now, because the second most fundamental ingredient of any political public sphere is a political discourse (the first, of course, being a voluntarily attentive public of participants), something must be said about the strategically transgressive political discourse of the Zapatistas. John Holloway points out that, in their communiqués, the Zapatistas always made the concept of "dignity" a centerpiece. There are no persons anywhere, however you define the term "dignity," who do not want it and who fail to understand that they want to live with it. A demand for dignity is an exceptionally "thin" demand, whose specific meaning may vary greatly from one context to the next, and it is a demand that, inasmuch as it is heard and understood as such, lends itself to widespread resonance. To thicken this demand a bit we could say that a dignified life entails respect, recognition, equal treatment and rights, and to be treated with fairness (of course, we could make each of these terms thicker too). One cannot live with dignity without any of these things. Indigenous peoples do fight for dignity, but it is easy to imagine that any person deprived of it would fight for it too. It is for this reason, that Holloway insists that "'Zapatismo' is not a movement restricted to Mexico but is central to the struggle of thousands of millions of people all over the world to live a human life against and in an increasingly inhuman society."[45]

And the transboundary resonance of the concept of dignity does not clash with, supplant or even diminish an orientation toward a state-bounded, national, political project. To be precise, I am thinking here not of the kind of nationalism invoked by

Habermas (chapter 5) but rather of the kind invoked by Calhoun (chapter 6)—a nationalism that gives cohesion and purpose to an otherwise marginalized politics seeking to become national, as the Zapatistas first had to do:

> The fact that the EZLN is an Army of National Liberation seems to give a clear definition to the movement. . . . Here we have what appears to be a clearly defined and well-established framework: national liberation movements typically aim to liberate a national territory from foreign influence (the control of a colonial or neo-colonial power), to establish a government of national liberation designed to introduce radical social changes and establish national economic autonomy. . . . Looked at more closely, however, the apparent definition of "Army of National Liberation" begins to dissolve. In the context of the uprising the term "national liberation" has more a sense of moving outwards than of moving inwards. . . . "Nation" is counterposed to the state, so that national liberation can even be understood as the liberation of Mexico from the Mexican state. Or the defence of Mexico (or indeed whatever territory) against the state. . . . That the Zapatista movement is a movement of national liberation does not, then, confine or restrict the movement to Mexico.[46]

What is so critical about this passage is that it reveals an important way in which the articulation of a national project is compatible with the articulation of a transnational project. "National interest" does not necessarily mean the interest of the national state, for it may mean the interest of a civil society at odds with its own state, even if that state is not a colonial power. And if the centerpiece of such a movement is dignity, that is, if a national movement frames itself in the public sphere as a part of broader struggles for human dignity, then it can be *a transnational movement of national liberation.*

The Zapatista public sphere teaches political theory, and particularly public sphere theory, an invaluable lesson about the shortcoming of national and transnational analytical rubrics. But the Zapatista public sphere has not taught movements how to win. The Zapatistas negotiated the San Andrés Accords in February 1996 with President Zedillo, accords on Indian rights and culture designed to grant and protect both, but the terms of these accords have been contested ever since they were agreed to. The accords have never been fully enforced, and have often appeared a safe concession to the Zapatistas that would not deeply affect the lives of Mayans.[47] The Zapatistas are still organized and exist in a dangerous tension with the Mexican state and military, and yet they have not been able to continue to captivate the attention of the public sphere they built in the years following the uprising. Their resistances to those who still seek to displace them from the biosphere reserves on which they live and depend are scarcely covered by the international media, and, since 1996, they have hardly found their way into headlines.[48] Politically, the Zapatistas have not revived their early more militaristic paradigm; they have remained more peaceful and less threatening, and no longer have the theatrical appeal that once seized public attention. Therefore, the Zapatistas are an example of a transgressive public sphere not how to use one to win.

But at the same time, their successes mustn't simply be ignored. Weinberg catalogs some of the Zapatistas' successes:

> [I]n the court of Mexican public opinion they are overwhelmingly perceived as occupying the moral high ground. The Zapatista rebel government continues, even after significant setbacks, to rule from below throughout much of Chiapas. It has stood up to the cattle oligarchy goons and instated its own agrarian reform; outmaneuvered the state and federal governments into accepting at least some land take-overs; instigated the fall of numerous local governments; challenged the institutional subservience of women; and changed the nature of political discourse in Mexico. It has made Indian autonomy a national issue, brought revolutionary ideas to the mainstream, and accelerated the rupture between organized labor and the ruling party. *New York Times* reporter Alan Riding admitted the Zapatista uprising "had thrown the entire political system into disarray and given Mexico a hefty shove towards becoming a real democracy."[49]

Jung adds to this: "Although the Zapatista movement no longer holds the conscience of the Mexican nation, even skeptics agree that the EZLN played an important role in ending more than

268 / Chapter 7

seventy years of PRI one-party rule. It did so in part by multi-
plying the sites and terms of political contestation beyond state
control, issuing new challenges to party legitimacy."[50]

Of course, assessing the successes and failures of the Zapatistas has not been the goal of this chapter. The Zapatista public sphere presents a picture of a public that cannot be
characterized as exclusively national or exclusively transnational in terms of its *character or composition* (C). And yet, its first
participants were in and of indigenous communities who had
historically asserted an ethnonationalist politics. Their nationalism was not obliterated, but rather, it was transformed (as per
Holloway and the discussion above). Ultimately, this was a public sphere with a multifarious, international composition that
nevertheless retained a clear focus on immediate crises facing
subnational, marginalized populations. Components of patriotism and cosmopolitanism complementarily defined the Zapatista public sphere.

The *function or orientation* (F) of the Zapatista public sphere
was also simultaneously national and transnational. It aimed to
win recognition, rights, and self-determination for local communities in jeopardy, but also to bolster a transnational oppositional
dialogue to the present phase of global capitalism, which was
believed to place them in jeopardy.

And so what was the *location in the world* (L) of the Zapatista
public sphere? It was, in no abstract terms, concretely in the
mountains of Chiapas, concretely in Mexico's national discourse,
concretely in the in-boxes of countless e-mail accounts, and concretely in the streets of Seattle, among other places. For these reasons, such a public sphere can only be understood as
transgressive.

All of this has important implications for political identity.
Indigenous identity "goes beyond much of the existing literature
on identity formation by focusing particular attention on the role
of transnational forces, like the end of the Cold War, the rise of
neoliberalism, and the expansion of the international human
rights framework, in shifting the terms of politics at a domestic
level."[51] Indigeneity is a subject position that is to some extent always inextricably linked to traditional, cultural, lifeways and a
sense of connectivity to particular places. But at the same time,

by the shifting of the terms of its domestic struggle, indigeneity reconstructs itself transgressively, opening up a historically exclusive subject position without annihilating it, and creating a transgressive political identity. Such constructions of political identity will be the topic of the following chapter.

Notes

1. See, for example, Bill Weinberg's *Homage to Chiapas: The New Indigenous Struggles in Mexico*; John Womack, Jr.'s; *Rebellion in Chiapas: An Historical Reader*, John Ross' *War against Oblivion: The Zapatista Chronicles*; Courtney Jung's *Critical Liberalism: What Normative Political Theory Has to Learn from the Mexican Indigenous Rights Movement*, and *Mayan Lives, Mayan Utopias: The Indigenous Peoples of Chiapas and Zapatista Rebellion*, edited by Jan Rus, Rosalva Aída Hernández Castillo, and Shannan L. Mattiace, just to name some excellent accounts in English.

2. If the reader takes my discussion of pre-Zapatista indigenous rights politics from chapter 6 together with my discussion in the present chapter, I expect that he or she will follow this story well. The texts listed in the above note should provide sufficient supplemental information on historical context and analysis.

3. John Womack, Jr., *Rebellion in Chiapas: An Historical Reader*, 9.

4. Ibid., 10.

5. From the National Commission, cited in Gustavo Esteva, "The Meaning and Scope of the Struggle for Autonomy," 244.

6. See Esteva, "The Meaning and Scope of the Struggle for Autonomy," 247. See also John Ross, *The War against Oblivion: The Zapatista Chronicles*, 39–40. "México profundo," or "deep Mexico," also refers to remote Indian communities, their lands, and lifeways.

7. Esteva, 247.

8. See Ana Esther Ceceña and Andrés Barreda, "Chiapas and the Global Restructuring of Capital," 39–63. Also see Bill Weinberg, *Homage to Chiapas: The New Indigenous Struggles in Mexico*, 66–93.

9. Esteva, 251.

10. Rosalva Aída Hernández Castillo, "Between Civil Disobedience and Silent Rejection," 72–73.

11. See chapter 6 for my first, preliminary discussion of this openness to outsiders.

12. Weinberg, *Homage to Chiapas: The New Indigenous Struggles in Mexico*, 99.

13. Ibid., 128.

14. Ibid., 130–31.

15. Womack, *Rebellion in Chiapas*, 23.

16. Octavio Paz, "The Media Spectacle Comes to Mexico," 33.

17. Cited in Ross, *The War against Oblivion: The Zapatista Chronicles*, 21.

18. Ibid., 295.

19. Ibid., 319.

20. Ibid., 34.

21. Ibid., 40.

22. Jürgen Habermas, *Between Fact and Norms*, 359.

23. That the Zapatistas have been resolute in not wanting to seize state power, but rather, to establish a democratic process that all Mexicans could participate in, situates them beyond the "old" and "new" social movement formats of overtaking institutions of governance and making them accountable, respectively. Perhaps their interest in democracy can be said to fall under the rubric of demanding accountability, but in the case of the Zapatistas, the demand for democracy involves the deep restructuring of the systems of governance. This is what I will continue to refer to, particularly in chapter 9, as a "radical democratic politics."

24. Also called the *Intergalácticas*.

25. Courtney Jung, "The Politics of Indigenous Identity: Neoliberalism, Cultural Rights, and The Mexican Zapatistas," 459.

26. Harry Cleaver, "The Zapatistas and the Electronic Fabric of Struggle," 81.

27. Ilan Stavans, "Unmasking Marcos," 388–89.

28. See, for example, Octavio Paz's "The Media Spectacle Comes to Mexico," *New Perspectives Quarterly* 11:2 (Spring 1994), and Jorge G. Castañeda's "The Chiapas Uprising," *Los Angeles Times* (January 3, 1994).

29. See Michel Foucault, *Power/Knowledge: Selected Interviews and Other Writings, 1972–1977*, Pantheon Books, 1980, Part 6: Truth and Power.

30. Manuel Callahan, "Zapatismo and the Politics of Solidarity," 37.

31. Weinberg, *Homage to Chiapas*, 189.

32. See Antonio Gramsci, *The Gramsci Reader: Selected Writings 1916–1935*, New York: New York University Press, 2000, 223–30.

33. Saul Landau, "The Zapatista Army of National Liberation," 151.

34. Womack, *Rebellion in Chiapas*, 299.

35. As cited in Womack, *Rebellion in Chiapas*, 325–26.

36. Please note that I capitalize the word "Zapatismo" but not the words "indianismo" or "indigenismo." This is for two reasons. First, I am reusing the conventions employed in the studied texts. Second, and more importantly, Zapatismo has at its root the proper name of Emiliano Zapata.

37. Weinberg, *Homage to Chiapas*, 161.

38. Massimo de Angelis, "Zapata in Europe," 82.

39. Habermas, *Between Fact and Norms*, 365.

40. Also see Ross, *The War against Oblivion*, 328.

41. Callahan, "Zapatismo and the Politics of Solidarity," 38.

42. Carlo Manzo, "Civil Society and the EZLN," 43.

43. I shall argue in chapter 9 that not all public spheres that assume this formal construction can be transgressive public spheres. Indeed, I will argue that if the classical, single, national public sphere was required by definition to

increase inclusion, the transgressive public sphere more radically deepens the commitment to inclusion. Hence, exclusivist, fundamentalist, or ethnonationalist groups could not employ a transgressive public sphere toward their political ends.

44. Nationalism, national political identity, and a nationally conceived political project "should be" impediments to cosmopolitanism according to Habermas, Janna Thompson, and others, discussed in chapter 9 below.

45. John Holloway, "Dignity's Revolt," 160.

46. Ibid., 167.

47. For fuller discussions of the San Andrés Accords and these issues, see Weinberg, *Homage to Chiapas*, 153–63. Also see Andrés Aubry, "Autonomy in the San Andrés Accords: Expression and Fulfillment of a New Federal Pact."

48. This is more or less the case. However, there have been some notable exceptions, including recently, in the summer of 2005, over ten years after the initial uprising. Marcos announced in the summer of 2005 that the EZLN would be severely rethinking its political aims, and, because of the 2006 presidential election, there was a good deal of press coverage about the possibility that the EZLN might get involved in electoral politics. After it became clear that their new political proposal would neither support any candidate for the presidency of Mexico in 2006, and that nor would the EZLN run their own candidate, there was sufficient mystery about the nature of the EZLN's new political program to keep the international press attentive to a deluge of new communiqués.

49. Weinberg, *Homage to Chiapas*, 188.

50. Jung, *Critical Liberalism: What Normative Political Theory Has to Learn from the Mexican Indigenous Rights Movement*, chapter 1, 10 (unpublished manuscript).

51. Ibid., chapter 6, 5.

8

Indigenous Identity and the Recasting of Subject Positions

I have argued in chapter 7 that the Zapatista public sphere exemplifies a transgressive public sphere. A transgressive public sphere, I maintain, cannot be properly understood as national or transnational because it occupies both of these supposedly clear and distinct arenas with an explicit simultaneity. Yet this has raised a new question, which has been periodically presented and postponed, about the political self-understanding of participants in a transgressive public sphere. Specifically, what happens to their sense of national identity, since it is not simply replaced, and what kind of cosmopolitan identity do they achieve, since cosmopolitanism is not their sole or primary aim? Here, I address these questions directly and argue that indigenous identity illustrates the possibility of recasting subject positions for a transgressive political identity.

I argue that transgressive political public spheres entail a transgressive political identity, and that this identity enables actors and theorists to see the ongoing importance of the national framework within the context of transnational politics. Transgressive public spheres, like all public spheres, do not simply subsist in any gathering of people. The public sphere in my conception, as well as in classical conceptions, is understood as a political mechanism, a means of forming political opinion, a means of argumentation and contestation. Because of this, the voluntary participants of any public sphere have a political identity that is shaped in and of that public sphere, or that is represented in some defining way by the comportment of that public. That is, nationalist public spheres exist because nationalists populate them, and transnational public spheres exist because cosmopolitans or self-identified "global citizens" populate them. Likewise, the Zapatista public sphere exists only so long as there are Zapatistas to populate it, and this is true no matter how much what it means to be a Zapatista is thrown into question. So *who* makes a transgressive public sphere? In short, its constituents must maintain a national and transnational comportment simultaneously; they must have strong self-identifications at both levels.

To be clear, I do not intend to make a "chicken or egg" argument here, claiming that transgressive identity precedes transgressive public spheres, or vice versa. I do not make such a claim largely because both scenarios are entirely plausible. It is entirely possible that people could first form a transgressive political identity and then come together to form a transgressive public sphere later on.[1] On the other hand, it is also possible that people may enter a transgressive public sphere (or be addressed by one) for one reason or another, and then, in the process of participation become more transgressive in their own self-understanding. While there is no hard and fast rule regarding what comes first, the political identity or the public sphere, I maintain that one cannot be sustained without the other.

I ultimately argue that transgression is the most preferable complex identity for two reasons: First, it centralizes the importance of both the thick and thin dimensions of political identity, maintaining that one dimension should never have too much primacy over the other. The thick, more parochial, national or subnational identity preserves peoples' roots in the communities in which they live. The thin, more abstract ties (or principles) that link us to others elsewhere enlarge the very fabric of our community and expand our sphere of affection. Second, a transgressive political identity, much like a transgressive public sphere, implies certain normative commitments that stem from its imbricated construction. For example, transgressive identity incorporates and appreciates what is distinct about cultures and lifeways, and even calls for the self-defense of such particularity wherever it is meaningful to people and placed in jeopardy by external forces. At the same time, transgressive identity calls for a larger project than such a localized defense—it calls first for imagining community with others elsewhere, and then for making such community real. At the heart of transgressive identity is a commitment to inclusion without assimilation, to building larger political communities without the dissolution of smaller ones. Yet identity all by itself is not an actual mechanism of political change—the transgressive public sphere, I maintain, is.[2]

In this chapter, I move between (1) discussions of different theories of political identity and (2) explications of indigenous identity and its transgressive subject position. As with chapter 7, the point here is not so much to say something about the Zapatistas as it is to exemplify and extrapolate the ways in which their transgressive public sphere entails a transgressive political identity. In weaving together these two considerations (of theories of identity and of the particular case of indigenous identity), I ultimately show what the former can learn from the latter. Consequently, I make a case for a more complex kind of political identity than that which is more or less national or transnational.

The example of the Zapatista public sphere has continuing relevance here because it is remarkably rich with insights and opportunities for a profound rethinking of political identity. The significance of wearing masks, of an intentionally confusing political discourse about who is the "we" that the Zapatistas are, and of the peculiar invitations for outside participation and even for membership in indigenous community, is that these things are pregnant with serious implications for political identity (especially given that we are talking about indigeneity, a subject position that historically implied a very particular identification with geographic locales and lifeways). To grasp these implications more fully, I look (1) at some influential works on the malleability of political identity in general, (2) at how indigenous identity takes advantage of such malleability, and (3) at Courtney Jung's work on the subject, which directly confronts the question of the malleability of political identity as it is raised by the case of the Zapatistas and indigenous identity. From this, I develop the idea of a transgressive political identity and argue for its importance.

A member of the EZLN, Major Ana María, said in the opening speech of the first Intercontinental meeting:

> Behind us are the we that are you. Behind our balaclavas is the face of all the excluded women. Of all the forgotten indigenous people. Of all the persecuted homosexuals. Of all the despised youth. Of all the beaten migrants. Of all those imprisoned for their word and thought. Of all the humiliated workers. Of all those who have died from being forgotten. Of all the simple and ordinary men and women who do not count, who are not seen, who are not named, who have no tomorrow.[3]

Something about this polemical claim that the masked anonymity of the Zapatistas enabled them to serve as placeholders for marginalized people of countless kinds has had a very popular appeal. In solidarity protests all over Mexico and outside, the chants "We are all Marcos" and "We are all Zapatistas" were common refrains.[4] But there is also something fantastical about this.

In the first place, this language is a tactical framing, a call for solidarity and support that suggests that if you too are among the excluded, persecuted, forgotten, despised, beaten, imprisoned, humiliated, uncounted, unseen, and/or unnamed, then you too are a part of the movement of the Zapatistas. But it is rather obvious that, no matter how I might feel and no matter how warmly I might be invited, while I am sitting here writing at a desk in New York, it is a bit silly to think that I am *in* the struggle of the Zapatistas. My reality and the set of problems I face each week, are, quite simply, wholly different than those faced by indigenous peoples living all over the world. But that I am not a woman discriminated against as such does not necessarily mean that I cannot be a part of the woman's movement, that I cannot be a feminist. Moreover, there is no necessary or accurate assumption that all feminists share a social and political reality, that all feminists share an ethnicity, class position, sexuality, etc. It is in light of this that I reject any impulse to treat the Zapatistas' discourse of radical inclusion and representation dismissively.

If one considers the indigenous a new proletarian subject, as Jung suggests,[5] their amorphous and strangely inclusive parameters appear more substantive than strictly tactical. The proletariat was always an international class, though it was to be organized concretely within each nation, in accordance with very different material conditions and very different developmental junctures in the industrialization of capitalism. Likewise, there is something about indigeneity that necessitates community with others, geographically disparate—people you may never meet but whom share similar stakes and a similar disposition in facing a similar opponent. This, as it was for the proletariat of the nineteenth century, has to do with the identification of a transnational problematic in which the group finds itself to be one subordinate contender in community with others. Industrial capitalism, according to Marx in the nineteenth century, was stripping the workers of their national identity, dehumanizing them into and as the machinery they operated, machinery that was being used for mass production, for export, and which was no more German in Germany than it was in France or the United States.

Today's story is not the same. Living communities of indigenous people are not a mechanism or a special product *of* neoliberalism and capitalist globalization; they are a pre-existing impediment to capitalism. Indigenous peoples (to varying degrees) share a contestatory comportment toward neoliberalism and capitalist globalization because they more or less occupy resource-rich lands that could be profitably mined by capitalists if these lands were vacated. As well, indigenous communities do not form much of the active consumer base in the modern markets of capitalist societies. Indigenous communities thus encumber capitalist development and demarcate outliers to the economy and to dominant culture. In this way, indigenous peoples everywhere are, in a fragmented yet objective and tangible way, part of a single and resistant transnational community.

This part of the picture makes sense of the idea of a community of communities of indigenous peoples, but it does not account for the more lofty appeal of the Zapatistas to make theirs a community including others too. This more expansive part of their discourse, I think, can be understood with the appropriate seriousness with the help of some reference to cosmopolitanism, whose suggestion that we become citizens of the world has also often sounded a bit lofty. Yet, as we have seen in chapter 5, governments and people all over the world at least try, rhetorically if not in actual practice, to represent a cosmopolitan posture. It is indeed a norm today that people and governments should try to be or at least to be considered good world citizens. It is meaningful and important today, in a world with highly integrated global markets and transnational communications technologies, to strive to be a good world citizen, even if you never leave the country or the town you were born in.

Cosmopolitanism emerges in our thinking first. It cannot be achieved in any other way until it is achieved in our own self-understanding (the self-understanding of civil societies and of governments). A fundamental goal of cosmopolitanism is to break down the walls that enable us to remain estranged and indifferent to the crises others face. Indigenous peoples face losing the land they live and depend on. They face the prospects of not being able to secure the space to continue their lifeways in future generations. But there are others than the indigenous themselves who do not want this space taken away, who, perhaps for other reasons, favor and encourage the triumph of living impediments to capitalist development. And such people could see themselves in community with indigenous peoples, perhaps even as actual members of such communities. With the earnest invitation of the Zapatistas, they could be conferred as such (though the Zapatistas by no means speak for all indigenous communities, they are one such community in community with others). With these qualifications, we have sufficient cause to take seriously those more extreme declarations of identity that have framed much of the discourse of the Zapatista public sphere.

Courtney Jung has written extensively about both political identity and the Zapatistas, and has recently addressed the juncture between the two by considering questions of indigenous identity directly. An engagement with her work shall, therefore, be particularly fruitful for my present inquiry into transgressive political identity. Jung writes that the Mexican Zapatistas have raised "the domestic and international profile of indigenous rights, in expanding the terms of the indigenous subject position, and in linking indigenous rights to an emerging global opposition."[6] She argues that, "the rise of indigenous identity is implicated with neoliberal economic and political initiatives that have rede-fined the role of the state."[7] The Zapatistas have been able to ef-fectively open up indigenous identity in important ways largely because the subject position of other materially and/or ideologi-cally subordinate groups implicates a similar opposition to ne-oliberal economic and political initiatives. Express linkages of solidarity between these groups bring into sharp relief the collec-tivity of a global opposition. The Zapatista public sphere sought to multiply and express these linkages as much as possible.

Mexican indigenous rights activists initially denied that the Zapatistas were really indigenous because they had traveled to and settled in Chiapas coming from outside of it—they were not its native inhabitants. But the Zapatistas, from their earliest com-muniqués, always worked toward an expanded indigenous identity, calling their movement that of "the dispossessed" with-out ever delimiting any particular form of dispossession.[8] Being dispossessed could, therefore, mean being ousted, displaced, or alienated, or perhaps even anyone opposed to neoliberalism and capitalist globalization.

Recall Habermas' argument that "the political public sphere can fulfill its function of perceiving and thematizing encompass-ing social problems only insofar as it develops out of the com-munication taking place among *those who are potentially affected*."[9] The Zapatistas, it must be noted, do not contradict this claim, but they do radically expand what would be conventionally seen as the sphere of potential affection. But what does it mean, if any-thing at all, to understand oneself as affected by the struggles of the Zapatistas if one is not directly engaged in that struggle? To answer this question more fully, and to move more resolutely to-ward an explication of transgressive identity, we must consider important theories of political identity that can help us to make sense of our example.

In her *Then I Was Black: South African Political Identities in Transition*, Jung writes about the ongoing negotiation and rene-gotiation of political identity—of the subject and the context in which the subject's self-understanding is formed. She summa-rizes that there have been two general ways to speak of political identity. First, is the "constitution" argument, which maintains that identity is constituted, that our political identity is made up of many parts, that it is something we can unravel or analyze. In order to understand constituted identities, we need to understand their constitutive parts. But, according to the constitution argument, identity is not something we can change, or recast time and time again. Jung agrees with this argument up to a point. Identities *are* constituted, and it is important, she maintains, to understand and analyze the ways that identities are constituted.

However, we must also understand the degree to which the choices we make effect the "construction" of our identity. Jung insists that there is always a limited but important kind of choosing involved in assessing our position in varying contexts of struggle over power, and that these choices are a major part of the construction of our identity. This point requires further qualification. Jung does not mean that "choosing," in the common sense of the term, is the key to construction. Indeed, she neither assumes that we can simply nor always choose our political identifications. Rather, Jung's point is that the fluidity and malleability of political identities must be understood and taken into account, and that because the constitution argument does not do this it denies a critical degree of choice that we do often have. Political identity must be self-conscious, because how others identify you does not necessarily indicate how you identify yourself politically. This account of the self-conscious "settling" of political identifications distinguishes the constructivist approach to understanding and speaking about political identity.[10] Construction therefore assumes a certain amount of constitution, but it rejects the strong thesis that we can hold no sway at all in the recasting of our political identity.

Jung identifies five different independent variables in the construction of political identity. First are *political institutions*, which order, group, and classify people, thus constructing demarcations of identity. Second are *mobilizing discourses*, each of which refers to a discursive repertoire of a world of meaning in which the delineation, identification, and reification of groups is established and continually evoked. Mobilizing discourses are tied to political institutions because, Jung maintains, the discourses of political elites provide incentives to mobilize some discourses over others and have the greatest mobilizing effect.

Hence, the lexicon with which powerholders talk about distinctive groups works to bring such groups into sharp relief and to bring their members together. Third are *material conditions*, meaning the economic status of individuals in a social system— that is, peoples' understanding of their material position in society. In other words, people have work-defined roles that determine, at least in part, their class position, that determine their place in the economic system. People often (not always) understand themselves according to what they do, what status they have, and, as a result of this, what community or social group they belong to. Fourth is *organization*, which refers to organized and maintained social and political networks, social movements, or any other organized idiom of participation and/or membership (environmentalism, for example) that may question or support political institutions, mobilizing discourses, and material conditions. Fifth and finally is *available ideology*, which refers to our access to articulated worldviews, how we comport ourselves ideologically, negotiate and ultimately claim certain political beliefs. All of these variables determine, more or less, our political identities.

But Jung also identifies a dependent variable, what she calls *resonance*, or "the extent to which individuals internalize the political meanings and boundaries that elites mobilize. It functions as a gauge of political identity at the mass level. Resonance operates on the plane of interaction between political elites and their potential constituents. . . . Discourse that failed to mobilize a constituent base at time X may succeed at time $X+1$."[11] Thus, there is a multiplicity of sources from which political identity is constituted and constructed, and in the realm of these things, we do and can make choices that uproot and recast our identity. However, whether or not a potential political identity becomes an actual one on a mass level has to do with how resonant it is, how widely and how deeply it resonates with groups of people. So political identity is not simply an inherited and unchangeable matter of fact, but is malleable according to the appeal, influence, and incorporation of the independent variables, and is made effective on a mass level by resonance.

Jung's general picture of the construction of identities provides a model that will work well for the present inquiry, and we shall see that she applies it herself, in other texts, to the case of the Zapatistas and indigenous identity. In any case, the above discussion can only be a starting point, for I want to consider the construction of a transgressive political identity in the public sphere. In *Then I Was Black*, Jung is addressing the specific case of political identities in South Africa and not the question of transnational or transgressive political identities. And because I am focusing on the public sphere as a formative terrain for the construction of political identity, I focus more on mobilizing discourses, available ideologies, and organization than on the other independent variables. Specifically, I am interested in how the mobilizing discourses of marginalized groups innovatively expand their resonance. This follows from the fact that Zapatismo introduced a mobilizing discourse that simultaneously challenged Mexican powerholders' traditional indigenismo as well as the indigenous peoples' own traditional indianismo.

But before we delineate a distinctive theory of transgressive political identity from the case of the Zapatistas, it will be helpful to consider some other contributions to understanding the malleability of political identity in the context of contemporary politics. Richard Falk, for example, in his *Predatory Globalization: A Critique*, makes some very useful observations about the potential not only to recast political identity but citizenship as well, particularly in light of what he sees as a withering role of the nation and of nationalism to provide us with new political identifications well suited to contemporary political realities. He points out that nationalism has historically served as the centerpiece for the political identities that ground most modern forms of citizenship. By nationalism, Falk means "a geographically bounded ideal of political community."[12]

Falk argues that the impact of economic globalization has weakened territorial links between people and their state in significant ways, and that even though transnational links remain very thin and are not yet sufficient to serve as the grounding for global citizenship, nationalism seems categorically, and by definition, incapable of doing so. Globalization, he maintains, causes the "deterritorializing of citizenship."[13] And because it is citizenship, and particularly national citizenship, which has traditionally been the locus of political identity, we necessarily see a deterritorializing of political identity too. Indeed, deterritorializing political identity is an important part of understanding how Zapatismo renegotiates indigenous identity, although the Zapatistas do not find it necessary to simply transcend national identity, but to reinvigorate and redefine it.

But Falk contends that economic globalization is creating and will continue to create a decline in the sense of national citizenship that traditionally binds people to a state. One way to defend citizenship, he suggests is, if

> the idea of political membership and existential identity can be effectively transferred to the global village realities of community and participation in a post-statist or postmodern world. If such a process is to succeed, it must proceed in a manner that is able to engage non-Western as well as Western social and political forces, one that is psychologically meaningful for large numbers of people at all levels of society.[14]

The idea of citizenship is so important to Falk because it has historically provided people with the leverage to claim recognition, protections, and rights. If one can invoke citizenship, conferred by a political institutional authority, then one has a basis for holding that institution accountable to her. The problem, however, is that *we do not live* in a post-statist or postmodern world where the deterritorializing of citizenship has made struggles for citizenship within the national framework superfluous. To the contrary, for many people, including many indigenous, the need for such struggles cannot be overstated.

Despite this, Falk's use of the terms "existential identity" and "psychological meaning" is quite helpful. Extremely thin transnational ties are understood by most people to already exist, especially in the context of an integrated world market, but these ties are not yet resonant enough; they are not yet psychologically meaningful enough to large enough numbers of people. Existential identity refers not to a national or legal political identity, but to an identity that we feel in a deep and abiding way, that gets to the core of how we understand who we are and the meaning of our lives. Existential identity does not necessarily imply a shared rootedness in particular topical common spaces, so it is an identity that can in principle reach across state boundaries. If a transnational community of people who share an existential identity can be substantively assessed, then we can assess the basis for a kind of transboundary citizenship. Recognition and rights cannot be expected without citizenship, and a global recasting of citizenship is possible from Falk's standpoint.

The aim of a transnational politics, Falk maintains, must therefore be to bring the foundational basis for claim making (i.e., citizenship), onto a transnational terrain. Falk calls this the "aspirational side of citizenship," which

> involves a movement from an emphasis on *space* to an emphasis on *time*. Such a shift corresponds to the decline of territoriality as the foundation for political identity and the seeming exhaustion of government as a source of creative problem solving with respect to fundamental social concerns. It also reflects the impact of economic globalization and the current absence of countervailing ideological and political possibilities, yet the need for alternatives with normative content, both to moderate the cruelest effects of the global market and to give impetus to reformist perspectives. Time becomes, then, the essential component in a search for solutions.[15]

The ultimate challenge, he concludes is to eventuate a kind of global civil society that could serve as a post-statist grounding for global citizenship. Falk's argument is helpful in some regards, but also suffers from the kind of mistake we have been striving to remedy. His argument about citizenship is helpful because a public sphere forms, makes demands, and then eventually dissipates in died down communication. If, however, such a public sphere could demand and achieve citizenship for its participants, for its human basis (or raw material), then this geographically disparate community could subsist as such in the absence of active discussion; it could claim citizenship as the basis for the fulfillment of needs.

At the same time, Falk's "aspirational side of citizenship" aims to anchor itself anew to a transnational framework in light of the outflanked citizenship conferred by single national states. Falk does not object to national citizenship writ large, but he does fail to see the need for a transgressive project of struggling for a "dual citizenship" in which the rights of peoples in states are sought in conjunction with and aided by a transnational project of existential identity. Also, unfortunately, Falk does not further develop this idea of moving from an emphasis on space to an emphasis on time. The idea, it seems, is that rather than holding onto a more parochial or geographic basis, a space-basis, for political community, we should look toward the future, the increasing deterritorializing of economics and politics and the need for an alternative grounding, a time-basis. Rather than a wholesale shift from space to time, however, it seems to me that there will always be a need for an emphasis on space (short-term and already present problems and solutions fitted to existing spaces) *and* time (long-term, emergent problems and solutions developed to match the scale of growing problems and solutions).

In his *Sources of the Self: The Making of Modern Identity*, Charles Taylor discusses varying frameworks within which we identify ourselves. He too takes on a constructivist approach, although in a different way than we've seen in Jung and Falk. Taylor argues that we do indeed settle our identities one way or another based on the context of our social existences and our moral dispositions. Taylor states that to know who one is, is to know how one stands on what is good and bad, admirable and worthwhile, or neither: "My identity is defined by the commitments and identifications which provide the frame or horizon within which I can try to determine from case to case what is good, or valuable, or what ought to be done, or what I endorse or oppose. In other words, it is the horizon within which I am capable of taking a stand."[16]

Taylor goes on to state flatly that to *not* know where one stands is a kind of identity crisis. But for Taylor, we cannot simply identify *as* Zapatistas because we take a stand *with* Zapatistas. Identity must be fixed, and fixing our identity comes from taking a stand in a horizon of possibility, but we stand *with* others who take similar stands, not *as* them. We have multiple identifications, and when we enjoin another's movement our political identity is shaped by this participation, but we simultaneously retain the previous identifications that distinguish us. This is a critical point because it underlines the fact that we can affirm our more parochial, even nationalist identifications while affirming transnational cosmopolitan ones. In fact, it is the multiplicity of such political identifications in a single subject that makes transgressive identity possible.

In his essay, "Struggles for Recognition in the Democratic Constitutional State," Habermas makes some rare but helpful comments about the malleability of cultural identities and the political need to reconstruct such identities generationally. He objects to the protectionist politics of many democratic states toward their cultural minorities or otherwise marginal populations. He argues that cultural heritages and cultural identities cannot be approached in the same manner as the natural scientist or ecologist approaches species conservation. That is, cultures cannot be preserved as if they are endangered species (more on this in chapter 9). But it is the reason why such an approach is unfitting that interests us the most here. Habermas argues that the heritages and identities of cultural minorities, and we may imagine the Maya Indians of Chiapas here, are only reproduced to the degree that subsequent generations choose to reproduce them as such. A reflexive culture, he maintains, must give each generation the space to reproduce, to redefine, and even to reject cultural practices and identifications. Traditions will be modified generationally, and thus, so will the identities and political self-understandings of cultural minorities (one example of this has been discussed: the transition from indianismo to Zapatismo).

So Habermas suggests that cultures can and must be allowed (and expected) to radically rethink themselves in light of the changing social and political contexts in which they exist. But he is not suggesting that new generations adapt and ultimately assimilate. The difference between these points may be difficult to discern: "The accelerated pace of change in modern societies explodes all stationary forms of life. Cultures survive only if they draw the strength to transform themselves from criticism and secession."[17] Hence, it is not that Indians in Mexico should assimilate, ceding to indigenismo policies, for doing this would not be any kind of cultural survival at all. But criticisms from outside must be constructively managed, and a culture will need to account for generational secession, and doing these things with a long view for the survival of cultural lifeways means that the culture must change itself and not simply defend itself as such.

Static resistance is not a forward-looking stance, an insight that accounts for the Zapatistas recasting the indigenous subject position. The Zapatistas understood that indianismo, the more static defense of traditional cultures as such, would not be enough in the changing contexts of neoliberalism and economic globalization. They would have to recast their movement and their self-understanding in a different way, and specifically on a different scale, or else they could face an eventual cultural extinction.

Furthermore, and in another rare moment, Habermas concedes in this essay that nationalism is not necessarily synonymous with fundamentalism or ethnonationalism, as it has appeared before in his writing (see chapter 5). The tendency for nationalism to become fundamentalism, he maintains, is still a threat: "Nationalism too can turn into fundamentalism, but it should not be confused with it. The nationalism of the French Revolution allied itself with the universalistic principles of the democratic constitutional state; at that time nationalism and republicanism were kindred spirits."[18] We are by now used to harsher words from Habermas about the need for cosmopolitanism to overcome and replace nationalism. But indeed, we can find in the nationalism of the EZLN a kinship with republicanism and cosmopolitanism; thus, such a kinship is not simply a possibility that has been incontrovertibly closed off by history. Inasmuch as republicanism refers to a politics that emphasizes the power of and ultimately locates its own authority in a body of citizens that chooses its representatives, the Zapatistas' discourse on national liberation was very much tied to republican ideals. And the Zapatistas, like the French revolutionaries, allied themselves with universalistic principles of democracy, self-determination, and human rights.

In order to understand just how indigenous identity can be transgressive, it is helpful to imagine the different shared characteristics among any group of people, and how any one characteristic could be used as the basis for a collective identity. That is, in any group of any people there will likely be many shared characteristics, but few of these, or perhaps none of them, may end up establishing a collective identity. Kwame Anthony Appiah points out, for example, that there is "a logical but no social category of the witty, or the clever, or the charming, or the greedy. People who share these properties do not constitute a social group, in the relevant sense."[19] Yet there are relevant social categories for sexuality, "races," and religious groups, among other things. There is a good deal of choice and active construction involved in the formation of politically relevant social groups. This is important for my argument, although for a reason unintended by Appiah. Namely, it illustrates that it is entirely possible to construct collective identities on the basis of unconventionally selected but nevertheless shared attributes. It is perfectly logical to say that there is a group of people who are greedy, but something else has to happen for this group to somehow become political *as a group*.

For example, people with physical disabilities have always existed as such, at least objectively. But politically, an external mobilizing discourse is necessary to make them a socially relevant collectivity. People with disabilities, because of unequal treatment, blatant disregard, and difficulties with recognition, have politicized themselves as a group, making a salient political identity out of a formally shared attribute, which, although radically divergent in content (there are, of course, a broad range of different disabilities), effectively classifies them as a collectivity.[20] This underlines Jung's contention that political identity must be self-conscious. Others have often identified people with disabilities as such, but the classification of one group by another is not necessarily enough for political identity. Choice, construction, resonance, and self-conscious self-understanding play a major role. But given these qualifications, it is always possible, at least in principle, for any logically shared attribute to be made socially relevant. The radical expansion of indigeneity pursued by the Zapatistas centrally involved an effort to make a political collectivity out of the resonant shared attribute of taking a stand "against neoliberalism" and "for humanity." This also underlines Taylor's idea of identity formed by taking stands.

Appiah agrees with Habermas that generations of relevant social groups must have the freedom to resist, to redefine, or to reject their culture. Appiah takes other examples. He points out that African-Americans after the "Black Power" movement in America, and gays after Stonewall, redefined their self-understandings in important ways—the old scripts of self-hatred from previous generations were discarded and the next generations of African-

Americans and gays would have, in important ways, very different political identifications.[21] After the Zapatistas, we could say, many indigenous similarly redefined themselves, throwing out the old script of indianismo and parochial ethnic exclusivity, and choosing instead a new script of transnational solidarity and inclusion.

Appiah points out that it is possible to have a political identity based on an unconventional attribute, and to feel it as profoundly as others feel more common ethnic identities. Appiah takes the example, following Taylor, of francophone Quebecois, which evidences that speaking a particular language in a certain historical and political context can, and in this case does, deeply and thickly bind a community. People can and do feel "ethnically" francophone, that is, that *being* a francophone Quebecois is like *being* a member of a particular "racial" or a sexual group. Appiah contends that it is not right for francophone Quebecois to teach their children only in French as a means to generationally guarantee the continuation of francophone Quebecois ethnicity over time. He argues "that the desire of some Quebecois to require people who are 'ethnically' francophone to teach their children in French steps over a boundary . . . this is, in some sense, the same boundary that is crossed by someone who demands that I organize my life around my 'race' or my sexuality."[22]

But I would like to emphasize a slightly different point here. Speaking French in Quebec is *not* a thin kind of bond. To the contrary, it is so thick that it resonates on the deep and abiding existential level of many ethnic identities. Given a particular historical and political context, such as that of francophone Quebecois, it is possible for a thick political identity to be formed around unconventionally singled-out commonalities. In other words, the commonality of speaking French, which countless strangers all over the world share, would not immediately represent a thick existential bond without a particular historical and political context such as that of francophone Quebecois. But within a particular historical and political context, apparently thin commonalities can in fact provide the basis for thick political community (with the help of an effective binding discourse in the public sphere).

The Zapatistas have mined this possibility in a vivid and innovative way. In her essay, "The Politics of Indigenous Identity: Neoliberalism, Cultural Rights, and the Mexican Zapatistas," Jung explains that the Zapatistas have expanded the terms of the indigenous subject position and have effectively linked "indigenous rights to an emerging global opposition."[23] Jung focuses primarily on the achievement of a new kind of indigenous identity, on the way in which indigenous identity has been innovatively expanded by the Zapatistas. She points out that

> indigenous identity is the condition of participation in a global political dialogue. Indigenous identity claims a political voice for many of those who have been most marginalized and oppressed by modernity, and asserts for this group the "right to have rights." Indigenous identity has forged new political spaces, strategies, and alliances that insert new political actors into the public discourse.[24]

The point here is not at all that every indigenous group seeks to overcome its own parochialism or that any person anywhere can achieve indigenous identity. Jung is referring to the achievement of indigenous identity *by* Mexican peasants, who, in becoming publicly acknowledged representatives and vigorous proponents of an indigenous rights agenda, were finally able to enter their political discourse into a global political dialogue that had previously excluded their voices.

As well, my argument is not that any person can achieve indigenous identity directly. Rather, that indigenous identity has opened up new political spaces and forged new alliances that insert new and diverse political actors into the same public sphere, and that these actors include both the indigenous and nonindigenous people in solidarity elsewhere. But the innovation in this is in the development of a transgressive identity that necessarily emerges from "standing with" others in a political public sphere on the grounds of a shared critique of neoliberalism and economic globalization (which the public sphere circulates). The Zapatista public sphere is transgressive, and those who participate in it, at least for the duration of their active participation, must assume a transgressive identity. Transgressive identity is necessary in this case because if the political identity of the participants is understood as strictly nationalist on the one hand, or wholly transnational or cosmopolitan on the other, then the participants' political disposition (the stand that is taken) is ultimately misunderstood.

This last point, regarding the transgressive construction of political identity, is applicable, at least in principle, to other public spheres, whether or not it is realized in practice. When participants in a political public sphere cannot be properly understood to be maintaining a political comportment that is either strictly national or strictly transnational in terms of its scope and its content, then such participants *and* the public sphere they comprise can only be transgressive. Feminists, gay rights activists, environmentalists, and anticapitalists (in addition to indigenous rights activists) could all, certainly in principle, simultaneously self-understand as members of national and transnational political communities. A group of environmentalists, inasmuch as it objects to global warming trends and causes, or the pollution of air and water, for example, is never *just* American or German even when it *is* American or German. As group members, they also identify as members of a larger, transnational political community.

Environmentalists may locate numerous sites of contestation. Contestation regarding sites that are physically located clearly within the bounds of a single state (whether we are talking about a rainforest, a reservoir, garbage disposal site, or the Arctic wildlife refuge) can be framed in terms of national interest, in terms of the needed regulatory action of a single national state, and as an intrastate struggle or political project. Indeed, such a framing may prove indispensable to the defense of a rainforest, a particular body of water, or the Arctic wildlife refuge. But the national framing as such does not have to erode the transnational self-understanding of the environmentalists who do the framing, and it does not have to preclude a simultaneous and imbricated transnational framing. A transgressive framing is also possible, and it could be critical for mobilizing outside opinion and influence and bringing it to bear on those political actors in whose interest it is to deforest the rainforest or to drill for oil in the wildlife refuge. Transgressive framing is often desirable to environmentalists who cannot abandon their local sites of contestation, but who are in need of consolidated leverage. It is within the public spheres of environmentalists that such a framing can be articulated and can gain traction outside of itself.

The Zapatistas' first declaration on the day of the January 1 uprising declared the rebellion's historical lineage from earlier Mexican struggles against Spanish colonizers, North American imperialism, and the French Empire. But now both the opponent and the actors are different. The opponent is divided into a national target (the one-party PRI rule) and a transnational target (NAFTA and neoliberal development plans for Chiapas). The actors, initially, were those living in Mexico represented by the Zapatistas, but their subject position was proclaimed as "the dispossessed." Jung points out that their movement "identifies the Zapatistas simply as 'the dispossessed' without identifying the root of dispossession—as peasants, indigenous people, or other."[25] From the very first public address then, the composition of the Zapatistas was always intentionally imbricated with a broad range of historical and highly differentiated struggles, and with an ambiguous sense of membership and participation that suggested that anyone who was *on their side* could be *in their movement*.

These outreaches and redefinitions of political community were achieved in and by the Zapatista public sphere—mostly in and by reading publics, but occasionally in the topical common spaces of actual encounters with the EZLN. As outlined above, through the utilization of cyberspace (e-mail and Internet web pages), the reading public sphere of the Zapatistas was enlarged substantially. But the "others" who found themselves addressed by the Zapatistas were asked a question that went deeper than asking them where they stood on the question of indigenous rights, and asking for solidarity. The question was, "Will you join our political community and join our struggle?" This invitation would not be particularly attractive to those who occupy a distant, comfortable seat in the face of neoliberalism. But, to the world's poor, this invitation had wide resonance and immediate strategic appeal:

> Nevertheless, the claim to indigenous identity has proliferated throughout the world as a result of the development of a framework for indigenous rights located at the international

level. The world's rural poor have employed indigenous identity in order to carve out a space for political activism at the domestic level, and have been able, by invoking their identity as
indigenous people, to enter a global political dialogue. . . . In
contemporary politics, indigenous identity has provided the
terms of struggle for many of the world's poor and dispossessed.[26]

Entry into a global political dialogue is here described as a major political achievement, and the invocation of indigenous identity is described as a means to cast the makers of this dialogue as
a collectivity. This stresses the importance of both the public
sphere and political identity, and moreover, illustrates that the
former could not subsist without the latter.

The transgressive part was not only that there were no ethnic or geographic prerequisites for joining the Zapatista public
sphere. More importantly, the Zapatistas intentionally and effectively communicated an explicit discourse *against* all political exclusions and *for* radical inclusion without assimilation. Indeed,
one could say that "radical inclusion without assimilation" describes both the heart of Zapatista politics *and* of transgressive
public spheres. "Radical inclusion" enables the imagining and
forming of a transnational political community, and "without assimilation" enables the preservation and affirmation of subnational, national, and perhaps even nationalist orientations. This
also reveals something about the normative content of transgression: transgression is incompatible with any politics that
seeks exclusion or assimilation programmatically (more on this
in chapter 9).

Further, and finally, I now turn to consider the peculiar nature of the indigenous subject position in Jung's *Critical Liberalism: What Normative Political Theory has to Learn from the Mexican
Indigenous Rights Movement*. This work provides support for my
claims about the critical importance of a transgressive identity.
Jung begins by tracing the evolution of the terms of struggle for
Mexico's indigenous peoples, focusing first on the struggle to
transform peasant identity into indigenous identity. Indigenous
identity has collectivized peasants as a politically relevant social
group with a voice in the public sphere. Jung frames the work of

the EZLN along the lines of classical terms of legitimation—in this case, the democratic legitimacy of the PRI was contested. She argues,

> the EZLN played an important role in ending more than seventy years of PRI one-party rule. It did so by multiplying the sites and terms of political contestation beyond state control, issuing new challenges to party legitimacy. . . . Unlike "peasant," which was primarily constituted at the national level, indigenous political identity has emerged in a dialogue between local and international activists, organizations, and ideas.[27]

The previous peasant politics of indianismo, by definition, could not make the invitations to membership and participation that Zapatismo could make.

Indigenous identity, Jung argues, goes beyond existing literature on political identity, and it does so precisely by way of its unconventional focus on transnational political landmarks, "like the end of the Cold War, the rise of neo-liberalism, and the expansion of the international human rights framework, in shifting the terms of politics at a domestic level. It also focuses attention on the hard work of activists in building a political identity and linking it to a political and ideological framework."[28] Discursively, the EZLN tied their discussion of indigenous rights in Mexico to a broader political and ideological framework that was already engaged in a global discourse on neoliberalism and human rights after the Cold War. The Zapatistas understood that other people in an increasing number of places could identify with indigenous rights in myriad ways, and that their own political identity could be linked to that of others. At the same time, they understood that the location of their own struggle must not get lost in this, that they were facing and challenging a very specific political reality in Mexico, and that theirs was still a national movement with very clear national targets and achievable ends.

Now, as Taylor and Appiah have made clear, a political identity is shaped, at least to some extent, by the stands we are willing to take, and we can identify thickly as a part of a group in different ways, as the terms of struggle evolve. LGBTQ activists, for example, have to some extent, and certainly could have, a similarly transgressive political identity. There are no ethnic prerequisites, few ideological prerequisites, and there is not even any sexuality prerequisite (although it is probably necessary, for reasons of legitimacy, that the initiating and forerunning base of LGBTQ activism comes from the LGBTQ community). Yet there are many different sites of contestation for gay rights activists all over the world, and different societies represent a different comportment toward, and, therefore, a different crisis for, LGBTQ activism. In fact, LGBTQ rights activists will encounter a different kind of struggle, a more or less hostile opponent from one town to the next town, let alone from one nation to the next.

Gays and lesbians comprise a transnational collectivity, but it is another matter entirely to assess to what extent they are collectivized and politicized as such. Peasants are also a transnational collectivity *in principle*, but they cannot be effectively collectivized and politicized as such by parochial, ethnonationalist discourses. Today, the struggles of LGBTQ activists could remain more or less insulated from each other, their sites of contestation fought in relative isolation from one town or country to the next, in varying contexts. On the other hand, in a transgressive public sphere these struggles could continue to work in localized sites while simultaneously transcending them in order to accrue the leverage of transnational solidarity and participation.

Cosmopolitanism already implies a certain kind of transgression. But cosmopolitanism represents only a very weak transgression because it suggests that the national part of one's cosmopolitan identity serves mainly a practical, emotional, or psychological function, and that the real political achievement, the primary goal, must be a cosmopolitan self-understanding as a world citizen. But this could never be the approach of the Zapatistas (and it would not help LGBTQ activism much either). The politics of indigenous identity requires a rigorous dual focus, and the nationally framed domestic struggle cannot afford any degree of discursive deterioration. I imagine, as well, that those involved directly in gay rights activism, a fight for the right to civil unions in Connecticut, let's say, will not be terribly eager to utilize a cosmopolitan political and ideological framework. Why diminish the focus of the fight for a cosmopolitan vantage? A transgressive political and ideological framework, however, makes no such prioritization necessary. It insists on retaining the focus of the more parochial fight, but expands the subject position of the actors so that others may be pooled in.

Jung speaks of the indigenous subject position as one that is today

> widely recognized as a political location from which it is possible to make strategic alliances and demands. What holds 'indigenous' together as an identity is a common structural position of discrimination and exclusion from full rights in citizenship by the modern state. By inhabiting an indigenous subject position, many of the world's poor have been able to develop their capacity to contest such exclusion.[29]

The indigenous subject position is therefore inhabitable by a wide range of people who are seeking to expand their presence in politics and to fight against exclusion.

Jung speaks about the historical tendency of political theorists to, following Foucault, understand the production of political identities as a result of the production of political boundaries. A transboundary political terrain, for example, is understood precisely in relation to existing boundaries. So a transboundary political terrain and a transboundary politics do not simply evaporate the categories of "us" and "them": "The sense of 'us' is constitutively dependent on the sense of 'them.' The subject is only produced through differentiation, which sometimes takes the form of exclusion or repression, likely as differentiation is to be bound up with struggles for power."[30]

Even in the realm of ideology, we can discover enough differentiation to construct a sense of "us" and "them." Political discourses can draw the lines of political communities. Debates about abortion, physician assisted suicide, war, globalization, and same-gender marriage, for example, have brought into stark relief many of the dark lines of differentiation that distinguish numerous "us" and "them" subgroups. If "for" and "against" prefigure "us" and "them," then the public sphere must be understood to play a major role in the construction of new political identities.

The Zapatista public sphere has understood this, and while it has provided a means for poor and excluded people to speak with some degree of consolidated authority and resonance, it has also tried to go further. It is not just the material conditions of poverty and political exclusion that wrench open the subject position of indigeneity. But also, there are the lines drawn by political discourses that give shape to new political communities. This has been an ongoing and characteristic part of the strategic plea of the EZLN, and they have tried to make as much as possible out of it, to make a political community comprised not just of all the world's poor and excluded, but also of those who stand on the same side of the ideological dividing line about neoliberalism and the rights of cultures.

Jung refers to Ian Shapiro's principle of affected interest from his *Democratic Justice*.[31] She summarizes that the

> principle of affected interest entails that everyone whose interests are affected by a particular decision or set of policies should have a right to be involved, to have their voice heard, in the decision-making process. . . . For Shapiro, the principle of affected interest means that participatory entitlement can reach across borders, to people who may be affected by decisions made in another country. . . . Most normative theories of democracy remain wedded to the borders of the nation as the limit of political engagement and responsibility, in ways that limit their capacity to offer meaningful comments on contemporary political reality.[32]

Cosmopolitanism suggests that the principle of affected interest could be radically rethought. If the relevant affected polity that ought to be drawn into decisionmaking processes can include any of those who are or are potentially affected, then it is important to ask what constitutes "affection"? Does caring, for example, constitute affection? Does publicly taking a side constitute affection? Do agreement and solidarity constitute affection? Or is the sphere of affection limited to those who hold personal or directly felt communal stakes? We cannot take up these questions here. But we can certainly say, without any doubt at all, that the Zapatistas posed these questions and tried to expand the sphere of affection, arguing in part that everyone is potentially affected by economic globalization, albeit in very different ways than the indigenous communities of Mexico.

Subcomandante Marcos described the Zapatista uprising as that of "those without faces and without histories."[33] This polemical remark would be a common feature of the poetic discourses of the Zapatistas. But it is of course not true. As we have seen in chapters 6 and 7, the Zapatistas come out of a very particular history of struggle in Mexico and their faces would be eventually unmasked as the years wore on. But, on another level, we must take Marcos' refrain seriously. After all, the Zapatista public sphere, particularly in the form of the encuentros and on the terrain of cyberspace, did demarcate a broad sphere of affection consisting of those who fought similar struggles, faced similar perils, or who agreed with the political resistance of the EZLN.

The signification of being masked had some other important implications for political identity. President Ernesto Zedillo made the unmasking of Marcos and the revealing of his actual identity into a mission aimed to eliminate the appealing mystique of the mask. Zedillo sought to do this precisely because the confusion of Marcos' actual identity effectively portrayed the Zapatista leadership in a romantic light, and their anonymity and mystery were an important part of the reason why they were so favorably received and celebrated by the public in general. Eventually, Marcos was both debatably and controversially unmasked as Rafael Guillén, a man believed to have taught philosophy at the Autonomous Metropolitan University's Xochimilco campus.[34]

In response to his unmasking, Marcos released the following reply: "I'm gay in San Francisco . . . a Black in South Africa . . . an Asian in Europe . . . a Chicano in San Ysidro . . . an anarchist in Spain . . . a pacifist in Bosnia . . . a Palestinian in Israel . . . a *chava banda* (gang member) in Nezahualcóyotl . . . a woman alone in the metro after 10 p.m . . . an Indian in San Cristóbal."[35] At the same time, Mexican civil society started to protest about the unmasking debacle, and the protest cry coming from the streets was "Todos somos Marcos!"[36] This exhortation, "We are all Marcos," echoed Marcos' speech.

Zedillo's intent in unmasking Marcos was to obliterate his romanticized anonymity. The failed objective was to diminish wide political identifications with the EZLN's celebrated spokesperson, fragmenting solidarity for the Zapatistas in the Mexican public sphere and elsewhere. Another way to say this would be to say that Zedillo understood that the ability of the Zapatistas to open up their political identification to claimants from outside of Chiapas was a major part of their strength.

Zedillo's preferred opponent would have been a more insulated opponent, the old opponent of indianismo. If those who identify as members of the political community consist of a large sector of the mainstream of civil society, then that political community will have more leverage than if it were identifiable as a community of violent terrorists.

This political identification would be further abstracted during the 1996 encuentro, when one woman in attendance would proclaim, "We are all Indians."[37] The basic idea behind this seemingly absurd proclamation was to bind a political community with Zapatismo, to declare a community consisting of anyone in attendance during the event. Although this sentiment meant a degree of shifted focus away from the Zapatistas, the "indefinition was helpful to the Zapatistas. It made Zapatismo very plug-in-able all over the globe to fight local struggles. In a globalized world, where international opinion is far more important than national, this adaptability gave the EZLN many allies who protected them from annihilation."[38] The struggle for the favor of international public opinion takes place in the public sphere, and in this case, the democratic legitimacy of the PRI government was also at risk—in addition to the future of the Zapatistas.

That the members of the Zapatista public sphere may not have all been poor or politically excluded does not mean that Mexico's Indian population loses its distinction as such within the Zapatista public sphere. There is nothing about a transgressive political community that requires the denial of internal differentiations. Just as in the movement for equal rights for gays and lesbians, for example, there is no qualification that requires the denial of its members' other political identifications, such as their "race," being feminist, rich or poor, or francophone Quebecois. Likewise, student participants in the Zapatista public sphere living in El Paso, Texas are in no way claiming to be Maya Indians. Manzo calls the indigenous "an innovative historical subject . . . arising out of an indigenous worldview and its interaction with 'the rest of the world.'"[39] And Julio Moguel agrees: "the EZLN has been able to show an extraordinary novel way of 'subject construction' which, at the same time, includes a way of constituting discourse."[40]

Ultimately then, the key innovation of the indigenous subject position is that it does not reify the strict definition of indigeneity as an exclusive, native connection to some geographic locale as much as it emphasizes a shareable worldview that can be associated with indigeneity. This innovative indigenous subject position neither undermines nor belittles the unique vantage point of the directly lived experiences of indigenous peoples; rather, it relies on a political discourse that transgresses the usual dichotomies between thick and thin, between national and transnational. The case of the Zapatistas reveals that a choice between nationalism or cosmopolitanism, in terms of the status and scale of public spheres and political identities, should not be a simple either/or choice.

Political actors take on a transgressive identity, which is to say that they identify as themselves, where they are, and also that they identify as members of a larger community, inclusive of other people around the world who share a common political orientation. These two identifications are not divided up as stronger or weaker according to which one is more thick, or according to whether or not one is more of a cosmopolitan, according to which one is thinner and resonates more widely. Rather, these two identifications are combined and centralized to the extent that one's political self-understanding depreciates and something of the "self" is lost, when one component of political identity is stressed to the exclusion of the other. Recalling our discussion of the constitution and construction of political identity, it must be acknowledged that one cannot simply choose to have a transgressive identity. To really understand oneself in this way, for transgression to be a deep "existential identity" and "psychologically meaningful," requires hard, conscious effort and the active and ongoing support of others.[41]

In this chapter, I have tried to understand how those who populate and activate transgressive political public spheres must also take on a complex transgressive political identity. As well, I have argued that this transgressive political identity provides a way to foster a new and deeper transnational, cosmopolitan self-understanding among political actors that does not in any way pit the transnational, cosmopolitan comportment against a self-consciously national one.

Yet transgression must be understood as more than structurally innovative and strategically important. It remains to be addressed whether or not any political movement, good or bad, can construct its public sphere, political community, and identity transgressively. That is, it is not yet clear why an exclusionary political movement could not utilize transgression to its own benefit. I thus turn to the ninth and final chapter, in which I shall make the case that transgression is normatively and categorically incompatible with any exclusionary politics.

Notes

1. The "cosmopolitan patriots" I discuss in chapter 9, vis-à-vis Charles Taylor, may form a transgressive public sphere in this way.
2. Identity is a major factor at play in processes of social and political change. Thus, in this chapter I explore some of the ways that identity is shaped and reshaped, and I discuss why it matters. Nevertheless, the simple fact that one has a particular identity, no mater how complex that identity may be, is not a political act in and of itself. Further action must be taken to affect discourses on the recognition, rights, and respect of people with particular political identities, and that is where the public sphere comes in.
3. Cited in John Holloway, "Dignity's Revolt," 189.
4. Ibid.
5. Jung, *Critical Liberalism*, chapter 6, 38.
6. Jung, "The Politics of Indigenous Identity: Neoliberalism, Cultural Rights, and the Mexican Zapatistas," in *Social Research: Selected Essays* 70, no. 2, summer 2003, 437.
7. Ibid., 436.
8. Ibid., 454.
9. Habermas, *Between Facts and Norms*, 365.
10. See Courtney Jung, *Then I Was Black: South African Political Identities in Transition*, 18–20.
11. Ibid., 34–35.
12. Richard Falk, *Predatory Globalization: A Critique*, 153.
13. Ibid., 154.
14. Ibid., 155.
15. Ibid., 165–66.
16. Charles Taylor, *Sources of the Self: The Making of the Modern Identity*, 27.
17. Jürgen Habermas, "Struggles for Recognition in the Democratic Constitutional State," 132.
18. Ibid., 132.
19. Kwame Anthony Appiah, "Identity, Authenticity, Survival, Multicultural Societies and Social Reproduction," 151.

20. See Paul K. Longmore and Lauri Umansky, *The New Disability History: American Perspectives*, New York: New York University Press, 2000.

21. Appiah, "Identity, Authenticity, Survival, Multicultural Societies and Social Reproduction," 161–62.

22. Ibid., 163.

23. Jung, "The Politics of Indigenous Identity: Neoliberalism, Cultural Rights, and the Mexican Zapatistas," 437.

24. Ibid., 436.

25. Ibid., 454.

26. Ibid., 460.

27. Jung, *Critical Liberalism: What Normative Political Theory Has to Learn from the Mexican Indigenous Rights Movement*, chapter 1, 10 (unpublished manuscript).

28. Ibid., chapter 6, 5.

29. Ibid., chapter 6, 25.

30. Ibid., chapter 6, 28.

31. See Ian Shapiro, *Democratic Justice*, New Haven, Conn./London: Yale University Press, 1999.

32. Jung, *Critical Liberalism*, chapter 7, 31.

33. In John Ross, *The War against Oblivion: The Zapatista Chronicles*, 48.

34. Ibid., 108.

35. Ibid., 109.

36. Ibid.

37. Ibid., 191.

38. Ibid.

39. Carlo Manzo, "Civil Society and the EZLN," 26.

40. Julio Moguel, "Civil Society and the EZLN," 32–33.

41. In fact, Jung points out: "Because political identity is an achievement and not an accident of birth—being born into some culture does not automatically confer political identity—many people lack political identities altogether." In Jung, *Critical Liberalism*, chapter 6, 7.

9

The Case for Transgressive Public Spheres

The Normative Case for Transgression

We now have a concept of the transgressive public sphere, of transgressive political identity, and we understand these in contrast to various concepts of national and transnational public spheres and political identities. However, I have not introduced this third model only to show that it has been and could be, but also to recommend it wherever practically and theoretically possible. But it is hard to make a case for transgression if what I mean by it is an intrinsically neutral organizational structure, a strategic deployment of political identity and political solidarity. Transgression, as I have mainly discussed it thus far (as the transgression the national/transnational boundaries), invites such a criticism indeed. However, it is not the case that any group, regardless of their ideologies and objectives, can utilize transgressive public spheres. Only those committed to democratization, radical democracy, or revolutionary schemes that challenge structural inequality, social and economic injustice, and political exclusion will be well suited for transgression.

In this chapter, I set out to argue precisely this point, ultimately showing that a fundamentalist, exclusivist, antidemocratic politics is wholly incompatible with the transgressive paradigm. Thus, the transgressive public sphere not only provides civil society with a means of transnationalizing the public sphere without losing any of the critical focus of much needed intrastate political projects, but also, it *necessarily* works toward increased inclusivity without assimilation, the democratization of existing institutions and societies, and the overthrow of political institutions that resist inclusion or democracy. In fact, these normative commitments of the transgressive public sphere derive originally from the historical and classical conceptions of the public sphere, and are only made more resolute with the concept of transgression.

Let us begin with an example. Wahhabism is a conservative, highly exclusive, and intolerant form of Islam known for its staunch insistence on a strict observance of the Koran. Wahhabism flourishes in some Arab countries, and is most powerful in Saudi Arabia. Politically, Wahhabism sees concrete projects within the states in which its members reside, and yet it simultaneously sees itself as a part of a global project, a project that resists the encroachments of Western political and religious ideologies that aim to modernize Arab countries and weaken traditional cultures. There is something transgressive about Wahhabism in that it is a nationally oriented politics that seeks to establish an Islamic state in each country in which it is organized, and yet it never loses sight of the global arena in which it is situated; its political discourse is always imbricated with both of these foci. Moreover, this two-pronged focus is a major source of the strength of Wahhabism, although it is worth noting that in all of its strength, Wahhabism is a political movement that has not achieved many of its objectives.[1]

Transgression, to the extent that it means misfit with the national and transnational frameworks as clear and distinct arenas, could be used to describe Wahhabism, but transgression in our context has never had this simple definition. That is, I have not been arguing for and have never intended to argue for transgression as an unqualified relation. Rather, my subject has been the transgressive public sphere and a correlated, complex political identity that preserves and transcends national identity. Wahhabism may employ a kind of unqualified transgression, but it is, by definition, incapable of forming a transgressive public sphere—it is incapable of opening up its political identifications to claimants outside of the purview of its religious community (it opposes secularism by definition).

A public sphere can only be understood as such if it is more or less, or at least in principle, open to participation from the whole civil society, or, as in Habermas' ideal-typical bourgeois public sphere, represents the interests of the whole society and not just those of a particular sect. The public sphere in the works of Kant, Arendt, and Habermas is defined by the ideals of inclusion and openness and serves the function of legitimating or contesting the representative quality of political institutions (for Kant, this legitimating function took the form of the concept of public right in his "Perpetual Peace: A Philosophical Sketch"). To be transgressive, the public sphere must be more inclusive than any national public sphere that focuses solely on citizens associating in topical common space. That is, unlike the public sphere of classical accounts, the transgressive public sphere cannot exist without transnational participation by a multiplicity of speakers, hearers, and actors from the global community.

To speak of a "Wahhabi public sphere" then is a contradiction in terms, for this would have to mean a public sphere demarcated by strict parameters of exclusion, including the exclusion of women, and even of other Islamic sects, such as the Shiites and the Muslim Brotherhood.[2] And for Wahhabism to recast itself transgressively, in terms of the political identity of its participants and members, it would have to at least be able to include other Islamic sects, as well as others elsewhere. So, even if Wahhabism transgresses the national/transnational dichotomy in the most basic sense of transgression, it is not, properly speaking, a transgressive public sphere and neither can it recast its political self-understanding transgressively.

Certainly, we do need to understand the strategic and paradigmatic response to globalization represented by the transgressive public sphere. However, the fact that the transgressive public sphere is normatively committed to the ideals of democratization and inclusion (and to a further extent than any national public sphere) characteristic of early accounts of the public sphere (those we examined in chapters 1–3) differentiates the theory of transgression from an assessment of new instruments.[3]

Indeed, the theory of transgressive public spheres must be understood as a part of a radical democratic politics that positions itself against exclusionary, antidemocratic politics and that is not satisfied with the degree of influence afforded by existing mechanisms of democracy in highly technological capitalist societies, or elsewhere in predemocratic developing societies. That is to say, transgressive public spheres offer willing parts of civil societies a means to innovatively rethink themselves as a heterogeneous political community and to proliferate a critical discourse in between and outside of electoral processes, to bring its opinion and will to bear on domestic and other institutions. And the normative commitments of transgressive public spheres are not only held in place by definition. More importantly, it is the internal logic of the concept of transgression that most resolutely prohibits its use for antidemocratic and exclusionary politics.

But it is precisely because the concept of the public sphere has been historically and increasingly defined by its inclusivity that public spheres cannot simply ban all exclusivist political movements or a consideration of their discourses. So, for example, Wahhabi or neo-Nazi political discourses can be and are in fact engaged in numerous public spheres. Surely, many public spheres have provided a space for the consideration of such political discourses. Yet, at the same time, the contents of these discourses are irreconcilable with the defining comportment of the public sphere.

As I have discussed variously throughout this work, publicity, inclusion, pluralism, reciprocity, rational-critical attention to new discourses, democratic legitimation, and democratization have all been ideals of the public sphere from classical to current theories. These ideals reflect the normative position of the public sphere. Thus, while exclusivist political movements, such as Wahhabism or neo-Nazism, may enter themselves and their discourses into the public sphere, no public sphere can adopt the normative positions of these discourses without collapsing.

An exclusivist, reactionary, fundamentalist, antidemocratic public sphere is paradoxical because a members-only group that has already made up its collective mind about the issues it discusses, that refuses to open itself up to and/or advocate for nonmembers, violates the defining principles of the conception of the public sphere as understood from Kant to Arendt, to Habermas, and beyond (more on this below). This is why such groups, even when they engage in aggressive recruitment, cut themselves off from heterogeneous, populist movements. They are marginal contenders, and they may indeed grow in size, but their marginality is unlike that of despised and forcibly marginalized subsets of the population; their marginality reflects their principled exclusivity, an ideological opposition to political pluralism.

Of course, none of this is to say that Wahhabism or neo-Nazism cannot accumulate political leverage and constitute a real threat. Indeed, they can. It is, therefore, necessary to ask: Why should anyone care that exclusivist political movements are normatively in conflict with the public sphere? The answer is that, because the internal logic of the conception of the public sphere is diametrically opposed to such politics, even when exclusivist discourses enter the public sphere, the terrain of the public sphere challenges them, destabilizing the grounds on which they stand. The foundational principles of the public sphere do not abide by the foundational principles of exclusivist political movements. The more vibrant and transgressive the public spheres, the less such movements can thrive.

In fact, transgression makes the public sphere even more open and more welcoming to "distinctive outsiders" than its national and transnational counterparts, so the transgressive public sphere poses yet a deeper challenge to exclusivist groups. Transgressive identity requires us to identify with other people who are not like us in any thick, cultural sense; entering into such community with radically differentiated others is objectionable in principle to exclusivist groups. Still, this tension between the transgressive public sphere and exclusivist political movements does not dissolve the potential threat of the latter. But it does suggest something more than a simple contradiction in terms—it suggests that the population of and participation in transgressive public spheres works concretely against exclusivist tendencies.[4]

To further explore the normative commitments of the transgressive public sphere, let us return to some of the defining features of earlier kinds of public spheres that are retained in our new model. Remember in part I, in our discussion of Kant's "Perpetual Peace," we saw that Kant links justice to openness. Kant understood the public realm as a realm open to international and cosmopolitan participation, and he insisted that political right must satisfy the will and needs of the general public. As he put it: "For if they [all political maxims] can only attain their end by being publicised, they must conform to the universal aim of the public (which is happiness), and it is the particular task of politics to remain in harmony with the aim of the public through making it satisfied with its condition."[5] Political institutions must have their maxims and initiatives conferred in public opinion. What is right politically conforms to the public right, and the more widely a maxim is conferred by public opinion, the more suitable it is for wider publics. The transgressive public sphere agrees with this principle and acts on it. In an initially national project, such as the fight for indigenous rights for Mexico's Indians, the transgressive public sphere tries to find and publicize the maxims within this struggle that conform to the universal aim of the public, or that have the furthest and widest resonance—both nationally and transnationally. For Kant, the public sphere is the testing ground for political maxims, it is a discursive arena where the acceptability of principles is evaluated, and where the wider the approval of the public, the wider the validity of the principles.

Also in part I, we saw that Arendt defined the public realm as the space in civil society that is open to all citizens, as opposed to private realms, that is, as opposed to those exclusive spaces that are guarded and managed as "off limits" to unauthorized citizens, or to those who do not or cannot bear the qualifications of "members." For Arendt, the more public person places herself in common spaces with others, speaks and acts publicly, and spends more time in open rather than in closed, private spaces. (As we have seen, making a public sphere transgressive requires placing oneself in the same public sphere as others.) For Arendt, then, the public sphere can only be understood as such inasmuch as it is open, shared, and opposed to exclusions. The transgressive public sphere not only accords with the basic disposition of openness that Arendt associated with the public realm, but, also, it deepens this disposition to a further extent than she imagined, by the implications of a complex, transgressive identity.

Habermas, again as discussed in part I, did take into account the possibility for exclusion in the public sphere. He characterized exclusion in the public sphere as its deformation and manipulation, as what ultimately undermines the public sphere's structural function of political legitimation. If the public sphere becomes exclusionary that means that its discourse is now ruled by bias and special interests (what Habermas calls distortion). Hence, even though Habermas' bourgeois public sphere was not as inclusive as other formulations, it was still juxtaposed to exclusionary politics. Its discursive contents were distorted to some degree by any infiltration of bias and special interest. But the bourgeois public sphere, even while excluding participation from more plebeian sectors of civil society, did nevertheless effectively "put the state in touch with the needs of society."[6]

I recount these defining features of earlier conceptions of the political public sphere (Kant's, Arendt's, and Habermas') in order to emphasize that the principle of inclusion has always been inextricably linked to the meaning of publicity and the public sphere. In Arendt's and, more explicitly, in Habermas' early conception of the political public sphere, the public is an arena that correlates to a national state, voluntarily populated by members of a civil society defined as a society of legally conferred citizens. These early national formulations are more exclusive, on a continuum of gradations, than transnational and/or cosmopolitan public spheres that rethink civil society more broadly and take up transnational institutions as addressees. So the historical-theoretical development of the political public sphere has only made it a more inclusive conception over time.

But inclusion was not the only part of the concept's normative content. Even in its strictly national formulation, the public sphere strove to democratize society and political processes by inputting pressure and influence outside of and in between the formal democratic mechanisms of a single state. In other words, the public sphere considered maxims, assessed a public will and opinion, and articulated and registered a critique with political institutions, thereby revealing the degree to which those institutions harmonized with public opinion—and it performed these

310 / Chapter 9

functions on an ongoing basis, whenever and however it com-
menced the circulation of its critique. Thus, democratization and
its fitness for a radical democratic politics were prefigured in the
early theorization of the public sphere.

These normative commitments of the public sphere have
been preserved but reformulated in theories of transnational
public spheres, and often, newer theories have expanded the
public sphere's commitments to inclusion and democratization.
Indeed, my theory of the transgressive public sphere deepens
and extends these commitments in multiple directions, and in
directions typically mistaken as mutually exclusive (hence the
transgression).

Recall our discussion in chapter 5 of John A. Guidry and
Mark Q. Sawyer's theory of "contentious pluralism." The "pluralism" part of this term is what imbues their concept with its
normative commitments, what guarantees the concept's compatibility with a progressive, liberal political theory. Contentious
pluralism, because it is pluralistic, refers only to contention that
contests exclusionary and intolerant practices. Contentious pluralism is, therefore, unusable by a fascist, sexist, or religious fundamentalist politics. Because such politics oppose pluralism writ
large, they cannot qualify as contentious pluralism no matter
how contentious they might be. Likewise, the "transgressive"
part of the concept of the transgressive public sphere invokes
both the preservation *and* the transcendence of national political
projects and national identities, thus requiring the transgressive
political community to loosen up its parameters of inclusion and
exclusion, to open up its self-understanding. And because the
transgressive public sphere is a sphere of many spheres, it is also
necessarily pluralistic and, therefore, wholly incompatible with
a fascist, sexist, or religious fundamentalist politics.

In the foregoing discussion, I have briefly recalled the inclusionary character of the public sphere, pointing out how inclusion has been rethought and ultimately made more expansive by
subsequent formulations. As well, I have recalled the public
sphere's fitness for a radical democratic politics, contending that
the transgressive public sphere must also be understood as a
part of a radical democratic politics. At this juncture, I would
like to explicate more fully what I mean by this latter point.

Following Negt and Kluge and Cohen and Arato, I have already defined radical democracy in chapter 3. There, I described radical democracy as consisting of processes of democratization that look elsewhere than to state-sanctioned formal mechanisms of hearing and responding to public opinion. A radical democratic politics sees itself somewhere in between reform and revolution. It is more contestatory, challenging, and uninvited than voting or letter-writing or strictly textual or speech-based addresses in the public sphere. But, at the same time, it ultimately seeks the restructuring of existing institutions, not their wholesale overthrow or overtaking. That is, a radical democratic politics seeks to challenge, compel, and demand rather than to ask for reforms, and it uses various forms of protest and political action including but by no means limited to voting or letter-writing or strictly textual or speech-based addresses in the public sphere. At its best, radical democracy is both deconstructive and transformative. It deconstructs the hard lines of group differentiation and the walls of narrow political identities, and it transforms the underlying structures, or the root causes, of inequality—and this is the conception of revolution envisioned in theories of radical democracy.

Our example of the Zapatistas serves well to illustrate this kind of radical democratic politics. Even in their most insurrectionary moments, the Zapatistas were ultimately demanding deconstruction (of indianismo) and transformation (of the political system's hostile regard toward indigenous people), and were not attempting to overtake the state. Cohen and Arato's treatment of civil disobedience as a way to enact a radical democratic politics is well demonstrated by the case of the Zapatistas. The Zapatistas could not have won the attention of the state and the favor of civil society that they did win were it not for the theatrical way in which their agenda was originally introduced as a guerilla uprising.

The public sphere tries to restructure valuations in the culture, to transform political community and identity, and to influence and change political institutions—but it does not seek to do these things simply by working through political parties and existing democratic processes. Ernesto Laclau and Chantal Mouffe, two theorists of radical democracy, explain that radical

democracy is essentially about the abolition of relations of subordination. They point out that "[c]ertain contemporary feminist
practices, for example, tend to transform the relationship between
masculinity and femininity without passing in any way through
parties or the State."[7] The aim of a radical democratic politics is to
utilize political discourses in innovative ways—not simple, conversational invitations for dialogue with an opponent—in order to
challenge social inequalities and relations of subordination.

Laclau and Mouffe develop their theory following Antonio
Gramsci's idea of hegemony and a "war of position," which I
have briefly mentioned in chapters 3 and 7. That is, a radical
democratic politics is primarily about fighting a war of position,
not a war of movement. Fighting a war of position means fighting to change peoples' thinking, to win the favor of public opinion, to make a marginalized political critique more hegemonic,
whereas a war of movement means a frontal assault on powerholders, the seizing of the state apparatus. Even though Laclau
and Mouffe wholly ignore the concept of the public sphere, the
public sphere is the necessary terrain for radical democratic politics. This is because the public sphere is where thinking is transformed, where public opinion is made and won over, and where
a prevailing hegemony secedes for the emergence of new thinking. For Laclau and Mouffe, discursive contestations must be antagonistic to the prevailing, dominant, hegemonic discourses
that condition and strengthen exclusionary practices and relations of subordination.

Hence, although it is not at all their aim, Laclau and Mouffe
get to the heart of the idea of a transgressive public sphere and a
transgressive political identity. Reaffirming principles of inclusion, pluralism, and democracy, they suggest that the politics

> of the Left should consist of locating itself fully in the field of
> democratic revolution and expanding the chain of equivalents
> between the different struggles against oppression. *The task of
> the Left therefore cannot be to renounce liberal-democratic ideology,
> but on the contrary, to deepen and expand it in the direction of a rad-
> ical and plural democracy.*[8]

A radical democratic politics is incompatible with exclusionary politics and practices, and goes far to describe the politics
of transgressive public spheres such as that of the Mexican

Zapatistas or, for example, transgressive gay and lesbian rights and feminist public spheres. In other words, indigenous rights, gay and lesbian rights, and feminist public spheres could not maintain their status as *transgressive* public spheres if they excluded the participation and membership of outside activists, heterosexuals, and men. Such transgressive public spheres expand the chain of equivalents between different struggles and are therefore necessarily pluralistic.

Linkages between geographically separated sites of political struggle and of different types of struggle are helpful for a radical democratic politics, and necessary for the transgressive public sphere. These linkages can be made nowhere else but in the public sphere. Laclau and Mouffe insist that

> there are not . . . necessary links between anti-sexism and anti-capitalism, and a unity between the two can only be the result of hegemonic articulation. It follows that it is only possible to construct this articulation on the basis of separate struggles, which only exercise their equivalential and overdetermining effects in *certain* spheres of the social. This requires the autonomization of the spheres of struggle and the multiplication of political spaces.[9]

In other words, what is distinct about individuated struggles must be retained, but at the same time, autonomous spheres of struggle that can be bound together for their mutual benefit should be so bound by effective political discourses.

It is worth noting that the Zapatista public sphere did just this—it multiplied the number of spaces in which its political discourses were taken up using what Laclau and Mouffe would call a hegemonic articulation to ultimately link separate struggles. It is also worth noting that a person's self-understanding as both antisexist and anticapitalist entails a complex political identity that has implications at both intrastate and transnational levels. Such a person's politics, for example, will imbricate a general critique of neoliberalism and the WTO or the IMF with a particular critique of the sexual division and valuation of labor as these are practiced in concrete locales.

Making such linkages between different political communities and cultures may, therefore, require the internal transformation of those cultures. For this reason, it is useful to recall

Habermas' insistence that it is not right to approach cultural minorities in an era of capitalist globalization as if the issue of their survival was an issue of the preservation of species: "The ecological perspective on species conservation cannot be transferred to cultures. Cultural heritages and the forms of life articulated in them normally reproduce themselves by convincing those whose personality structures they shape, that is, by motivating them to appropriate productively and continue the traditions."[10] Cultures must be given the room to critically re-assess their traditional practices and their own self-understanding. For it is only in the malleability of culture that some of the linkages between distinct political communities can be made.

We already encountered this idea in chapter 8. But here, a commitment to radical democracy, which entails a commitment to inclusion, pluralism, and democratization, not only necessitates the linking of distinct struggles in the articulation of a chain of equivalencies as Laclau and Mouffe point out. But also, as Habermas notes, a commitment to radical democracy may necessitate a transformation of traditional cultural practices, which might otherwise be too conservative. This is a complicated point, because it is not the interest or the aim of a radical democratic politics to level out differentiations in cultural practices making them all uniformly harmonious with some standard for liberal democratic lifeways. Indeed, pluralism opposes the elimination of differentiations and thrives on their actual and equal right to coexistence. However, traditional cultures that exclude women from their own internal political organization cannot effectively invite and incorporate the political action of women elsewhere. Recasting their problematic as a shared problematic that links them to other struggles elsewhere compels traditional cultures to confront their own exclusive practices.

The crux of this observation is that exclusivist political cultures cannot be integrated very well with more inclusive pluralistic cultures, that they will not have a very wide resonance, and that they will not do very well in achieving transgression. It is, therefore, necessary for subcultures fighting for inclusion externally to be more inclusive internally. Inclusion, pluralism and the deepening and expanding of democracy are not compatible with exclusionary political cultures of any kind, whether these cultures are dominant or marginal.

This helps to underline the normativity of transgression in a new way. A transgressive public sphere functions in multiple spaces simultaneously, and understands its progress in smaller spheres as being a part of the progress of the pluralistic larger sphere. Because of this, an ethnonationalist or religious fundamentalist subgroup *cannot* situate itself transgressively. For many subgroups to achieve transgression, a transformation of their own practices is necessary—transgression thus holds up a mirror. Achieving transgression requires the dissolution of a group's own exclusionary character and practices.

It is for these reasons that Wahhabism and other exclusionary and antidemocratic political movements cannot appropriate the model of a transgressive public sphere for their own strategic benefit. This is not at all to say that we should not be worried about such movements. Certainly, we should be concerned wherever such movements increase their traction, and the fact that they are not using transgressive public spheres to do so is not much of a consolation. Wahhabism and other exclusionary and antidemocratic political movements may find other means by which to accrue political power. However, it is a contradiction in terms for them to do so utilizing a transgressive public sphere. If the Wahhabis "insist on the inclusive character of their own political culture" (as Habermas says a pluralistic culture must do)[11] and locate themselves "fully in the field of democratic revolution and expanding the chain of equivalents between the different struggles against oppression . . . *not to renounce liberal-democratic ideology, but to deepen and expand it*" (as Laclau and Mouffe put it above), they will be forced to repudiate their own political philosophy. Stated bluntly, the radical democratic politics of the transgressive public sphere are antithetical to the politics of exclusivist groups. And though my public sphere theory does not detail concrete steps for undermining the popularity of exclusivist groups, we can say this: the proliferation of transgressive identity and transgressive public spheres functions as a counterforce to exclusivist politics in the world.

I now turn to conclude with some brief reflections on the indispensable strength of a transboundary politics with an intrastate focus—that is to say, we conclude by taking stock of the special capabilities of and the vital need for transgressive public spheres.

Unbounded but Not Unfocused

In the final turn of this book I shall (1) consider some of the actual terrain on which transgressive public spheres form and function today and (2) discuss some concrete examples of why the transgressive public sphere is important for politics. Following my argument that the transgressive public sphere represents a better normative political philosophy than its national and transnational counterparts, the task remains to show more fully that and how my conception is not merely a philosophical abstraction. This has of course been part of the reason for my focus in chapters 7 and 8 on the Zapatista public sphere—to understand the transgressive public sphere as an extant phenomenon, as more than an ideal. Here, I argue that the transgressive public sphere represents, fosters, or actually creates a transboundary politics with an intrastate focus that serves a critical purpose in the world.

The major work of restructuring political identities, of forming new collectivities first, and then a collective opinion and will, takes place in the public sphere. If transnational institutions such as the European Union or WTO, for example, cannot find a clearly defined body in civil society to confer their democratic legitimacy, then such institutions face a legitimation crisis. Yet the legitimating body that institutions require for their own legitimacy cannot be established simply because institutions want or need it. As with the case of the European Union, which requires a strong, supportive European public, much of the work of forming such a body must take place in the public sphere.[12] In other words, if states continue to exclude certain groups from politics, or are moving toward a more exclusionary politics (i.e., immigration policy, cultural-valuational attitudes toward gays and lesbians, ethnonationalist and racist feelings toward Muslims in Bosnia), then much of the work of formulating and circulating a challenger discourse will take place in the public sphere. The ongoing importance of the public sphere today is well understood by all political institutions and social movements that fight for the favor of public opinion.

But to make the case specifically for a transgressive public sphere requires something further. The compatibility of certain forms of patriotism and cosmopolitanism (which I discuss below), for example, helps to exemplify the case for transgression. It illustrates the benefit and possibility of simultaneously inhabiting both national and transnational frameworks and the fact that the self-defining parameters of public spheres can, in principle, draw and redraw the lines of political community. Indeed, because of this, not only people, but also otherwise isolated movements and political discourses can be brought together by and in the public sphere. And specifically, it is by and in the transgressive public sphere that national political identities can be retained and continually invoked but also opened up to transnational solidarities and cosmopolitan identities. Giving up one project for the other, choosing between one framework and the other, have only appeared to be choices as a result of a false opposition of frameworks.

We have seen from the above section on the normative comportment of the transgressive public sphere that it is, by definition, incompatible with exclusionary politics, both for historical reasons pertaining to the history of the concept of the public realm and because of the implications of transgression itself (for political identity and political theory). Yet, as I have previously discussed, not all of the political discourses of all political movements can be recast transgressively. The competing political discourses of the Republican and Democratic parties in the run up to local or national elections are not easily made transgressive, nor are contestatory discourses advocating tax legislation (excluding the Tobin tax or other international tax schemes, for example), or rent stabilization or a lower subway fare in New York City. It is not simply that the issues central to these discourses do not or cannot have transboundary resonance, for they certainly could, but that (1) the solidarity of *other* political communities elsewhere would be more intellectual than existential, and that (2) a transgressive construction may not even be useful here.

What I mean by the first point is that the transgressive public sphere requires more than intellectual solidarity, but rather a deep and abiding existential solidarity of some kind such that the construction of complex political identities is both possible and desirable. The second point is simply a tactical observation about when transgression is helpful. For example, the political discourses of local elections, and debates about state taxes, rent, and subway fare are more parochial issues that may have no need or appeal for transnational influence. Instead, we might think again of feminism, gay and lesbian rights movements, environmentalism, anticapitalism, and indigenous rights movements, all of which could benefit from a transgressive construction.[13]

And I have argued that the main political discourses associated with these latter examples are, at least in principle, open to a transgressive construction, that their transnationalization can be achieved in the transgressive public sphere without the abandonment of national interests, national projects, or even national political identities.[14] Furthermore, I have argued that this construction is sometimes necessary (as it was in the case of women's rights, universal suffrage, and other examples treated in chapter 3 in the consideration of nonbourgeois public spheres) and that it is other times a choice aimed to increase the emancipatory potential of a political movement, deepening the terms of inclusion, and consolidating leverage (as in the case of the Zapatistas).

With this idea of the transgressive public sphere fresh in mind, I'd like now to consider its terrain and vital importance. To begin with the question of its terrain, I shall consider briefly a relevant discussion of a relatively new kind of political space in Saskia Sassen's *Globalization and Its Discontents: Essays on the New Mobility of People and Money.*

Sassen speaks of the struggle over electronic space, by which she means Internet cyberspace. Cyberspace is, in some ways, the primary terrain of the present phase of economic globalization. But cyberspace has been typically characterized as an open and decentralized terrain for human communications. Despite this characterization, cyberspace has been and is being increasingly seized by private corporations. Thus, sections of cyberspace have been increasingly "firewalled" off to nonmember access, and thereby made less public. The use of cyberspace by the public sphere is impeded by privatization and firewalling, which effectively makes large segments of it closed off and exclusive. To the extent that it is exclusionary it is incompatible with the public sphere. Sassen speaks of cyberspace as being segmented in three general ways: "One is the commercializing of access, a familiar subject. A second is the emergence of intermediaries to sort, choose, and evaluate information for paying customers. A third is the formation of privatized 'firewalled' corporate networks on the Web."[15]

Given this picture, we can see that cyberspace is only a potential terrain for transboundary public spheres of various kinds, but that the potentiality of cyberspace could be effectively undermined by its seizure, privatization, and commercialization. We must remember that the public sphere is typified by its nonexclusive character—by its participatory openness to citizens. Yet large regions of cyberspace still provide the terrain for numerous public spheres, even though vast regions are exclusive and closed off to nonmember usage. The terrain of public spheres was certainly not unimportant to Habermas, who saw the emergence of the ideal bourgeois public sphere linked to the communicative terrains of salons and cafes, and Kant, Arendt, and C. Wright Mills made much of the terrains of the print media shared by reading publics, public parks, and the televisional and broadcast terrains where disparate viewing and listening publics came together.

But with cyberspace we see a terrain that better lends itself to the openness and direct participatory action of the public sphere than earlier terrains. It is not easy to be widely published and read in print media, and it is harder still to get on television or the radio. These terrains, therefore, limit the participation of the public sphere to a more passive role. People could actively participate in collective group discussion, but their first role is listening, reading, or watching privileged, publicized discourses—not introducing new themes of their own. Earlier reading and viewing publics could not as easily become distributors of their own discourses as they now can in the blogospheres of cyberspace. Simply put, cyberspace invites more voices to travel farther distances. Even so, this openness does not guarantee anything politically. While it is easy to start a blog of political commentary, it is hard to get anyone other than family and friends to read it. In a sense, the radical openness of cyberspace (as seen with forums like blogs) subverts the authority and seriousness guarded in and by previous forms of communication. Today, anyone can and does say anything, and everyone is speaking at once; so much that is said in cyberspace appears as a desperate call for attention in a sea of other such calls, and we can only attend to so much—in the end, few end up with a serious audience.

Sassen points out that the main occupiers and users of cyberspace are (1) civil society and (2) corporations. Corporations have used the Internet so effectively that it is fair to say that most of the major activities of the global capitalist economy have in some way been embedded in cyberspace: "Electronic space has emerged not simply as a means for transmitting information, but as a major new theater for capital accumulation and the operations of global capital."[16] And the commercializing, privatizing, and firewalling of cyberspace are not the effects of civil society's use, but of corporations' use of the Internet.

Sassen also points out that the political system is not one of the two major users of cyberspace even in highly advanced technological countries. Simply put, the activities of governments are not nearly as embedded in cyberspace as are the activities of civil societies and corporations. Sassen has said that the "political system, even in the most highly developed countries, is operating in a predigital era."[17] Whereas,

> civil society has been an energetic user, but this also means that the full range of social forces will use it, from environmentalists to fundamentalists such as the Christian Coalition in the United States. It becomes a democratic space for many opposing views and drives. . . . We are at a particular moment in the history of electronic space, one when powerful corporate actors and high-performance networks are strengthening the role of private electronic space and altering the structure of public electronic space. But it is also a moment when we are seeing the emergence of a fairly broad-based—though as yet a demographic minority—civil society in electronic space. This sets the stage for contestation.[18]

To call cyberspace "a democratic space for many opposing views and drives" that is "energetically used by civil society" is to speak of a vibrant terrain for public spheres. Users, whenever possible in terms of the normative content and the resonance of their political discourses, can organize in cyberspace to make a transgressive public sphere (one example, massive protest demonstrations against the war on Iraq were coordinated to take place in cities around the world on February 15, 2003, by organizing done in cyberspace). And indeed, the Zapatista public sphere could not have achieved its transgression without the use of Internet communications.

I introduce cyberspace because no public sphere can form without a communicative terrain, and because the contemporary need for transgressive public spheres is contemporaneous with the innovations of electronic communications technologies. Opportunities for transgression are linked to and bolstered by new possibilities opened up by new communicative terrains. But these technological terrains are not sufficiently protected from privatization, and the prospects for civil society's political deployment of and within the new communicative terrain of cyberspace will diminish with its commercialization, privatization, and firewalling.

At the same time, as mentioned above, leaving cyberspace open and public does not guarantee anything either. The Internet is so heavily populated by so many competing voices and groups, and those who use the space for political purposes represent every possible position, from religious fundamentalists who circulate exclusionary political discourses to progressive organizations and projects with liberal or left wing biases. Moreover, users have access to so many millions of sites that there is little reason to be very confident that one site will garner more attention than another. Related to this, users in cyberspace are not addressed against their will (excluding ads and spam e-mails, etc.). Hence, at least for the most part, users discover in cyberspace precisely what they have gone there looking for. Given these remarks, the political potential of public spheres in cyberspace is uncertain and difficult to predict.

Yet we know that the Zapatista public sphere did utilize cyberspace for circulating communiqués and refutations of the

Mexican government's portrayal of them as terrorists. And they continued to use cyberspace during and after the encuentros. Cyberspace can increase the communicative reach of contestatory discourses that might otherwise be trapped in the vacuum of domestic political affairs. For the Zapatista public sphere, cyberspace was a critical means of transgression, and it was their transgressive status that protected them from their own government for years.

I raise these qualifications in order to acknowledge that the formation of an effective political public sphere is not easy. Not all of the political discourses of all political movements can be recast transgressively. The formation of public spheres always depends on some communicative terrain, and the privatization of the means of communication, throughout history, has severely weakened the prospects for political public spheres. But new electronic communications technologies are evolving quickly and these developments continually set and reset the stage for contestation. Inasmuch as geographically disparate civil societies can meet in new metatopical common spaces, the terms of political community and political identity are opened up to redefinition, and, most importantly for our purposes, to transgressive construction. This gives us some sense of "where" and "how" transgressive construction is possible, in light of electronic space, the public sphere's latest communicative terrain.

In conclusion, I shall move from a special emphasis on the "where" and the "how" of transgression back to the "why," to the task of making the case for transgression. A short essay by Charles Taylor, "Why Democracy Needs Patriotism," will help us to bear out the case. There, Taylor argues both *for* cosmopolitanism and *for* patriotism, rejecting the formulation of a choice between them. We have seen that cosmopolitanism and patriotism, respectively, map out over the transnational and national frameworks for understanding politics. As discussed in chapter 5, cosmopolitanism is often pitted against patriotism, in arguing that politics must supersede a national framework and that, because of the transnational scale of the problems of our time, the national framework for political action has been effectively outflanked.

Indeed, the collection of essays in which Taylor's short piece is published (*For Love of Country?*) staunchly reifies this false opposition. The book contains a host of essays written in response to a feature by Martha Nussbaum, "Patriotism and Cosmopolitanism," and in general, throughout Nussbaum's essay and elsewhere in the collection, we encounter the basic dichotomy discussed at great length in my work.[19] The dichotomy is that which maintains a necessary antagonism between cosmopolitanism and patriotism, between the transnational and national frameworks, and is subsequently represented by theorists as a choice, more or less, between the patriotic or cosmopolitan, between the national or transnational. Toward the end of this collection, Taylor addresses the dichotomy.

He argues, as Calhoun has (see chapter 6), that patriotism does not need to mean a crude and elitist kind of national pride. Taylor wants to discuss the importance of a strong national identity that exists for good, inclusionary, democratic political purposes. Indeed, if a key part of our broader politics is the democratization of existing societies, which have (to varying degrees) still very far to go, a national and even patriotic politics could be helpful.[20] To create strong, free, democratic, and egalitarian societies, it is necessary that a collectivity of people identify as such and with a determined allegiance to a common project. Taylor points out that "Nussbaum sometimes seems to be proposing cosmopolitan identity as an alternative to patriotism. If so, then I think she is making a mistake. . . . The societies we are striving to create—free, democratic, willing to some degree to share equally—require strong identification on the part of their citizens."[21] Transgressive public spheres are in large part based on this insight, on the enduring need for mobilized citizens with national identifications and nationally framed projects. What transgression poses is that national and patriotic identifications and framings do not need to preclude transnational and cosmopolitan identifications and framings.

Although Taylor does not formulate a theory of transgression, he too is unconvinced of the mutual exclusivity of the two frameworks. Taylor is suggesting that in addition to the laudable aims of cosmopolitanism there are still aims of intrastate democratization all over the world. More localized struggles for democratization are not incompatible with more transnational efforts to produce cosmopolitanism in the thinking and behavior of peoples and states. What Taylor wants to emphasize is that a comportment as "world citizens" is not necessarily incompatible with a national or even nationalist comportment. In a sense, Taylor is arguing here for a kind of dual citizenship, a kind of dual self-understanding, as a means of retaining and utilizing what makes sense in both cosmopolitanism and patriotism.

Taylor raises the example of India to illustrate this point:

> The present drive towards Hindu chauvinism of the Bharatiya Janata Party comes as an alternative to the Nehru-Gandhi secular definition of Indian national identity. And what in the end can defeat this chauvinism but some reinvention of India as a secular republic with which people can identify? I shudder to think of the consequences of abandoning the issue of Indian identity altogether to the perpetrators of the Ayodhya disaster. In sum, I am saying that we have no choice but to be cosmopolitans and patriots, which means to fight for the kind of patriotism that is open to universal solidarities against other, more closed kinds.[22]

So there is a real, pressing need in India today for a particular kind of national political identity, one that can collectivize people under the banner of making India a more secular republic in the face of a now-spreading Hindu chauvinism. It is not ethnonationalist fundamentalists who will make this national project and work toward the kind of Indian national identity that Taylor is speaking of. Such a national project could only be made in the contestation of exclusion and the struggle for a more democratic, secular society. Yet Taylor is never simply defending nationalism. Instead, he concludes the passage above by insisting that we must be both cosmopolitans *and* patriots. The patriotism we invoke, he says, should not be closed but should be open to universal solidarities.[23]

Finally, it will be helpful to consider Kwame Anthony Appiah's contributions to the rethinking of nationalism and cosmopolitanism. Appiah presents a similar (he also seeks to negotiate the compatibility of nationalism and cosmopolitanism), but importantly different theory of "rooted cosmopolitanism."[24] He joins Calhoun and Taylor in rejecting the caricature of nationalism as necessarily exclusivist and ethnonationalist.

But Appiah's rejection challenges common thinking about the concept of nationalism in a new way.

Appiah does not accept the idea that topical common space maps out over intrastate, in-person associations while metatopical common space maps out over transnational, electronically mediated associations. Rather, he stresses that even within the bounds of any single nation, it is in metatopical common space, and not in topical common space, that nationalism is formed and maintained: "Everyone knows you cannot have face-to-face relations with six billion people. But you cannot have face-to-face relations with ten million or a million or a hundred thousand people (with your fellow Swazis or Swahilis or Swedes) either; and we humans have long had practice in identifying, in nations, cities, and towns, with groups on this grander scale."[25] This seemingly simple observation is very important because it points out that the organizational and identity-based work needed to build cosmopolitan community and identity is the same kind of work required for the formation of national community and identity. In other words, feeling a deep and abiding solidarity and a sense of community with Americans, since we will only ever meet such a minute number of them, is not very different than feeling solidarity and community with others elsewhere. This observation locates the possibility for cosmopolitanism (and for transgression) in the extant identifications and collective self-understandings of nationalism. Hence, these supposedly antithetical identifications can have much in common in both form and content.

Appiah is a committed cosmopolitan. Yet he does not believe, as I do not, that a choice between the national and transnational frameworks is necessary. He defends what is good about nationalism and insists on its compatibility with (and its potential to strengthen) cosmopolitanism. Appiah contends that a

> tenable cosmopolitanism, in the first instance, must take seriously the value of human life, and the value of particular human lives, the lives people have made for themselves, within the communities that help lend significance to those lives. This prescription captures the challenge. A cosmopolitanism with prospects must reconcile a kind of universalism with the legitimacy of at least some forms of partiality.[26]

What is so unique about Appiah's prescription is that he does not defend the defensible forms of partiality only by showing their ongoing political import and fitness with universalism. In fact, he does not think it necessary to find political functions for the national framework in order to justify its continuing usefulness as a framework for identity. Instead, he points to the meaning of peoples' lives and insists that nations can sometimes foster deep yet politically unobjectionable meanings. In such instances, we have enough justification already for national (even some nationalist) identifications in the meaningful existential attachments of individuals. We may insist, therefore, on the importance of rooting our cosmopolitanism in the locales that give our lives value, community and meaning precisely because we get these things from them.[27]

Moreover, Appiah maintains that human beings live better lives on a smaller scale. He insists that cosmopolitans must acknowledge this, that not just the whole country, but also the county, town, street, business, and family, all outline communities that often make our lives better.[28] And the cosmopolitan does not need to belittle or subordinate these communities to transnational communities and identities because smaller communities such as these will not necessarily resist or react negatively to cosmopolitanism. Appiah thus proposes that the "cosmopolitan patriot can entertain the possibility of a world in which everyone is a rooted cosmopolitan, attached to a home of his or her own, with its own cultural particularities, but taking pleasure from the presence of other, different, places that are home to other, different, people."[29]

This picture captures well the kind of rooted cosmopolitanism that the Zapatistas espoused. In chapters 7 and 8, we discussed the existential meaning of human attachments to specific cultural lifeways and the importance of simultaneously transcending those lifeways in reaching out to others elsewhere and in the making of new communities. However, we also discussed something else in the case of the Zapatistas—something that problematically falls by the wayside in critical discussions about cosmopolitanism and patriotism such as Taylor's and Appiah's. And that something else is the public sphere. The Zapatistas achieved their transgression of the national/transnational boundary by positively invoking nationalism and transnationalism in the public sphere. But Taylor's and Appiah's observations, however much my own argument resonates with them, fail to acknowledge the critical importance of the public sphere in the "where," "how," and "why" part of their analyses and recommendations. I maintain that it is only in public spheres that the tenets of rooted cosmopolitanism could be evaluated and that people all over the globe could come to understand themselves as rooted cosmopolitans or cosmopolitan patriots.

Let us explore this claim a bit further. Imagine for a moment what kinds of mechanisms would be necessary for developing rooted cosmopolitanism or cosmopolitan patriotism in the world. A few things, at least, are clear even if implicit. For example, achieving rooted cosmopolitanism requires rethinking national orientations versus transnational ones, and particularly rethinking the assumption of their mutual exclusivity. More concrete is the necessity to evolve real political solidarities across boundaries, to evolve deep and abiding political identifications with others elsewhere. All of this must happen in numerous societies around the globe. My emphasis on civil society here is not meant to be in lieu of or to the exclusion of institutional developments toward cosmopolitanism. But institutions, we must remember, seek to confer their own legitimacy in correlated and beholden publics, so their own cosmopolitan development *cannot really* occur on a separate track from that of civil societies (at least not if we are talking about political institutions that purport to be representative).

Building rooted cosmopolitanism or cosmopolitan patriotism in the real world clearly requires (1) the *circulation* of a political discourse on the compatibility of nationalism/patriotism and transnationalism/cosmopolitanism that (2) resonates well and has a sympathetic *reception* where it travels, and (3) ultimately leads to the *production* of new political discourses, new identities, and new collectivities.[30]

This *circulation, reception,* and *production* describes directly the parts of the process of creating rooted cosmopolitanism in the world, and this process can only occur in public spheres, by the work of public spheres. In fact, the concept of the public sphere has mostly been an "absent referent" in discussions about

328 / Chapter 9

the commensurability of nationalism and transnationalism.[31] By "absent referent," I mean that we cannot imagine a politics of rooted cosmopolitanism winning traction without imagining political public spheres as the terrain for that process—so the public sphere is a necessary referent, but it is mostly left out of theorizations on the subject.[32] I argue that the transgressive public sphere is the "where" and the "how" of, and provides the normative grounds for (the "why") rooted cosmopolitanism, and that it therefore cannot be excluded from these discussions. The transgressive public sphere is inevitably the arena in which cosmopolitans would work to increase the traction of rooted cosmopolitanism.

Now, it has not been my goal to identify wherever the public sphere is an absent referent in others' texts. But one way to sum up what I have tried to do in this work would be to say that I have tried to reformulate a public sphere theory to make it compatible with the best arguments in debates about the beneficial commensurability of the national and transnational frameworks (Calhoun, Taylor, Appiah—those whom I think have "gotten it right"). I have tried, in other words, to rethink the concept of the public sphere *against* its national and transnational formulations in the same way that others have tried to rethink political identity against its patriotic and "rootless" cosmopolitan formulations. Ultimately, I contend that the transgressive public sphere's indispensable role in any plan to bring about rooted cosmopolitanism in the world cannot remain an absent referent for two reasons:

First is a pragmatic consideration: The transgressive public sphere is the place where the restructuring of a transgressive political identity occurs. The rooted cosmopolitanism of the Zapatistas, for example, was evolved in a transgressive public sphere, in a public sphere that was simultaneously, consciously, and resolutely indigenous, Mexican, and transnational. Thus, the pragmatic reason why we must account for the transgressive public sphere has two sharper points: public sphere theory needs to be informed and revised by the innovations of social movements that employ public spheres in ways unaccounted for by theorists, and the strongest arguments about the compatibility of national and transnational frameworks need to understand the public sphere as a principal terrain on which their aspirations can win traction.

Second is the normative point: It is good and necessary to insist on the voluntary continuation of cultural particularities inasmuch as they do not violate shared ideals of inclusion, democracy, and universal human rights. Indeed, cosmopolitanism itself already contains a normative commitment to these ideals. One cannot truly see oneself as a world citizen and at the same time justify the political exclusion, mistreatment, or worse, the killing of other people who were born in another part of the world. Rather, these "others" must be included in one's sphere of affection, their political will and opinion must be taken seriously, and the human rights that we would demand for ourselves must also be demanded for them. Cosmopolitanism, we must acknowledge, upholds these ideals all by itself, by its own internal logic. But the public spheres in which cosmopolitanism fights for political traction are more than important terrains.

How and why? Because the public sphere, unlike rooted cosmopolitanism, does not refer solely to one's comportment in the world, that is, to a political identity; public sphere theory has certain normative commitments, but it does more than outline a position. The public sphere requires collective action and functions only by engaging other publics or powerholders—it requires dialogue or contestation with the state, and is a mechanism of social and political change. As observed in the history of the concept, the public sphere has always worked toward inclusion. The inclusivity of public spheres was redefined, deepened, and opened up (along with the concept of civil society) in the theorization of transnational public spheres.

This is because the concept of transnational publics goes beyond the concept of a public of people who share the same legal status as citizens of a particular nation. But with transgressive public spheres, the inclusivity of the public sphere is even more radically opened up to identifications with others, further deepened, and redefined once again. This happens because transgressive identity is more complex, consisting of more layers of political identification. Instead of *abandoning* strong identification with a particular culture or community, transgression retains and reinforces such identity while also *transcending* it in order to join into community with others abroad. Hence, the transgressive public spheres in which and with which rooted cosmopolitanism may win traction are always more than an instrument—they must also always serve as mechanisms of and for inclusion, for the rethinking of political identities and the generation of new, pluralistic collectivities that engage in collective action.

Previous and influential arguments explored in earlier chapters, including but not only Habermas' arguments in chapter 5, have maintained that cosmopolitanism must confront and eventually defeat a resilient, emotionally charged, and thickly rooted politics of patriotism tied to an outflanked national framework. The public sphere, it has been argued, must move from the national framework to the transnational framework if it is to provide civil society with any useful means to collectivize on a transnational scale and thereby to remain relevant in the arena of transboundary politics today. But we have seen, to the contrary, that this either/or choice depends on a deeply problematic dichotomy that distorts theorists' assessments of public spheres. Many public spheres can approach and have approached questions of their participants' political identifications and the varying scales of contestation with creativity and finally with transgression.

We live in a world marked by ever-increasing disparities of wealth and grave imbalances in military and political power. The means of production, the means of communication, and other means of the distribution of cultural products are far from being managed by democratic steering, as privatization takes over many of the functions historically assigned to public institutions. We live in a world where accelerated trends of globalization threaten local and traditional lifeways, as we have seen with the case of the Zapatistas. We live in a world where capitalism has outflanked politics and the former cannot guarantee democracy. We live in a world where the crises of peak oil, AIDS, global warming, pollution, and nuclear weapons, among other things, represent problems that do not belong to any one national community by itself, and cannot be resolved by any single government or single concerned public. We live in a world where forced and voluntary migrations, both leading to complex transformations in political identity, have produced innumerable diasporas and increasing group differentiation. It is precisely in our world, then, where political action from transgressive public spheres matters most.

Notes

1. I cannot get into this discussion here. See Olivier Roy, *The Failure of Political Islam* for an excellent analysis of the different strains of political Islam, including Wahhabi fundamentalism, and its difficulty winning political traction.

2. Ibid., 123 and 197.

3. What I mean by "new instrument" is an intrinsically neutral tool that can be used for increasing the leverage of any political movement (a website, for example). The transgressive public sphere cannot be instrumentalized as such because it is not intrinsically neutral. It has normative commitments that it cannot be stripped of (or else it loses its meaning as a transgressive public sphere), and these commitments guarantee its partiality for and usability by certain political movements.

4. For one example of this, the reader should recall my discussion of indigenous rights, indigeneity, and the Zapatista public sphere in chapters 6, 7, and 8 and the effect these had on the exclusivist tendencies of indianismo.

5. Immanuel Kant, *Political Writings*, 130.

6. Jürgen Habermas, *The Structural Transformation of the Public Sphere: An Inquiry into a Category of Bourgeois Society*, 31.

7. Ernesto Laclau and Chantal Mouffe, *Hegemony and Socialist Strategy: Towards a Radical Democratic Politics*, 153.

8. Ibid., 176.

9. Ibid., 178.

10. Habermas, "Struggles for Recognition in the Democratic Constitutional State," 130

11. "The right to democratic self-determination does indeed include the right of citizens to insist on the inclusive character of their own political culture; it safeguards the society from the danger of segmentation—from the exclusion of alien subcultures and from a separatist disintegration into unrelated subcultures. As I indicated above, political integration also excludes fundamentalist immigrant cultures." In Habermas, "Struggles for Recognition in the Democratic Constitutional State," 139.

12. See my discussion of the European Union and the question of a European public sphere in chapters 5 and 6.

13. Each of these latter examples has been discussed at some length in the course of this project beginning with the examples of feminism and anticapitalism in chapter 3.

14. I say that transgression can be achieved here *in principle*, because *in practice* it is not always possible to achieve a transgressive construction. Movements

do need a substantial communicative reach, sufficient opportunities for the proliferation of their political discourse, and a highly resonant politics, none of which are simply there for the taking. Resources, access, and timing may (and often do) prevent movements that seek transgression from achieving it. Although it is not the aim of my study to explore how much communicative reach, how many opportunities, and how much resonance are needed to achieve transgression, this indeed points out an area for further research.

15. Saskia Sassen, *Globalization and Its Discontents: Essays on The New Mobility of People and Money*, 185.

16. Ibid., 190.

17. Ibid., 192.

18. Ibid., 194.

19. See Martha Nussbaum, "Patriotism and Cosmopolitanism," 3–17.

20. I would add, in addition to the point about democratization, that national movements have fought for the inclusion of ethnic and/or other social minorities, such as that of the Algerian movement against French colonization or other national movements aimed at the contestation of colonial occupying powers.

21. Charles Taylor, "Why Democracy Needs Patriotism," 119.

22. Ibid., 121.

23. We have, of course, already explored an actual project of this kind in the case of the Zapatistas, who invoked a Mexican patriotism imbued and bolstered with cosmopolitan solidarity.

24. There are basically two places to look for Appiah's idea of "rooted cosmopolitanism." A brief overview of the argument appears as "Cosmopolitan Patriots" in the collection of essays *For Love of Country?* (2002), and a fuller discussion appears as chapter 6 of his *Ethics of Identity* (2005).

25. Kwame Anthony Appiah, *The Ethics of Identity*, 216–17.

26. Ibid., 222–23.

27. Appiah does not endorse all cultural practices simply because they carry meaning within a community. Indeed, he is very much in favor of globalizing human rights on the grounds of universal principles and opposing cultural practices such as the infibulation ("Pharaonic circumcision") of young females in Africa (see ibid., 246–54 and 259–67). The point is that many cultural practices *do not* violate human rights underwritten by universal principles, and often, such practices give deep meaning and value to human lives.

28. Ibid., 246.

29. Appiah, "Cosmopolitan Patriots," 22.

30. The role of the public sphere in the *circulation, reception,* and *production* of new political discourses was discussed in detail in chapter 3.

31. I take the term "absent referent" from Carol J. Adams' *Sexual Politics of Meat: A Feminist-Vegetarian Critical Theory,* see 40–48. Adams uses the term in a different context there, but it is a fitting idea for the present discussion.

32. For example, we might point out that the collection of essays *For Love of Country?* (2002) takes up the question of patriotism/nationalism versus cosmopolitanism/transnationalism from multiple perspectives, none of which considers the role of the public sphere. As well, Appiah's *Ethics of Identity* (2005) leaves the concept of the public sphere wholly unaccounted for.

Conclusion

In many ways, this book began with the usually concluding question of "What is to be done?" At bottom, we have asked what civil societies have done in order to wield political influence in varying contexts, what they can and should do. We have focused specifically on discursive processes—our unit of study throughout has been the public sphere, its changing scale and function, and the changing terrains on which new ideas are produced, circulated, and received. We have pursued this course with the express purpose of understanding how public spheres have historically held and can continue to hold sway in politics. And I have answered the latter part of this project by proposing the theory of transgressive public spheres.

By way of conclusion, then, I shall not simply restate my recommendations for political theory and practice. Instead, I offer some reflections on the intended and proper context in which we should see the theory of transgressive public spheres. Of course, I do this in anticipation of a certain objection. I suspect that my analytical distinction of the transgressive public sphere from the national and transnational paradigms has left an outstanding tension between my theory and cosmopolitanism. How different, really, is a transgressive public sphere from a cosmopolitan one, and is my theory as importantly distinct from cosmopolitan theories as I have contended? Whether or not I am right that these questions still stand, further remarks on the distinction shall make a fitting conclusion.

The theory of transgressive public spheres *is* a cosmopolitan theory, but it is not just any. Recall my discussions in chapter 9 of Appiah's theory of "rooted cosmopolitanism" and Taylor's theory of "cosmopolitan patriotism." Transgressive public spheres are wholly compatible with and indeed foster these kinds of cosmopolitanisms. A transgressive politics encourages the evolution of a global civil society, democratic transnational organizations (these may be governmental and nongovernmental), and a cosmopolitan politics. But at the same time, a transgressive politics insists on the enduring importance of more parochial roots and identifications, and it understands that nationalism and patriotism can mobilize critical state-bounded political movements (such as struggles against colonialism and neoliberalism) that work to deepen democracy and to expand the terms of inclusion at home. A transgressive politics always searches for the imbricated coexistence of these larger and smaller scale components in a single political identity or political project.

Because of this, transgressive public spheres are incompatible with and work against any cosmopolitanism that seeks to destabilize and subordinate peoples' subnational interests and problems, that tries to undermine all patriotism and nationalism writ large as if these were necessarily chauvinistic and narrow, as if they were necessary impediments to cosmopolitan projects. A transgressive politics acknowledges that all nations are unfinished projects, but that national projects do not effectively address contemporary transnational problems in and of themselves; hence, opening them up for linkages to, solidarities with, and participation from people elsewhere can bolster their domestic leverage *and* enter them into a contentious global dialogue against broader injustices and exclusions.

So, we must qualify the tension between transgressive public spheres and cosmopolitanism in this way. However, even though transgressive public spheres work with and promote rooted cosmopolitanism, it would be wrong to conclude that my theory is just another theory of rooted cosmopolitanism. I have specifically developed a public sphere theory, situating my recommendations in relation to the historical development of this concept. This is a crucial distinction. Existing literature on cosmopolitanisms of various kinds can go and has gone very far without much devoted attention to the vital role of the public sphere (i.e., Nussbaum, 1996; Archibugi, 2003; Appiah, 2005). Meanwhile the public sphere, as I have suggested, remains an absent referent in much of this literature. That is, the public sphere is a key terrain on which cosmopolitanisms must struggle to take hold, and yet it is insufficiently explored in the major debates about cosmopolitanism.

I have insisted on centralizing the importance of the public sphere for two reasons: Not only does this compel us to think about the public spaces in which new political proposals are (or should be) evaluated, but also, making the public sphere a focal point imbues the whole discussion about patriotism and cosmopolitanism with particular and valuable normative commitments. For example, in neglecting the role of the public sphere, many cosmopolitan theorists take for granted a key insight of Kant's that touches on both of these scores, the pragmatic and the normative. Kant understood cosmopolitanism as an enlightened and ultimate achievement of the public use of reason; but the public use of reason was not only necessary for achieving cosmopolitanism. Also, the publicity of maxims and their agreeability in public opinion was necessary for determining and testing universal right and for fostering peace among different states and peoples.[1] And (as we have seen in other discussions, from Habermas' account of the bourgeois public sphere to my own account of the Zapatista public sphere) cosmopolitans who ignore the vital role of the public sphere are ignoring an important mechanism for democratization, increasing inclusion, mobilizing new political actors, entering the opinion and will of subordinated and excluded people into public discourse, and generating new political identities and solidarities.

It is for these reasons that one of the overarching claims of this book has been that we should always keep the concept and the question of the public sphere closely and explicitly linked to debates about patriotism, cosmopolitanism, global civil society, transnational politics, and new political identities.

Nevertheless, it is not enough to simply insert the concept of the public sphere into existing debates about patriotism and cosmopolitanism. The fact that the public sphere is an absent referent in these debates is only a part of the problem. Public sphere theories have been so resolutely tied to either a national or a transnational framework that they only map out over those arguments regarding patriotism and cosmopolitanism that I believe have gotten it *wrong*. In other words, the strictly national public sphere is and has been a fine model for certain patriots, nationalists, and groups fighting for citizenship rights; the strictly transnational public sphere works well for cosmopolitans and those who, like Habermas, speak of a "postnational constellation."[2] But neither of these public spheres is suitable for rooted cosmopolitans or cosmopolitan patriots, who do not understand their politics as either strictly national or strictly transnational. The theory of transgressive public spheres understands and deals with the problems of the national/transnational dichotomy in the same way that the theory of rooted cosmopolitanism understands and deals with the problems of the patriotism/cosmopolitanism dichotomy—namely, transgression maintains that one without the other is at best a theoretical mistake and at worst a dangerous political practice.

Indeed, transgression matters for politics. We saw how transgressing the boundaries between national and transnational worked for the Zapatistas (which, once again, is not to say that they have been categorically successful) and how it has worked in part and could work further for others such as socialists, feminists, and gay and lesbian rights activists. But I would like now to conclude by highlighting how the basic insights underlying the theory of transgressive public spheres are pertinent to a number of other questions as well.

Let us take, for example, one of the responses to the disastrous effects of Hurricane Katrina in late August 2005. The mayor of Biloxi, Mississippi, A. J. Holloway, told reporters, "This is our tsunami."[3] This comment was intended to compare the devastation of the hurricane to that of the tsunami that hit southern Asia in December of 2004, the latter of which killed over 226,000 people.[4] But the remark implies more than a comparison. The sentiment of Mayor Holloway's comment was that Hurricane Katrina was *our* disaster of *that* kind. Cosmopolitans, of course, would point out that there is something peculiar, perhaps even absurd, about saying that one disaster is "ours" on the grounds that it impacted the lives of Americans, most of whom most other Americans do not know any more personally than they know the Indonesian victims of the tsunami in Asia.

Appiah has pointed out that most Americans are strangers to most Americans, that "you cannot have face-to-face relations with ten million or a million or a hundred thousand people," but that "we humans have long had practice in identifying, in nations, cities, and towns, with groups on this grander scale."[5] We commonly identify with American strangers as "our people," and while there is nothing wrong with this in principle, it demonstrates that we should be able to identify with Indonesian strangers as "our people" too. This cosmopolitan insight is just as (or perhaps more) valuable for thinking about wars than for natural disasters. Whenever civilians are killed, for example, how sensible is it to differentiate "our" dead from "theirs?" On what grounds and toward what end do we determine that the loss of American lives is more meaningful than the loss of Iraqi or Afghani lives? From the cosmopolitan point of view, one principle remains firm—it is a dangerous thing to underwrite policies with the devaluation of some lives over others.

Where I now live and work, in Springfield, Illinois, some days before July 4, 2007, one of my neighbors stuck an American flag in our front yard (and everyone else's yard in the neighborhood), free of charge and without any consultation. The gesture bothered me, and I felt some degree of misrecognition, so I pulled the flag out of our yard. Why should anyone object to an American flag in America? Isn't patriotism something all Americans can express, regardless of how differently we may view what makes us patriotic? I did not uproot the flag because I don't identify as an American on any meaningful level, or because I am "anti-American" writ large. Indeed, I self-identify as an American and would probably choose to live here over anywhere else, at least as far and as well as I know other places. The content of my feeling of misrecognition, however, is not difficult to explain.

The American flag has taken on particular signification in our particular time. In most places in the United States, and certainly in Springfield, this signification is immediately comprehended. To some extent, the American flag still stands for ideals of freedom and democracy, but its meaning has been heavily re-cast by the particularities of our place (both locally, in our communities, and in geopolitical terms) and time (both historically and under the aegis of the present regime). Most Americans readily recognize that the American flag signifies a defense of the integrity of American programs abroad, that the country and its foreign policy, and certainly its military, are noble and just and deserving of support and political solidarity. Indeed, it is sensible to imagine that within the homes and cars on which American flags are seen, in the years after 9/11 and during the Iraq War, that you will find people who value American soldiers, even American people, more than they value Iraqi soldiers and civilians; you will find the contention that we should be a leading example for the rest of the world in matters of morality, economic development, culture, and politics. Admittedly, this is a generalization and not everyone waves the flag for these reasons. But today, the flag is manufactured with captions: "United We Stand," "Support Our Troops," "God Bless America," and "Freedom Isn't Free," among other phrases that clearly identify an articulated, familiar political discourse. Whatever one may say about this discourse, it is certainly not a cosmopolitan one, and from a cosmopolitan perspective it is even offensive.

These discursive contents, embodied as they are in symbols and slogans, cannot simply be done away with because I do not like them. The cultural-valuational norms that enable us to read a specific patriotic discourse in the image of the American flag are established by a national conversation, a collectivity of people who read them the same way. So if I would like to hang a flag as a statement that dissent is patriotic, no one will read it as such without additional context.

To take another example, consider the "Support Our Troops" ribbon magnet frequently seen on cars in America during the Iraq War. I do not think it is possible to support our troops and to support the Bush administration and its foreign policy in Iraq simultaneously. From my point of view, the two positions are mutually exclusive because to support the war effort represents an ultimate willingness to suffer the loss of even more troops in battle even though the casualties continue to escalate every year since the start of the war, and despite the fact that the administration is increasingly incapable of satisfying the test of public justification.

If by "supporting troops," we mean protecting their lives, safeguarding them against violent death, then "support" is much better achieved through opposition to the war and withdrawal of troops from Iraq. Still, if I put a "Support Our Troops" ribbon magnet on my car, no one will read my point of view in it, precisely because "Support Our Troops" has come to take on a very particular and singular signification. My point of view will only be signified for me, privately, while publicly, the ribbon magnet is certain to signify a meaning that betrays my position, that represents a position that I find deeply disagreeable—the magnet announces solidarity with the war effort that the administration has deployed our troops to fight. To change the "Support Our Troops" signification, much hard work must be done in the public sphere. Arguments challenging the generally accepted meaning need to take flight and take hold on a mass scale. This step cannot be bypassed by the intention or action of an isolated individual; only collective action in the public sphere can deconstruct the prevailing signification.

On the other hand, and as an example of such collective action, in May 2006, starting on May Day and running for weeks after, I marched in the massive immigration rally in New York City, and witnessed similar rallies throughout the country in the press. Masses of people with partial, unstable, or no legal citizenship waved American flags in the streets, along with the flags of their native countries. Many of these protestors thus proclaimed a multifarious identity; waving the American flag was a way of claiming a contested national identity, of challenging exclusion and a tenuous existence in America. But they were not *only* claiming an American identity. They were announcing a complex transgressive identity in the streets, with cosmopolitan and diasporic contents. This was a transgressive political identity because it simultaneously asserted both national identity with a native country and transnational cosmopolitan and diasporic identities. If I were an undocumented worker in America, with unstable citizenship, I too might wave the American flag in the streets. In the context of collective action and specific stakes, signification can be changed. Complex identity is complicated.

At the same time, some populations are not *only* threatened by the prejudicial comportment of foreign governments and publics abroad. Some live under the tyranny, the neglect, or the incompetence of their own government, are threatened by the disposition of their own leaders, or by the presence of foreign governments in occupation. Cases such as these can be seen throughout the history of colonialism, we have studied an example in the case of the Zapatistas, and Taylor has pointed out another in the present threat of Hindu chauvinism in India.[6] In addition to these, we might also think about the drafting of a new constitution in Iraq and what is at stake for sectors of the Iraqi population if the new government is not a secular one founded on principles of inclusion and pluralism.

In cases such as these, cosmopolitanism is necessary but insufficient at best; groups may do better to invoke a kind of nationalism at home as a way to contest the unjust treatment of their own populations. Indeed, we may go so far as to suggest that for any democracy (for longstanding ones as well as for newly democratizing countries), it is important for the domestic population to self-identify as a national body—as a collectivity that takes further democratization at home to be a permanent national project. Most cosmopolitans will not deny these claims. To the contrary, many would agree. However, few cosmopolitans centralize these claims about the enduring importance of a national framework, of national identity, and of formulations of certain kinds of nationalisms, in the crux of their arguments. Why? Because among the most central, key goals of cosmopolitanism are transcending national identifications with identifications as world citizens, looking further than the limited purview of domestic affairs, and expanding our spheres of affection beyond state boundaries.

Transgressive public spheres are formed when publics discover that cosmopolitanism and nationalism are each insufficient on their own, that they will be more effective and more inclusive by inextricably linking the national and transnational dimensions of their dilemma in a political discourse that travels domestically and abroad. It is not always possible or easy to frame one's case as bearing both national and transnational significance, both national and transnational magnitude. But some public spheres can do it, and can benefit (strategically and normatively) from a transgressive framing of their politics. And, inasmuch as public spheres do achieve this double-occupancy, analysts will need to apply a transgressive paradigm in order to properly understand them.

The grounds for the possibility of transgressive public spheres have become clearer in light of recent phases of globalization, which have revealed some of the ways that the problems distinctive communities face today are exacerbated or even caused by larger, transnational processes.[7] And yet many of these communities still see a clear role for their own government, they still find good reason to hold their own state at least partly accountable. Thus, they too have helped to reveal the possibility and importance of transgressive public spheres. And the response of some communities disaffected by globalization, such as that of the Zapatistas, has explicitly made their movements simultaneously national and transnational. In some cases it is not just possible, but necessary to take the path of transgression. In such instances, we cannot continue to analyze and act within the confines of discourses that do not map out over our own or others' lived experiences.

Notes

1. See part II of the appendix to Immanuel Kant's "Perpetual Peace: A Philosophical Sketch," the section titled "On the Agreement Between Politics and Morality According to the Transcendental Concept of Public Right." As well, review our discussion of Kant on this subject in chapter 1.

2. Or who, like Richard Falk, speak of a "post-statist" world. See Richard Falk, *Predatory Globalization: A Critique*, 155.

3. This quotation appeared in Reuters, August 30, 2005, CBS News, August 30, 2005, *The Washington Post*, August 31, 2005, and *The LA Times*, August 31, 2005, among others.

4. "Global Tsunami Death Toll Tops 226,000," Reuters, January 20, 2005.

5. Kwame Anthony Appiah, *The Ethics of Identity*, 216–17.

6. See my treatment of Taylor on India in chapter 9.

7. These problems and processes were discussed in chapter 4.

Bibliography

Adams, Carol J. 1990. *The Sexual Politics of Meat: A Feminist-Vegetarian Critical Theory*. New York: The Continuum Publishing Company.

Adorno, Theodor, and Max Horkheimer. 1997 [1944]. *Dialectic of Enlightenment*. John Cumming, trans. New York: The Continuum Publishing Company.

Anderson, Benedict. 1991 [1983]. *Imagined Communities: Reflections on the Origin and Spread of Nationalism*. London and New York: Verso.

Appiah, Kwame Anthony. 1994. "Identity, Authenticity, Survival, Multicultural Societies and Social Reproduction." In Taylor and Gutmann, eds., *Multiculturalism*. Princeton, N.J.: Princeton University Press, 1994.

———. 2002 [1996]. "Cosmopolitan Patriots." In Nussbaum and Cohen, eds., *For Love of Country*? Boston: Beacon Press, 2002.

———. 2005. *The Ethics of Identity*. Princeton, N.J.: Princeton University Press.

Archibugi, Daniele. 2003a. "Cosmopolitical Democracy." In Archibugi, ed., *Debating Cosmopolitics*. London/New York: Verso, 2003.

———. 2003b. "Demos and Cosmopolis." In Archibugi, ed., *Debating Cosmopolitics*. London/New York: Verso, 2003.

Arendt, Hannah. 1958. *The Human Condition*. Chicago and London: University of Chicago Press.

———. 1969. *On Violence*. New York: Harcourt, Brace and World, Inc.

———. 1977 [1963]. *On Revolution*. Kingsport, Tenn.: Penguin Books.

———. 1985 [1950]. *The Origins of Totalitarianism*. San Diego and New York: Harcourt, Inc.

———. 1986 [1969]. "Communicative Power." In Lukes, ed., *Power*. New York: New York University Press, 1986.

Aubry, Andrés. 2003. "Autonomy in the San Andrés Accords: Expression and Fulfillment of a New Federal Pact." Barbara Metzger and Linda L. Grabner-Coronel, trans. In Rus, Castillo, and Mattiace, eds., *Mayan Lives, Mayan*

Utopias: The Indigenous Peoples of Chiapas and the Zapatista Rebellion. Oxford: Rowman & Littlefield, 2003.

Benhabib, Seyla. 1992. "Models of Public Space: Hannah Arendt, the Liberal Tradition, and Jürgen Habermas." In Calhoun, ed., *Habermas and the Public Sphere.* Cambridge, Mass.: MIT Press, 1992.

Bohman, James. 1997. "The Public Spheres of the World Citizen." In Bohman and Lutz-Bachmann, eds., *Perpetual Peace: Essays on Kant's Cosmopolitan Ideal.* Cambridge, Mass.: MIT Press, 1997.

Brysk, Alison. 1995. "Acting Globally: Indian Rights and International Politics in Latin America." In Van Cott, ed., *Indigenous Peoples and Democracy in Latin America.* New York: St. Martin's Press, 1995.

Burke, Edmund. 2000 [1783]. "Speech on Fox's East India Bill." In Bromwich, ed., *On Empire, Liberty, and Reform: Speeches and Letters.* New Haven, Conn.: Yale University Press, 2000.

———. 2000 [1788]. "Speech in Opening the Impeachment of Warren Hastings." In Bromwich, ed., *On Empire, Liberty, and Reform: Speeches and Letters.* New Haven, Conn.: Yale University Press, 2000.

Calhoun, Craig. 1992. "Habermas and the Public Sphere." In Calhoun, ed., *Habermas and the Public Sphere.* Cambridge, Mass.: MIT Press, 1992.

———. 2002. "Constitutional Patriotism and the Public Sphere: Interests, Identity, and Solidarity in the Integration of Europe." In De Greiff and Cronin, eds., *Global Justice and Transnational Politics: Essays on the Moral and Political Challenges of Globalization.* Cambridge, Mass.: MIT Press, 2002.

Callahan, Manuel. 2002. "Zapatismo and the Politics of Solidarity." In Yuen, Katsiaficas, and Burton Rose, eds., *The Battle of Seattle: The New Challenge to Capitalist Globalization.* New York: Soft Skull Press, 2002.

Castillo, Rosalva Aída Hernández. 2003. "Between Civil Disobedience and Silent Rejection: Differing Responses by Mam Peasants to the Zapatista Rebellion." Francine Cronshaw, trans. In Rus, Castillo, and Mattiace, eds., *Mayan Lives, Mayan Utopias: The Indigenous Peoples of Chiapas and the Zapatista Rebellion.* Oxford: Rowman & Littlefield, 2003.

Castoriadis, Cornelius. 1998 [1947]. *Political & Social Writings, Volume 1, 1946–1955: From the Critique of Bureaucracy to the Positive Content of Socialism.* David Ames Curtis, trans. Minneapolis: University of Minnesota Press.

Ceceña, Ana Esther, and Andrés Barreda. "Chiapas and the Global Restructuring of Capital." In Holloway and Peláez, eds., *Zapatista! Reinventing Revolution in Mexico.* London: Pluto Press, 1998.

Cleaver, Harry. 1998 [1994]. "The Zapatistas and the Electronic Fabric of Struggle." In Holloway and Peláez, eds., *Zapatista! Reinventing Revolution in Mexico.* London: Pluto Press, 1998.

Cohen, Jean, and Andrew Arato. 1999 [1992]. *Civil Society and Political Theory.* Cambridge, Mass./London: The MIT Press.

Cott, Nancy F. 1987. *The Grounding of Modern Feminism.* New Haven, Conn./London: Yale University Press.

Danaher, Kevin, and Roger Burbach, eds. 2000. *Globalize This! The Battle against the World Trade Organization and Corporate Rule.* Monroe, Maine: Common Courage Press.

de Angelis, Massimo. 2001. "Zapata in Europe." In Barchiesi, Brennan, Caffentzis, Colatrella, Coughlin, Linebaugh, Neill, Riker, Roosa, Street, Vance, and Willshire-Carrera, eds., *Auroras of the Zapatistas: Local and Global Struggles of the Fourth World War*, second edition. New York: Autonomedia, 2001.

Debord, Guy. 1995 [1967]. *The Society of the Spectacle*. Donald Nicholson-Smith, trans. New York: Zone Books.

———. 2007 [1957]. "Report on the Construction of Situations." Ken Knabb, trans. In Knabb, ed., *Situationist International Anthology: Revised and Expanded Edition*. Berkeley, Calif.: Bureau of Public Secrets, 2006.

Eley, Geoff. 1992. "Nations, Publics and Political Cultures: Placing Habermas in the Nineteenth Century." In Calhoun, ed., *Habermas and the Public Sphere*. Cambridge, Mass.: MIT Press, 1992.

Esteva, Gustavo. 2003. "The Meaning and Scope of the Struggle for Autonomy." Carlos Pérez, trans. In Rus, Castillo, and Mattiace, eds., *Mayan Lives, Mayan Utopias: The Indigenous Peoples of Chiapas and the Zapatista Rebellion*. Oxford: Rowman & Littlefield, 2003.

Falk, Richard. 1999. *Predatory Globalization: A Critique*. Malden, Mass.: Polity Press.

Forgacs, David, ed. 2000. *The Gramsci Reader*. New York: New York University Press.

Foucault, Michel. 1980. *Power/Knowledge: Selected Interviews and Other Writings, 1972–1977*. Colin Gordon, Leo Marshall, John Mepham, Kate Soper, trans. New York: Pantheon Books.

———. 1990 [1984]. *The History of Sexuality, Vol. 2: The Use of Pleasure*. Robert Hurley, trans. New York: Vintage Books.

Fraser, Nancy. 1997. *Justice Interruptus: Critical Reflections on the "Postsocialist" Condition*. New York and London: Routledge.

———. 2002. "Transnationalizing the Public Sphere." New York: Manuscript.

Gramsci, Antonio. 1971. *Selections from the Prison Notebooks of Antonio Gramsci*. Quintin Hoare and Geoffrey Nowell Smith, trans. and eds. New York: International Publishers.

———. 2000. *The Gramsci Reader: Selected Writings 1916–1935*. David Forgacs, ed. New York: New York University Press.

Guidry, John A., Michael D. Kennedy, and Mayer N. Zald. 2000. "Globalizations and Social Movements." In Guidry, Kennedy, and Zald, eds., *Globalizations and Social Movements: Culture, Power, and the Transnational Public Sphere*. Ann Arbor: University of Michigan Press, 2000.

Guidry, John A., and Mark Q. Sawyer. 2003. "Contentious Pluralism: The Public Sphere and Democracy." *Perspectives on Politics* (1:2).

Habermas, Jürgen. 1962. *Strukturwandel der Öffentlichkeit*. Neuwied: Hermann Luchterhand Verlag.

———. 1975 [1973]. *Legitimation Crisis*. Thomas McCarthy, trans. Boston: Beacon Press.

———. 1984 [1981]. *The Theory of Communicative Action, Volume 1: Reason and the Rationalization of Society*. Thomas McCarthy, trans. Boston: Beacon Press.

———. 1986 [1977]. "Hannah Arendt's Communications Concept of Power." In Lukes, ed., *Power*. New York: New York University Press, 1986.

———. 1987 [1981]. *The Theory of Communicative Action, Volume 2: Lifeworld and System: A Critique of Functionalist Reason.* Thomas McCarthy, trans. Boston: Beacon Press.

———. 1989 [1962]. *The Structural Transformation of the Public Sphere: An Inquiry into a Category of Bourgeois Society.* Thomas Burger, trans. Cambridge, Mass.: The MIT Press.

———. 1992. "Further Reflections on the Public Sphere." Thomas Burger, trans. In Calhoun, ed., *Habermas and the Public Sphere.* Cambridge, Mass.: MIT Press, 1992.

———. 1994. "Struggles for Recognition in the Democratic Constitutional State." Shierry Weber Nicholsen, trans. In Taylor and Gutmann, eds., *Multiculturalism.* Princeton, N.J.: Princeton University Press, 1994.

———. 1997. "Kant's Idea of Perpetual Peace, with the Benefit of Two Hundred Years' Hindsight." James Bohman, trans. In Bohman and Lutz-Bachmann, eds., *Perpetual Peace: Essays on Kant's Cosmopolitan Ideal.* Cambridge, Mass.: MIT Press, 1997.

———. 1998 [1992]. *Between Facts and Norms: Contributions to a Discourse Theory of Law and Democracy.* William Rehg, trans. Cambridge, Mass.: The MIT Press.

———. 2001 [1998]. *The Postnational Constellation: Political Essays.* Max Pensky, trans. Cambridge, Mass.: The MIT Press.

———. 2002a. "On Legitimation through Human Rights." William Rehg, trans. In De Greiff and Cronin, eds., *Global Justice and Transnational Politics: Essays on the Moral and Political Challenges of Globalization.* Cambridge, Mass.: MIT Press, 2002.

———. 2002b. "The European Nation-State and the Pressures of Globalization." G. M. Goshgarian, trans. In De Greiff and Cronin, eds., *Global Justice and Transnational Politics: Essays on the Moral and Political Challenges of Globalization.* Cambridge, Mass.: MIT Press, 2002.

Hardt, Michael. 2000. "The Withering of Civil Society." In Hill and Montag, eds., *Masses, Classes, and the Public Sphere.* London: Verso, 2000.

Hegel, G. W. F. 1999. *Political Writings.* H. B. Nisbet, trans. Dickey and Nisbet, eds. Cambridge: Cambridge University Press.

Held, David. 1998. "Democracy and Globalization." In Archibugi, Held, and Köhler, eds., *Re-imagining Political Community: Studies in Cosmopolitan Democracy.* Stanford, Calif.: Stanford University Press, 1998.

Hill, Mike, and Warren Montag. 2000. "What Was, What Is, the Public Sphere? Post–Cold War Reflections." In Hill and Montag, eds., *Masses, Classes, and the Public Sphere.* London: Verso, 2000.

Holloway, John. 1998. "Dignity's Revolt." In Holloway and Peláez, eds., *Zapatista! Reinventing Revolution in Mexico.* New York: Pluto Press, 1998.

Jung, Courtney. 2000. *Then I Was Black: South African Political Identities in Transition.* New Haven, Conn./London: Yale University Press.

———. 2003. "The Politics of Indigenous Identity: Neoliberalism, Cultural Rights, and the Mexican Zapatistas." *Social Research: Selected Essays* (70:2).

———. 2005. *Critical Liberalism: What Normative Political Theory Has to Learn from the Mexican Indigenous Rights Movement.* New York: Manuscript.

Kant, Immanuel. 1983 [1797]. "The Metaphysics of Morals." James W. Ellington, trans. In Ellington, ed., *Kant's Ethical Philosophy*. Indianapolis: Hackett Publishing Company, 1983.

———. 1999. *Political Writings*. H. B. Nisbet, trans. Dickey and Nisbet, eds. Cambridge: Cambridge University Press.

Keck, Margaret E., and Kathryn Sikkink. 1998. *Activists Beyond Borders: Advocacy Networks in International Politics*. Ithaca and London: Cornell University Press.

Köhler, Martin. 1998. "From the National to the Cosmopolitan Public Sphere." In Archibugi, Held, and Köhler, eds., *Re-imagining Political Community: Studies in Cosmopolitan Democracy*. Stanford, Calif.: Stanford University Press, 1998.

Laclau, Ernesto, and Chantal Mouffe. 1985. *Hegemony and Socialist Strategy: Towards a Radical Democratic Politics*. London and New York: Verso.

Landau, Saul. 2002. "The Zapatista Army of National Liberation: Part of the Latin American Revolutionary Tradition—But Also Very Different." In Hayden, ed., *The Zapatista Reader*. New York: Thunder's Mouth Press/Nation Books, 2002.

Longmore, Paul K., and Lauri Umansky. 2000. *The New Disability History: American Perspectives*. New York: New York University Press.

Mannheim, Karl. 1985 [1936]. *Ideology and Utopia: An Introduction to the Sociology of Knowledge*. Louis Wirth and Edward Shils, trans. San Diego, New York, and London: Garcourt Brace and Company.

Manzo, Carlo. 2001. "Civil Society and the EZLN." In Barchiesi, Brennan, Caffentzis, Colatrella, Coughlin, Linebaugh, Neill, Riker, Roosa, Street, Vance, and Willshire-Carrera, eds., *Auroras of the Zapatistas: Local and Global Struggles of the Fourth World War*, second edition. New York: Autonomedia, 2001.

Marx, Karl. 1983 [1848]. "Manifesto of the Communist Party." Eugene Kamenka, trans. In Kamenka, ed., *The Portable Karl Marx*. New York: Penguin Books, 1983.

———. 2002 [1875]. *Critique of the Gotha Programme*. New York: International Publishers.

McAdam, Doug, Sidney Tarrow, and Charles Tilly. 2001. *Dynamics of Contention*. Cambridge: Cambridge University Press.

Mills, C. Wright. 1956. *The Power Elite*. New York: Oxford University Press.

———. 1967. *Power, Politics and People: The Collected Essays of C. Wright Mills*. Irving Louis Horowitz, ed. New York: Oxford University Press.

Moguel, Julio. 2001. "Civil Society and the EZLN." In Barchiesi, Brennan, Caffentzis, Colatrella, Coughlin, Linebaugh, Neill, Riker, Roosa, Street, Vance, and Willshire-Carrera, eds., *Auroras of the Zapatistas: Local and Global Struggles of the Fourth World War*, second edition. New York: Autonomedia, 2001.

Montag, Warren. 2000. "The Pressure of the Street: Habermas's Fear of the Masses." In Hill and Montag, eds., *Masses, Classes, and the Public Sphere*. London: Verso, 2000.

Negt, Oskar, and Alexander Kluge. 1993 [1972]. *Public Sphere and Experience: Toward an Analysis of the Bourgeois and Proletarian Public Sphere*. Peter Labanyi,

Jamie Owen Daniel, and Assenka Oksiloff, trans. Minneapolis and London: University of Minnesota Press.

Nussbaum, Martha. 2002 [1996]. "Patriotism and Cosmopolitanism." In Nussbaum and Cohen, eds., *For Love of Country?* Boston: Beacon Press, 2002.

Parenti, Michael. 1995. *Against Empire.* San Francisco: City Lights Books.

Paz, Octavio. 2002 [1994]. "The Media Spectacle Comes to Mexico." In Hayden, ed., *The Zapatista Reader.* New York: Thunder's Mouth Press/Nation Books, 2002.

Ross, John. 2000. *The War against Oblivion: The Zapatista Chronicles 1994–2000.* Monroe, Maine: Common Courage Press.

Rousseau, Jean-Jacques. 1968 [1762]. *The Social Contract.* Maurice Cranston, trans. London: Penguin Books.

Roy, Olivier. 1996 [1992]. *The Failure of Political Islam.* Carol Volk, trans. Cambridge, Mass.: Harvard University Press.

Rus, Jan, Rosalva Aída Hernández Castillo, and Shannan L. Mattiace, eds. 2003. *Mayan Lives, Mayan Utopias: The Indigenous Peoples of Chiapas and the Zapatista Rebellion.* Oxford: Rowman & Littlefield Publishers, Inc.

Sassen, Saskia. 1998. *Globalization and Its Discontents: Essays on the New Mobility of People and Money.* New York: The New Press.

Scarry, Elaine. 2002 [1996]. "The Difficulty of Imagining Other People." In Nussbaum and Cohen, eds., *For Love of Country?* Boston: Beacon Press, 2002.

Scott, James C. 1990. *Domination and the Arts of Resistance: Hidden Transcripts.* New Haven, Conn./London: Yale University Press.

Shapiro, Ian. 1999. *Democratic Justice.* New Haven, Conn./London: Yale University Press.

Stavans, Ilan. 2002 [1996]. "Unmasking Marcos." In Hayden, ed., *The Zapatista Reader.* New York: Thunder's Mouth Press/Nation Books, 2002.

Taylor, Charles. 1989. *Sources of the Self: The Making of the Modern Identity.* Cambridge, Mass.: Harvard University Press.

———. 1997. *Philosophical Arguments.* Cambridge, Mass./London: Harvard University Press.

———. 2002 [1996]. "Why Democracy Needs Patriotism." In Nussbaum and Cohen, eds., *For Love of Country?* Boston: Beacon Press, 2002.

Thompson, E. P. 1963. *The Making of the English Working Class.* New York: Vintage Books.

———. 2001. *The Essential E. P. Thompson.* Dorothy Thompson, ed. New York: The New Press.

Thompson, Janna. 1998. "Community Identity and World Citizenship." In Archibugi, Held, and Köhler, eds., *Re-imagining Political Community: Studies in Cosmopolitan Democracy.* Stanford, Calif.: Stanford University Press, 1998.

Tresierra, Julio C. 1995. "Mexico: Indigenous Peoples and the Nation-State." Charles Roberts, trans. In Van Cott, ed., *Indigenous Peoples and Democracy in Latin America.* New York: St. Martin's Press, 1995.

UN Human Development Report 1999. New York and Oxford: Oxford University Press.

UN Human Development Report 2002: Deepening Democracy in a Fragmented World. New York and Oxford: Oxford University Press.

Walzer, Michael. 1994. *Thick and Thin: Moral Argument at Home and Abroad*. Notre Dame, Ind.: University of Notre Dame Press.

Warner, Michael. 2002. *Publics and Counterpublics*. New York: Zone Books.

Weber, Max. 1958 [1921]. *Politics as a Vocation*. In Gerth and Mills, eds., *From Max Weber: Essays in Sociology*. New York: Oxford University Press.

Weinberg, Bill. 2002. *Homage to Chiapas: The New Indigenous Struggles in Mexico*. London and New York: Verso.

Womack, John, Jr. 1999. *Rebellion in Chiapas: An Historical Reader*. New York: The New Press.

Index

boomerang effect, 212, 213–14, 220
bourgeois public sphere, xii;
    effectiveness of early, 73–74. *See
    also* Habermas, Jürgen;
    nonbourgeois public sphere
Boutros-Ghali, Boutros, 161
Brown, Mark Malloch, 144n18
Brysk, Alison, 215–16, 218, 220
Burke, Edmund, 140
Bush, George W., 83, 199n16

Calhoun, Craig, 97, 111n31, 205–6,
    222n3, 259, 260, 323, 324–25, 328
Callahan, Manuel, 253
capitalism: anticapitalism, 119–20,
    138–39, 291, 313, 318; indigenous
    people as impediment to, 277
Castañeda, Jorge G., 253
Castoriadis, Cornelius, 42n30, 66n22
categorical identities, 210
character (C), 109n3, 133, 234–35, 240,
    268
Chartist/Chartism, 68, 92, 94
Chiapas. *See* Zapatistas
Chinese democracy, 150, 151
circulation, reception, 327
citizenship: aspirational side of, 284;
    classical, 78; dual, 171, 284–85,
    324; problemization of, as
    national, 171
civil disobedience, 99–100
civil society: collective identity in, 15,
    71–72, 77–78, 287–88; defining, 15,
    16, 61; public realm as subset of,
    16–17, 18, 19–20; *vs.* public sphere,
    71–72
Civil Society Organization (CSO),
    160–64, 174; as cosmopolitan
    sphere, 162–63; as state-bounded
    sphere, 161–62
civitas gentium (international state),
    24, 58
classical theory. *See* Habermas,
    Jürgen

Cleaver, Harry, 252
Cohen, Jean, 11n4, 98, 100–101, 255,
    311
Cold War, 56, 57, 63, 64, 131, 180, 294
collateral damage, 157, 158,
    199–200n17
collective identity, xv, 15, 71–72,
    77–78, 287–88
collectivity, 15, 79, 249, 259
communism, 27–28, 60–61, 61–62,
    66n22, 139, 186
communitarianism, 156
communities of birth, 153
communities of choice, 153
community of communities, 277
community of fate, 129, 132, 135, 136
complex identity, 153, 154, 155, 176
Congressional Human Rights
    Caucus, 217
constitutional patriotism, 207–8
"Constitutional Patriotism and the
    Public Sphere" (Calhoun), 205–10
constructionism, 285
contained *vs.* transgressive
    contention, 230
contentious pluralism, 172, 173–74,
    310
"Contentious Pluralism" (Guidry
    and Sawyer), 172–73
The Contest of Faculties (Kant), 25
cosmopolitanism, 228, 334; complex
    identity of, 153, 154, 155, 176; of
    Habermas, 185, 188–89, 197,
    271n44; of Kant, 23, 26, 48, 335;
    and nationalism, 323–26; as
    transgressive, 295; of Zapatistas,
    262, 277–78, 326–27
cosmopolitan patriotism. *See* rooted
    cosmopolitanism
cosmopolitan patriots, 301n1
cosmopolitan solidarity, 178
Critical Liberalism (Jung), 293–94
critical theory, 28, 42n30, 147
cultural products, 31, 42n34

national public sphere, xi, xiii,
110n14, 112n40, 162; *vs.*
transnational public sphere, 204,
205–6
native inhabitance, 237n9
Negt, Oskar, 11n4, 89, 94, 95, 311
neoliberalism, 236, 248, 251, 277, 292,
294, 334
Neo-Nazism, 229, 306, 307
nonbourgeois public sphere, xiv, xvi,
5–6, 9–10; character (C) of, 234–35,
240; function (F) of, 234–35, 240;
location (L) of, 234–35, 240;
suffrage, 94, 103–5, 106, 108, 186,
214, 222n10. *See also* Zapatista
public sphere
"non-ethnic" national identities,
222n3
nongovernmental organizations
(NGOs), 160, 194, 197, 216;
transnational advocacy networks,
213–15
Nussbaum, Martha, 125n2, 323

occasional publics, 184, 186–87
On Violence (Arendt), 9, 36–37, 47, 52
openness, 8, 24, 35, 107, 173, 244, 305,
308–9, 319–20
organization, as political identity
variable, 281
The Origins of Totalitarianism
(Arendt), 47, 53, 54, 64

Parenti, Michael, 144n18
patriotism, 323, 324, 334, 335;
cosmopolitan, 327–30, 332n24,
334–35
"Patriotism and Cosmopolitanism"
(Nussbaum), 323
Paz, Octavio, 247, 253
Peoples' Global Action (PGA), 161,
259
perlocutionary discourse, 49, 50, 51,
53

"Perpetual Peace: A Philosophical
Sketch" (Kant), 17, 23–24, 129,
164, 185, 305, 308
Philosophy of Right (Hegel), 19
plebeian public sphere, 67–68, 68,
111n26
polis, 43n45, 52
political identity, 204; based on
unconventional attribute, 287–89,
294–95; constitution argument,
279–80; construction argument,
280–82; of Jung, 279–82; lack of,
302n41; malleability of, 282;
transgressive construction of,
287–89, 291
political institutions, as political
identity variable, 280
political public sphere, 42n34, 56–65;
defining, 15–16
politics: accountability, 214
"The Politics of Indigenous Identity:
Neoliberalism, Cultural Rights,
and the Mexican Zapatistas"
(Jung), 290
postnational constellation, 138,
192–93, 336
The Postnational Constellation
(Habermas), 105, 178, 190, 192
postnational cosmopolitan public
sphere, 192–93, 195–96, 198,
200n37–201n38
postnational public spheres, xi
post-Westphalian national publics,
222n3
potestas in populo, 37
The Power Elite (Mills), 29
power-violence relationship, 37–38
Predatory Globalization: A Critique
(Falk), 282
"The Pressure of the Street"
(Montag), 107
privatization, 330
propaganda, 53
protectionism, 286

Zapatistas, xv, 41n13, 66n21; appeal
of, 247–48, 250–51, 276, 277–78;
cosmopolitanism of, 277–78,
326–27; nationalist rhetoric of,
208–9; radical democratic politics

of, 253, 270n23, 311–12; and
republican ideals, 287; rhetoric of
indigenous identity, 278–79
Zedillo, Ernesto, 298–99
zones of citizenship criteria, 110n14